Death Penalty Cases

Death Penalty Cases

Leading U.S. Supreme Court Cases on Capital Punishment

Second Edition

Barry Latzer
Professor of Government
John Jay College of Criminal Justice
The Graduate Center of the City University of New York

BUTTERWORTH
HEINEMANN

An Imprint of Elsevier
Amsterdam   Boston   London   New York   Oxford   Paris   San Diego
San Francisco   Singapore   Sydney   Tokyo

Butterworth–Heinemann is an imprint of Elsevier.

Copyright © 2002, Elsevier. All rights reserved.

♾ Recognizing the importance of preserving what has been written, Elsevier prints its books on acid-free paper whenever possible.

Library of Congress Cataloging-in-Publication Data
A catalog record for this book is available from the Library of Congress.

ISBN-13: 978-0-7506-7594-9   ISBN-10: 0-7506-7594-2

British Library Cataloguing-in-Publication Data
A catalogue record for this book is available from the British Library.

The publisher offers special discounts on bulk orders of this book.
For information, please contact:

Manager of Special Sales
Elsevier
200 Wheeler Road
Burlington, MA 01803
Tel: 781-221-2212
Fax: 781-221-1615

For information on all Butterworth–Heinemann publications available, contact our World Wide Web home page at: http://www.bh.com

10 9 8 7 6 5 4 3 2

Printed in the United States of America

For Miriam, my best kid

Contents

Preface

As the title indicates, this book consists mainly of excerpts from U.S. Supreme Court cases on the death penalty. In ruling on such cases, the Supreme Court does much more than decide whether or not a defendant may be executed; it really participates in a national debate over the appropriateness of imposing the ultimate punishment for some of the most reprehensible crimes.

Although duty-bound to limit their decisions to the resolution of legal claims based upon the U.S. Constitution, the Justices freely discuss the widest possible range of issues surrounding capital punishment—from philosophical questions on the justification of punishment, to social science questions on the deterrent effects of executions, to the history of murder laws in America. There are candid discussions on race, and sometimes soul-wrenching dialogues about death. The result is an extremely rich offering, one which can serve as the basis for a number of university courses or portions thereof—in criminal justice, sociology, political science, legal studies, or philosophy. Indeed, since the subject is both controversial and fascinating, there is no good reason why any intelligent citizen would not find this material edifying and rewarding.

I have chosen what I believe to be the 25 most significant Supreme Court pronouncements on capital punishment. The reader (or instructor) should be able, simply by using the Table of Contents, to select cases either by case name or by the main issue resolved.

The cases were edited with an eye toward balance and completeness, with all of the major views of the Justices fairly represented. Most of the footnotes in the original were omitted; where they are reprinted the Court's own footnote numbers were retained. Case citations, always plentiful in Supreme Court opinions, were shortened or eliminated. Brackets in the original text were converted to parentheses so they would not be confused with the editor's brackets. Brief textual deletions are indicated by ellipses, longer ones by three asterisks.

Because of constraints on the size of this book, some of the narrative had to be excised as well, occasionally even full opinions of some of the Justices. But by and large, *Death Penalty Cases* presents accurately and fully the Supreme Court's own words on the subject of capital punishment.

Nearly all the case selections are preceded by brief introductory commentaries, to give the reader the essential legal background for full comprehension of the material. In addition, I prepared an Introduction intended to provide general background information on capital punishment. The Introduction covers the history of the Eighth Amendment Cruel and Unusual Punishments Clause, the laws and procedures governing contemporary capital case adjudication (including murder statutes and the latest changes in habeas corpus), and the modern-day penological, philosophical, and social debate over capital punishment. I have tried to present the death penalty debate material as impartially as I could; if there are any biases in this book, they probably appear here.

For this second edition of *Death Penalty Cases* I have added four cases and updated the Introduction and the statistical appendix (now Appendix A), and created a new appendix, Appendix B, that contains excerpts from selected death penalty statutes.

The new cases include *Jurek v. Texas* (Chapter 4), which upheld the Texas death penalty law. This case is especially interesting because Texas law differs from most other state statutes, and because Texas carries out the most death sentences.

The second new case is *Simmons v. South Carolina* (Chapter 17), which concerns the need to inform the sentencing jury about the parole ineligibility of a death penalty defendant—information that could have an impact on the jury's decision to impose a death sentence.

Third, I have added *Herrera v. Collins* (Chapter 26), which provides a fascinating discussion of the right to use federal habeas corpus to claim innocence, along with some insights into the clemency power of the president and state governors.

Finally, I replaced *Penry v. Lynaugh* (1989) with the case that overruled it: *Atkins v. Virginia* (2002) (Chapter 24). *Atkins* makes it unconstitutional to execute mentally retarded criminals.

Acknowledgments

I wish to express my appreciation to Professor Roger McDonald of John Jay College of Criminal Justice, Professor John Cochran of the University of South Florida, and Dana Greene, doctoral candidate in Criminal Justice at City University of New York, for reviewing the manuscript for this book and making many excellent suggestions. Many of the changes made for the second edition were recommended by Professor David McCord of Drake University Law School. I am very grateful to him.

Chapter 1

Capital Punishment: The Law and the Issues

Most of the cases in this book determine whether or not the procedures used to impose the death penalty violate the Eighth Amendment Cruel and Unusual Punishments Clause. In a minority of cases, some other provision of the United States Constitution is invoked, such as the Fourteenth Amendment (which guarantees due process of law and the equal protection of the laws), or the Fifth Amendment (which prohibits double jeopardy) or the Sixth Amendment (which establishes the right to an impartial jury and to the effective assistance of counsel). As will become readily apparent, the Supreme Court's treatment of these cases rarely is confined to arid discourse on legal abstractions. The death penalty cases before the Court frequently trigger quite lively debates among the Justices on the penological, philosophical, social, and social scientific issues implicated by capital punishment.

The aim of this introduction is to give the reader a guide to the legal and extralegal issues surrounding the death penalty controversy. There will be three focal points:

1. The history of the Eighth Amendment,
2. The laws and procedures governing the adjudication of current-day capital cases,
3. The extralegal (penological, philosophical, and social) debate over capital punishment.

A BRIEF HISTORY OF THE EIGHTH AMENDMENT

The Eighth Amendment to the United States Constitution was ratified in 1791, along with the rest of the Bill of Rights. It says:

> Excessive bail shall not be required, nor excessive fines imposed, nor cruel and unusual punishments inflicted.

1

The Cruel and Unusual Punishments Clause derives from the English Bill of Rights of 1689. The English bill was a response to the cruelty of King James II, who savagely suppressed a revolution against him. Hundreds of rebels were captured, tried before special courts (the "Bloody Assizes"), and brutally executed by being hanged, cut down before death, disemboweled, beheaded, and hacked to pieces. Use of the rack, drawing and quartering, and burning alive also were common in Europe prior to the 18th century.

When the United States Constitution was adopted in 1789, some of these barbaric punishments still were used abroad, and the framers of the Constitution apparently were determined to prohibit their imposition in America. However, branding, whipping, and the cropping of ears were commonly used in the United States before and after the adoption of the Eighth Amendment, until, by 1850, they were virtually abolished by the state legislatures.

It is clear that the Cruel and Unusual Punishments Clause was *not* intended to abolish capital punishment. Some proof of this is provided by other language in the Constitution; the Fifth Amendment in particular implies that the death penalty was constitutionally acceptable.[a] It was intended (in part) to forbid the infliction of more pain than was necessary to extinguish life. Therefore, the focus of the few death penalty cases before the Supreme Court in the 19th century was not whether a death sentence could be imposed, but *how* it was to be carried out.[b]

No punishments were held unconstitutional by the Supreme Court until 1910, when a *non*capital punishment was struck down in *Weems v. United States*, 217 U.S. 349 (1910). In the *Weems* case, the Philippines, then under U.S. control, imposed 12 years' imprisonment in heavy chains at hard and painful labor for falsifying government documents. For the first time, the Court indicated that the Eighth Amendment does more than simply ban barbarous punishment; it also prohibits punishments that are disproportionate to the offense. This opened the door to arguments that the death penalty was disproportionate punishment, at least for some crimes—a view ultimately adopted by the Supreme Court in the 1970's.[c]

---

[a] The Fifth Amendment, which was adopted the same day as the Eighth, says, among other things, that "No person shall be held for a *capital* or otherwise infamous crime, unless on a presentment or indictment of a Grand Jury." It also states: "nor shall any person be subject for the same offence to be twice put in jeopardy of *life* or limb." Finally, it declares: "nor [shall any person] be deprived of *life*, liberty, or property, without due process of law." (Emphases added.)

[b] The first Supreme Court case invoking the Cruel and Unusual Punishments Clause was *Wilkerson v. Utah*, 99 U.S. 130, 25 L. Ed. 345 (1879), in which the Court unanimously upheld a sentence of death by public shooting. (Although the Eighth Amendment was not then applicable to the states, it was enforceable in federal territory such as Utah at the time of Wilkerson's case. See footnote e.)

In *In re Kemmler*, 136 U.S. 436, 10 S. Ct. 930, 34 L. Ed. 519 (1890), the Court, again without dissent, approved New York's use of the electric chair, finding no violation of the Fourteenth Amendment. In a nonbinding dictum, the *Kemmler* Court said: "Punishments are cruel when they involve torture or a lingering death; but the punishment of death is not cruel within the meaning of that word as used in the Constitution." *Id.* 136 U.S. at 447, 10 S. Ct. at 933.

[c] In *Coker v. Georgia*, 433 U.S. 584 (1977) (see Chapter 5), the Court held that imposing the death penalty for the rape of an adult woman violates the Eighth Amendment.

The disproportionate punishment theory of the Eighth Amendment recently has led courts to occasionally strike down prison sentences that are considered too long for the offense committed. In the leading case, *Solem v. Helm*, 463 U.S. 277 (1983), the Supreme Court overturned a sentence of life without parole for writing a bad $100 check, the defendant's seventh felony. Even prison conditions, as opposed to sentences, have been successfully attacked on the ground that they amount to cruel and unusual punishment.[d]

Recently, however, Supreme Court Justice Antonin Scalia and Chief Justice William Rehnquist wrote that according to their historical research, the Eighth Amendment was not intended to prohibit disproportionate punishments, but rather, was aimed at particular modes of punishment, *i.e.*, cruel methods of punishment that are not regularly or customarily employed. (See *Harmelin v. Michigan*, 501 U.S. 957 [1991].) The Court does not accept Scalia's position, and continues to strike down death sentences that it considers "excessive" (see, for example, *Atkins v. Virginia*, Chapter 24).

In *Robinson v. California*, 370 U.S. 660 (1962), the Supreme Court held that the Cruel and Unusual Punishments Clause restricts the states, not just the federal government.[e] Consequently, the states must observe Eighth Amendment limitations established by the Supreme Court.[f] This is significant because the overwhelming majority of murder prosecutions, and therefore of capital cases, take place at the state level.

The contemporary Supreme Court does not feel bound by the original 18th-century understanding of the meaning of the word *cruel*. After all, we would no longer tolerate pillorying, branding, or cropping or nailing of the ears—acceptable punishments during the colonial era. The modern Supreme Court construes the Eighth Amendment by "evolving standards of decency."[g] In other words, the Cruel and Unusual Punishments Clause is interpreted in accordance with con-

---

[d] See, for example, *Hudson v. McMillian*, 503 U.S. 1, 9, 1000 (1992) ("When prison officials maliciously and sadistically use force to cause harm, contemporary standards of decency always are violated."). As will be shown, "contemporary standards of decency" is the modern yardstick for Eighth Amendment violations.

[e] The Bill of Rights, standing alone, limits only the national government. By a process known as *incorporation*, the Supreme Court has gradually applied nearly all provisions of the Bill of Rights to the states. This was accomplished by interpreting the Fourteenth Amendment, which expressly restricts the states, as requiring most of the same rights as the Bill of Rights. See footnote b.

[f] However, the state courts may go further than the Supreme Court and find that the punishment provisions in the state constitutions require even greater restrictions on state government. Indeed, in *People v. Anderson*, 493 P.2d 880 (Cal. 1972) the California Supreme Court, construing the California cruel or unusual punishments clause, became the first American tribunal to declare the death penalty per se unconstitutional. Opponents of the death penalty often seek to establish broader rights for capital defendants by couching their arguments in state constitutional terms.

Forty-one state constitutions prohibit cruel and unusual (or "cruel *or* unusual") punishments. Six bar only "cruel" punishments. Nine state constitutions require that punishments be proportionate to the offense, and three say that punishment must be based on the principle of "reformation"; that is, rehabilitation. At least three state constitutions expressly authorize the death penalty.

[g] "The [Eighth] Amendment must draw its meaning from the evolving standards of decency that mark the progress of a maturing society." *Trop v. Dulles*, 356 U.S. 86, 100–101 (1958) (plurality opinion). *Trop* held that it is cruel and unusual punishment to take away the citizenship of a wartime deserter.

temporary standards, not 18th-century standards. The Supreme Court has had difficulty determining how to measure contemporary standards of decency. It frequently relies on "objective" indicators, such as laws passed by state legislatures and Congress, and the decisions of juries. (See, for example, *Stanford v. Kentucky*, Chapter 22.)

In *Furman v. Georgia*, 408 U.S. 238 (1972) (Chapter 2), the Supreme Court, for the first time in American history, declared the death penalty to be cruel and unusual. But the judges were sharply divided in their reasoning, and an examination of their positions reveals that only a minority of the Court was categorically opposed to capital punishment. The rest of the *Furman* majority was concerned mainly with the arbitrariness of death sentences. Four years after *Furman*, in *Gregg v. Georgia*, 428 U.S. 153 (1976) (Chapter 3), the Court rejected the view that the death penalty is always (per se) cruel and unusual. *Gregg* upheld a Georgia capital punishment law that utilized certain trial procedures and appeals designed to prevent the penalty from being imposed arbitrarily. Although *Gregg* eliminated the most broad-gauged attack on capital punishment, many years of litigation followed in an effort to clarify the Court's procedural demands. By the late 1980s, the principal requirements for imposing the death penalty in the United States were fairly well settled. Those requirements are discussed on the pages that follow. The key Supreme Court cases are reprinted in this book.

CAPITAL LAWS AND PROCEDURES

Since 1976, when capital punishment was reinstated in the United States, it has been applied only to murder in the first degree. Other crimes, such as treason or certain terrorist acts, also may warrant the death penalty, but the Supreme Court has not yet made clear whether this would be constitutionally acceptable.

Currently, 38 states and the federal government authorize a death penalty; 12 states and the District of Columbia do not. (See Appendix A for details.) Once the police determine that a *homicide* (defined as the killing of a living human being by another human being) has occurred, it will be up to the prosecutor to decide whether or not the killing was a crime and, if so, whether or not to treat it as a capital offense. A great deal of discretion is lodged in American prosecutors; even within a capital punishment state, the same crime might be prosecuted capitally or not depending on the county in which it occurred (Rosenberg 1995).

Note as well that some homicides are not crimes at all and therefore cannot be punished. One example is *justifiable homicide*, which includes killings in self-defense and certain killings by law enforcement agents, such as to arrest a dangerous felon. Likewise, a homicide may be "excused" if the person who did it was not blameworthy. An insane defendant, for instance, may not be punished, although he may be committed to a mental institution. In most states, insanity means that the defendant, due to a mental disease or defect, did not know he was killing someone or thought that such conduct was acceptable by society's moral (or legal) standards. Very few people can meet this definition, and very few defendants are found insane. In some cases, the prosecutor (and grand jury) may not believe that the killing was justified or excused. Consequently, the defendant must stand trial and offer justification or an excuse as a trial defense.

Where the apparent killer is suffering from mental disease at the time of trial, such that he cannot understand the proceedings or consult with his lawyer, he will be considered incompetent to stand trial and will be involuntarily committed. If his sanity is restored, the now-competent person may be required to stand trial.

A defendant who is mentally retarded may be considered sane, but, under Supreme Court rulings is ineligible for the death penalty. (See *Atkins v. Virginia*, Chapter 24.) Furthermore, all states must permit the defendant to offer evidence of mental problems or intoxication to persuade the sentencers not to impose the death penalty.

Finally, a defendant who is sentenced to death may not be executed if, despite his sanity during the trial, he had become insane at the time the sentence was to be imposed. (See *Ford v. Wainwright*, Chapter 23.)

Criminal homicides are defined by the legislatures of each state and, for federal offenses, by the United States Congress. Since each legislature may adopt whatever statutory scheme it wishes (subject to constitutional restrictions) significant variations are found in murder laws around the country. Generally speaking, criminal homicides fall into three categories: murder in the first degree, murder in the second degree, and manslaughter. The purpose of dividing murder into "degrees" is to establish punishments of different levels of severity depending on the reprehensibility of the crime. Only first degree murder may be punished by death, and this is true only for "aggravated" first degree murders, as will be explained later. Second degree murder and manslaughter are punishable by no more than a term of imprisonment. Manslaughter, the least reprehensible of the criminal homicides, carries the lightest sentence. Most criminal homicides will not be classified as murder in the first degree and therefore will not be eligible for the death penalty.

Intentional Murder

First degree murder usually has two subcategories: intent-to-kill murder and felony murder. Intent-to-kill or intentional murder means simply that at the time of the homicide the actor had as his purpose the death of the victim. Intent must generally be inferred from all of the circumstances. For example, if the actor knowingly used a deadly weapon on the victim, aware of its capacity to cause harm, the inference that he intended the death of the victim will not be difficult to draw. This is sometimes called the *deadly weapon doctrine*: a jury may infer an intent to kill from such use of a deadly weapon.

If, on the other hand, evidence suggests that the defendant intended only to injure the victim, although the act actually caused the victim's death, he is not guilty of intentional murder, but may be guilty of second degree murder. Likewise, reckless or extremely negligent killings are second degree murder, sometimes called *depraved heart* murder. Examples include: shooting into an occupied room or at passing vehicles, throwing heavy objects from a tall building to the street below, driving at high speeds on city streets, violently shaking an infant, or playing "Russian roulette" with another person. In these examples, the defendant, who does not intend to kill anyone, is not guilty of first degree murder and cannot get the death penalty.

For a conviction of first degree murder, most states require proof of premeditation and deliberation in addition to proof of an intent to kill. Premeditation and deliberation derive from the old English common law crime of murder with "malice aforethought," which was a capital offense. In such states, the prosecutor will have to prove, in addition to the intent to kill at the time of the murder, that the defendant reflected about the killing in a cool state of mind (*i.e.*, not uncontrollably excited) prior to the homicidal act. Some premeditation-deliberation states do not require proof of any significant time lapse between the premeditation and the fatal act. Other states require proof that the murder was actually planned in advance.

Finally, some states categorize as first degree murder certain specific types of intentional homicide. These include killings (1) by certain methods, such as by bombing; (2) of certain victims, such as on-duty police; (3) by particular actors, such as hired agents, or defendants with prior murder convictions; or (4) of more than one person in a single incident. If the death penalty is sought, some of these circumstances also may serve as aggravating factors, which (as explained later) must be proven in order to justify the ultimate punishment.

Felony Murder

The other type of first degree murder is felony murder, which is a murder for which intent to kill need not be proved. If the actor commits certain felonies and that felonious conduct causes the death of another person, he may be guilty of felony murder. The underlying ("predicate") felonies usually are dangerous to life and the danger is foreseeable (and usually foreseen); hence, the perpetrator is guilty of first degree murder even though he may not have intended to kill.

Statutes usually list the kinds of felonies to which felony murder applies; typically, rape, robbery, kidnapping, arson, and burglary. Felonies not specified in the felony murder statute, usually nonviolent crimes such as grand larceny, may not serve as the predicate for felony murder, but they may serve as the basis for second degree murder.

Under felony murder concepts a defendant may be guilty of murder without actually performing the homicidal act. For instance, crimes are often committed by coperpetrators, such as when A and B together rob C. If A purposely shoots and kills C, then both A and B may be guilty of murder. A is guilty of intent-to-kill murder, and B, although not the shooter, is guilty of felony murder. (B, of course, must be proven guilty of the underlying felony of robbery.) Likewise, if

A accidentally shoots C to death during the robbery, A and B are guilty of felony murder.

The logic behind finding B culpable of murder is that he is guilty of a dangerous felony (armed robbery) that foreseeably could, and indeed did, cause a death. But there may be moral problems with convicting of murder a person who did not have homicidal intent and may not personally have done the killing. This seems especially true where B's involvement in the felony was relatively minor (*e.g.*, he served as the lookout). Where capital punishment is the potential penalty, these moral problems are heightened. The Supreme Court addressed this issue from a constitutional perspective in *Enmund v. Florida* (Chapter 11) and *Tison v. Arizona* (Chapter 12). The effect of these cases was to restrict (but not eliminate) capital punishment for felony murder.

We now turn to a description of the various stages in contemporary death penalty prosecutions, emphasizing those proceedings that are different from non-capital cases. (See *Gregg v. Georgia*, Chapter 3, where the Supreme Court first endorsed what became the model for death penalty procedures.) We have divided the capital case into eight stages. The proceedings described are typical of death penalty cases in the United States, but there are, of course, variations from state-to-state.

Stage 1. Investigation and Filing of Charges

As previously noted, whether or not a homicide is treated as a capital case is largely a matter of prosecutorial discretion. Usually, a thorough investigation will be undertaken by both prosecutors and defense attorneys to determine whether or not aggravating or mitigating factors (discussed later) are likely to be proven. If mental condition is a potential issue, this will include an examination by psychologists or psychiatrists. Prosecutors usually have a fixed time period (*e.g.*, 120 days after the filing of formal charges) to notify the court and the defendant of their intent to seek the death penalty.

Stage 2. Jury Selection

After all of the usual pretrial proceedings are completed (*e.g.*, hearings to determine the admissibility of evidence), the jury must be selected. Prospective jurors will be questioned by both prosecutors and defense attorneys to determine their competence to serve, a process known as *voir dire*. In capital cases, the jurors must be "death qualified." That is, a prospective juror, whose views on the death penalty are determined to be so strong that they would interfere with the ability to render an impartial verdict or fairly determine the sentence, may be excused "for cause." Both the defense and prosecution have an unlimited number of challenges "for cause" and a limited number (*e.g.*, 20 per side) of "peremptory challenges," for which no explanation need be given (see *Witherspoon v. Illinois*, Chapter 13, and *Lockhart v. McCree*, Chapter 14). Interracial murders may require special questions to potential jurors on race prejudice (see *Turner v. Murray*, Chapter 15).

Stage 3. Bifurcated Trial

Capital trials are *bifurcated*; in other words, divided into two phases: the guilt stage and the penalty stage. Ordinarily, the same jury sits for both phases. (However, see *Spaziano v. Florida*, Chapter 19, on the legitimacy of capital sentencing by a judge.) The purpose of bifurcation is to permit the jury to consider evidence relevant to the sentence that would be inappropriate for the jury to consider when deciding guilt.

The guilt phase runs like an ordinary trial. Should the jury acquit or find the defendant guilty of a homicide ineligible for the death penalty, there will be no penalty hearing. If the verdict is that the defendant is guilty of a capital crime, the penalty phase is conducted. To get a death sentence, the prosecution must prove that the murder was committed under *aggravating circumstances*. The jury must unanimously find that at least one aggravating circumstance from a list established by statute was proven beyond a reasonable doubt.

In *Ring v. Arizona*, 122 S. Ct. 2428 (2002), the Supreme Court held that the Sixth Amendment right to a jury trial prohibits assigning to a judge the determination of the existence of aggravating factors. Aggravating factors generally fall into three categories: (1) the killing of certain victims, such as law enforcement officers or young children; (2) murders by certain defendants, such as prisoners serving life sentences or defendants with previous murder convictions; and (3) murders committed in a certain manner, such as contract killings, serial murders, murders accompanied by torture, or murders during the commission of a violent felony (see *Godfrey v. Georgia*, Chapter 8).

If an aggravating factor is not proven, the death penalty may not be imposed, and a term of imprisonment, usually life or life without parole, is mandated instead. However, even if an aggravator is proven, the sentencer must also consider any *mitigating evidence*—factors favoring leniency—presented by the defense. Relevant mitigating evidence may not be restricted by law; therefore the defense may present almost any evidence it wishes to convince the jury to spare the accused's life (see *Lockett v. Ohio*, Chapter 9). Mitigating evidence usually concerns either characteristics of the accused or circumstances surrounding the crime. In the former category are such factors as the mental or emotional impairment of the defendant (insufficient for a finding of insanity, which would have precluded a penalty phase), the influence of alcohol or drugs, youthfulness, or the lack of a criminal history. Mitigating crime circumstances include such things as the defendant's relative lack of responsibility for the victim's death, such as where he was dominated by another person or where someone else did the actual killing.

Assuming that the jurors find beyond a reasonable doubt that an aggravating circumstance existed, they must, in most states, balance the aggravator against the mitigating circumstances, if any are found. The jury need not be unanimous with respect to mitigating factors; indeed, each juror can determine the existence of such evidence (see *McKoy v. North Carolina*, Chapter 10). Some states *require* the sentencing jury to impose the death penalty if the aggravating circumstances outweigh the mitigating circumstances. Other states *permit* a death sentence if the aggravators sufficiently outweigh the mitigators, but require a separate unanimous decision on the sentence (see *Blystone v. Pennsylvania*, Chapter 7).

Stage 4. Expedited Appeal

A defendant sentenced to death usually may appeal directly to the state court of last resort, bypassing the state intermediate appeals court. Nearly all states require review of a capital case by the state's highest court even if the convict does not wish to appeal. On appeal, the defendant—who is assigned state-paid counsel if indigent—may challenge the conviction or sentence on any number of grounds. Appeals courts do not ordinarily reconsider the guilt or sentence of the defendant. They review a transcript of the trial for procedural errors alleged by the defendant, such as violations of state rules of evidence or federal constitutional guarantees. If they conclude that such errors occurred and that they were serious enough to have resulted in an unfair trial or sentencing hearing, they will reverse the conviction or death sentence.

If there are no further appeals (see Stage 5, below), the case will then be *remanded* to the trial court so that the defective proceeding can be done over before a new jury. If, as often happens, the error occurred in the sentencing phase alone, only the punishment hearing will be repeated. (For double jeopardy considerations, see *Arizona v. Rumsey*, Chapter 21.)

Stage 5. Appeal to the United States Supreme Court

A defendant who claims that his federal constitutional rights were denied may petition the United States Supreme Court for a *writ of certiorari*. If the writ is granted the Supreme Court will review the case on appeal. Review is discretionary with the Justices of the Court (four of the nine must agree to take the case) and is conferred only in cases raising issues of national significance. About 1 percent (80 cases) of the nearly 8,000 annual certiorari petitions are successful, and even a death penalty case has a slim chance of being heard by the Supreme Court. If the Court denies certiorari the last lower court decision stands.

Stage 6. State Habeas Corpus

The direct appeal process ends when the United States Supreme Court denies certiorari or reviews the case on appeal. At this point, the capital defendant usually will seek further review of the case through state habeas corpus (also known as *postconviction review* or *collateral attack*). Although state habeas corpus technically is a civil proceeding rather than a continuation of the criminal case, as a practical matter, it is akin to another appeal. While appeals or habeas petitions (state or federal) are pending, the convict may not be executed.

Although the postconviction process varies from state to state, the following generally are true. Generally, the prisoner must first seek the writ from the trial court judge. If denied, he may appeal the denial to (or seek a new writ from) the state intermediate appeals court and then the state court of last resort.

The defendant must raise claims that could not be (or at least were not) raised on direct appeal. These may include federal or state constitutional arguments. The most popular claim is "ineffective assistance of counsel," which means that the trial attorney did not provide an adequate defense. (See *Burger v. Kemp*, Chapter 18, for an example of an effective assistance claim.) If the writ is granted, the trial court judgment (conviction or sentence) is reversed and the case remanded. The defendant may then be retried or resentenced.

If unsuccessful in the state courts (and if his habeas claim includes federal constitutional issues), the prisoner may (for the second time) seek United States Supreme Court review by writ of certiorari. Depending on state rules, the defendant may be able to file successive state habeas petitions, provided he raises different claims each time. The indigent prisoner has no federal constitutional right to free counsel for the preparation of state habeas petitions; the right to counsel, if any, is a matter of state law.

Stage 7. Federal Habeas Corpus

Once a state prisoner has "exhausted" all of his state remedies (direct appeals, which includes appeals to the U.S. Supreme Court, and state habeas petitions), he may seek federal habeas corpus review. (One consequence of the "exhaustion" requirement is that given the time needed for completing state postconviction review, only inmates under long prison or death sentences will be eligible for federal habeas.)

Federal habeas corpus is a civil action brought by an inmate against the prison authorities to challenge the legality of his incarceration. The purpose is to ensure that those accused of crimes are not convicted and punished in violation of the United States Constitution or other federal law. Federal habeas corpus is governed by federal statutes (28 U.S.C. §§ 2241–2266) and some rather complex Supreme Court decisions interpreting these acts. The writ may be issued by federal judges to state prisoners "in custody in violation of the Constitution or laws or treaties of the United States." 28 U.S.C. § 2241(c)(3). (State criminal cases rarely are affected by federal laws or treaties. Thus, habeas claims almost always involve alleged violations of constitutional rights.) If the writ issues, the prisoner must be released, retried, or resentenced, depending on the legal defect.

Federal habeas petitions must be filed with the United States District Court (single-judge federal courts) in the district in which the prisoner is incarcerated. The claims raised on federal habeas must have already been reviewed (and rejected) by the state courts during the direct appeals or state habeas process. This redundancy is intended to permit state courts to correct their own constitutional errors and to minimize federal court interference in state criminal prosecutions. Although there is no federal constitutional right to counsel for collateral review, federal statutes authorize U.S. district courts to appoint counsel at public expense for indigent habeas applicants under a death sentence.

If the application for the writ is denied, the prisoner may appeal the denial to the appropriate United States Court of Appeals and if unsuccessful there, may seek review of the denial of the writ by the United States Supreme Court. (This is likely to be a death row inmate's third Supreme Court certiorari petition, including the petitions on direct appeal and on state habeas.)

In recent years, federal district courts have received from state inmates approximately 21,000 habeas petitions annually. Fewer than 300 of these are filed by state prisoners under sentence of death. The overall success rate for all habeas petitioners (writ granted) has been very low—around 2 percent—but the rate is much higher for capital defendants. How high is a matter of dispute. A study by the National Center for State Courts (1994) found a 17 percent success rate for capital petitioners, and a one-year survey by the Justice Department (for 1995) produced a 12 percent rate, but some experts say that if one counts appeals of initially unsuccessful petitions, death row inmates ultimately obtain 40 percent of the writs they seek.[h]

Even unsuccessful petitions are helpful to death-sentenced inmates, however, as they delay the execution. Until the recent reform of habeas law (see below for discussion of the Antiterrorism and Effective Death Penalty Act of 1996), prisoners could file as many petitions as they or their lawyers could formulate, subject only to the rather ineffectual limitations of the Supreme Court's "abuse of the writ" doctrine. There were no time limits on filings and no bars to successive petitions, including eleventh hour applications just before scheduled executions. To many, federal habeas corpus had become a major source of inefficiency and lack of finality in the administration of criminal justice.[i]

---

[h] U.S. Dept. of Justice, Bureau of Justice Statistics, Prisoner Petitions in the Federal Courts, 1980–96 at 9 (1997) (12 percent of petitions that were not dismissed were concluded favorably to death row inmates by U.S. district courts); James S. Liebman, Jeffrey Fagan & Valerie West, "A Broken System: Error Rates in Capital Cases, 1973–1995," at http://www.law.columbia.edu/instructionalservices/liebman/liebman_final.pdf (June 2000) at App. A-8 (40 percent of death row petitions finally decided by U.S. district courts, U.S. courts of appeals or the Supreme Court between 1973 and 1995 were successful).

[i] See the report of the special committee created by Chief Justice Rehnquist and headed by then-retired Supreme Court Justice Lewis F. Powell, Jr. "Committee Report and Proposal from the Judicial Conference of the United States Ad Hoc Committee on Federal Habeas Corpus in Capital Cases," Aug. 23, 1989, reprinted in 135 Cong. Rec. S13482 (October 16, 1989).

THE ANTITERRORISM AND EFFECTIVE DEATH PENALTY ACT OF 1996

Despite strenuous opposition by death penalty abolitionists, Congress approved and President Clinton signed into law the Antiterrorism and Effective Death Penalty Act of 1996 ("AEDPA").

AEDPA was intended to expedite the federal habeas corpus process by shortening the time allowed for submitting applications, narrowing the legal grounds for issuing petitions, and discouraging appeals and successive petitions. If it proves effective, this legislation should speed up executions and decrease the number of overturned death sentences.

The act survived its first significant court challenge almost immediately after it went into effect. In *Felker v. Turpin*, 518 U.S. 1051 (1996), the Supreme Court held that modifying the requirements for habeas corpus did not amount to a suspension of the writ in violation of Article I, § 9 of the Constitution. (Article I, § 9 says, "The privilege of the Writ of Habeas Corpus shall not be suspended, unless when in Cases of Rebellion or Invasion the public Safety may require it.")

Whether AEDPA will be successful remains an open question.[j] There are also unresolved legal issues involving the interpretation and constitutionality of AEDPA's complex provisions. (See Chapter 26, *Herrera v. Collins*.)

Highlights of the Antiterrorism and Effective Death Penalty Act

- *Imposes time limits for filing habeas petitions.* Previously no time limits existed. Prisoners now must file within one year of the conclusion of direct appeals.
- *Mandates deference by the federal habeas judges to state court rulings.* Habeas claims must be denied unless the state court made an unreasonable application of federal law or an unreasonable determination of the facts. Factual determinations by the state courts must be presumed correct.
- *Discourages appeals by unsuccessful habeas petitioners.* The petitioner may only appeal when an appeals court judge or a Supreme Court Justice issues a "certificate of appealability" indicating that the applicant made a substantial showing of the denial of a constitutional right.
- *Bars, with a few narrow exceptions, multiple habeas petitions.* Second or successive petitions must be authorized by a federal court of appeals and only for newly discovered facts sufficient to undercut guilt or new rules of constitutional law made retroactive by the Supreme Court.

---

[j] See U.S. Dept. of Justice, Bureau of Justice Statistics, Prisoner Petitions Filed in U.S. District Courts, 2000, with Trends, 1980–2000 at 1, 5 (2001) (finding that AEDPA caused an *increase* in the number of habeas petitions filed by state inmates).

Stage 8. Executive Clemency

Once all judicial options have been unsuccessfully pursued, the death row inmate may apply for executive clemency. Traditionally in English law, the King had the authority to grant clemency: full or conditional pardon, commutation (shortening) of sentence, remissions of fines, and reprieves. In America, Article II, § 2 of the Constitution bestows upon the President the "Power to grant Reprieves and Pardons for Offences against the United States." (For a discussion, see Chapter 26, *Herrera v. Collins.*) Similarly, state constitutions vest the governors with sole clemency authority or final authority to act upon the recommendations of a clemency board. This authority is rarely subject to judicial review or legislative control, although the Supreme Court recently held that minimal due process must be accorded capital inmates in clemency proceedings. (*Ohio Adult Parole Authority v. Woodard*, 523 U.S. 272 [1998].) From 1976 to the end of 2000, there were 105 commutations of death sentences (during which time 6,441 death sentences were imposed and 683 were executed).[k]

THE EXTRALEGAL DEBATE

Much of the legal debate over the death penalty is intertwined with extralegal matters: penological, philosophical, and social. The aim of this section is to describe, as impartially as possible, the contours of this debate. We will note throughout the contributions of social scientists who have attempted to shed light on those aspects of the controversy that are amenable to empirical analysis.

Five key issues are discussed, in the following order: deterrence, retribution, incapacitation, mistake, and race.

Deterrence

A fundamental assumption of the criminal law is that punishing criminals discourages other potential offenders from committing crime. This is known as *general deterrence.* A key question is whether the death penalty is more effective as a crime preventative than less harsh punishments (such as life in prison)—what may be called the marginal deterrence benefit.

Proponents of capital punishment contend that deterrence is based on fear and that, since death is feared the most (among constitutionally permissible punishments—torture unto death being prohibited), it will deter the best. Opponents counter that murder often is an impulsive act and that killers do not think about punishment before committing their crimes. Consequently, they argue, those who engage in murder are singularly unlikely to be deterred by the threat of execu-

---

[k] See U.S. Dept. of Justice, Bureau of Justice Statistics, Capital Punishment 2000 at 13 (2001).

tion. Proponents respond that perhaps *some* killers cannot be deterred but other would-be murderers can (*e.g.*, those who plan the murder), and that justifies the most effective deterrence. Abolitionists question the assumption that death sentences are better deterrents than, say, life without parole. Their adversaries point out that although there is scant proof that longer prison sentences deter more than shorter ones, a fundamental premise of the criminal justice system is that harsher sentences deter more, and this same assumption supports the ultimate penalty (van den Haag and Conrad 1983).

Last, those opposed to the death penalty doubt that much deterrence is possible when so few executions actually take place. Death penalty advocates agree that more executions would be better, but add that, like the lottery, selecting only a few is enough so long as the target audience believes that they too might be chosen.

The major social science studies of deterrence were done by Isaac Ehrlich (1975a, 1975b) and Thorsten Sellin (1980). Sellin, who compared murder rates in states with and without a death penalty, concluded that there was no deterrent effect, but his work did not take account of the many factors other than the death penalty (*e.g.*, drug-related killings) that could affect murder rates. Ehrlich, using multiple regression analysis, was able to isolate the effect of executions on murder rates. He found that each execution in the United States, from 1933 to 1967, deterred eight murders. But Ehrlich's complex statistical methods have been sharply criticized, for, among other things, relying on national data even though many states had no death penalty.

Most empirical analyses of the death penalty have found no deterrent effect, heartening capital punishment opponents. (For a summary of the leading studies of deterrence, including Sellin's and Ehrlich's, see Bailey and Peterson 1994.) But those who favor the death penalty argue that the empirical evidence is contradictory and that if ultimate proof of deterrence (or nondeterrence) is unattainable, it is better to err in favor of capital punishment. After all, they reason, if the death penalty deters (though we cannot prove it), then employing it will save lives. If it doesn't deter, then justice still is served by the execution of murderers. One response to this is that society values present lives (even the lives of murderers) more than hypothetical future lives (those who might be saved because of deterrence). Furthermore, if there is no deterrence, then the advantage of the death penalty in terms of justice for murderers must be weighed against all of its disadvantages, including the risk of executing innocents.

There are those who claim not only that the death penalty does not deter, but that it actually *encourages* murder. At least two social scientists have contended that the death penalty has a reverse-deterrent, or "brutalization" effect; that is, that the number of murders actually increases after each execution (Bowers and Pierce 1980). Critics respond that only the long-term (*e.g.*, annual) effect on murder rates is significant. Moreover, conceding that some people are stimulated to violence by seeing it, they doubt that contemporary executions serve as that kind of stimulus. Executions no longer are public spectacles. They are held behind closed doors before a small number of selected observers and (so far, at least) are not televised.

Closely related to deterrence is the question of whether the death penalty provides marginal (*i.e.*, greater than imprisonment) reinforcement of moral inhibitions against murder. That is, do executions prevent murder—not by engendering fear (deterrence), but by strengthening the norms that restrain law-abiding citizens?

Proponents are fond of quoting the 19th-century English jurist Sir James Fitzjames Stephen: "Some men, probably, abstain from murder because they fear that if they committed murder they would be hanged. Hundreds of thousands abstain from it because they regard it with horror. One great reason why they regard it with horror is that murderers are hanged" (Stephen 1863, vol. 2, p. 99). That is, deterrence holds some in check, internal moral constraints (conscience) restrain most of us, and punishment fortifies or reinforces these moral constraints. But would our strong revulsion against murder diminish if there were no death penalty? Opponents doubt it, whereas proponents believe that it could happen over time and that the size of the morally inhibited population could be reduced. In other words, the question is whether, in the absence of the death penalty, there would be an increase in the number of people who would not regard murder "with horror" and therefore would engage in it.

Retribution

Retribution, or "just deserts," is a normative (nonempirical) justification of punishment and therefore is impervious to social science findings. In essence, the retributivist argument for the death penalty states that some crimes are so heinous, so profoundly reprehensible, that only the severest constitutionally acceptable penalty is appropriate for the perpetrator. Such an assertion can be neither proven nor disproven, but for death penalty opponents, life without parole is more than sufficient to the task. Justice, abolitionists argue, is amply served by condemning such criminals to a life of confinement, with its accompanying regimentation, degradation, boredom, abuse, assault, and fear.

All of us have, at one time or other, been horrified by newspaper or television accounts of especially shocking murders—the blowing up of buildings or airplanes with scores of occupants, savage rape-murders or torture-killings of young children, the assassination of a beloved national figure, and the like. Death penalty advocates believe that only the harshest penalty can provide justice for such horrific crimes. Opponents contend that most capital murderers (*i.e.*, murderers eligible for the death penalty), while properly condemned, are not nearly as blameworthy as those who commit the kinds of acts just described; they are more likely to be jittery armed robbers who shoot on impulse. Even if they concede (and they usually do not) that *some* criminals deserve to die, abolitionists doubt that the death penalty can be limited to the most reprehensible crimes.

They would rather lock up the most contemptible offenders for life than risk executing the less blameworthy.

A related—but strictly speaking, not a retributivist—argument is that the public's sense of justice demands a death penalty for the vilest crimes. This is not a retributivist claim because retribution theory asks only whether the punishment fits the crime and not whether it satisfies public sentiment or, for that matter, has any other instrumental effect. Nonetheless, perhaps because of the impossibility of proving that a punishment is "just," the public demand may serve as the measure of justice. One might also argue that in a democratic system, the punishments provided by the criminal law ought to reflect public sentiment, at least within constitutional boundaries.

To the abolitionists, any argument that the criminal law should gratify the public clamor for death is barbaric; it is vengeance in disguise—a catering to the darkest of human instincts. But retentionists are apt to share the view that "it is morally right to hate criminals" and that satisfying the public's "healthy natural sentiment" is "advantageous to the community" (Stephen 1883, vol. 2, pp. 81–82). As Émile Durkheim put it, punishing criminals "maintain[s] social cohesion intact" and conserves the "moral conscience" (Durkheim 1964, pp. 108–109). This is similar to the argument, considered earlier, that the death penalty provides reinforcement of moral inhibitions against murder.

A related advantage to the community of assuaging the public demand for justice is said to be the prevention of vigilantism, for if people come to feel that the authorities are incapable of providing justice, they may decide to provide it themselves. Death penalty opponents consider these arguments greatly overdrawn. They think that the realities of life in prison are harsh enough to satisfy the public, maintain community norms against murder, and prevent any widespread resort to "street justice."

Incapacitation

Whereas retributivism looks to punish people for their completed misdeeds, incapacitation justifies punishment on the grounds of public protection from *future* crimes. Incapacitation, in other words, looks ahead to the likelihood of recidivism by the offender. Clearly, death is the ultimate incapacitator, but is execution necessary if the offender is locked up for life, especially life without parole? Retentionists point out that even lifers pose a threat to fellow inmates and prison personnel, and there is always the possibility of the commutation of a sentence by a governor, retroactive liberalization of the parole laws, and (however remote) an escape from confinement. The opposition considers these events too unlikely to warrant executions and adds two other arguments.

First, they contend, murderers do not recidivate as often as most other offenders. Hugo A. Bedau (1982, p. 176) reports that of a sample of 2,646 released murderers (released from 12 states from 1900 to 1976), 16 were subsequently convicted of another homicide. Bedau considers this number very small, but at the standardized rate it comes to 605 per 100,000, a rate roughly 23 times higher than the recidivism rate for 18- to 24-year-olds, the most homicidal age group (see Appendix A).

Second, abolitionists reason that, since the death penalty applies to only a small percentage of murderers, the incapacitation benefit will likewise be small.

Mistake

For many, the possibility that an innocent person could be executed is sufficient in itself to warrant an end to capital punishment. While there is no compelling evidence that an innocent person has been executed since 1976, when the Supreme Court reinstated the death penalty, there have been numerous cases of death row inmates obtaining conviction reversals.[l] Some of these cases—the precise number is difficult to determine—appear to be true miscarriages of justice. In January 2000, following the thirteenth reversal of a death penalty conviction in Illinois, the Governor announced a death penalty moratorium in that state.

There are significantly more reversals on appeal in capital than noncapital cases. It is estimated that nationwide, noncapital convictions are overturned 15 percent of the time, whereas for death penalty cases the reversal rate may be as high as 68%.[m] Some see this as an indicator of a high risk of mistaken executions. However, most of the reversals are sentence-reversals due to errors in the penalty phase of the capital trial—errors which have no bearing upon guilt. The guilt portions of capital trials are overturned at a 20 percent rate, only five points higher than the reversal rate for non-capital prosecutions.

More significantly, reversal on appeal rarely connotes innocence. Appeals courts do not ordinarily re-examine the evidence or take new testimony; they review trial transcripts for procedural errors. If a conviction is reversed on appeal, a retrial is usually permitted. Even a failure to reprosecute, however, may not be a sign of factual innocence; it may simply reflect weakness in the state's case due to the passage of time. A reversal of the death sentence alone (due to procedural error in the penalty phase of the trial) is even more equivocal, as it leaves the murder conviction intact.

---

[l] Data from the Death Penalty Information Center, an anti-death penalty organization, indicate 93 cases from 1976 to the end of 2001 in which capital prosecutions were terminated following a reversal on appeal." See http://www.deathpenaltyinfo.org.

[m] A study of death penalty appeals found a 68 percent capital reversal rate. James S. Liebman, Jeffrey Fagan & Valerie West, "A Broken System: Error Rates in Capital Cases, 1973–1995," at http://www.law.columbia.edu/instructionalservices/liebman/liebman_final.pdf (June 2000). However, that figure may have been inflated. On recalculation using the same data, the rate was shown to be 52 percent. Barry Latzer & James N.G. Cauthen, "Another Recount: Appeals in Capital Cases," The Prosecutor 35: 25–28 (2001).

In exceptional cases there may be evidence uncovered after trial that strongly suggests innocence. (See Chapter 26, *Herrera v. Collins*, where several Supreme Court Justices expressed skepticism about defendant's innocence claim.) These unusual but disturbing cases are proof that despite all of the safeguards employed in contemporary capital cases—bifurcated trials, vigilant and numerous appeals—the risk that an innocent may be executed cannot be eliminated.

Death penalty retentionists are not without a response (see van den Haag and Conrad 1983). Many public policies—from war to space exploration—entail risks of innocent deaths. Whether the policy is worth pursuing requires a cost-benefit analysis, a weighing of the risk of harm against the benefits. The same analysis should apply to capital punishment. Is the remote risk of wrongful execution worth the advantages gained in innocent lives saved through deterrence and in justice for the truly blameworthy? The answer, of course, depends in part on one's views on the retributive and deterrent effects of the death penalty (see above).

In one of the few serious empirical studies of innocence and capital punishment, Bedau and Radelet (1987) concluded that 350 persons were wrongly convicted of capital or "potentially capital" crimes in the United States from 1900 to 1985 and that 23 of these cases resulted in the execution of an innocent person (before 1976). But their method of determining "innocence" was vigorously challenged in a rebuttal by Markman and Cassell (1988). The latter also observed that over 7,000 executions occurred during the time period studied, and even accepting that 23 persons were wrongfully executed, the rate of error is only one-third of one percent. Markman and Cassell consider this rate quite low, especially when balanced against the benefits of the death penalty in terms of incapacitation, deterrence, just punishment, and the fulfillment of society's duty to the victims.

Race

The data on executions show that blacks have constituted 52 percent of those put to death since 1930, 37 percent since 1976 (see Appendix A). These figures are way out of proportion to the black population, which is approximately 12 percent of the nation. The disparity is not necessarily due to race discrimination, however; rates of murder by blacks are seven to eight times those of whites, and roughly half of all murderers in the United States have been black (see Appendix A). It is possible that these figures may be slightly inflated by race prejudice on the part of the police or juries; it is not likely, however, that racism could explain much of the high incidence of murder by blacks.

Studies on the administration of the death penalty prior to the 1960's show that in the Southern states, blacks were much more likely than whites to be executed for rape, especially for raping white women (Wolfgang and Riedel 1973). The inference that racism influenced the imposition of the death penalty—at least during this period, for this crime, and in these states—is difficult to resist. Analyses of capital punishment for *murder*—even in the South, and especially after the 1950's—show that whites are *more* likely than blacks to be given the death penalty for the same offense (Rothman and Powers 1994). This remains true today. But—and this has been the focal point of the recent controversy—these studies also show that killers of whites are sentenced to death more often than killers of blacks, especially if the killer was black (U.S. GAO 1990). The best-known study, by David C. Baldus, Charles Pulaski, and George Woodworth, was the basis for the *McCleskey* case, in which the Supreme Court held that the research offered insufficient proof of a constitutional defect (see Chapter 25).

Opponents of capital punishment say that the studies prove that racist prosecutors or juries undervalue the lives of black murder victims. Defenders of the death penalty respond as follows. First, they say, these studies, which are based on sophisticated statistical techniques, are methodologically flawed. In McCleskey's case, the lower federal court relied on such a critique of the Baldus-Pulaski-Woodworth research in denying the writ of habeas corpus. *McCleskey v. Zant*, 580 F. Supp. 338 (N.D. Ga. 1984).

Second, critics claim, there may be a nonracial explanation for the disparity: murders of blacks are less often "aggravated," therefore they lack one of the legal requirements (the aggravating factor) for the death penalty. Murders are overwhelmingly intraracial; that is, blacks are usually killed by blacks, whites by whites (see Appendix A). Many of the killings of blacks, it is contended, are a result of quarrels among acquaintances, and these are less likely to be aggravated. By contrast, the victims of the most commonplace aggravated murders—robbery-murders of strangers and killings of police officers—are more likely to be white (Rothman and Powers 1994). Defenders of the studies deny that aggravating factors explain the racial differential, insisting that racial disparities remain even after controlling for such factors.

Finally, critics of the studies find it odd that allegedly racist juries discriminate against dead black victims but not against the black defendants (or in favor of the white defendants) sitting before them. That is, juries—the racial makeup of which is not taken into account in most studies—are more likely to impose death sentences on white defendants than black defendants, belying charges of racism. Critics also add that since murders are overwhelmingly intraracial, efforts to increase the number of death sentences imposed on killers of blacks would, ironically, result in the execution of more black defendants.

The response to these objections is that the studies prove that there *is* discrimination against black defendants—black defendants charged with killing whites. For many, this is reason enough to abolish capital punishment. As a fallback position, some anti-death penalty activists favor the development of prosecutorial guidelines restricting capital prosecutions to the most aggravated murders, as the studies show that these are least affected by racial motivations. However, proposals to limit the discretion of American prosecutors have not gotten much support.

REFERENCES

Bailey, William C., and Ruth D. Peterson. "Murder, Capital Punishment, and Deterrence: A Review of the Evidence and an Examination of Police Killings." *Journal of Social Issues* 50 (1994): 53–74.

Bedau, Hugo A. *The Death Penalty in America*, 3d ed. Oxford: Oxford University Press, 1982.

Bedau, Hugo A., and Michael L. Radelet. "Miscarriages of Justice in Potentially Capital Cases." *Stanford Law Review* 40 (1987): 21–90.

Bowers, William J., and Glenn L. Pierce. "Deterrence or Brutalization: What Is the Effect of Executions?" *Crime and Delinquency* 26 (1980): 453–484.

Durkheim, Émile. *The Division of Labor in Society*, translated by George Simpson. New York: The Free Press, 1964.

Ehrlich, Isaac. "The Deterrent Effect of Capital Punishment: A Question of Life and Death." *American Economic Review* 65 (1975a): 397–417.

Ehrlich, Isaac. "Deterrence: Evidence and Inference." *Yale Law Journal* 85 (1975b): 209–227.

Ellsworth, Phoebe C., and Samuel R. Gross. "Hardening of the Attitudes: Americans' Views on the Death Penalty." *Journal of Social Issues* 50 (1994): 19–52.

Latzer, Barry, and James N.G. Cauthen, "Another Recount: Appeals in Capital Cases." *The Prosecutor* 35 (2001): 25–28.

Liebman, James S., Jeffrey Fagan, and Valerie West, "A Broken System: Error Rates in Capital Cases, 1973–1995." http://www.law.columbia.edu/instructionalservices/liebman/liebman_final.pdf (June 2000).

Markman, Steven J., and Paul G. Cassell. "Protecting the Innocent: A Response to the Bedau-Radelet Study." *Stanford Law Review* 41 (1988): 121–160.

National Center for State Courts. *Habeas Corpus in State and Federal Courts*. Williamsburg, VA: National Center for State Courts, 1994.

Rosenberg, Tina. "Deadliest D.A." *The New York Times Magazine* (July 16, 1995), pp. 21 ff.

Rothman, Stanley, and Stephen Powers. "Execution by Quota?" *The Public Interest* 116 (1994): 3–17.

Sellin, Thorsten. *The Penalty of Death*. Beverly Hills, CA: Sage Publications, 1980.

Stephen, Sir James Fitzjames. *A General View of the Criminal Law of England*. London: Macmillan, 1863.

Stephen, Sir James Fitzjames. *A History of the Criminal Law of England*. London: Macmillan, 1883.

United States General Accounting Office [U.S. GAO]. *Death Penalty Sentencing: Research Indicates Pattern of Racial Disparities*. Washington, DC: GPO, 1990.

van den Haag, Ernest, and John P. Conrad. *The Death Penalty, A Debate*. New York and London: Plenum Press, 1983.

Wolfgang, Marvin E., and Marc Riedel. "Race, Judicial Discretion, and the Death Penalty." *The Annals of the American Academy of Political and Social Science* 407 (1973): 119–133.

Chapter 2

Cruel and Unusual as Applied—*Furman v. Georgia* (1972)

Furman v. Georgia, 408 U.S. 238, 92 S. Ct. 2726, 33 L. Ed.2d 346 (1972) (5–4, the death penalty, as administered at the time, violates the Eighth Amendment).

Editor's comment: In the *Furman* case, the Supreme Court, for the first time in American history, found that capital punishment violates the cruel and unusual punishments provision of the Eighth Amendment. But each Justice wrote an opinion, and the grounds for the decision were left unclear. The absence of agreement among the Justices also is reflected in the use of a "per curiam" opinion—a concise unsigned opinion "for the Court." Only two Justices (Brennan and Marshall) expressly contended that the death penalty was, in and of itself (per se), unconstitutional. Justices Stewart and White, although part of the five-Justice majority, rejected this absolute position. Given reforms acceptable to Stewart and White, their votes, along with those of the four dissenters, could yield a potential future majority of the Court in support of the death penalty. The question was, what reforms were necessary? The disparate opinions, most of which are reprinted here, left the state legislatures in a quandary as to what kind of changes had to be made. Some states enacted mandatory death penalty laws (declared unconstitutional in *Woodson v. North Carolina*, 428 U.S. 280 [1976]). Others adopted procedures to restrict jury discretion in capital cases. This approach won Court approval in *Gregg v. Georgia*, 428 U.S. 153 (1976).

❖   ❖   ❖

PER CURIAM OPINION

Petitioner in No. 69–5003 was convicted of murder in Georgia and was sentenced to death. . . . Petitioner in No. 69–5030 was convicted of rape in Georgia and was sentenced to death. . . . Petitioner in No. 69–5031 was convicted of rape in Texas and was sentenced to death. . . . Certiorari was granted limited to the following question: "Does the imposition and carrying out of the death penalty in (these cases) constitute cruel and unusual punishment in violation of the Eighth and Fourteenth Amendments?" The Court holds that the imposition and carrying out of the death penalty in these cases constitute cruel and unusual punishment in violation of the Eighth and Fourteenth Amendments. The judgment in each case is therefore reversed insofar as it leaves undisturbed the death sentence imposed, and the cases are remanded for further proceedings.

CONCURRING OPINION OF JUSTICE DOUGLAS

The generality of a law inflicting capital punishment is one thing. What may be said of the validity of a law on the books and what may be done with the law in its application do, or may, lead to quite different conclusions. It would seem to be incontestable that the death penalty inflicted on one defendant is "unusual" if it discriminates against him by reason of his race, religion, wealth, social position, or class, or if it is imposed under a procedure that gives room for the play of such prejudices. . . .

The words "cruel and unusual" certainly include penalties that are barbaric. But the words, at least when read in light of the English proscription against selective and irregular use of penalties, suggest that it is "cruel and unusual" to apply the death penalty—or any other penalty—selectively to minorities whose numbers are few, who are outcasts of society, and who are unpopular, but whom society is willing to see suffer though it would not countenance general application of the same penalty across the board. . . .

There is increasing recognition of the fact that the basic theme of equal protection is implicit in "cruel and unusual" punishments. "A penalty . . . should be considered 'unusually' imposed if it is administered arbitrarily or discriminatorily." . . .

We cannot say from facts disclosed in these records that these defendants were sentenced to death because they were black. Yet our task is not restricted to an effort to divine what motives impelled these death penalties. Rather, we deal with a system of law and of justice that leaves to the uncontrolled discretion of judges or juries the determination whether defendants committing these crimes should die or be imprisoned. Under these laws no standards govern the selection of the penalty. People live or die, dependent on the whim of 1 man or of 12. . . .

Those who wrote the Eighth Amendment knew what price their forebears had paid for a system based, not on equal justice, but on discrimination. In those days the target was not the blacks or the poor, but the dissenters, those who opposed absolutism in government, who struggled for a parliamentary regime, and who opposed governments' recurring efforts to foist a particular religion on the people. But the tool of capital punishment was used with vengeance against the opposition and those unpopular with the regime. One cannot read this history without realizing that the desire for equality was reflected in the ban against "cruel and unusual punishments" contained in the Eighth Amendment.

In a Nation committed to equal protection of the laws there is no permissible "caste" aspect of law enforcement. Yet we know that the discretion of judges and juries in imposing the death penalty enables the penalty to be selectively applied, feeding prejudices against the accused if he is poor and despised, and lacking political clout, or if he is a member of a suspect or unpopular minority, and saving those who by social position may be in a more protected position. In ancient Hindu law a Brahman was exempt from capital punishment, and under that law, "[g]enerally, in the law books, punishment increased in severity as social status diminished." We have, I fear, taken in practice the same position, partially as a result of making the death penalty discretionary and partially as a result of the ability of the rich to purchase the services of the most respected and most resourceful legal talent in the Nation.

The high service rendered by the "cruel and unusual" punishment clause of the Eighth Amendment is to require legislatures to write penal laws that are evenhanded, nonselective, and nonarbitrary, and to require judges to see to it that general laws are not applied sparsely, selectively, and spottily to unpopular groups.

A law that stated that anyone making more than $50,000 would be exempt from the death penalty would plainly fall, as would a law that in terms said that blacks, those who never went beyond the fifth grade in school, those who made less than $3,000 a year, or those who were unpopular or unstable should be the only people executed. A law which in the overall view reaches that result in practice has no more sanctity than a law which in terms provides the same.

Thus, these discretionary statutes are unconstitutional in their operation. They are pregnant with discrimination and discrimination is an ingredient not compatible with the idea of equal protection of the laws that is implicit in the ban on "cruel and unusual" punishments.

Any law which is nondiscriminatory on its face may be applied in such a way as to violate the Equal Protection Clause of the Fourteenth Amendment.... Such conceivably might be the fate of a mandatory death penalty, where equal or lesser sentences were imposed on the elite, a harsher one on the minorities or members of the lower castes. Whether a mandatory death penalty would otherwise be constitutional is a question I do not reach.

CONCURRING OPINION OF JUSTICE BRENNAN

There are, then, four principles by which we may determine whether a particular punishment is "cruel and unusual."... If a punishment is unusually severe, if there is a strong probability that it is inflicted arbitrarily, if it is substantially rejected by contemporary society, and if there is no reason to believe that it serves any penal purpose more effectively than some less severe punishment, then the continued infliction of that punishment violates the command of the Clause that the State may not inflict inhuman and uncivilized punishments upon those convicted of crimes. . . .

III

The question, then, is whether the deliberate infliction of death is today consistent with the command of the Clause that the State may not inflict punishments that do not comport with human dignity. I will analyze the punishment of death in terms of the principles set out above and the cumulative test to which they lead: It is a denial of human dignity for the State arbitrarily to subject a person to an unusually severe punishment that society has indicated it does not regard as acceptable, and that cannot be shown to serve any penal purpose more effectively than a significantly less drastic punishment. Under these principles and this test, death is today a "cruel and unusual" punishment.

Death is a unique punishment in the United States. In a society that so strongly affirms the sanctity of life, not surprisingly the common view is that death is the ultimate sanction. This natural human feeling appears all about us. There has been no national debate about punishment, in general or by imprisonment, comparable to the debate about the punishment of death. No other punishment has been so continuously restricted, nor has any State yet abolished prisons, as some have abolished this punishment. And those States that still inflict death reserve it for the most heinous crimes. Juries, of course, have always treated death cases differently, as have governors exercising their commutation powers. Criminal defendants are of the same view. . . . Some legislatures have required particular procedures, such as two-stage trials and automatic appeals, applicable only in death cases. . . . This Court, too, almost always treats death cases as a class apart. And the unfortunate effect of this punishment upon the functioning of the judicial process is well known; no other punishment has a similar effect.

The only explanation for the uniqueness of death is its extreme severity. Death is today an unusually severe punishment, unusual in its pain, in its finality, and in its enormity. No other existing punishment is comparable to death in terms of physical and mental suffering. Although our information is not conclusive, it appears that there is no method available that guarantees an immediate and painless death. Since the discontinuance of flogging as a constitutionally permissible punishment, death remains as the only punishment that may involve the conscious infliction of physical pain. In addition, we know that mental pain is an inseparable part of our practice of punishing criminals by death, for the prospect of pending execution exacts a frightful toll during the inevitable long wait between the imposition of sentence and the actual infliction of death. . . .

The unusual severity of death is manifested most clearly in its finality and enormity. Death, in these respects, is in a class by itself. . . .

Death is truly an awesome punishment. The calculated killing of a human being by the State involves, by its very nature, a denial of the executed person's humanity. The contrast with the plight of a person punished by imprisonment is evident. An individual in prison does not lose "the right to have rights." . . . His punishment is not irrevocable. Apart from the common charge, grounded upon the recognition of human fallibility, that the punishment of death must inevitably be inflicted upon innocent men, we know that death has been the lot of men whose convictions were unconstitutionally secured in view of later, retroactively applied, holdings of this Court. The punishment itself may have been unconstitutionally inflicted, see *Witherspoon v. Illinois*, yet the finality of death precludes relief. . . .

In comparison to all other punishments today, then, the deliberate extinguishment of human life by the State is uniquely degrading to human dignity. I would not hesitate to hold, on that ground alone, that death is today a "cruel and unusual" punishment, were it not that death is a punishment of long-standing usage and acceptance in this country. I therefore turn to the second principle— that the State may not arbitrarily inflict an unusually severe punishment.

The outstanding characteristic of our present practice of punishing criminals by death is the infrequency with which we resort to it. The evidence is conclusive that death is not the ordinary punishment for any crime. There has been a steady decline in the infliction of this punishment in every decade since the 1930's, the earliest period for which accurate statistics are available. In the 1930's, executions averaged 167 per year; in the 1940's, the average was 128; in the 1950's, it was 72; and in the years 1960–1962, it was 48. There have been a total of 46 executions since then, 36 of them in 1963–1964. Yet our population and the number of capital crimes committed have increased greatly over the past four decades. The contemporary rarity of the infliction of this punishment is thus the end result of a long-continued decline. . . .

When a country of over 200 million people inflicts an unusually severe punishment no more than 50 times a year, the inference is strong that the punishment is not being regularly and fairly applied. To dispel it would indeed require a clear showing of nonarbitrary infliction.

Although there are no exact figures available, we know that thousands of murders and rapes are committed annually in States where death is an authorized punishment for those crimes. However the rate of infliction is characterized—as "freakishly" or "spectacularly" rare, or simply as rare—it would take the purest sophistry to deny that death is inflicted in only a minute fraction of these cases. How much rarer, after all, could the infliction of death be?

When the punishment of death is inflicted in a trivial number of the cases in which it is legally available, the conclusion is virtually inescapable that it is being inflicted arbitrarily. Indeed, it smacks of little more than a lottery system. The States claim, however, that this rarity is evidence not of arbitrariness, but of informed selectivity: Death is inflicted, they say, only in "extreme" cases.

Informed selectivity, of course, is a value not to be denigrated. Yet presumably the States could make precisely the same claim if there were 10 executions per year, or 5, or even if there were but 1. That there may be as many as 50 per year does not strengthen the claim. When the rate of infliction is at this low level, it is highly implausible that only the worst criminals or the criminals who commit the worst crimes are selected for this punishment. No one has yet suggested a rational basis that could differentiate in those terms the few who die from the many who go to prison. Crimes and criminals simply do not admit of a distinction that can be drawn so finely as to explain, on that ground, the execution of such a tiny sample of those eligible. Certainly the laws that provide for this punishment do not attempt to draw that distinction; all cases to which the laws apply are necessarily "extreme." Nor is the distinction credible in fact. If, for example, petitioner Furman or his crime illustrates the "extreme," then nearly all murderers and their murders are also "extreme."

Furthermore, our procedures in death cases, rather than resulting in the selection of "extreme" cases for this punishment, actually sanction an arbitrary selection. For this Court has held that juries may, as they do, make the decision whether to impose a death sentence wholly unguided by standards governing that decision. *McGautha v. California*, 402 U.S. 183, 196–208 (1971). In other words, our procedures are not constructed to guard against the totally capricious selection of criminals for the punishment of death.

Although it is difficult to imagine what further facts would be necessary in order to prove that death is, as my Brother Stewart puts it, "wantonly and . . . freakishly" inflicted, I need not conclude that arbitrary infliction is patently obvious. I am not considering this punishment by the isolated light of one principle. The probability of arbitrariness is sufficiently substantial that it can be relied upon, in combination with the other principles, in reaching a judgment on the constitutionality of this punishment.

When there is a strong probability that an unusually severe and degrading punishment is being inflicted arbitrarily, we may well expect that society will disapprove of its infliction. I turn, therefore, to the third principle. An examination of the history and present operation of the American practice of punishing criminals by death reveals that this punishment has been almost totally rejected by contemporary society.

. . . From the beginning of our Nation, the punishment of death has stirred acute public controversy. Although pragmatic arguments for and against the punishment have been frequently advanced, this longstanding and heated controversy cannot be explained solely as the result of differences over the practical wisdom of a particular government policy. At bottom, the battle has been waged on moral grounds. The country has debated whether a society for which the dignity of the individual is the supreme value can, without a fundamental inconsistency, follow the practice of deliberately putting some of its members to death. . . .

Our practice of punishing criminals by death has changed greatly over the years. One significant change has been in our methods of inflicting death. Although this country never embraced the more violent and repulsive methods employed in England, we did for a long time rely almost exclusively upon the gallows and the firing squad. Since the development of the supposedly more humane methods of electrocution late in the 19th century and lethal gas in the

20th, however, hanging and shooting have virtually ceased. Our concern for decency and human dignity, moreover, has compelled changes in the circumstances surrounding the execution itself. No longer does our society countenance the spectacle of public executions, once thought desirable as a deterrent to criminal behavior by others. Today we reject public executions as debasing and brutalizing to us all.

Also significant is the drastic decrease in the crimes for which the punishment of death is actually inflicted. While esoteric capital crimes remain on the books, since 1930 murder and rape have accounted for nearly 99 percent of the total executions, and murder alone for about 87 percent. In addition, the crime of capital murder has itself been limited. As the Court noted in *McGautha v. California*, there was in this country a "rebellion against the common-law rule imposing a mandatory death sentence on all convicted murderers." . . . In consequence, virtually all death sentences today are discretionarily imposed. Finally, it is significant that nine States no longer inflict the punishment of death under any circumstances, and five others have restricted it to extremely rare crimes.

Thus, although "the death penalty has been employed throughout our history," *Trop v. Dulles*, in fact the history of this punishment is one of successive restriction. What was once a common punishment has become, in the context of a continuing moral debate, increasingly rare. The evolution of this punishment evidences, not that it is an inevitable part of the American scene, but that it has proved progressively more troublesome to the national conscience. The result of this movement is our current system of administering the punishment, under which death sentences are rarely imposed and death is even more rarely inflicted. . . .

The progressive decline in, and the current rarity of, the infliction of death demonstrate that our society seriously questions the appropriateness of this punishment today. The States point out that many legislatures authorize death as the punishment for certain crimes and that substantial segments of the public, as reflected in opinion polls and referendum votes, continue to support it. Yet the availability of this punishment through statutory authorization, as well as the polls and referenda, which amount simply to approval of that authorization, simply underscores the extent to which our society has in fact rejected this punishment. When an unusually severe punishment is authorized for wide-scale application but not, because of society's refusal, inflicted save in a few instances, the inference is compelling that there is a deep-seated reluctance to inflict it. Indeed, the likelihood is great that the punishment is tolerated only because of its disuse. The objective indicator of society's view of an unusually severe punishment is what society does with it, and today society will inflict death upon only a small sample of the eligible criminals. Rejection could hardly be more complete without becoming absolute. At the very least, I must conclude that contemporary society views this punishment with substantial doubt.

The final principle to be considered is that an unusually severe and degrading punishment may not be excessive in view of the purposes for which it is inflicted. This principle, too, is related to the others. When there is a strong probability that the State is arbitrarily inflicting an unusually severe punishment that is subject to grave societal doubts, it is likely also that the punishment cannot be shown to be serving any penal purpose that could not be served equally well by some less severe punishment.

The States' primary claim is that death is a necessary punishment because it prevents the commission of capital crimes more effectively than any less severe punishment. The first part of this claim is that the infliction of death is necessary to stop the individuals executed from committing further crimes. The sufficient answer to this is that if a criminal convicted of a capital crime poses a danger to society, effective administration of the State's pardon and parole laws can delay or deny his release from prison, and techniques of isolation can eliminate or minimize the danger while he remains confined.

The more significant argument is that the threat of death prevents the commission of capital crimes because it deters potential criminals who would not be deterred by the threat of imprisonment. The argument is not based upon evidence that the threat of death is a superior deterrent. Indeed, as my Brother Marshall establishes, the available evidence uniformly indicates, although it does not conclusively prove, that the threat of death has no greater deterrent effect than the threat of imprisonment. The States argue, however, that they are entitled to rely upon common human experience, and that experience, they say, supports the conclusion that death must be a more effective deterrent than any less severe punishment. Because people fear death the most, the argument runs, the threat of death must be the greatest deterrent.

It is important to focus upon the precise import of this argument. It is not denied that many, and probably most, capital crimes cannot be deterred by the threat of punishment. Thus the argument can apply only to those who think rationally about the commission of capital crimes. Particularly is that true when the potential criminal, under this argument, must not only consider the risk of punishment, but also distinguish between two possible punishments. The concern, then, is with a particular type of potential criminal, the rational person who will commit a capital crime knowing that the punishment is long-term imprisonment, which may well be for the rest of his life, but will not commit the crime knowing that the punishment is death. On the face of it, the assumption that such persons exist is implausible.

In any event, this argument cannot be appraised in the abstract. We are not presented with the theoretical question whether under any imaginable circumstances the threat of death might be a greater deterrent to the commission of capital crimes than the threat of imprisonment. We are concerned with the practice of punishing criminals by death as it exists in the United States today. Proponents of this argument necessarily admit that its validity depends upon the existence of a system in which the punishment of death is invariably and swiftly imposed. Our system, of course, satisfies neither condition. A rational person contemplating a murder or rape is confronted, not with the certainty of a speedy death, but with the slightest possibility that he will be executed in the distant future. The risk of death is remote and improbable; in contrast, the risk of long-term imprisonment is near and great. In short, whatever the speculative validity of the assumption that the threat of death is a superior deterrent, there is no reason to believe that as currently administered the punishment of death is necessary to deter the commission of capital crimes. Whatever might be the case were all or substantially all eligible criminals quickly put to death, unverifiable possibilities are an insufficient basis upon which to conclude that the threat of death today has any greater deterrent efficacy than the threat of imprisonment.

There is, however, another aspect to the argument that the punishment of death is necessary for the protection of society. The infliction of death, the States urge, serves to manifest the community's outrage at the commission of the crime. It is, they say, a concrete public expression of moral indignation that inculcates respect for the law and helps assure a more peaceful community. Moreover, we are told, not only does the punishment of death exert this widespread moralizing influence upon community values, it also satisfies the popular demand for grievous condemnation of abhorrent crimes and thus prevents disorder, lynching, and attempts by private citizens to take the law into their own hands.

The question, however, is not whether death serves these supposed purposes of punishment, but whether death serves them more effectively than imprisonment. There is no evidence whatever that utilization of imprisonment rather than death encourages private blood feuds and other disorders. Surely if there were such a danger, the execution of a handful of criminals each year would not prevent it. The assertion that death alone is a sufficiently emphatic denunciation for capital crimes suffers from the same defect. If capital crimes require the punishment of death in order to provide moral reinforcement for the basic values of the community, those values can only be undermined when death is so rarely inflicted upon the criminals who commit the crimes. Furthermore, it is certainly doubtful that the infliction of death by the State does in fact strengthen the community's moral code; if the deliberate extinguishment of human life has any effect at all, it more likely tends to lower our respect for life and brutalize our values. That, after all, is why we no longer carry out public executions. In any event, this claim simply means that one purpose of punishment is to indicate social disapproval of crime. To serve that purpose our laws distribute punishments according to the gravity of crimes and punish more severely the crimes society regards as more serious. That purpose cannot justify any particular punishment as the upper limit of severity.

There is, then, no substantial reason to believe that the punishment of death, as currently administered, is necessary for the protection of society. The only other purpose suggested, one that is independent of protection for society, is retribution. Shortly stated, retribution in this context means that criminals are put to death because they deserve it. . . . As administered today, however, the punishment of death cannot be justified as a necessary means of exacting retribution from criminals. When the overwhelming number of criminals who commit capital crimes go to prison, it cannot be concluded that death serves the purpose of retribution more effectively than imprisonment. The asserted public belief that murderers and rapists deserve to die is flatly inconsistent with the execution of a random few. As the history of the punishment of death in this country shows, our society wishes to prevent crime; we have no desire to kill criminals simply to get even with them.

In sum, the punishment of death is inconsistent with all four principles: Death is an unusually severe and degrading punishment; there is a strong probability that it is inflicted arbitrarily; its rejection by contemporary society is virtually total; and there is no reason to believe that it serves any penal purpose more effectively than the less severe punishment of imprisonment. The function of these principles is to enable a court to determine whether a punishment comports with human dignity. Death, quite simply, does not.

CONCURRING OPINION OF JUSTICE STEWART

The penalty of death differs from all other forms of criminal punishment, not in degree but in kind. It is unique in its total irrevocability. It is unique in its rejection of rehabilitation of the convict as a basic purpose of criminal justice. And it is unique, finally, in its absolute renunciation of all that is embodied in our concept of humanity.

For these and other reasons, at least two of my Brothers have concluded that the infliction of the death penalty is constitutionally impermissible in all circumstances under the Eight and Fourteenth Amendments. Their case is a strong one. But I find it unnecessary to reach the ultimate question they would decide. . . .

In the first place, it is clear that these sentences are "cruel" in the sense that they excessively go beyond, not in degree but in kind, the punishments that the state legislatures have determined to be necessary. *Weems v. United States*. In the second place, it is equally clear that these sentences are "unusual" in the sense that the penalty of death is infrequently imposed for murder, and that its imposition for rape is extraordinarily rare. But I do not rest by conclusion upon these two propositions alone.

These death sentences are cruel and unusual in the same way that being struck by lightning is cruel and unusual. For, of all the people convicted of rapes and murders in 1967 and 1968, many just as reprehensible as these, the petitioners are among a capriciously selected random handful upon whom the sentence of death has in fact been imposed. My concurring Brothers have demonstrated that, if any basis can be discerned for the selection of these few to be sentenced to die, it is the constitutionally impermissible basis of race. But racial discrimination has not been proved, and I put it to one side. I simply conclude that the Eighth and Fourteenth Amendments cannot tolerate the infliction of a sentence of death under legal systems that permit this unique penalty to be so wantonly and so freakishly imposed.

CONCURRING OPINION OF JUSTICE WHITE

The facial constitutionality of statutes requiring the imposition of the death penalty for first-degree murder, for more narrowly defined categories of murder, or for rape would present quite different issues under the Eighth Amendment than are posed by the cases before us. In joining the Court's judgments, therefore, I do not at all intimate that the death penalty is unconstitutional *per se* or that there is no system of capital punishment that would comport with the Eighth Amendment. That question, ably argued by several of my Brethren, is not presented by these cases and need not be decided.

The narrower question to which I address myself concerns the constitutionality of capital punishment statutes under which (1) the legislature authorizes the imposition of the death penalty for murder or rape; (2) the legislature does not itself mandate the penalty in any particular class or kind of case (that is, legislative will is not frustrated if the penalty is never imposed), but delegates to judges or juries the decisions as to those cases, if any, in which the penalty will be utilized; and (3) judges and juries have ordered the death penalty with such infrequency that the odds are now very much against imposition and execution of the penalty with respect to any convicted murderer or rapist. It is in this context that we must consider whether the execution of these petitioners would violate the Eighth Amendment.

I begin with what I consider a near truism: that the death penalty could so seldom be imposed that it would cease to be a credible deterrent or measurably to contribute to any other end of punishment in the criminal justice system. It is perhaps true that no matter how infrequently those convicted of rape or murder are executed, the penalty so imposed is not disproportionate to the crime and those executed may deserve exactly what they received. It would also be clear that executed defendants are finally and completely incapacitated from again committing rape or murder or any other crime. But when imposition of the penalty reaches a certain degree of infrequency, it would be very doubtful that any existing general need for retribution would be measurably satisfied. Nor could it be said with confidence that society's need for specific deterrence justifies death for so few when for so many in like circumstances life imprisonment or shorter prison terms are judged sufficient, or that community values are measurably reinforced by authorizing a penalty so rarely invoked.

Most important, a major goal of the criminal law—to deter others by punishing the convicted criminal—would not be substantially served where the penalty is so seldom invoked that it ceases to be the credible threat essential to influence the conduct of others. For present purposes I accept the morality and utility of punishing one person to influence another. I accept also the effectiveness of punishment generally and need not reject the death penalty as a more effective deterrent than a lesser punishment. But common sense and experience tell us that seldom-enforced laws become ineffective measures for controlling human conduct and that the death penalty, unless imposed with sufficient frequency, will make little contribution to deterring those crimes for which it may be exacted.

The imposition and execution of the death penalty are obviously cruel in the dictionary sense. But the penalty has not been considered cruel and unusual punishment in the constitutional sense because it was thought justified by the social ends it was deemed to serve. At the moment that it ceases realistically to further these purposes, however, the emerging question is whether its imposition in such circumstances would violate the Eighth Amendment. It is my view that it would, for its imposition would then be the pointless and needless extinction of life with only marginal contributions to any discernible social or public purposes. A penalty with such negligible returns to the State would be patently excessive and cruel and unusual punishment violative of the Eighth Amendment.

It is also my judgment that this point has been reached with respect to capital punishment as it is presently administered under the statutes involved in these cases. Concededly, it is difficult to prove as a general proposition that capital punishment, however administered, more effectively serves the ends of the criminal law than does imprisonment. But however that may be, I cannot avoid the conclusion that as the statutes before us are now administered, the penalty is so infrequently imposed that the threat of execution is too attenuated to be of substantial service to criminal justice. . . .

The short of it is that the policy of vesting sentencing authority primarily in juries—a decision largely motivated by the desire to mitigate the harshness of the law and to bring community judgment to bear on the sentence as well as guilt or innocence—has so effectively achieved its aims that capital punishment within the confines of the statutes now before us has for all practical purposes run its course.

CONCURRING OPINION OF JUSTICE MARSHALL

[A] punishment may be deemed cruel and unusual for any one of four distinct reasons.

First, there are certain punishments that inherently involve so much physical pain and suffering that civilized people cannot tolerate them—*e.g.*, use of the rack, the thumbscrew. . . .

Second, there are punishments that are unusual, signifying that they were previously unknown as penalties for a given offense. . . . If these punishments are intended to serve a humane purpose, they may be constitutionally permissible. . . . Prior decisions leave open the question of just how much the word "unusual" adds to the word "cruel." I have previously indicated that use of the word "unusual" in the English Bill of Rights of 1689 was inadvertent, and there is nothing in the history of the Eighth Amendment to give flesh to its intended meaning. In light of the meager history that does exist, one would suppose that an innovative punishment would probably be constitutional if no more cruel than that punishment which it superseded. We need not decide this question here, however, for capital punishment is certainly not a recent phenomenon.

Third, a penalty may be cruel and unusual because it is excessive and serves no valid legislative purpose. *Weems v. United States*. The decisions previously discussed are replete with assertions that one of the primary functions of the cruel and unusual punishments clause is to prevent excessive or unnecessary penalties, *e.g.*, *Wilkerson v. Utah*; *O'Neil v. Vermont*; *Weems v. United States*; *Louisiana ex rel. Francis v. Resweber*; these punishments are unconstitutional even though popular sentiment may favor them. . . .

Fourth, where a punishment is not excessive and serves a valid legislative purpose, it still may be invalid if popular sentiment abhors it. For example, if the evidence clearly demonstrated that capital punishment served valid legislative purposes, such punishment would, nevertheless, be unconstitutional if citizens found it to be morally unacceptable. A general abhorrence on the part of the public would, in effect, equate a modern punishment with those barred since the adoption of the Eighth Amendment. There are no prior cases in this Court striking down a penalty on this ground, but the very notion of changing values requires that we recognize its existence.

It is immediately obvious, then, that since capital punishment is not a recent phenomenon, if it violates the Constitution, it does so because it is excessive or unnecessary, or because it is abhorrent to currently existing moral values. . . .

V

In order to assess whether or not death is an excessive or unnecessary penalty, it is necessary to consider the reasons why a legislature might select it as punishment for one or more offenses, and examine whether less severe penalties would satisfy the legitimate legislative wants as well as capital punishment. If they would, then the death penalty is unnecessary cruelty, and, therefore, unconstitutional.

There are six purposes conceivably served by capital punishment: retribution, deterrence, prevention of repetitive criminal acts, encouragement of guilty pleas and confessions, eugenics, and economy. These are considered *seriatim* below.

A. The concept of retribution is one of the most misunderstood in all of our criminal jurisprudence. The principal source of confusion derives from the fact that, in dealing with the concept, most people confuse the question "why do men in fact punish?" with the question "what justifies men in punishing?" Men may punish for any number of reasons, but the one reason that punishment is morally good or morally justifiable is that someone has broken the law. Thus, it can correctly be said that breaking the law is the *sine qua non* of punishment, or, in other words, that we only tolerate punishment as it is imposed on one who deviates from the norm established by the criminal law.

The fact that the State may seek retribution against those who have broken its laws does not mean that retribution may then become the State's sole end in punishing. Our jurisprudence has always accepted deterrence in general, deterrence of individual recidivism, isolation of dangerous persons, and rehabilitation as proper goals of punishment. See *Trop v. Dulles*. Retaliation, vengeance, and retribution have been roundly condemned as intolerable aspirations for a government in a free society.

Punishment as retribution has been condemned by scholars for centuries, and the Eighth Amendment itself was adopted to prevent punishment from becoming synonymous with vengeance. . . .

Retribution surely underlies the imposition of some punishment on one who commits a criminal act. But, the fact that *some* punishment may be imposed does not mean that *any* punishment is permissible. If retribution alone could serve as a justification for any particular penalty, then all penalties selected by the legislature would by definition be acceptable means for designating society's moral approbation of a particular act. The "cruel and unusual" language would thus be read out of the Constitution and the fears of Patrick Henry and the other Founding Fathers would become realities.

To preserve the integrity of the Eighth Amendment, the Court has consistently denigrated retribution as a permissible goal of punishment. It is undoubtedly correct that there is a demand for vengeance on the part of many persons in a community against one who is convicted of a particularly offensive act. At times a cry is heard that morality requires vengeance to evidence society's abhorrence of the act. But the Eighth Amendment is our insulation from our baser selves. The "cruel and unusual" language limits the avenues through which vengeance can be channeled. Were this not so, the language would be empty and a return to the rack and other tortures would be possible in a given case. . . .

The history of the Eighth Amendment supports only the conclusion that retribution for its own sake is improper.

B.   The most hotly contested issue regarding capital punishment is whether it is better than life imprisonment as a deterrent to crime. . . .

It must be kept in mind, then, that the question to be considered is not simply whether capital punishment is a deterrent, but whether it is a better deterrent than life imprisonment. There is no more complex problem than determining the deterrent efficacy of the death penalty. "Capital punishment has obviously failed as a deterrent when a murder is committed. We can number its failures. But we cannot number its successes. No one can ever know how many people have refrained from murder because of the fear of being hanged." This is the nub of the problem and it is exacerbated by the paucity of useful data. . . .

Despite the fact that abolitionists have not proved nondeterrence beyond a reasonable doubt, they have succeeded in showing by clear and convincing evidence that capital punishment is not necessary as a deterrent to crime in our society. This is all that they must do. We would shirk our judicial responsibilities if we failed to accept the presently existing statistics and demanded more proof. It may be that we now possess all the proof that anyone could ever hope to assemble on the subject. But, even if further proof were to be forthcoming, I believe there is more than enough evidence presently available for a decision in this case.

In light of the massive amount of evidence before us, I see no alternative but to conclude that capital punishment cannot be justified on the basis of its deterrent effect.

C.   Much of what must be said about the death penalty as a device to prevent recidivism is obvious—if a murderer is executed, he cannot possibly commit another offense. The fact is, however, that murderers are extremely unlikely to commit other crimes either in prison or upon their release. For the most part, they are first offenders, and when released from prison they are known to become model citizens. Furthermore, most persons who commit capital crimes are not executed. With respect to those who are sentenced to die, it is critical to note that the jury is never asked to determine whether they are likely to be recidivists. In light of these facts, if capital punishment were justified purely on the basis of preventing recidivism, it would have to be considered to be excessive; no general need to obliterate all capital offenders could have been demonstrated, nor any specific need in individual cases. . . .

E.   There is but one conclusion that can be drawn from all of this—*i.e.*, the death penalty is an excessive and unnecessary punishment that violates the Eighth Amendment. . . .

VI

In addition, even if capital punishment is not excessive, it nonetheless violates the Eighth Amendment because it is morally unacceptable to the people of the United States at this time in their history. . . .

While a public opinion poll obviously is of some assistance in indicating public acceptance or rejection of a specific penalty, its utility cannot be very great. This is because whether or not a punishment is cruel and unusual depends, not on whether its mere mention "shocks the conscience and sense of justice of the people," but on whether people who were fully informed as to the purposes of the penalty and its liabilities would find the penalty shocking, unjust, and unacceptable. . . .

Some of the conclusions arrived at in the preceding section and the supporting evidence would be critical to an informed judgment on the morality of the death penalty: *e.g.*, that the death penalty is no more effective a deterrent than life imprisonment, that convicted murderers are rarely executed, but are usually sentenced to a term in prison; that convicted murderers usually are model prisoners, and that they almost always become law-abiding citizens upon their release from prison; that the costs of executing a capital offender exceed the costs of imprisoning him for life; that while in prison, a convict under sentence of death performs none of the useful functions that life prisoners perform; that no attempt is made in the sentencing process to ferret out likely recidivists for execution; and that the death penalty may actually stimulate criminal activity.

This information would almost surely convince the average citizen that the death penalty was unwise, but a problem arises as to whether it would convince him that the penalty was morally reprehensible. This problem arises from the fact that the public's desire for retribution, even though this is a goal that the legislature cannot constitutionally pursue as its sole justification for capital punishment, might influence the citizenry's view of the morality of capital punishment. The solution to the problem lies in the fact that no one has ever seriously advanced retribution as a legitimate goal of our society. Defenses of capital punishment are always mounted on deterrent or other similar theories. This should not be surprising. It is the people of this country who have urged in the past that prisons rehabilitate as well as isolate offenders, and it is the people who have injected a sense of purpose into our penology. I cannot believe that at this stage in our history, the American people would ever knowingly support purposeless vengeance. Thus, I believe that the great mass of citizens would conclude on the basis of the material already considered that the death penalty is immoral and therefore unconstitutional.

But, if this information needs supplementing, I believe that the following facts would serve to convince even the most hesitant of citizens to condemn death as a sanction: capital punishment is imposed discriminatorily against certain identifiable classes of people; there is evidence that innocent people have been executed before their innocence can be proved; and the death penalty wreaks havoc with our entire criminal justice system. . . .

Assuming knowledge of all the facts presently available regarding capital punishment, the average citizen would, in my opinion, find it shocking to his conscience and sense of justice. For this reason alone capital punishment cannot stand.

DISSENTING OPINION OF CHIEF JUSTICE BURGER, JOINED BY JUSTICES POWELL, BLACKMUN, AND REHNQUIST

. . . There are no obvious indications that capital punishment offends the conscience of society to such a degree that our traditional deference to the legislative judgment must be abandoned. It is not a punishment such as burning at the stake that everyone would ineffably find to be repugnant to all civilized standards. Nor is it a punishment so roundly condemned that only a few aberrant legislatures have retained it on the statute books. Capital punishment is authorized by statute in 40 States, the District of Columbia, and in the federal courts for the commission of certain crimes. On four occasions in the last 11 years Congress has added to the list of federal crimes punishable by death. In looking for reliable indicia of contemporary attitude, none more trustworthy has been advanced.

One conceivable source of evidence that legislatures have abdicated their essentially barometric role with respect to community values would be public opinion polls, of which there have been many in the past decade addressed to the question of capital punishment. Without assessing the reliability of such polls, or intimating that any judicial reliance could ever be placed on them, it need only be noted that the reported results have shown nothing approximating the universal condemnation of capital punishment that might lead us to suspect that the legislatures in general have lost touch with current social values.

Counsel for petitioners rely on a different body of empirical evidence. They argue, in effect, that the number of cases in which the death penalty is imposed, as compared with the number of cases in which it is statutorily available, reflects a general revulsion toward the penalty that would lead to its repeal if only it were more generally and widely enforced. It cannot be gainsaid that by the choice of juries—and sometimes judges—the death penalty is imposed in far fewer than half the cases in which it is available. To go further and characterize the rate of imposition as "freakishly rare," as petitioners insist, is unwarranted hyperbole. And regardless of its characterization, the rate of imposition does not impel the conclusion that capital punishment is now regarded as intolerably cruel or uncivilized.

It is argued that in those capital cases where juries have recommended mercy, they have given expression to civilized values and effectively renounced the legislative authorization for capital punishment. At the same time it is argued that where juries have made the awesome decision to send men to their deaths, they have acted arbitrarily and without sensitivity to prevailing standards of decency. This explanation for the infrequency of imposition of capital punishment is unsupported by known facts, and is inconsistent in principle with everything this Court has ever said about the functioning of juries in capital cases. . . .

The selectivity of juries in imposing the punishment of death is properly viewed as a refinement on, rather than a repudiation of, the statutory authorization for that penalty. Legislatures prescribe the categories of crimes for which the death penalty should be available, and, acting as "the conscience of the community," juries are entrusted to determine in individual cases that the ultimate punishment is warranted. Juries are undoubtedly influenced in this judgment by myriad factors. The motive or lack of motive of the perpetrator, the degree of injury or suffering of the victim or victims, and the degree of brutality in the commission of the crime would seem to be prominent among these factors. Given the general awareness that death is no longer a routine punishment for the crimes for which it is made available, it is hardly surprising that juries have been increasingly meticulous in their imposition of the penalty. But to assume from the mere fact of relative infrequency that only a random assortment of pariahs are sentenced to death, is to cast grave doubt on the basic integrity of our jury system.

It would, of course, be unrealistic to assume that juries have been perfectly consistent in choosing the cases where the death penalty is to be imposed, for no human institution performs with perfect consistency. There are doubtless prisoners on death row who would not be there had they been tried before a different jury or in a different State. In this sense their fate has been controlled by a fortuitous circumstance. However, this element of fortuity does not stand as an indictment either of the general functioning of juries in capital cases or of the integrity of jury decisions in individual cases. There is no empirical basis for concluding that juries have generally failed to discharge in good faith the responsibility described in *Witherspoon*—that of choosing between life and death in individual cases according to the dictates of community values.

The rate of imposition of death sentences falls far short of providing the requisite unambiguous evidence that the legislatures of 40 States and the Congress have turned their backs on current or evolving standards of decency in continuing to make the death penalty available. For, if selective imposition evidences a rejection of capital punishment in those cases where it is not imposed, it surely evidences a correlative affirmation of the penalty in those cases where it is imposed. Absent some clear indication that the continued imposition of the death penalty on a selective basis is violative of prevailing standards of civilized conduct, the Eighth Amendment cannot be said to interdict its use. . . .

IV

Capital punishment has also been attacked as violative of the Eighth Amendment on the ground that it is not needed to achieve legitimate penal aims and is thus "unnecessarily cruel." As a pure policy matter, this approach has much to recommend it, but it seeks to give a dimension to the Eighth Amendment that it was never intended to have and promotes a line of inquiry that this Court has never before pursued.

The Eighth Amendment, as I have noted, was included in the Bill of Rights to guard against the use of torturous and inhuman punishments, not those of limited efficacy. . . .

Apart from . . . isolated uses of the word "unnecessary," nothing in the cases suggests that it is for the courts to make a determination of the efficacy of punishments. . . .

By pursuing the necessity approach, it becomes even more apparent that it involves matters outside the purview of the Eighth Amendment. Two of the several aims of punishment are generally associated with capital punishment— retribution and deterrence. It is argued that retribution can be discounted because that, after all, is what the Eighth Amendment seeks to eliminate. There is no authority suggesting that the Eighth Amendment was intended to purge the law of its retributive elements, and the Court has consistently assumed that retribution is a legitimate dimension of the punishment of crimes. See *Williams v. New York*, 337 U.S. 241, 248 (1949); *United States v. Lovett*, 328 U.S. 303, 324 (1946) (Frankfurter, J., concurring). Furthermore, responsible legal thinkers of widely varying persuasions have debated the sociological and philosophical aspects of the retribution question for generations, neither side being able to convince the other. It would be reading a great deal into the Eighth Amendment to hold that the punishments authorized by legislatures cannot constitutionally reflect a retributive purpose.

The less esoteric but no less controversial question is whether the death penalty acts as a superior deterrent. Those favoring abolition find no evidence that it does. Those favoring retention start from the intuitive notion that capital punishment should act as the most effective deterrent and note that there is no convincing evidence that it does not. Escape from this empirical stalemate is ought by placing the burden of proof on the States and concluding that they have failed to demonstrate that capital punishment is a more effective deterrent than life imprisonment. Numerous justifications have been advanced for shifting the burden, and they are not without their rhetorical appeal. However, these arguments are not descended from established constitutional principles, but are born of the urge to bypass an unresolved factual question. Comparative deterrence is not a matter that lends itself to precise measurement; to shift the burden to the states is to provide an illusory solution to an enormously complex problem. If it were proper to put the States to the test of demonstrating the deterrent value of capital punishment, we could just as well ask them to prove the need for life imprisonment or any other punishment. Yet I know of no convincing evidence that life imprisonment is a more effective deterrent than 20 years' imprisonment, or even that a $10 parking ticket is a more effective deterrent than a $5 parking ticket. In fact, there are some who go so far as to challenge the notion that any punishments deter crime. If the States are unable to adduce convincing proof rebutting such assertions, does it then follow that all punishments are suspect as being "cruel and unusual" within the meaning of the Constitution? On the contrary, I submit that the questions raised by the necessity approach are beyond the pale of judicial inquiry under the Eighth Amendment.

. . . As I have earlier stated, the Eighth Amendment forbids the imposition of punishments that are so cruel and inhumane as to violate society's standards of civilized conduct. The Amendment does not prohibit all punishments the States are unable to prove necessary to deter or control crime. The Amendment is not concerned with the process by which a State determines that a particular punishment is to be imposed in a particular case. And the Amendment most assuredly does not speak to the power of legislatures to confer sentencing discretion on juries, rather than to fix all sentences by statute.

The critical factor in the concurring opinions of both Mr. Justice Stewart and Mr. Justice White is the infrequency with which the penalty is imposed. This factor is taken not as evidence of society's abhorrence of capital punishment— the inference that petitioners would have the Court draw—but as the earmark of deteriorated system of sentencing. It is concluded that petitioners' sentences must be set aside, not because the punishment is impermissibly cruel, but because juries and judges have failed to exercise their sentencing discretion in acceptable fashion. . . .

The decisive grievance of the opinions—not translated into Eighth Amendment terms—is that the present system of discretionary sentencing in capital cases has failed to produce evenhanded justice; the problem is not that too few have been sentenced to die, but that the selection process has followed no rational pattern. This claim of arbitrariness is not only lacking in empirical support, but also it manifestly fails to establish that the death penalty is a "cruel and unusual" punishment. The Eighth Amendment was included in the Bill of Rights to assure that certain types of punishments would never be imposed, not to channelize the sentencing process. The approach of these concurring opinions has no antecedent in the Eighth Amendment cases. It is essentially and exclusively a procedural due process argument.

This ground of decision is plainly foreclosed as well as misplaced. Only one year ago, in *McGautha v. California*, the Court upheld the prevailing system of sentencing in capital cases. . . .

While I would not undertake to make a definitive statement as to the parameters of the Court's ruling, it is clear that if state legislatures and the Congress wish to maintain the availability of capital punishment, significant statutory changes will have to be made. Since the two pivotal concurring opinions turn on the assumption that the punishment of death is now meted out in a random and unpredictable manner, legislative bodies may seek to bring their laws into compliance with the Court's ruling by providing standards for juries and judges to follow in determining the sentence in capital cases or by more narrowly defining the crimes for which the penalty is to be imposed. If such standards can be devised or the crimes more meticulously defined, the result cannot be detrimental. However, Mr. Justice Harlan's opinion for the Court in *McGautha* convincingly demonstrates that all past efforts "to identify before the fact" the cases in which the penalty is to be imposed have been "uniformly unsuccessful." 402 U.S., at 197. One problem is that "the factors which determine whether the sentence of death is the appropriate penalty in particular cases are too complex to be compressed within the limits of a simple formula . . ." Report of Royal Commission on Capital Punishment.

Real change could clearly be brought about if legislatures provided mandatory death sentences in such a way as to deny juries the opportunity to bring in a verdict on a lesser charge; under such a system, the death sentence could only be avoided by a verdict of acquittal. If this is the only alternative that the legislatures can safely pursue under today's ruling, I would have preferred that the Court opt for total abolition.

It seems remarkable to me that with our basic trust in lay jurors as the keystone in our system of criminal justice, it should now be suggested that we take the most sensitive and important of all decisions away from them. I could more easily be persuaded that mandatory sentences of death, without the intervening and ameliorating impact of lay jurors, are so arbitrary and doctrinaire that they violate the Constitution. . . .

[The dissenting opinion of Justice Blackmun is omitted.]

DISSENTING OPINION OF JUSTICE POWELL, JOINED BY CHIEF JUSTICE BURGER AND JUSTICES BLACKMUN AND REHNQUIST

. . . Although determining the range of available punishments for a particular crime is a legislative function, the very presence of the Cruel and Unusual Punishments Clause within the Bill of Rights requires, in the context of a specific case, that courts decide whether particular acts of the Congress offend that Amendment. The Due Process Clause of the Fourteenth Amendment imposes on the judiciary a similar obligation to scrutinize state legislation. But the proper exercise of that constitutional obligation in the cases before us today must be founded on a full recognition of the several considerations set forth above—the affirmative references to capital punishment in the Constitution, the prevailing precedents of this Court, the limitations on the exercise of our power imposed by tested principles of judicial self-restraint, and the duty to avoid encroachment on the powers conferred upon state and federal legislatures. In the face of these considerations, only the most conclusive of objective demonstrations could warrant this Court in holding capital punishment *per se* unconstitutional. The burden of seeking so sweeping a decision against such formidable obstacles is almost insuperable. Viewed from this perspective, as I believe it must be, the case against the death penalty falls far short.

Petitioners' contentions are premised, as indicated above, on the long-accepted view that concepts embodied in the Eighth and Fourteenth Amendments evolve. They present, with skill and persistence, a list of "objective indicators" which are said to demonstrate that prevailing standards of human decency have progressed to the final point of requiring the Court to hold, for all cases and for all time, that capital punishment is unconstitutional.

Briefly summarized, these proffered indicia of contemporary standards of decency include the following: (i) a worldwide trend toward the disuse of the death penalty; (ii) the reflection in the scholarly literature of a progressive rejection of capital punishment founded essentially on moral opposition to such treatment; (iii) the decreasing numbers of executions over the last 40 years and especially over the last decade; (iv) the small number of death sentences rendered in relation to the number of cases in which they might have been imposed; and (v) the indication of public abhorrence of the penalty reflected in the circumstance that executions are no longer public affairs. The foregoing is an incomplete summary but it touches the major bases of petitioners' presentation. Although they are not appropriate for consideration as objective evidence, petitioners strongly urge two additional propositions. They contend, first, that the penalty survives public condemnation only through the infrequency, arbitrariness, and discriminatory nature of its application, and, second, that there no longer exists any legitimate justification for the utilization of the ultimate penalty. These contentions, which have proved persuasive to several of the Justices constituting the majority, deserve separate consideration and will be considered in the ensuing sections. Before turning to those arguments, I first address the argument based on "objective" factors.

Any attempt to discern contemporary standards of decency through the review of objective factors must take into account several overriding considerations which petitioners choose to discount or ignore. In a democracy the first indicator of the public's attitude must always be found in the legislative judgments of the people's chosen representatives. Mr. Justice Marshall's opinion today catalogues the salient statistics. Forty States, the District of Columbia, and the

Federal Government still authorize the death penalty for a wide variety of crimes. That number has remained relatively static since the end of World War I. That does not mean, however, that capital punishment has become a forgotten issue in the legislative arena. . . .

[After discussing recent federal, state, and foreign legislative activity on the death penalty Justice Powell concludes as follows.] This recent history of activity with respect to legislation concerning the death penalty abundantly refutes the abolitionist position.

The second and even more direct source of information reflecting the public's attitude toward capital punishment is the jury. . . . Any attempt to discern, therefore, where the prevailing standards of decency lie must take careful account of the jury's response to the question of capital punishment. During the 1960's juries returned in excess of a thousand death sentences, a rate of approximately two per week. Whether it is true that death sentences were returned in less than 10 percent of the cases as petitioners estimate or whether some higher percentage is more accurate, these totals simply do not support petitioners' assertion at oral argument that "the death penalty is virtually unanimously repudiated and condemned by the conscience of contemporary society." It is also worthy of note that the annual rate of death sentences has remained relatively constant over the last 10 years and that the figure for 1970—127 sentences—is the highest annual total since 1961. It is true that the sentencing rate might be expected to rise, rather than remain constant, when the number of violent crimes increases as it has in this country. And it may be conceded that the constancy in these statistics indicates the unwillingness of juries to demand the ultimate penalty in many cases where it might be imposed. But these considerations fall short of indicating that juries are imposing the death penalty with such rarity as to justify this Court in reading into this circumstance a public rejection of capital punishment.

One must conclude, contrary to petitioners' submission, that the indicators most likely to reflect the public's view—legislative bodies, state referenda and the juries which have the actual responsibility—do not support the contention that evolving standards of decency require total abolition of capital punishment. Indeed, the weight of the evidence indicates that the public generally has not accepted either the morality or the social merit of the views so passionately advocated by the articulate spokesmen for abolition. But however one may assess the amorphous ebb and flow of public opinion generally on this volatile issue, this type of inquiry lies at the periphery—not the core—of the judicial process in constitutional cases. The assessment of popular opinion is essentially a legislative, not a judicial, function.

V

Petitioners seek to salvage their thesis by arguing that the infrequency and discriminatory nature of the actual resort to the ultimate penalty tend to diffuse public opposition. We are told that the penalty is imposed exclusively on uninfluential minorities—"the poor and powerless, personally ugly and socially unacceptable." It is urged that this pattern of application assures that large segments of the public will be either uninformed or unconcerned and will have no reason to measure the punishment against prevailing moral standards. . . .

Apart from the impermissibility of basing a constitutional judgment of this magnitude on such speculative assumptions, the argument suffers from other defects. If, as petitioners urge, we are to engage in speculation, it is not at all certain that the public would experience deep-felt revulsion if the States were to execute as many sentenced capital offenders this year as they executed in the mid-1930's. It seems more likely that public reaction, rather than being characterized by undifferentiated rejection, would depend upon the facts and circumstances surrounding each particular case.

Members of this Court know, from the petitions and appeals that come before us regularly, that brutish and revolting murders continue to occur with disquieting frequency. Indeed, murders are so commonplace in our society that only the most sensational receive significant and sustained publicity. It could hardly be suggested that in any of these highly publicized murder cases—the several senseless assassinations or the too numerous shocking multiple murders that have stained this country's recent history—the public has exhibited any signs of "revulsion" at the thought of executing the convicted murderers. The public outcry, as we all know, has been quite to the contrary. . . . Nor is there any rational basis for arguing that the public reaction to any of these crimes would be muted if the murderer were "rich and powerful." The demand for the ultimate sanction might well be greater, as a wealthy killer is hardly a sympathetic figure. While there might be specific cases in which capital punishment would be regarded as excessive and shocking to the conscience of the community, it can hardly be argued that the public's dissatisfaction with the penalty in particular cases would translate into a demand for absolute abolition.

. . . But the discrimination argument does not rest alone on a projection of the assumed effect on public opinion of more frequent executions. Much also is made of the undeniable fact that the death penalty has a greater impact on the lower economic strata of society, which include a relatively higher percentage of persons of minority racial and ethnic group backgrounds. The argument drawn from this fact is two-pronged. In part it is merely an extension of the speculative approach pursued by petitioners, *i.e.*, that public revulsion is suppressed in callous apathy because the penalty does not affect persons from the white middle class which constitutes the majority in this country. This aspect, however, adds little to the infrequency rationalization for public apathy which I have found unpersuasive.

As Mr. Justice Marshall's opinion today demonstrates, the argument does have a more troubling aspect. It is his contention that if the average citizen were aware of the disproportionate burden of capital punishment borne by the "poor, the ignorant, and the underprivileged," he would find the penalty "shocking to his conscience and sense of justice" and would not stand for its further use. . . .

Certainly the claim is justified that this criminal sanction falls more heavily on the relatively impoverished and underprivileged elements of society. The "have-nots" in every society always have been subject to greater pressure to commit crimes and to fewer constraints than their more affluent fellow citizens. This is, indeed, a tragic by-product of social and economic deprivation, but it is not an argument of constitutional proportions under the Eighth or Fourteenth Amendment. The same discriminatory impact argument could be made with equal force and logic with respect to those sentenced to prison terms. The Due Process Clause admits of no distinction between the deprivation of "life" and the deprivation of "liberty." If discriminatory impact renders capital punishment cruel and unusual, it likewise renders invalid most of the prescribed penalties for crimes of violence. The root causes of the higher incidence of criminal penalties on "minorities and the poor" will not be cured by abolishing the system of penalties. Nor, indeed, could any society have a viable system of criminal justice if sanctions were abolished or ameliorated because most of those who commit crimes happen to be underprivileged. The basic problem results not from the penalties imposed for criminal conduct but from social and economic factors that have plagued humanity since the beginning of recorded history, frustrating all efforts to create in any country at any time the perfect society in which there are no "poor," no "minorities" and no "underprivileged." The causes underlying this problem are unrelated to the constitutional issue before the Court. . . .

VI

Petitioner[s] . . . urge that capital punishment is cruel and unusual because it no longer serves any rational legislative interests. Before turning to consider whether any of the traditional aims of punishment justify the death penalty, I should make clear the context in which I approach this aspect of the cases.

First, I find no support—in the language of the Constitution, in its history, or in the cases arising under it—for the view that this Court may invalidate a category of penalties because we deem less severe penalties adequate to serve the ends of penology. While the cases affirm our authority to prohibit punishments that are cruelly inhumane (*e.g., Wilkerson v. Utah; In re Kemmler*), and punishments that are cruelly excessive in that they are disproportionate to particular crimes, the precedents of this Court afford no basis for striking down a particular form of punishment because we may be persuaded that means less stringent would be equally efficacious.

Secondly, if we were free to question the justifications for the use of capital punishment, a heavy burden would rest on those who attack the legislatures' judgments to prove the lack of rational justifications. This Court has long held that legislative decisions in this area, which lie within the special competency of that branch, are entitled to a presumption of validity.

I come now to consider, subject to the reservations above expressed, the two justifications most often cited for the retention of capital punishment. The concept of retribution—though popular for centuries—is now criticized as unworthy of a civilized people. Yet this Court has acknowledged the existence of a retributive element in criminal sanctions and has never heretofore found it impermissible. . . .

While retribution alone may seem an unworthy justification in a moral sense, its utility in a system of criminal justice requiring public support has long been recognized. Lord Justice Denning, now Master of the Rolls of the Court of Appeal in England, testified on this subject before the British Royal Commission on Capital Punishment:

> Many are inclined to test the efficacy of punishment solely by its value as a deterrent: but this is too narrow a view. Punishment is the way in which society expresses its denunciation of wrong doing; and, in order to maintain respect for law, it is essential that the punishment inflicted for grave crimes should adequately reflect the revulsion felt by the great majority of citizens for them. It is a mistake to consider the objects of punishment as being deterrent or reformative or preventive and nothing else. If this were so, we should not send to prison a man who was guilty of motor manslaughter, but only disqualify him from driving; but would public opinion be content with this?
>
> The truth is that some crimes are so outrageous that society insists on adequate punishment, because the wrong-doer deserves it, irrespective of whether it is a deterrent or not.

The view expressed by Lord Denning was cited approvingly in the Royal Commission's Report, recognizing "a strong and widespread demand for retribution." Mr. Justice Stewart makes much the same point in his opinion today when he concludes that expression of man's retributive instincts in the sentencing process "serves an important purpose in promoting the stability of a society governed by law." The view, moreover, is not without respectable support in the jurisprudential literature in this country, despite a substantial body of opinion to the contrary. And it is conceded on all sides that, not infrequently, cases arise that are so shocking or offensive that the public demands the ultimate penalty for the transgressor.

Deterrence is a more appealing justification, although opinions again differ widely. Indeed, the deterrence issue lies at the heart of much of the debate between the abolitionists and retentionists. Statistical studies based primarily on trends in States that have abolished the penalty, tend to support the view that the death penalty has not been proved to be a superior deterrent. Some dispute the validity of this conclusion, pointing out that the studies do not show that the death penalty has no deterrent effect on any categories of crimes. On the basis of the available evidence, I find myself in agreement with the conclusions drawn by the Royal Commission following its exhaustive study of this issue:

> The general conclusion which we reach, after careful review of all the evidence we have been able to obtain as to the deterrent effect of capital punishment, may be stated as follows. *Prima facie* the penalty of death is likely to have a stronger effect as a deterrent to normal human beings than any other form of punishment, and there is some evidence (though no convincing statistical

evidence) that this is in fact so. But this effect does not operate universally or uniformly, and there are many offenders on whom it is limited and may often be negligible. It is accordingly important to view this question in a just perspective and not base a penal policy in relation to murder on exaggerated estimates of the uniquely deterrent force of the death penalty.

As I noted at the outset of this section, legislative judgments as to the efficacy of particular punishments are presumptively rational and may not be struck down under the Eighth Amendment because this Court may think that some alternative sanction would be more appropriate. Even if such judgments were within the judicial prerogative, petitioners have failed to show that there exist no justifications for the legislative enactments challenged in these cases. While the evidence and arguments advanced by petitioners might have proved profoundly persuasive if addressed to a legislative body, they do not approach the showing traditionally required before a court declares that the legislature has acted irrationally. . . .

VIII

I now return to the overriding question in these cases: whether this Court, acting in conformity with the Constitution, can justify its judgment to abolish capital punishment as heretofore known in this country. It is important to keep in focus the enormity of the step undertaken by the Court today. Not only does it invalidate hundreds of state and federal laws, it deprives those jurisdictions of the power to legislate with respect to capital punishment in the future, except in a manner consistent with the cloudily outlined views of those Justices who do not purport to undertake total abolition. . . .

With deference and respect for the views of the Justices who differ, it seems to me that . . . as a matter of policy and precedent, this is a classic case for the exercise of our oft-announced allegiance to judicial restraint. I know of no case in which greater gravity and delicacy have attached to the duty that this Court is called on to perform whenever legislation—state or federal—is challenged on constitutional grounds. It seems to me that the sweeping judicial action undertaken today reflects a basic lack of faith and confidence in the democratic process. Many may regret, as I do, the failure of some legislative bodies to address the capital punishment issue with greater frankness or effectiveness. Many might decry their failure either to abolish the penalty entirely or selectively, or to establish standards for its enforcement. But impatience with the slowness, and even the unresponsiveness, of legislatures is no justification for judicial intrusion upon their historic powers. . . .

[The dissenting opinion of Justice Rehnquist is omitted.]

Chapter 3

Not Inherently Unconstitutional— *Gregg v. Georgia* (1976)

Gregg v. Georgia, 428 U.S. 153, 96 S. Ct. 2909, 49 L. Ed.2d 859 (1976) (7–2, the death penalty is not a *per se* violation of the Eighth Amendment).

Editor's comment: *Furman v. Georgia*, 408 U.S. 238 (1972), invalidated most of the capital punishment statutes in this country and sowed great confusion for a number of years. Death penalty statutes were rewritten in 35 states in an effort to conform to Supreme Court guidelines— if anyone could determine what they were. Some states enacted mandatory death penalty laws, but these were declared unconstitutional in *Woodson v. North Carolina*, 428 U.S. 280 (1976). Death sentences were no longer imposed in some states (such as New York) where the statutes were not revised, and in states where death sentences were imposed they were often not carried out because of lengthy legal challenges and uncertainties regarding capital punishment law.

Four years after *Furman*, in *Gregg v. Georgia*, 428 U.S. 153 (1976), the Court rejected, over the protests of Justices Brennan and Marshall, the view that the death penalty is *per se* cruel and unusual. *Gregg* upheld a Georgia capital punishment law that utilized certain trial procedures and appeals designed to prevent the penalty from being imposed arbitrarily. (Recall that arbitrariness was the main objection to the death penalty voiced by Justices Stewart and White, the pivotal votes in the *Furman* case.) The concept was that trial judges and juries would be permitted to sentence a defendant to death only for homicides having certain characteristics, called *aggravating factors*, and only where there were insufficiently *mitigating factors*. Aggravating factors make a murder more reprehensible than other homicides and thus support the death penalty. Mitigating factors are circumstances of the crime or characteristics of the defendant that make the offense less reprehensible and therefore support a less harsh punishment. The Georgia statute approved in *Gregg* provided that aggravating and mitigating factors must be proven at a separate penalty proceeding, conducted after (and only if) the defendant is found guilty. Such two-part proceedings are called *bifurcated trials*. Georgia also provided for direct appeal of a capital conviction to the state's highest court. The Georgia statute became the model for death penalty laws in the United States.

❖　❖　❖

OPINION OF JUSTICE STEWART, JOINED BY JUSTICES POWELL AND STEVENS

The issue in this case is whether the imposition of the sentence of death for the crime of murder under the law of Georgia violates the Eighth and Fourteenth Amendments.

I

The petitioner, Troy Gregg, was charged with committing armed robbery and murder. In accordance with Georgia procedure in capital cases, the trial was in two stages, a guilt stage and a sentencing stage. The evidence at the guilt trial established that on November 21, 1973, the petitioner and a traveling companion, Floyd Allen, while hitchhiking north in Florida were picked up by Fred Simmons and Bob Moore. Their car broke down, but they continued north after Simmons purchased another vehicle with some of the cash he was carrying.

While still in Florida, they picked up another hitchhiker, Dennis Weaver, who rode with them to Atlanta, where he was let out about 11 P.M. A short time later the four men interrupted their journey for a rest stop along the highway. The next morning the bodies of Simmons and Moore were discovered in a ditch nearby ... The jury found the petitioner guilty of two counts of armed robbery and two counts of murder.

At the penalty stage, which took place before the same jury, neither the prosecutor nor the petitioner's lawyer offered any additional evidence. Both counsel, however, made lengthy arguments dealing generally with the propriety of capital punishment under the circumstances and with the weight of the evidence of guilt. The trial judge instructed the jury that it could recommend either a death sentence or a life prison sentence on each count. The judge further charged the jury that in determining what sentence was appropriate the jury was free to consider the facts and circumstances, if any, presented by the parties in mitigation or aggravation.

Finally, the judge instructed the jury that it "would not be authorized to consider [imposing] the penalty of death" unless it first found beyond a reasonable doubt one of these aggravating circumstances:

One—That the offense of murder was committed while the offender was engaged in the commission of two other capital felonies, to-wit the armed robbery of [Simmons and Moore].

Two—That the offender committed the offense of murder for the purpose of receiving money and the automobile described in the indictment.

Three—The offense of murder was outrageously and wantonly vile, horrible and inhuman, in that they [*sic*] involved the depravity of [the] mind of the defendant.

Finding the first and second of these circumstances, the jury returned verdicts of death on each count.

The Supreme Court of Georgia affirmed the convictions and the imposition of the death sentences for murder.

II

Before considering the issues presented it is necessary to understand the Georgia statutory scheme for the imposition of the death penalty. The Georgia statute, as amended after our decision in *Furman v. Georgia*, retains the death penalty for six categories of crime: murder, kidnapping for ransom or where the victim is harmed, armed robbery, rape, treason, and aircraft hijacking. The capital defendant's guilt or innocence is determined in the traditional manner, either by a trial judge or a jury, in the first stage of a bifurcated trial. . . . After a verdict, finding, or plea of guilty to a capital crime, a presentence hearing is conducted before whoever made the determination of guilt. The sentencing procedures are essentially the same in both bench and jury trials. At the hearing:

[T]he judge [or jury] shall hear additional evidence in extenuation, mitigation, and aggravation of punishment, including the record of any prior criminal convictions and pleas of guilty or pleas of nolo contendere of the defendant, or the absence of any prior conviction and pleas: Provided, however, that only such evidence in aggravation as the State has made known to the defendant prior to his trial shall be admissible. The judge [or jury] shall also hear argument by the defendant or his counsel and the prosecuting attorney . . . regarding the punishment to be imposed.

The defendant is accorded substantial latitude as to the types of evidence that he may introduce. Evidence considered during the guilt stage may be considered during the sentencing stage without being resubmitted. In the assessment of the appropriate sentence to be imposed the judge is also required to consider or to include in his instructions to the jury "any mitigating circumstances or aggravating circumstances otherwise authorized by law and any of [10] statutory aggravating circumstances which may be supported by the evidence . . ." The scope of the nonstatutory aggravating or mitigating circumstances is not delineated in the statute. Before a convicted defendant may be sentenced to death, however, except in cases of treason or aircraft hijacking, the jury, or the trial judge in cases tried without a jury, must find beyond a reasonable doubt one of the 10 aggravating circumstances specified in the statute.[9] The sentence of death may be imposed only if the jury (or judge) finds one of the statutory aggravating circumstances and then elects to impose that sentence. If the verdict is death, the jury or judge must specify the aggravating circumstance(s) found. In jury cases, the trial judge is bound by the jury's recommended sentence.

In addition to the conventional appellate process available in all criminal cases, provision is made for special expedited direct review by the Supreme Court of Georgia of the appropriateness of imposing the sentence of death in the particular case. The court is directed to consider "the punishment as well as any errors enumerated by way of appeal," and to determine:

(1) Whether the sentence of death was imposed under the influence of passion, prejudice, or anything arbitrary factor, and
(2) Whether, in cases other than treason or aircraft hijacking, the evidence supports the jury's or judge's finding of a statutory aggravating circumstance . . . , and
(3) Whether the sentence of death is excessive or disproportionate to the penalty imposed in similar cases, considering both the crime and the defendant.

If the court affirms a death sentence, it is required to include in its decision reference to similar cases that it has taken into consideration. A transcript and complete record of the trial, as well as a separate report by the trial judge, are transmitted to the court for its use in reviewing the sentence. The report is in the form of a 6½-page questionnaire, designed to elicit information about the defendant, the crime, and the circumstances of the trial. It requires the trial judge to characterize the trial in several ways designed to test for arbitrariness and disproportionality of sentence. Included in the report are responses to detailed questions concerning the quality of the defendant's representation, whether race

---

[9] The statute provides in part:
(a) The death penalty may be imposed for the offenses of aircraft hijacking or treason, in any case.
(b) In all cases of other offenses for which the death penalty may be authorized, the judge shall consider, or he shall include in his instructions to the jury for it to consider, any mitigating circumstances or aggravating circumstances otherwise authorized by law and any of the following statutory aggravating circumstances which may be supported by the evidence:
  (1) The offense of murder, rape, armed robbery, or kidnapping was committed by a person with a prior record of conviction for a capital felony, or the offense of murder was committed by a person who has a substantial history of serious assaultive criminal convictions.
  (2) The offense of murder, rape, armed robbery, or kidnapping was committed while the offender was engaged in the commission of another capital felony, or aggravated battery, or the offense of murder was committed while the offender was engaged in the commission of burglary or arson in the first degree.
  (3) The offender by his act of murder, armed robbery, or kidnapping knowingly created a great risk of death to more than one person in a public place by means of a weapon or device which would normally be hazardous to the lives of more than one person.

played a role in the trial, and, whether, in the trial court's judgment, there was any doubt about the defendant's guilt or the appropriateness of the sentence. A copy of the report is served upon defense counsel. Under its special review authority, the court may either affirm the death sentence or remand the case for resentencing. In cases in which the death sentence is affirmed there remains the possibility of executive clemency.

III

We address initially the basic contention that the punishment of death for the crime of murder is, under all circumstances, "cruel and unusual" in violation of the Eighth and Fourteenth Amendments of the Constitution. . . .

The petitioners in the capital cases before the Court today renew the "standards of decency" argument, but developments during the four years since *Furman* have undercut substantially the assumptions upon which their argument rested. Despite the continuing debate, dating back to the 19th century, over the morality and utility of capital punishment, it is now evident that a large proportion of American society continues to regard it as an appropriate and necessary criminal sanction.

The most marked indication of society's endorsement of the death penalty for murder is the legislative response to *Furman*. The legislatures of at least 35 States have enacted new statutes that provide for the death penalty for at least some crimes that result in the death of another person. And the Congress of the United States, in 1974, enacted a statute providing the death penalty for aircraft piracy that results in death. These recently adopted statutes have attempted to address the concerns expressed by the Court in *Furman* primarily (i) by specifying the factors to be weighed and the procedures to be followed in deciding when to impose a capital sentence, or (ii) by making the death penalty mandatory for specified crimes. But all of the post-*Furman* statutes make clear that capital punishment itself has not been rejected by the elected representatives of the people. . . .

---

(4) The offender committed the offense of murder for himself or another, for the purpose of receiving money or any other thing of monetary value.

(5) The murder of a judicial officer, former judicial officer, district attorney or solicitor or former district attorney or solicitor during or because of the exercise of his official duty.

(6) The offender caused or directed another to commit murder or committed murder as an agent or employee of another person.

(7) The offense of murder, rape, armed robbery, or kidnapping was outrageously or wantonly vile, horrible or inhuman in that it involved torture, depravity of mind, or an aggravated battery to the victim.

(8) The offense of murder was committed against any peace officer, corrections employee or fireman while engaged in the performance of his official duties.

(9) The offense of murder was committed by a person in, or who has escaped from, the lawful custody of a peace officer or place of lawful confinement.

(10) The murder was committed for the purpose of avoiding, interfering with, or preventing a lawful arrest or custody in a place of lawful confinement, of himself or another.

The jury also is a significant and reliable objective index of contemporary values because it is so directly involved. . . . The Court has said that "one of the most important functions any jury can perform in making . . . a selection [between life imprisonment and death for a defendant convicted in a capital case] is to maintain a link between contemporary community values and the penal system." *Witherspoon v. Illinois*, 391 U.S. 510, 519 n. 15 (1968). It may be true that evolving standards have influenced juries in recent decades to be more discriminating in imposing the sentence of death. But the relative infrequency of jury verdicts imposing the death sentence does not indicate rejection of capital punishment *per se*. Rather, the reluctance of juries in many cases to impose the sentence may well reflect the humane feeling that this most irrevocable of sanctions should be reserved for a small number of extreme cases. . . . Indeed, the actions of juries in many States since *Furman* are fully compatible with the legislative judgments, reflected in the new statutes, as to the continued utility and necessity of capital punishment in appropriate cases. At the close of 1974 at least 254 persons had been sentenced to death since *Furman*, and by the end of March 1976, more than 460 persons were subject to death sentences.

As we have seen, however, the Eighth Amendment demands more than that a challenged punishment be acceptable to contemporary society. The Court also must ask whether it comports with the basic concept of human dignity at the core of the Amendment. *Trop v. Dulles*, 356 U.S., at 100 (plurality opinion). Although we cannot "invalidate a category of penalties because we deem less severe penalties adequate to serve the ends of penology," *Furman v. Georgia*, 408 U.S., at 451, (Powell, J., dissenting), the sanction imposed cannot be so totally without penological justification that it results in the gratuitous infliction of suffering. Cf. *Wilkerson v. Utah; In re Kemmler*.

The death penalty is said to serve two principal social purposes: retribution and deterrence of capital crimes by prospective offenders. In part, capital punishment is an expression of society's moral outrage at particularly offensive conduct. This function may be unappealing to many, but it is essential in an ordered society that asks its citizens to rely on legal processes rather than self-help to vindicate their wrongs.

> The instinct for retribution is part of the nature of man, and channeling that instinct in the administration of criminal justice serves an important purpose in promoting the stability of a society governed by law. When people begin to believe that organized society is unwilling or unable to impose upon criminal offenders the punishment they "deserve," then there are sown the seeds of anarchy of self-help, vigilante justice, and lynch law. *Furman v. Georgia*, 408 U.S., at 308 (Stewart, J., concurring).

"Retribution is no longer the dominant objective of the criminal law," *Williams v. New York*, 337 U.S. 241, 248 (1949), but neither is it a forbidden objective nor one inconsistent with our respect for the dignity of men. . . . Indeed, the decision that capital punishment may be the appropriate sanction in extreme cases is an expression of the community's belief that certain crimes are themselves so grievous an affront to humanity that the only adequate response may be the penalty of death.

Statistical attempts to evaluate the worth of the death penalty as a deterrent to crimes by potential offenders have occasioned a great deal of debate. The results simply have been inconclusive. As one opponent of capital punishment has said:

> [A]fter all possible inquiry, including the probing of all possible methods of inquiry, we do not know, and for systematic and easily visible reasons cannot know, what the truth about this "deterrent" effect may be. . . .
>
> The inescapable flaw is . . . that social conditions in any state are not constant through time, and that social conditions are not the same in any two states. If an effect were observed (and the observed effects, one way or another, are not large) then one could not at all tell whether any of this effect is attributable to the presence or absence of capital punishment. A "scientific" that is to say, a soundly based conclusion is simply impossible, and no methodological path out of this tangle suggests itself. C. Black, *Capital Punishment: The Inevitability of Caprice and Mistake* 25–26 (1974).

Although some of the studies suggest that the death penalty may not function as a significantly greater deterrent than lesser penalties, there is no convincing empirical evidence either supporting or refuting this view. We may nevertheless assume safely that there are murderers, such as those who act in passion, for whom the threat of death has little or no deterrent effect. But for many others, the death penalty undoubtedly is a significant deterrent. There are carefully contemplated murders, such as murder for hire, where the possible penalty of death may well enter into the cold calculus that precedes the decision to act. And there are some categories of murder, such as murder by a life prisoner, where other sanctions may not be adequate.

The value of capital punishment as a deterrent of crime is a complex factual issue the resolution of which properly rests with the legislatures, which can evaluate the results of statistical studies in terms of their own local conditions and with a flexibility of approach that is not available to the courts. . . . Indeed, many of the post-*Furman* statutes reflect just such a responsible effort to define those crimes and those criminals for which capital punishment is most probably an effective deterrent.

In sum, we cannot say that the judgment of the Georgia Legislature that capital punishment may be necessary in some cases is clearly wrong. Considerations of federalism, as well as respect for the ability of a legislature to evaluate, in terms of its particular State, the moral consensus concerning the death penalty and its social utility as a sanction, require us to conclude, in the absence of more convincing evidence, that the infliction of death as a punishment for murder is not without justification and thus is not unconstitutionally severe.

Finally, we must consider whether the punishment of death is disproportionate in relation to the crime for which it is imposed. There is no question that death as a punishment is unique in its severity and irrevocability. . . . When a defendant's life is at stake, the Court has been particularly sensitive to insure that every safeguard is observed. . . . But we are concerned here only with the imposition of capital punishment for the crime of murder, and when a life has been taken deliberately by the offender, we cannot say that the punishment is invariably disproportionate to the crime. It is an extreme sanction, suitable to the most extreme of crimes.

We hold that the death penalty is not a form of punishment that may never be imposed, regardless of the circumstances of the offense, regardless of the character of the offender, and regardless of the procedure followed in reaching the decision to impose it.

IV

We now consider whether Georgia may impose the death penalty on the petitioner in this case. . . .

A.   While *Furman* did not hold that the infliction of the death penalty *per se* violates the Constitution's ban on cruel and unusual punishments, it did recognize that the penalty of death is different in kind from any other punishment imposed under our system of criminal justice. Because of the uniqueness of the death penalty, *Furman* held that it could not be imposed under sentencing procedures that created a substantial risk that it would be inflicted in an arbitrary and capricious manner. . . . *Furman* mandates that where discretion is afforded a sentencing body on a matter so grave as the determination of whether a human life should be taken or spared, that discretion must be suitably directed and limited so as to minimize the risk of wholly arbitrary and capricious action. . . .

Jury sentencing has been considered desirable in capital cases in order "to maintain a link between contemporary community values and the penal system—a link without which the determination of punishment could hardly reflect 'the evolving standards of decency that mark the progress of a maturing society.'" But it creates special problems. Much of the information that is relevant to the sentencing decision may have no relevance to the question of guilt, or may even be extremely prejudicial to a fair determination of that question. This problem, however, is scarcely insurmountable. Those who have studied the question suggest that a bifurcated procedure—one in which the question of sentence is not considered until the determination of guilt has been made—is the best answer. . . . When a human life is at stake and when the jury must have information prejudicial to the question of guilt but relevant to the question of penalty in order to impose a rational sentence, a bifurcated system is more likely to ensure elimination of the constitutional deficiencies identified in *Furman*.

But the provision of relevant information under fair procedural rules is not one sufficient to guarantee that the information will be properly used in the position of punishment, especially if sentencing is performed by a jury. Since the members of a jury will have had little, if any, previous experience in sentencing, they are unlikely to be skilled in dealing with the information they are given. ... To the extent that this problem is inherent in jury sentencing, it may not be totally correctable. It seems clear, however, that the problem will be eviated if the jury is given guidance regarding the factors about the crime and the defendant that the State, representing organized society, deems particularly relevant to the sentencing decision. ...

While some have suggested that standards to guide a capital jury's sentencing deliberations are impossible to formulate, the fact is that such standards have been developed. When the drafters of the Model Penal Code faced this problem, they concluded "that it is within the realm of possibility to point to the main circumstances of aggravation and of mitigation that should be weighed *and weighed against each other* when they are presented in a concrete case." ALI, Model Penal Code § 201.6, Comment 3, p. 71 (Tent. Draft No. 9, 1959) (emphasis original). While such standards are by necessity somewhat general, they do provide guidance to the sentencing authority and thereby reduce the likelihood that it will impose a sentence that fairly can be called capricious or arbitrary. Where the sentencing authority is required to specify the factors it relied upon in reaching its decision, the further safeguard of meaningful appellate review is available to ensure that death sentences are not imposed capriciously or in a reakish manner.

In summary, the concerns expressed in *Furman* that the penalty of death not be imposed in an arbitrary or capricious manner can be met by a carefully drafted statute that ensures that the sentencing authority is given adequate information and guidance. As a general proposition these concerns are best met by a system that provides for a bifurcated proceeding at which the sentencing authority is apprised of the information relevant to the imposition of sentence and provided with standards to guide its use of the information.

We do not intend to suggest that only the above-described procedures would be permissible under *Furman* or that any sentencing system constructed along these general lines would inevitably satisfy the concerns of *Furman*, for each distinct system must be examined on an individual basis. Rather, we have embarked upon this general exposition to make clear that it is possible to construct capital-sentencing systems capable of meeting *Furman*'s constitutional concerns.

B. We now turn to consideration of the constitutionality of Georgia's capital-sentencing procedures. ...

The petitioner contends ... that the changes in the Georgia sentencing procedures are only cosmetic, that the arbitrariness and capriciousness condemned by *Furman* continue to exist in Georgia—both in traditional practices that still remain and in the new sentencing procedures adopted in response to *Furman*.

First, the petitioner focuses on the opportunities for discretionary action that are inherent in the processing of any murder case under Georgia law. He notes that the state prosecutor has unfettered authority to select those persons whom he wishes to prosecute for a capital offense and to plea bargain with them. Further, at the trial the jury may choose to convict a defendant of a lesser included offense rather than find him guilty of a crime punishable by death, even if the evidence would support a capital verdict. And finally, a defendant who is convicted and sentenced to die may have his sentence commuted by the Governor of the State and the Georgia Board of Pardons and Paroles.

The existence of these discretionary stages is not determinative of the issues before us. At each of these stages an actor in the criminal justice system makes a decision which may remove a defendant from consideration as a candidate for the death penalty. *Furman*, in contrast, dealt with the decision to impose the death sentence on a specific individual who had been convicted of a capital offense. Nothing in any of our cases suggests that the decision to afford an individual defendant mercy violates the Constitution. *Furman* held only that, in order to minimize the risk that the death penalty would be imposed on a capriciously selected group of offenders, the decision to impose it had to be guided by standards so that the sentencing authority would focus on the particularized circumstances of the crime and the defendant. . . .

V

The basic concern of *Furman* centered on those defendants who were being condemned to death capriciously and arbitrarily. Under the procedures before the Court in that case, sentencing authorities were not directed to give attention to the nature or circumstances of the crime committed or to the character or record of the defendant. Left unguided, juries imposed the death sentence in a way that could only be called freakish. The new Georgia sentencing procedures, by contrast, focus the jury's attention on the particularized nature of the crime and the particularized characteristics of the individual defendant. While the jury is permitted to consider any aggravating or mitigating circumstances, it must find and identify at least one statutory aggravating factor before it may impose a penalty of death. In this way the jury's discretion is channeled. No longer can a jury wantonly and freakishly impose the death sentence; it is always circumscribed by the legislative guidelines. In addition, the review function of the Supreme Court of Georgia affords additional assurance that the concerns that prompted our decision in *Furman* are not present to any significant degree in the Georgia procedure applied here.

For the reasons expressed in this opinion, we hold that the statutory system under which Gregg was sentenced to death does not violate the Constitution. Accordingly, the judgment of the Georgia Supreme Court is affirmed. It is so ordered.

CONCURRING OPINION OF JUSTICE WHITE, JOINED BY CHIEF JUSTICE BURGER AND JUSTICE REHNQUIST

. . . Petitioner's argument that prosecutors behave in a standardless fashion in deciding which cases to try as capital felonies is unsupported by any facts.

Petitioner's simply asserts that since prosecutors have the power not to charge capital colonies they will exercise that power in a standardless fashion. This is untenable. Absent facts to the contrary it cannot be assumed that prosecutors will be motivated in their charging decision by factors other than the strength of their case and the likelihood that a jury would impose the death penalty if it convicts. Unless prosecutors are incompetent in their judgments the standards by which they decide whether to charge a capital felony will be the same as those by which the jury will decide the questions of guilt and sentence. Thus defendants will escape the death penalty through prosecutorial charging decisions only because the offense is not sufficiently serious; or because the proof is insufficiently strong. This does not cause the system to be standardless any more than the jury's decision to impose life imprisonment on a defendant whose crime is deemed insufficiently serious or its decision to acquit someone who is probably guilty but whose guilt is not established beyond a reasonable doubt. Thus the prosecutor's charging decisions are unlikely to have removed from the sample of cases considered by the Georgia Supreme Court any of which are truly "similar." If the cases really were "similar" in relevant respects it is unlikely that prosecutors would fail to prosecute them as capital cases; and I am unwilling to assume the contrary. Petitioner's argument that there is an unconstitutional amount of discretion in the system which separates those suspects who receive the death penalty from those who receive life imprisonment, a lesser penalty, or are acquitted or never charged, seems to be in final analysis an indictment of our entire system of justice. Petitioner has argued in effect that no matter how effective the death penalty may be as a punishment, government, created and run as it must be by humans, is inevitably incompetent to administer it. This cannot be accepted as a proposition of constitutional law. Imposition of the death penalty is surely an awesome responsibility for any system of justice and those who participate in it. Mistakes will be made and discriminations will occur which will be difficult to explain. However, one of society's most basic tasks is that of protecting the lives of its citizens and one of the most basic ways in which it achieves the task is through criminal laws against murder. I decline to interfere with the manner in which Georgia has chosen to enforce such laws on what is simply an assertion of lack of faith in the ability of the system of justice to operate in a fundamentally fair manner.

[Justice Blackmun concurred in the judgment, referring to his dissenting opinion in *Furman v. Georgia.*]

DISSENTING OPINION OF JUSTICE BRENNAN

In *Furman v. Georgia*, I read "evolving standards of decency" as requiring focus upon the essence of the death penalty itself and not primarily or solely upon the procedures under which the determination to inflict the penalty upon a particular person was made. That continues to be my view. . . .

My opinion in *Furman v. Georgia* concluded that our civilization and the law had progressed to this point and that therefore the punishment of death, for whatever crime and under all circumstances, is "cruel and unusual" in violation of the Eighth and Fourteenth Amendments of the Constitution. I shall not again canvass the reasons that led to that conclusion. I emphasize only that foremost among the "moral concepts" recognized in our cases and inherent in the Clause is the primary moral principle that the State, even as it punishes, must treat its citizens in a manner consistent with their intrinsic worth as human beings—a punishment must not be so severe as to be degrading to human dignity.

DISSENTING OPINION OF JUSTICE MARSHALL

In *Furman v. Georgia*, I set forth at some length my views on the basic issue presented to the Court in these cases. The death penalty, I concluded, is a cruel and unusual punishment prohibited by the Eighth and Fourteenth Amendments. That continues to be my view.

I have no intention of retracing the "long and tedious journey" that led to my conclusion in *Furman*. My sole purposes here are to consider the suggestion that my conclusion in *Furman* has been undercut by developments since then, and briefly to evaluate the basis for my Brethren's holding that the extinction of life is a permissible form of punishment under the Cruel and Unusual Punishments Clause.

In *Furman* I concluded that the death penalty is constitutionally invalid for two reasons. First, the death penalty is excessive. And second, the American people, fully informed as to the purpose of the death penalty and its liabilities, would in my view reject it as morally unacceptable. Since the decision in *Furman*, the legislatures of 35 States have enacted new statutes authorizing the imposition of the death sentence for certain crimes, and Congress has enacted a law providing the death penalty for air piracy resulting in death. I would be less than candid if I did not acknowledge that these developments have a significant bearing on a realistic assessment of the moral acceptability of the death penalty to the American people. But if the constitutionality of the death penalty turns, as I have urged, on the opinion of an *informed* citizenry, then even the enactment of new death statutes cannot be viewed as conclusive. In *Furman*, I observed that the American people are largely unaware of the information critical to a judgment on the morality of the death penalty, and concluded that if they were better informed they would consider it shocking, unjust, and unacceptable. A recent study, conducted after the enactment of the post-*Furman* statutes, has confirmed that the American people know little about the death penalty, and that the opinions of an informed public would differ significantly from those of a public unaware of the consequences and effects of the death penalty.[1]

---

[1] Sarat and Vidmar, "Public Opinion, the Death Penalty, and the Eighth Amendment: Testing the Marshall Hypothesis," 1976 Wis. L. Rev. 171.

Even assuming, however, that the post-*Furman* enactment of statutes authorizing the death penalty renders the prediction of the views of an informed citizenry an uncertain basis for a constitutional decision, the enactment of those statutes has no bearing whatsoever on the conclusion that the death penalty is unconstitutional because it is excessive. An excessive penalty is invalid under the Cruel and Unusual Punishments Clause "even though popular sentiment may favor" it. [*Furman*, 408 U.S.] at 331 [Marshall, J., concurring.] ... The inquiry there, then, is simply whether the death penalty is necessary to accomplish the legitimate legislative purposes in punishment, or whether a less severe penalty—life imprisonment—would do as well.

The two purposes that sustain the death penalty as nonexcessive in the Court's view are general deterrence and retribution. In *Furman*, I canvassed the relevant data on the deterrent effect of capital punishment. ... The available evidence, I concluded in *Furman*, was convincing that "capital punishment is not necessary as a deterrent to crime in our society."

The Solicitor General in his *amicus* brief in these cases relies heavily on a study by Isaac Ehrlich,[4] reported a year after *Furman*, to support the contention that the death penalty does deter murder. Since the Ehrlich study was not available at the time of *Furman* and since it is the first scientific study to suggest that the death penalty may have a deterrent effect, I will briefly consider its import.

The Ehrlich study focused on the relationship in the Nation as a whole between the homicide rate and "execution risk"—the fraction of persons convicted of murder who were actually executed. Comparing the differences in homicide rate and execution risk for the years 1933 to 1969, Ehrlich found that increases in execution risk were associated with increases in the homicide rate. But when he employed the statistical technique of multiple regression analysis to control for the influence of other variables posited to have an impact on the homicide rate, Ehrlich found a negative correlation between changes in the homicide rate and changes in execution risk. His tentative conclusion was that for the period from 1933 to 1967 each additional execution in the United States might have saved eight lives.

The methods and conclusions of the Ehrlich study have been severely criticized on a number of grounds. It has been suggested, for example, that the study is defective because it compares execution and homicide rates on a nationwide, rather than a state-by-state, basis. The aggregation of data from all States—including those that have abolished the death penalty—obscures the relationship between murder and execution rates. Under Ehrlich's methodology, a decrease in the execution risk in one State combined with an increase in the murder rate in another State would, all other things being equal, suggest a deterrent effect that quite obviously would not exist. Indeed, a deterrent effect would be suggested if, once again all other things being equal, one State abolished the death

---

[4] I. Ehrlich, "The Deterrent Effect of Capital Punishment: A Question of Life and Death" (Working Paper No. 18, National Bureau of Economic Research, Nov. 1973); Ehrlich, "The Deterrent Effect of Capital Punishment: A Question of Life and Death," 65 Am. Econ. Rev. 397 (June 1975).

penalty and experienced no change in the murder rate, while another State experienced an increase in the murder rate.

The most compelling criticism of the Ehrlich study is that its conclusions are extremely sensitive to the choice of the time period included in the regression analysis. Analysis of Ehrlich's data reveals that all empirical support for the deterrent effect of capital punishment disappears when the five most recent years are removed from his time series—that is to say, whether a decrease in the execution risk corresponds to an increase or a decrease in the murder rate depends on the ending point of the sample period. This finding has cast severe doubts on the reliability of Ehrlich's tentative conclusions. Indeed, a recent regression study, based on Ehrlich's theoretical model but using cross-section state data for the years 1950 and 1960 found no support for the conclusion that executions act as a deterrent.

The Ehrlich study, in short, is of little, if any, assistance in assessing the deterrent impact of the death penalty. . . . The evidence I reviewed in *Furman* remains convincing, in my view that "capital punishment is not necessary as a deterrent to crime in our society." The justification for the death penalty must be found elsewhere.

The other principal purpose said to be served by the death penalty is retribution. The notion that retribution can serve as a moral justification for the sanction of death finds credence in the opinion of my Brothers Stewart, Powell, and Stevens. . . . It is this notion that I find to be the most disturbing aspect of today's unfortunate decisions.

The concept of retribution is a multifaceted one, and any discussion of its role in the criminal law must be undertaken with caution. On one level, it can be said that the notion of retribution or reprobation is the basis of our insistence that only those who have broken the law be punished, and in this sense the notion is quite obviously central to a just system of criminal sanctions. But our recognition that retribution plays a crucial role in determining who may be punished by no means requires approval of retribution as a general justification for punishment. It is the question whether retribution can provide a moral justification for punishment—in particular, capital punishment—that we must consider.

. . . As my Brother Brennan stated in *Furman*, "[t]here is no evidence whatever that utilization of imprisonment rather than death encourages private blood feuds and other disorders." 408 U.S., at 303. It simply defies belief to suggest that the death penalty is necessary to prevent the American people from taking the law into their own hands.

In a related vein, it may be suggested that the expression of moral outrage through the imposition of the death penalty serves to reinforce basic moral values—that it marks some crimes as particularly offensive and therefore to be avoided. The argument is akin to a deterrence argument, but differs in that it contemplates the individual's shrinking from antisocial conduct, not because he fears punishment, but because he has been told in the strongest possible way that the conduct is wrong. This contention, like the previous one, provides no support for the death penalty. It is inconceivable that any individual concerned about conforming his conduct to what society says is "right" would fail to realize that murder is "wrong" if the penalty were simply life imprisonment.

The foregoing contentions—that society's expression of moral outrage through the imposition of the death penalty pre-empts the citizenry from taking the law into its own hands and reinforces moral values—are not retributive in the purest sense. They are essentially utilitarian in that they portray the death penalty as valuable because of its beneficial results. These justifications for the death penalty are inadequate because the penalty is, quite clearly I think, not necessary to the accomplishment of those results.

There remains for consideration, however, what might be termed the purely retributive justification for the death penalty—that the death penalty is appropriate, not because of its beneficial effect on society, but because the taking of the murderer's life is itself morally good. Some of the language of the opinion of my Brothers Stewart, Powell, and Stevens . . . appears positively to embrace this notion of retribution for its own sake as a justification for capital punishment. . . .

Of course, it may be that these statements are intended as no more than observations as to the popular demands that it is thought must be responded to in order to prevent anarchy. But the implication of the statements appears to me to be quite different—namely, that society's judgment that the murderer "deserves" death must be respected not simply because the preservation of order requires it, but because it is appropriate that society make the judgment and carry it out. It is this latter notion, in particular, that I consider to be fundamentally at odds with the Eighth Amendment. . . . The mere fact that the community demands the murderer's life in return for the evil he has done cannot sustain the death penalty, for as Justices Stewart, Powell, and Stevens remind us, "the Eighth Amendment demands more than that a challenged punishment be acceptable to contemporary society." To be sustained under the Eighth Amendment, the death penalty must "compor[t] with the basic concept of human dignity at the core of the Amendment;" the objective in imposing it must be "[consistent] with our respect for the dignity of [other] men." . . . Under these standards, the taking of life "because the wrongdoer deserves it" surely must fall, for such a punishment has as its very basis the total denial of the wrong-doer's dignity and worth.

The death penalty, unnecessary to promote the goal of deterrence or to further any legitimate notion of retribution, is an excessive penalty forbidden by the Eighth and Fourteenth Amendments. I respectfully dissent from the Court's judgment upholding the sentences of death imposed upon the petitioners in these cases.

Chapter 4

Texas Death Penalty Procedures—*Jurek v. Texas* (1976)

Jurek v. Texas, 428 U.S. 262, 96 S. Ct. 2950, 49 L. Ed.2d 929 (1976) (7-2, procedure that does not explicitly provide for aggravating or mitigating circumstances but adequately guides and focuses the jury does not violate the Eighth Amendment).

Editor's comment: *Jurek* was one of the four Supreme Court decisions accompanying the seminal case of *Gregg v. Georgia.* (See Chapter 3 for *Gregg* and Chapter 6 for *Woodson v. North Carolina.* The other cases were *Proffitt v. Florida,* 428 U.S. 242, and *Roberts v. Louisiana,* 428 U.S. 325.) The *Jurek* case is noteworthy because it involved death penalty procedures different from the processes approved in *Gregg.* The Texas law did not contain a list of aggravating factors (evidence that supports a death sentence) and did not expressly provide for consideration of mitigating circumstances (evidence that supports a nondeath sentence). Although *Jurek* upheld the Texas statute, the Supreme Court subsequently ruled that the instructions given to Texas juries were inadequate to enable them to properly consider mitigating evidence. See *Penry v. Lynaugh,* 492 U.S. 302 (1989); *Penry v. Johnson,* 531 U.S. 1003 (2001). Texas modified its death penalty law in 1991 to explicitly provide for the consideration of mitigating factors. (This statute is reprinted in Appendix B.)

Texas death penalty law is also of interest because Texas has carried out more executions since 1976 than any other state. At year-end 2001, Texas accounted for 256 of the 749 executed, a bit over one-third of the total. (See Appendix A.)

❖   ❖   ❖

OPINION OF JUSTICE STEVENS, JOINED BY JUSTICES STEWART AND POWELL

The issue in this case is whether the imposition of the sentence of death for the crime of murder under the law of Texas violates the Eighth and Fourteenth Amendments to the Constitution.

I

The petitioner in this case, Jerry Lane Jurek, was charged by indictment with the killing of Wendy Adams "by choking and strangling her with his hands, and by drowning her in water by throwing her into a river in the course of committing and attempting to commit kidnapping of and forcible rape upon the said Wendy Adams."

The evidence at his trial consisted of incriminating statements made by the petitioner, the testimony of several people who saw the petitioner and the deceased during the day she was killed, and certain technical evidence. This evidence established that the petitioner, 22 years old at the time, had been drinking beer in the afternoon. He and two young friends later went driving together in his old pickup truck. The petitioner expressed a desire for sexual relations with some young girls they saw, but one of his companions said the girls were too young. The petitioner then dropped his two friends off at a pool hall. He was next seen talking to Wendy, who was 10 years old, at a public swimming pool where her grandmother had left her to swim. Other witnesses testified that they later observed a man resembling the petitioner driving an old pickup truck through town at a high rate of speed, with a young blond girl standing screaming in the bed of the truck. The last witness who saw them heard the girl crying, "Help me, help me." The witness tried to follow them, but lost them in traffic. According to the petitioner's statement, he took the girl to the river, choked her, and threw her unconscious body in the river. Her drowned body was found downriver two days later.

At the conclusion of the trial the jury returned a verdict of guilty.

Texas law requires that if a defendant has been convicted of a capital offense, the trial court must conduct a separate sentencing proceeding before the same jury that tried the issue of guilt. Any relevant evidence may be introduced at this proceeding, and both prosecution and defense may present argument for or against the sentence of death. The jury is then presented with two (sometimes three) questions, the answers to which determine whether a death sentence will be imposed.

During the punishment phase of the petitioner's trial, several witnesses for the State testified to the petitioner's bad reputation in the community. The petitioner's father countered with testimony that the petitioner had always been steadily employed since he had left school and that he contributed to his family's support.

The jury then considered the two statutory questions relevant to this case: (1) whether the evidence established beyond a reasonable doubt that the murder of the deceased was committed deliberately and with the reasonable expectation that the death of the deceased or another would result, and (2) whether the evidence established beyond a reasonable doubt that there was a probability that the defendant would commit criminal acts of violence that would constitute a continuing threat to society. The jury unanimously answered "yes" to both questions, and the judge, therefore, in accordance with the statute, sentenced the petitioner to death. The Court of Criminal Appeals of Texas affirmed the judgment.

We granted certiorari to consider whether the imposition of the death penalty in this case violates the Eighth and Fourteenth Amendments of the United States Constitution.

II

The petitioner argues that the imposition of the death penalty under any circumstances is cruel and unusual punishment in violation of the Eighth and Fourteenth Amendments. We reject this argument for the reasons stated today in *Gregg v. Georgia.*

III

A. After this Court held Texas' system for imposing capital punishment unconstitutional in *Branch v. Texas,* decided with *Furman v. Georgia,* the Texas Legislature narrowed the scope of its laws relating to capital punishment. The new Texas Penal Code limits capital homicides to intentional and knowing murders committed in five situations: murder of a peace officer or fireman; murder committed in the course of kidnapping, burglary, robbery, forcible rape, or arson; murder committed for remuneration; murder committed while escaping or attempting to escape from a penal institution; and murder committed by a prison inmate when the victim is a prison employee.

In addition, Texas adopted a new capital-sentencing procedure. That procedure requires the jury to answer three questions in a proceeding that takes place subsequent to the return of a verdict finding a person guilty of one of the above categories of murder. The questions the jury must answer are these:

"(1) whether the conduct of the defendant that caused the death of the deceased was committed deliberately and with the reasonable expectation that the death of the deceased or another would result;
"(2) whether there is a probability that the defendant would commit criminal acts of violence that would constitute a continuing threat to society; and
"(3) if raised by the evidence, whether the conduct of the defendant in killing the deceased was unreasonable in response to the provocation, if any, by the deceased."

If the jury finds that the State has proved beyond a reasonable doubt that the answer to each of the three questions is yes, then the death sentence is imposed. If the jury finds that the answer to any question is no, then a sentence of life imprisonment results. The law also provides for an expedited review by the Texas Court of Criminal Appeals. . . .

While Texas has not adopted a list of statutory aggravating circumstances the existence of which can justify the imposition of the death penalty as have Georgia and Florida, its action in narrowing the categories of murders for which a death sentence may ever be imposed serves much the same purpose. In fact, each of the five classes of murders made capital by the Texas statute is encompassed in Georgia and Florida by one or more of their statutory aggravating circumstances. For example, the Texas statute requires the jury at the guilt-determining stage to consider whether the crime was committed in the course of a particular felony, whether it was committed for hire, or whether the defendant was an inmate of a penal institution at the time of its commission. Thus, in essence, the Texas statute requires that the jury find the existence of a statutory aggravating circumstance before the death penalty may be imposed. So far as consideration of aggravating circumstances is concerned, therefore, the principal difference between Texas and the other two States is that the death penalty is an available sentencing option even potentially for a smaller class of murders in Texas. Otherwise the statutes are similar. Each requires the sentencing authority to focus on the particularized nature of the crime.

But a sentencing system that allowed the jury to consider only aggravating circumstances would almost certainly fall short of providing the individualized sentencing determination that we today have held in *Woodson v. North Carolina* to be required by the Eighth and Fourteenth Amendments. For such a system would approach the mandatory laws that we today hold unconstitutional in *Woodson* and *Roberts v. Louisiana*. A jury must be allowed to consider on the basis of all relevant evidence not only why a death sentence should be imposed, but also why it should not be imposed.

Thus, in order to meet the requirement of the Eighth and Fourteenth Amendments, a capital-sentencing system must allow the sentencing authority to consider mitigating circumstances. In *Gregg v. Georgia*, we today hold constitutionally valid a capital-sentencing system that directs the jury to consider any mitigating factors, and in *Proffitt v. Florida* we likewise hold constitutional a system that directs the judge and advisory jury to consider certain enumerated mitigating circumstances. The Texas statute does not explicitly speak of mitigating circumstances; it directs only that the jury answer three questions. Thus, the constitutionality of the Texas procedures turns on whether the enumerated questions allow consideration of particularized mitigating factors.

The second Texas statutory question asks the jury to determine "whether there is a probability that the defendant would commit criminal acts of violence that would constitute a continuing threat to society" if he were not sentenced to death. The Texas Court of Criminal Appeals has yet to define precisely the meanings of such terms as "criminal acts of violence" or "continuing threat to society." In the present case, however, it indicated that it will interpret this second question so as to allow a defendant to bring to the jury's attention whatever mitigating circumstances he may be able to show:

"In determining the likelihood that the defendant would be a continuing threat to society, the jury could consider whether the defendant had a significant criminal record. It could consider the range and severity of his prior criminal conduct. It could further look to the age of the defendant and whether or not at the time of the commission of the offense he was acting under duress or under the domination of another. It could also consider whether the defendant was under an extreme form of mental or emotional pressure, something less, perhaps, than insanity, but more than the emotions of the average man, however inflamed, could withstand."

In the only other case in which the Texas Court of Criminal Appeals has upheld a death sentence, it focused on the question of whether any mitigating factors were present in the case. In that case the state appellate court examined the sufficiency of the evidence to see if a "yes" answer to question 2 should be sustained. In doing so it examined the defendant's prior conviction on narcotics charges, his subsequent failure to attempt to rehabilitate himself or obtain employment, the fact that he had not acted under duress or as a result of mental or emotional pressure, his apparent willingness to kill, his lack of remorse after the killing, and the conclusion of a psychiatrist that he had a sociopathic personality and that his patterns of conduct would be the same in the future as they had been in the past.

Thus, Texas law essentially requires that one of five aggravating circumstances be found before a defendant can be found guilty of capital murder, and that in considering whether to impose a death sentence the jury may be asked to consider whatever evidence of mitigating circumstances the defense can bring before it. It thus appears that, as in Georgia and Florida, the Texas capital-sentencing procedure guides and focuses the jury's objective consideration of the particularized circumstances of the individual offense and the individual offender before it can impose a sentence of death.

B. As in the Georgia and Florida cases, however, the petitioner contends that the substantial legislative changes that Texas made in response to this Court's *Furman* decision are no more than cosmetic in nature and have in fact not eliminated the arbitrariness and caprice of the system held in *Furman* to violate the Eighth and Fourteenth Amendments.

(1) The petitioner first asserts that arbitrariness still pervades the entire criminal justice system of Texas from the prosecutor's decision whether to charge a capital offense in the first place and then whether to engage in plea bargaining, through the jury's consideration of lesser included offenses, to the Governor's ultimate power to commute death sentences. This contention fundamentally misinterprets the *Furman* decision, and we reject it for the reasons set out in our opinion today in *Gregg v. Georgia.*

(2) Focusing on the second statutory question that Texas requires a jury to answer in considering whether to impose a death sentence, the petitioner argues that it is impossible to predict future behavior and that the question is so vague

as to be meaningless. It is, of course, not easy to predict future behavior. The fact that such a determination is difficult, however, does not mean that it cannot be made. Indeed, prediction of future criminal conduct is an essential element in many of the decisions rendered throughout our criminal justice system. The decision whether to admit a defendant to bail, for instance, must often turn on a judge's prediction of the defendant's future conduct. And any sentencing authority must predict a convicted person's probable future conduct when it engages in the process of determining what punishment to impose. For those sentenced to prison, these same predictions must be made by parole authorities. The task that a Texas jury must perform in answering the statutory question in issue is thus basically no different from the task performed countless times each day throughout the American system of criminal justice. What is essential is that the jury have before it all possible relevant information about the individual defendant whose fate it must determine. Texas law clearly assures that all such evidence will be adduced.

IV

We conclude that Texas' capital-sentencing procedures, like those of Georgia and Florida, do not violate the Eighth and Fourteenth Amendments. By narrowing its definition of capital murder, Texas has essentially said that there must be at least one statutory aggravating circumstance in a first-degree murder case before a death sentence may even be considered. By authorizing the defense to bring before the jury at the separate sentencing hearing whatever mitigating circumstances relating to the individual defendant can be adduced, Texas has ensured that the sentencing jury will have adequate guidance to enable it to perform its sentencing function. By providing prompt judicial review of the jury's decision in a court with statewide jurisdiction, Texas has provided a means to promote the evenhanded, rational, and consistent imposition of death sentences under law. Because this system serves to assure that sentences of death will not be "wantonly" or "freakishly" imposed, it does not violate the Constitution. *Furman.* Accordingly, the judgment of the Texas Court of Criminal Appeals is affirmed.

It is so ordered.

[Chief Justice Burger and Justice Blackmun concurred in the judgment. Justices Brennan and Marshall dissented for the reasons expressed in their opinions in *Gregg v. Georgia.*]

CONCURRING OPINION OF JUSTICE WHITE, JOINED BY CHIEF JUSTICE BURGER AND JUSTICE REHNQUIST

For the reasons stated in my dissent in *Roberts v. Louisiana*, I cannot conclude that the Eighth Amendment forbids the death penalty under any and all circumstances. I also cannot agree with petitioner's other major contention that under the new Texas statute and the State's criminal justice system in general, the criminal jury and other law enforcement officers exercise such a range of discretion that the death penalty will be imposed so seldom, so arbitrarily, and so freakishly that the new statute suffers from the infirmities which *Branch v. Texas* found in its predecessor. Under the revised law, the substantive crime of murder is defined; and when a murder occurs in one of the five circumstances set out in the statute, the death penalty must be imposed if the jury also makes the certain additional findings against the defendant. Petitioner claims that the additional questions upon which the death sentence depends are so vague that in essence the jury possesses standardless sentencing power; but I agree with Justices Stewart, Powell, and Stevens that the issues posed in the sentencing proceeding have a common-sense core of meaning and that criminal juries should be capable of understanding them. The statute does not extend to juries discretionary power to dispense mercy, and it should not be assumed that juries will disobey or nullify their instructions. As of February of this year, 33 persons, including petitioner, had been sentenced to death under the Texas murder statute. I cannot conclude at this juncture that the death penalty under this system will be imposed so seldom and arbitrarily as to serve no useful penological function and hence fall within reach of the decision announced by five Members of the Court in *Furman v. Georgia*.

Nor, for the reasons I have set out in *Roberts* and *Gregg*, am I convinced that this conclusion should be modified because of the alleged discretion which is exercisable by other major functionaries in the State's criminal justice system. Furthermore, as Justices Stewart, Powell, and Stevens state and as the Texas Court of Criminal Appeals has noted, the Texas capital punishment statute limits the imposition of the death penalty to a narrowly defined group of the most brutal crimes and aims at limiting its imposition to similar offenses occurring under similar circumstances.

I concur in the judgment of affirmance.

Chapter 5

Rape and the Death Penalty— *Coker v. Georgia* (1977)

Coker v. Georgia, 433 U.S. 584, 97 S. Ct. 2861, 53 L. Ed.2d 982 (1977) (7–2, a sentence of death for the rape of an adult woman is grossly disproportionate and excessive punishment forbidden by the Eighth Amendment).

❖ ❖ ❖

OPINION OF JUSTICE WHITE, JOINED BY JUSTICES STEWART, BLACKMUN, AND STEVENS

I

While serving various sentences for murder, rape, kidnapping, and aggravated assault, petitioner escaped from the Ware Correctional Institution near Waycross, Ga., on September 2, 1974. At approximately 11 o'clock that night, petitioner entered the house of Allen and Elnita Carver through an unlocked kitchen door. Threatening the couple with a "board," he tied up Mr. Carver in the bathroom, obtained a knife from the kitchen, and took Mr. Carver's money and the keys to the family car. Brandishing the knife and saying "you know what's going to happen to you if you try anything, don't you," Coker then raped Mrs. Carver. Soon thereafter, petitioner drove away in the Carver car, taking Mrs. Carver with him. Mr. Carver, freeing himself, notified the police; and not long thereafter petitioner was apprehended. Mrs. Carver was unharmed.

Petitioner was charged with escape, armed robbery, motor vehicle theft, kidnapping, and rape. Counsel was appointed to represent him. Having been found competent to stand trial, he was tried. The jury returned a verdict of guilty, rejecting his general plea of insanity. A sentencing hearing was then conducted in accordance with the procedures dealt with at length in *Gregg v. Georgia*, where this Court sustained the death penalty for murder when imposed pursuant to the statutory procedures. The jury was instructed that it could consider as aggravating circumstances whether the rape had been committed by a person with a prior record of conviction for a capital felony and whether the rape had been committed in the course of committing another capital felony, namely, the armed robbery of Allen Carver. The court also instructed, pursuant to statute, that even if aggravating circumstances were present, the death penalty need not be imposed if the jury found they were out-weighed by mitigating circumstances, that is, circumstances not constituting justification or excuse for the offense in question, "but which, in fairness and mercy, may be considered as extenuating or reducing the degree" of moral culpability or punishment. The jury's verdict on the rape count was death by electrocution. Both aggravating circumstances on which the court instructed were found to be present by the jury.

II

. . . In sustaining the imposition of the death penalty in *Gregg*, . . . the Court firmly embraced the holdings and dicta from prior cases, *Furman v. Georgia; Robinson v. California; Trop v. Dulles*; and *Weems v. United States*, to the effect that the Eighth Amendment bars not only those punishments that are "barbaric" but also those that are "excessive" in relation to the crime committed. Under *Gregg*, a punishment is "excessive" and unconstitutional if it (1) makes no measurable contribution to acceptable goals of punishment and hence is nothing more than the purposeless and needless imposition of pain and suffering; or (2) is grossly out of proportion to the severity of the crime. A punishment might fail the test on either ground. Furthermore, these Eighth Amendment judgments should not be, or appear to be, merely the subjective views of individual Justices; judgment should be informed by objective factors to the maximum possible extent. To this end, attention must be given to the public attitudes concerning a particular sentence—history and precedent, legislative attitudes, and the response of juries reflected in their sentencing decisions are to be consulted. In *Gregg*, after giving due regard to such sources, the Court's judgment was that the death penalty for deliberate murder was neither the purposeless imposition of severe punishment nor a punishment grossly disproportionate to the crime. But the Court reserved the question of the constitutionality of the death penalty when imposed for other crimes.

III

That question, with respect to rape of an adult woman, is now before us. We have concluded that a sentence of death is grossly disproportionate and excessive punishment for the crime of rape and is therefore forbidden by the Eighth Amendment as cruel and unusual punishment.

A. As advised by recent cases, we seek guidance in history and from the objective evidence of the country's present judgment concerning the acceptability of death as a penalty for rape of an adult woman. At no time in the last 50 years have majority of the States authorized death as a punishment for rape. In 1925, 18 States, the District of Columbia, and the Federal Government authorized capital punishment for the rape of an adult female. By 1971 just prior to the decision in *Furman v. Georgia,* that number had declined, but not substantially, to 16 States plus the Federal Government. *Furman* then invalidated most of the capital punishment statutes in this country, including the rape statutes, because, among other reasons, of the manner in which the death penalty was imposed and utilized under those laws.

With their death penalty statutes for the most part invalidated, the States were faced with the choice of enacting modified capital punishment laws in an attempt to satisfy the requirements of *Furman* or of being satisfied with life imprisonment as the ultimate punishment for any offense. Thirty-five States immediately reinstituted the death penalty for at least limited kinds of crime. . . . This public judgment as to the acceptability of capital punishment, evidenced by the immediate, post-*Furman* legislative reaction in a large majority of the States, heavily influenced the Court to sustain the death penalty for murder in *Gregg v. Georgia.*

But if the "most marked indication of society's endorsement of the death penalty for murder is the legislative response to *Furman,*" *Gregg,* it should also be a telling datum that the public judgment with respect to rape, as reflected in the statutes providing the punishment for that crime, has been dramatically different. In reviving death penalty laws to satisfy *Furman*'s mandate, none of the States that had not previously authorized death for rape chose to include rape among capital felonies. Of the 16 States in which rape had been a capital offense, only three provided the death penalty for rape of an adult woman in their revised statutes—Georgia, North Carolina, and Louisiana. In the latter two States, the death penalty was mandatory for those found guilty, and those laws were invalidated by *Woodson* and *Roberts.* When Louisiana and North Carolina, responding to those decisions, again revised their capital punishment laws, they reenacted the death penalty for murder but not for rape; none of the seven other legislatures that to our knowledge have amended or replaced their death penalty statutes since July 2, 1976, including four States (in addition to Louisiana and North Carolina) that had authorized the death sentence for rape prior to 1972 and had reacted to *Furman* with mandatory statutes, included rape among the crimes for which death was an authorized punishment.

Georgia argues that 11 of the 16 States that authorized death for rape in 1972 attempted to comply with *Furman* by enacting arguably mandatory death penalty legislation and that it is very likely that, aside from Louisiana and North Carolina, these States simply chose to eliminate rape as a capital offense rather than to require death for each and every instance of rape. The argument is not without force; but 4 of the 16 States did not take the mandatory course and also did *not* continue rape of an adult woman as a capital offense. Further, as we have indicated, the legislatures of 6 of the 11 arguably mandatory States have revised their death penalty laws since *Woodson* and *Roberts* without enacting a new death penalty for rape. And this is to say nothing of 19 other States that enacted nonmandatory, post-*Furman* statutes and chose not to sentence rapists to death.

It should be noted that Florida, Mississippi, and Tennessee also authorized the death penalty in some rape cases, but only where the victim was a child and the rapist an adult. The Tennessee statute has since been invalidated because the death sentence was mandatory. . . . The upshot is that Georgia is the sole jurisdiction in the United States at the present time that authorizes a sentence of death when the rape victim is an adult woman, and only two other jurisdictions provide capital punishment when the victim is a child.

The current judgment with respect to the death penalty for rape is not wholly unanimous among state legislatures, but it obviously weighs very heavily on the side of rejecting capital punishment as a suitable penalty for raping an adult woman.

B.   It was also observed in *Gregg* that "[t]he jury . . . is a significant and reliable objective index of contemporary values because it is so directly involved," and that it is thus important to look to the sentencing decisions that juries have made in the course of assessing whether capital punishment is an appropriate penalty for the crime being tried. Of course, the jury's judgment is meaningful only where the jury has an appropriate measure of choice as to whether the death penalty is to be imposed. As far as execution for rape is concerned, this is now true only in Georgia and in Florida; and in the latter State, capital punishment is authorized only for the rape of children.

According to the factual submissions in this Court, out of all rape convictions in Georgia since 1973—and that total number has not been tendered—63 cases had been reviewed by the Georgia Supreme Court as of the time of oral argument; and of these, 6 involved a death sentence, 1 of which was set aside, leaving 5 convicted rapists now under sentence of death in the State of Georgia. Georgia juries have thus sentenced rapists to death six times since 1973. This obviously is not a negligible number; and the State argues that as a practical matter juries simply reserve the extreme sanction for extreme cases of rape and that recent experience surely does not prove that jurors consider the death penalty to be a disproportionate punishment for every conceivable instance of rape, no matter how aggravated. Nevertheless, it is true that in the vast majority of cases, at least 9 out of 10, juries have not imposed the death sentence.

IV

These recent events evidencing the attitude of state legislatures and sentencing juries do not wholly determine this controversy, for the Constitution contemplates that in the end our own judgment will be brought to bear on the question of the acceptability of the death penalty under the Eighth Amendment. Nevertheless, the legislative rejection of capital punishment for rape strongly confirms our own judgment, which is that death is indeed a disproportionate penalty for the crime of raping an adult woman.

We do not discount the seriousness of rape as a crime. It is highly reprehensible, both in a moral sense and in its almost total contempt for the personal integrity and autonomy of the female victim and for the latter's privilege of choosing those with whom intimate relationships are to be established. Short of homicide, it is the "ultimate violation of self." It is also a violent crime because it normally involves force, or the threat of force or intimidation, to overcome the will and the capacity of the victim to resist. Rape is very often accompanied by physical injury to the female and can also inflict mental and psychological damage. Because it undermines the community's sense of security, there is public injury as well.

Rape is without doubt deserving of serious punishment; but in terms of moral depravity and of the injury to the person and to the public, it does not compare with murder, which does involve the unjustified taking of human life. Although it may be accompanied by another crime, rape by definition does not include the death of or even the serious injury to another person. The murderer kills; the rapist, if no more than that, does not. Life is over for the victim of the murderer; for the rape victim, life may not be nearly so happy as it was, but it is not over and normally is not beyond repair. We have the abiding conviction that the death penalty, which "is unique in its severity and irrevocability," *Gregg,* is an excessive penalty for the rapist who, as such, does not take human life.

This does not end the matter; for under Georgia law, death may not be imposed for any capital offense, including rape, unless the jury or judge finds one of the statutory aggravating circumstances and then elects to impose that sentence. . . . For the rapist to be executed in Georgia, it must therefore be found not only that he committed rape but also that one or more of the following aggravating circumstances were present: (1) that the rape was committed by a person with a prior record of conviction for a capital felony; (2) that the rape was committed while the offender was engaged in the commission of another capital felony, or aggravated battery; or (3) the rape "was outrageously or wantonly vile, horrible or inhuman in that it involved torture, depravity of mind, or aggravated battery to the victim." Here, the first two of these aggravating circumstances were alleged and found by the jury.

Neither of these circumstances, nor both of them together, change our conclusion that the death sentence imposed on Coker is a disproportionate punishment for rape. Coker had prior convictions for capital felonies—rape, murder, and kidnapping—but these prior convictions do not change the fact that the instant crime being punished is a rape not involving the taking of life.

It is also true that the present rape occurred while Coker was committing armed robbery, a felony for which the Georgia statutes authorize the death penalty. But Coker was tried for the robbery offense as well as for rape and received a separate life sentence for this crime; the jury did not deem the robbery itself deserving of the death penalty, even though accompanied by the aggravating circumstance, which was stipulated, that Coker had been convicted of a prior capital crime.

We note finally that in Georgia a person commits murder when he unlawfully and with malice aforethought, either express or implied, causes the death of another human being. He also commits that crime when in the commission of a felony he causes the death of another human being, irrespective of malice. But even where the killing is deliberate, it is not punishable by death absent proof of aggravating circumstances. It is difficult to accept the notion, and we do not, that the rapist, with or without aggravating circumstances, should be punished more heavily than the deliberate killer as long as the rapist does not himself take the life of his victim. The judgment of the Georgia Supreme Court upholding the death sentence is reversed, and the case is remanded to that court for further proceedings not inconsistent with this opinion. So ordered.

[Justices Brennan and Marshall concurred in the judgment.]

OPINION OF JUSTICE POWELL, CONCURRING IN THE JUDGMENT IN PART AND DISSENTING IN PART

I concur in the judgment of the Court on the facts of this case, and also in the plurality's reasoning supporting the view that ordinarily death is disproportionate punishment for the crime of raping an adult woman. Although rape invariably is a reprehensible crime, there is no indication that petitioner's offense was committed with excessive brutality or that the victim sustained serious or lasting injury. The plurality, however, does not limit its holding to the case before us or to similar cases. Rather, in an opinion that ranges well beyond what is necessary, it holds that capital punishment *always*—regardless of the circumstances—is a disproportionate penalty for the crime of rape. . . .

Today, . . . the plurality draws a bright line between murder and all rapes regardless of the degree of brutality of the rape or the effect upon the victim. I dissent because I am not persuaded that such a bright line is appropriate. As noted in *Snider v. Peyton*, 356 F.2d 626, 627 (CA4 1966), "[t]here is extreme variation in the degree of culpability of rapists." The deliberate viciousness of the rapist may be greater than that of the murderer. Rape is never an act committed accidentally. Rarely can it be said to be unpremeditated. There also is wide variation in the effect on the victim. The plurality opinion says that "[l]ife is over for the victim of the murderer; for the rape victim, life may not be nearly so happy as it was, but it is not over and normally is not beyond repair." But there is indeed "extreme variation" in the crime of rape. Some victims are so grievously injured physically or psychologically that life *is* beyond repair.

Thus, it may be that the death penalty is not disproportionate punishment for the crime of aggravated rape. Final resolution of the question must await careful inquiry into objective indicators of society's "evolving standards of decency," particularly legislative enactments and the responses of juries in capital cases. . . . The plurality properly examines these indicia, which do support the conclusion that society finds the death penalty unacceptable for the crime of rape in the absence of excessive brutality or severe injury. But it has not been shown that society finds the penalty disproportionate for all rapes. In a proper case a more discriminating inquiry than the plurality undertakes well might discover that both juries and legislatures have reserved the ultimate penalty for the case of an outrageous rape resulting in serious, lasting harm to the victim. I would not prejudge the issue. To this extent, I respectfully dissent.

DISSENTING OPINION OF CHIEF JUSTICE BURGER, JOINED BY JUSTICE REHNQUIST

. . . The Court today holds that the State of Georgia may not impose the death penalty on Coker. In so doing, it prevents the State from imposing any effective punishment upon Coker for his latest rape. The Court's holding, moreover, bars Georgia from guaranteeing its citizens that they will suffer no further attacks by this habitual rapist. In fact, given the lengthy sentences Coker must serve for the crimes he has already committed, the Court's holding assures that petitioner— as well as others in his position—will henceforth feel no compunction whatso- ever about committing further rapes as frequently as he may be able to escape from confinement and indeed even within the walls of the prison itself. To what extent we have left States "elbowroom" to protect innocent persons from depraved human beings like Coker remains in doubt.

My first disagreement with the Court's holding is its unnecessary breadth. The narrow issue here presented is whether the State of Georgia may constitu- tionally execute this petitioner for the particular rape which he has committed, in light of all the facts and circumstances shown by this record. The plurality opinion goes to great lengths to consider societal mores and attitudes toward the generic crime of rape and the punishment for it; however, the opinion gives little attention to the special circumstances which bear directly on whether imposition of the death penalty is an appropriate societal response to Coker's criminal acts: (a) On account of his prior offenses, Coker is already serving such lengthy prison sentences that imposition of additional periods of imprisonment would have no incremental punitive effect; (b) by his life pattern Coker has shown that he pre- sents a particular danger to the safety, welfare, and chastity of women, and on his record the likelihood is therefore great that he will repeat his crime at the first opportunity; (c) petitioner escaped from prison, only a year and a half after he commenced serving his latest sentences; he has nothing to lose by further escape attempts; and (d) should he again succeed in escaping from prison, it is reason- ably predictable that he will repeat his pattern of attacks on women—and with impunity since the threat of added prison sentences will be no deterrent.

. . . The question of whether the death penalty is an appropriate punishment for rape is surely an open one. It is arguable that many prospective rapists would be deterred by the possibility that they could suffer death for their offense; it is also arguable that the death penalty would have only minimal deterrent effect. It may well be that rape victims would become more willing to report the crime and aid in the apprehension of the criminals if they knew that community disapproval of rapists was sufficiently strong to inflict the extreme penalty; or perhaps they would be reluctant to cooperate in the prosecution of rapists if they knew that a conviction might result in the imposition of the death penalty. Quite possibly, the occasional, well-publicized execution of egregious rapists may cause citizens to feel greater security in their daily lives; or, on the contrary, it may be that members of a civilized community will suffer the pangs of a heavy conscience because such punishment will be perceived as excessive. We cannot know which among this range of possibilities is correct, but today's holding forecloses the very exploration we have said federalism was intended to foster. It is difficult to believe that Georgia would long remain alone in punishing rape by death if the next decade demonstrated a drastic reduction in its incidence of rape, an increased cooperation by rape victims in the apprehension and prosecution of rapists, and a greater confidence in the rule of law on the part of the populace.

. . . The clear implication of today's holding appears to be that the death penalty may be properly imposed only as to crimes resulting in death of the victim. This casts serious doubt upon the constitutional validity of statutes imposing the death penalty for a variety of conduct which, though dangerous, may not necessarily result in any immediate death, *e.g.*, treason, airplane hijacking, and kidnapping. In that respect, today's holding does even more harm than is initially apparent. We cannot avoid taking judicial notice that crimes such as airplane hijacking, kidnapping, and mass terrorist activity constitute a serious and increasing danger to the safety of the public. It would be unfortunate indeed if the effect of today's holding were to inhibit States and the Federal Government from experimenting with various remedies—including possibly imposition of the penalty of death—to prevent and deter such crimes. . . .

Chapter 6

Mandatory Death Penalty—
Woodson v. North Carolina
(1976)

Woodson v. North Carolina, 428 U.S. 280, 96 S. Ct. 2978, 49 L. Ed.2d 944 (1976) (5–4, mandatory death penalty for all first-degree murderers violates the Eighth Amendment).

Editor's comment: In the wake of *Furman*, a number of state legislatures apparently believed that a mandatory death penalty for certain types of murder would avoid the problem of the inconsistent application of the ultimate punishment. The Supreme Court disagreed and held that the Eighth Amendment forbade the mandatory imposition of death sentences. *Woodson* was decided on the same day as *Gregg* and *Roberts v. Louisiana*, 428 U.S. 325 (1976), which is cited in Justice White's *Woodson* dissent. In *Roberts*, the Court voided a Louisiana mandatory death law similar to the North Carolina statute.

❖　❖　❖

OPINION OF JUSTICE STEWART, JOINED BY JUSTICES POWELL AND STEVENS

The question in this case is whether the imposition of a death sentence for the crime of first-degree murder under the law of North Carolina violates the Eighth and Fourteenth Amendments.

I

The petitioners were convicted of first-degree murder as the result of their participation in an armed robbery of a convenience food store, in the course of which the cashier was killed and a customer was seriously wounded. . . .

III

... The [North Carolina murder] statute now reads as follows:

Murder in the first and second degree defined; punishment.—A murder which shall be perpetrated by means of poison, lying in wait, imprisonment, starving, torture, or by any other kind of willful, deliberate and premeditated killing, or which shall be committed in the perpetration or attempt to perpetrate any arson, rape, robbery, kidnapping, burglary or other felony, shall be deemed to be murder in the first degree and shall be punished with death. All other kinds of murder shall be deemed murder in the second degree, and shall be punished by imprisonment for a term of not less than two years nor more than life imprisonment in the State's prison.

It was under this statute that the petitioners, who committed their crime on June 3, 1974, were tried, convicted, and sentenced to death. North Carolina, unlike Florida, Georgia, and Texas, has thus responded to the *Furman* decision by making death the mandatory sentence for all persons convicted of first-degree murder. In ruling on the constitutionality of the sentences imposed on the petitioners under this North Carolina statute, the Court now addresses for the first time the question whether a death sentence returned pursuant to a law imposing a mandatory death penalty for a broad category of homicidal offenses[7] constitutes cruel and unusual punishment within the meaning of the Eighth and Fourteenth Amendments. The issue, like that explored in *Furman*, involves the procedure employed by the State to select persons for the unique and irreversible penalty of death.

A. ... Central to the application of the [Eighth] Amendment is the determination of contemporary standards regarding the infliction of punishment. As discussed in *Gregg v. Georgia*, ... indicia of societal values identified in prior opinions include history and traditional usage, legislative enactments, and jury determinations.

In order to provide a frame for assessing the relevancy of these factors in this case we begin by sketching the history of mandatory death penalty statutes in the United States. At the time the Eighth Amendment was adopted in 1791, the States uniformly followed the common-law practice of making death the exclusive and mandatory sentence for certain specified offenses. Although the range of capital offenses in the American Colonies was quite limited in comparison to the more than 200 offenses then punishable by death in England, the Colonies at the time of the Revolution imposed death sentences on all persons

---

[7] This case does not involve a mandatory death penalty statute limited to an extremely narrow category of homicide, such as murder by a prisoner serving a life sentence, defined in large part in terms of the character or record of the offender. We thus express no opinion regarding the constitutionality of such a statute. ...

convicted of any of a considerable number of crimes, typically including at a minimum, murder, treason, piracy, arson, rape, robbery, burglary, and sodomy. As at common law, all homicides that were not involuntary, provoked, justified, or excused constituted murder and were automatically punished by death. Almost from the outset jurors reacted unfavorably to the harshness of mandatory death sentences. The States initially responded to this expression of public dissatisfaction with mandatory statutes by limiting the classes of capital offenses.

This reform, however, left unresolved the problem posed by the not infrequent refusal of juries to convict murderers rather than subject them to automatic death sentences. In 1794, Pennsylvania attempted to alleviate the undue severity of the law by confining the mandatory death penalty to "murder of the first degree" encompassing all "wilful, deliberate and premediated" killings. . . . Other jurisdictions, including Virginia and Ohio, soon enacted similar measures, and within a generation the practice spread to most of the States.

Despite the broad acceptance of the division of murder into degrees, the reform proved to be an unsatisfactory means of identifying persons appropriately punishable by death. Although its failure was due in part to the amorphous nature of the controlling concepts of willfulness, deliberateness, and premeditation, a more fundamental weakness of the reform soon became apparent. Juries continued to find the death penalty inappropriate in a significant number of first-degree murder cases and refused to return guilty verdicts for that crime.

The inadequacy of distinguishing between murderers solely on the basis of legislative criteria narrowing the definition of the capital offense led the States to grant juries sentencing discretion in capital cases. Tennessee in 1838, followed by Alabama in 1841, and Louisiana in 1846, were the first States to abandon mandatory death sentences in favor of discretionary death penalty statutes. This flexibility remedied the harshness of mandatory statutes by permitting the jury to respond to mitigating factors by withholding the death penalty. By the turn of the century, 23 States and the Federal Government had made death sentences discretionary for first-degree murder and other capital offenses. During the next two decades 14 additional States replaced their mandatory death penalty statutes. Thus, by the end of World War I, all but eight States, Hawaii, and the District of Columbia either had adopted discretionary death penalty schemes or abolished the death penalty altogether. By 1963, all of these remaining jurisdictions had replaced their automatic death penalty statutes with discretionary jury sentencing.[25] The history of mandatory death penalty statutes in the United States thus reveals that the practice of sentencing to death all persons convicted of a partic-

---

[25] . . . The only category of mandatory death sentence statutes that appears to have had any relevance to the actual administration of the death penalty in the years preceding *Furman* concerned the crimes of murder or assault with a deadly weapon by a life-term prisoner. Statutes of this type apparently existed in five States in 1964. . . . In 1970, only five of the more than 550 prisoners under death sentence across the country had been sentenced under a mandatory death penalty statute. Those prisoners had all been convicted under the California statute applicable to assaults by life-term prisoners. We have no occasion in this case to examine the constitutionality of mandatory death sentence statutes applicable to prisoners serving life sentences.

ular offense has been rejected as unduly harsh and unworkably rigid. The two crucial indicators of evolving standards of decency respecting the imposition of punishment in our society—jury determinations and legislative enactments— both point conclusively to the repudiation of automatic death sentences. At least since the Revolution, American jurors have, with some regularity, disregarded their oaths and refused to convict defendants where a death sentence was the automatic consequence of a guilty verdict. As we have seen, the initial movement to reduce the number of capital offenses and to separate murder into degrees was prompted in part by the reaction of jurors as well as by reformers who objected to the imposition of death as the penalty for any crime. Nineteenth century journalists, statesmen, and jurists repeatedly observed that jurors were often deterred from convicting palpably guilty men of first-degree murder under mandatory statutes. Thereafter, continuing evidence of jury reluctance to convict persons of capital offenses in mandatory death penalty jurisdictions resulted in legislative authorization of discretionary jury sentencing—by Congress for federal crimes in 1897, by North Carolina in 1949, and by Congress for the District of Columbia in 1962.

As we have noted today in *Gregg v. Georgia*, legislative measures adopted by the people's chosen representatives weigh heavily in ascertaining contemporary standards of decency. The consistent course charted by the state legislatures and by Congress since the middle of the past century demonstrates that the aversion of jurors to mandatory death penalty statutes is shared by society at large.

Still further evidence of the incompatibility of mandatory death penalties with contemporary values is provided by the results of jury sentencing under discretionary statutes. In *Witherspoon v. Illinois*, 391 U.S. 510 (1968), the Court observed that "one of the most important functions any jury can perform" in exercising its discretion to choose "between life imprisonment and capital punishment" is "to maintain a link between contemporary community values and the penal system." *Id.*, at 519 and n. 15. Various studies indicate that even in first-degree murder cases juries with sentencing discretion do not impose the death penalty "with any great frequency." H. Kalven and H. Zeisel, The American Jury 436 (1966). The actions of sentencing juries suggest that under contemporary standards of decency death is viewed as an inappropriate punishment for a substantial portion of convicted first-degree murderers.

Although the Court has never ruled on the constitutionality of mandatory death penalty statutes, on several occasions dating back to 1899 it has commented upon our society's aversion to automatic death sentences. . . .

Although it seems beyond dispute that, at the time of the *Furman* decision in 1972, mandatory death penalty statutes had been renounced by American juries and legislatures, there remains the question whether the mandatory statutes adopted by North Carolina and a number of other States following *Furman* evince a sudden reversal of societal values regarding the imposition of capital punishment. In view of the persistent and unswerving legislative rejection of mandatory death penalty statutes beginning in 1838 and continuing for more than 130 years until *Furman*, it seems evident that the post-*Furman* enactments reflect attempts by the States to retain the death penalty in a form consistent with the Constitution, rather than a renewed societal acceptance of mandatory death sentencing. The fact that some States have adopted mandatory measures following *Furman* while others have legislated standards to guide jury discretion appears attributable to diverse readings of this Court's multi-opinioned decision in that case. . . .

It is now well established that the Eighth Amendment draws much of its meaning from "the evolving standards of decency that mark the progress of a maturing society." *Trop v. Dulles*, 356 U.S., at 101. As the above discussion makes clear, one of the most significant developments in our society's treatment of capital punishment has been the rejection of the common-law practice of inexorably imposing a death sentence upon every person convicted of a specified offense. North Carolina's mandatory death penalty statute for first-degree murder departs markedly from contemporary standards respecting the imposition of the punishment of death and thus cannot be applied consistently with the Eighth and Fourteenth Amendments' requirement that the State's power to punish "be exercised within the limits of civilized standards." *Id.*, at 100.[36]

B. A separate deficiency of North Carolina's mandatory death sentence statute is its failure to provide a constitutionally tolerable response to *Furman*'s rejection of unbridled jury discretion in the imposition of capital sentences. Central to the limited holding in *Furman* was the conviction that the vesting of standardless sentencing power in the jury violated the Eighth and Fourteenth Amendments. . . . It is argued that North Carolina has remedied the inadequacies of the death penalty statutes held unconstitutional in *Furman* by withdrawing all sentencing discretion from juries in capital cases. But when one considers the long and consistent American experience with the death penalty in first-degree murder cases, it becomes evident that mandatory statutes enacted in response to *Furman* have simply papered over the problem of unguided and unchecked jury discretion.

As we have noted in Part III-A, supra, there is general agreement that American juries have persistently refused to convict a significant portion of persons charged with first-degree murder of that offense under mandatory death penalty statutes. . . . In view of the historic record, it is only reasonable to assume that many juries under mandatory statutes will continue to consider the grave

---

[36] Dissenting opinions . . . argue that this conclusion is "simply mistaken" because the American rejection of mandatory death sentence statutes might possibly be ascribable to "some maverick juries or jurors." . . . Since acquittals no less than convictions required unanimity and citizens with moral reservations concerning the death penalty were regularly excluded from capital juries, it seems hardly conceivable that the persistent refusal of American juries to convict palpably guilty defendants of capital offenses under mandatory death sentence statutes merely "represented the intransigence of only a small minority" of jurors. . . . Moreover, the dissenting opinions simply ignore the experience under discretionary death sentence statutes indicating that juries reflecting contemporary community values . . . found the death penalty appropriate for only a small minority of convicted first-degree murderers. . . .

consequences of a conviction in reaching a verdict. North Carolina's mandatory death penalty statute provides no standards to guide the jury in its inevitable exercise of the power to determine which first-degree murderers shall live and which shall die. And there is no way under the North Carolina law for the judiciary to check arbitrary and capricious exercise of that power through a review of death sentences. Instead of rationalizing the sentencing process, a mandatory scheme may well exacerbate the problem identified in *Furman* by resting the penalty determination on the particular jury's willingness to act lawlessly. While a mandatory death penalty statute may reasonably be expected to increase the number of persons sentenced to death, it does not fulfill *Furman*'s basic requirement by replacing arbitrary and wanton jury discretion with objective standards to guide, regularize, and make rationally reviewable the process for imposing a sentence of death.

C.   A third constitutional shortcoming of the North Carolina statute is its failure to allow the particularized consideration of relevant aspects of the character and record of each convicted defendant before the imposition upon him of a sentence of death. In *Furman*, members of the Court acknowledge what cannot fairly be denied—that death is a punishment different from all other sanctions in kind rather than degree. . . . A process that accords no significance to relevant facets of the character and record of the individual offender or the circumstances of the particular offense excludes from consideration in fixing the ultimate punishment of death the possibility of compassionate or mitigating factors stemming from the diverse frailties of humankind. It treats all persons convicted of a designated offense not as uniquely individual human beings, but as members of a faceless, undifferentiated mass to be subjected to the blind infliction of the penalty of death.

This Court has previously recognized that "[f]or the determination of sentences, justice generally requires consideration of more than the particular acts by which the crime was committed and that there be taken into account the circumstances of the offense together with the character and propensities of the offender." . . . Consideration of both the offender and the offense in order to arrive at a just and appropriate sentence has been viewed as a progressive and humanizing development. . . . While the prevailing practice of individualizing sentencing determinations generally reflects simply enlightened policy rather than a constitutional imperative, we believe that in capital cases the fundamental respect for humanity underlying the Eighth Amendment . . . requires consideration of the character and record of the individual offender and the circumstances of the particular offense as a constitutionally indispensable part of the process of inflicting the penalty of death.

This conclusion rests squarely on the predicate that the penalty of death is qualitatively different from a sentence of imprisonment, however long. Death, in its finality, differs more from life imprisonment than a 100-year prison term differs from one of only a year or two. Because of that qualitative difference, there is a corresponding difference in the need for reliability in the determination that death is the appropriate punishment in a specific case.

For the reasons stated, we conclude that the death sentences imposed upon the petitioners under North Carolina's mandatory death sentence statute violated the Eighth and Fourteenth Amendments and therefore must be set aside.

[The concurring opinions of Justices Brennan and Marshall and the dissenting opinion of Justice Blackmun are omitted.]

DISSENTING OPINION OF JUSTICE WHITE, JOINED BY CHIEF JUSTICE BURGER AND JUSTICE REHNQUIST

. . . The issues in the case are very similar, if not identical, to those in *Roberts v. Louisiana*, 428 U.S. 325 [1976]. For the reasons stated in my dissenting opinion in that case, I reject petitioners' arguments that the death penalty in any circumstances is a violation of the Eighth Amendment and that the North Carolina statute, although making the imposition of the death penalty mandatory upon proof of guilt and a verdict of first-degree murder, will nevertheless result in the death penalty being imposed so seldom and arbitrarily that it is void under *Furman v. Georgia*. As is also apparent from my dissenting opinion in *Roberts v. Louisiana*, I also disagree with the two additional grounds which the plurality sua sponte offers for invalidating the North Carolina statute. I would affirm the judgment of the North Carolina Supreme Court.

DISSENTING OPINION OF JUSTICE REHNQUIST

I

. . . The plurality relies first upon its conclusion that society has turned away from the mandatory imposition of death sentences, and second upon its conclusion that the North Carolina system has "simply papered over" the problem of unbridled jury discretion which two of the separate opinions in *Furman v. Georgia* identified as the basis for the judgment rendering the death sentences there reviewed unconstitutional. The third "constitutional shortcoming" of the North Carolina statute is said to be "its failure to allow the particularized consideration of relevant aspects of the character and record of each convicted defendant before the imposition upon him of a sentence of death."

I do not believe that any one of these reasons singly, or all of them together, can withstand careful analysis. Contrary to the plurality's assertions, they would import into the Cruel and Unusual Punishments Clause procedural requirements which find no support in our cases. Their application will result in the invalidation of a death sentence imposed upon a defendant convicted of first-degree murder under the North Carolina system, and the upholding of the same sentence imposed on an identical defendant convicted on identical evidence of first-degree murder under the Florida, Georgia, or Texas systems—a result surely as "freakish" as that condemned in the separate opinions in *Furman.*

II

The plurality is simply mistaken in its assertion that "[t]he history of mandatory death penalty statutes in the United States thus reveals that the practice of sentencing to death all persons convicted of a particular offense has been rejected as unduly harsh and unworkably rigid." This conclusion is purported based on two historic developments: the first a series of legislative decisions during the 19th century narrowing the class of offenses punishable by death; the second a series of legislative decisions during both the 19th and 20th centuries, through which mandatory imposition of the death penalty largely gave way to jury discretion in deciding whether or not to impose this ultimate sanction. The first development may have some relevance to the plurality's argument in general but has no bearing at all upon this case. The second development, properly analyzed, has virtually no relevance even to the plurality's argument.

There can be no question that the legislative and other materials discussed in the plurality's opinion show a widespread conclusion on the part of state legislatures during the 19th century that the penalty of death was being required for too broad a range of crimes, and that these legislatures proceeded to narrow the range of crimes for which such penalty could be imposed. If this case involved the imposition of the death penalty for an offense such as burglary or sodomy the virtually unanimous trend in the legislatures of the States to exclude such offenders from liability for capital punishment might bear on the plurality's Eighth Amendment argument. But petitioners were convicted of first-degree murder, and there is not the slightest suggestion in the material relied upon by the plurality that there had been any turning away at all, much less any such unanimous turning away, from the death penalty as a punishment for those guilty of first-degree murder. The legislative narrowing of the spectrum of capital crimes, therefore, while very arguably representing a general societal judgment since the trend was so widespread, simply never reached far enough to exclude the sort of aggravated homicide of which petitioners stand convicted.

The second string to the plurality's analytical bow is that legislative change from mandatory to discretionary imposition of the death sentence likewise evidences societal rejection of mandatory death penalties. The plurality simply does not make out this part of its case, however, in large part because it treats as being of equal dignity with legislative judgments the judgments of particular juries and of individual jurors.

There was undoubted dissatisfaction, from more than one sector of 19th century society, with the operation of mandatory death sentences. One segment of that society was totally opposed to capital punishment, and was apparently willing to accept the substitution of discretionary imposition of that penalty for its mandatory imposition as a halfway house on the road to total abolition. Another segment was equally unhappy with the operation of the mandatory system, but for an entirely different reason. As the plurality recognizes, this second segment of society was unhappy with the operation of the mandatory system, not because of the death sentences imposed under it, but because people obviously guilty of criminal offenses were not being convicted under it. Change to a discretionary system was accepted by these persons not because they thought mandatory imposition of the death penalty was cruel and unusual, but because they thought that if jurors were permitted to return a sentence other than death upon the conviction of a capital crime, fewer guilty defendants would be acquitted. See *McGautha*, 402 U.S., at 199.

So far as the action of juries is concerned, the fact that in some cases juries operating under the mandatory system refused to convict obviously guilty defendants does not reflect any "turning away" from the death penalty, or the mandatory death penalty, supporting the proposition that it is "cruel and unusual." Given the requirement of unanimity with respect to jury verdicts in capital cases, a requirement which prevails today in States which accept a nonunanimous verdict in the case of other crimes, . . . it is apparent that a single juror could prevent a jury from returning a verdict of conviction. Occasional refusals to convict, therefore, may just as easily have represented the intransigence of only a small minority of 12 jurors as well as the unanimous judgment of all 12. The fact that the presence of such jurors could prevent conviction in a given case, even though the majority of society, speaking through legislatures, had decreed that it should be imposed, certainly does not indicate that society as a whole rejected mandatory punishment for such offenders; it does not even indicate that those few members of society who serve on juries, as a whole, had done so.

The introduction of discretionary sentencing likewise creates no inference that contemporary society had rejected the mandatory system as unduly severe. Legislatures enacting discretionary sentencing statutes had no reason to think that there would not be roughly the same number of capital convictions under the new system as under the old. The same subjective juror responses which resulted in juror nullification under the old system were legitimized, but in the absence of those subjective responses to a particular set of facts, a capital sentence could as likely be anticipated under the discretionary system as under the mandatory. And at least some of those who would have been acquitted under the mandatory system would be subjected to at least some punishment under the discretionary system, rather than escaping altogether a penalty for the crime of which they were guilty. That society was unwilling to accept the paradox presented to it by the actions of some maverick juries or jurors—the acquittal of palpably guilty defendants—hardly reflects the sort of an "evolving standard decency" to which the plurality professes obeisance.

Nor do the opinions in *Furman* which indicate a preference for discretionary sentencing in capital cases suggest in the slightest that a mandatory sentencing procedure would be cruel and unusual. The plurality concedes, as it must, that following *Furman* 10 States enacted laws providing for mandatory capital punishment. . . . These enactments the plurality seeks to explain as due to a wrongheaded reading of the holding in *Furman*. But this explanation simply does not wash. While those States may be presumed to have preferred their prior systems reposing sentencing discretion in juries or judges, they indisputably preferred mandatory capital punishment to no capital punishment at all. Their willingness to enact statutes providing that penalty is utterly inconsistent with the notion that they regarded mandatory capital sentencing as beyond "evolving standards of decency." The plurality's glib rejection of these legislative decisions as having little weight on the scale which it finds in the Eighth Amendment seems to me more an instance of its desire to save the people from themselves than a conscientious effort to ascertain the content of any "evolving standard of decency."

III

The second constitutional flaw which the plurality finds in North Carolina's mandatory system is that it has simply "papered over" the problem of unchecked jury discretion. The plurality states that "there is general agreement that American juries have persistently refused to convict a significant portion of persons charged with first-degree murder of that offense under mandatory death penalty statutes." The plurality also states, that "as a matter of historic fact, juries operating under discretionary sentencing statutes have consistently returned death sentences in only a minority of first-degree murder cases." The basic factual assumption of the plurality seems to be that for any given number of first-degree murder defendants subject to capital punishment, there will be a certain number of jurors who will be unwilling to impose the death penalty even though they are entirely satisfied that the necessary elements of the substantive offense are made out.

In North Carolina jurors unwilling to impose the death penalty may simply hang a jury or they may so assert themselves that a verdict of not guilty is brought in; in Louisiana they will have a similar effect in causing some juries to bring in a verdict of guilty of a lesser included offense even though all the jurors are satisfied that the elements of the greater offense are made out. Such jurors, of course, are violating their oath, but such violation is not only consistent with the majority's hypothesis; the majority's hypothesis is bottomed on its occurrence.

For purposes of argument, I accept the plurality's hypothesis; but it seems to me impossible to conclude from it that a mandatory death sentence statute such as North Carolina enacted is any less sound constitutionally than are the systems enacted by Georgia, Florida, and Texas which the Court upholds.

In Georgia juries are entitled to return a sentence of life, rather than death, for no reason whatever, simply based upon their own subjective notions of what is right and what is wrong. In Florida the judge and jury are required to weigh legislatively enacted aggravating factors against legislatively enacted mitigating factors, and then base their choice between life or death on an estimate of the result of that weighing. Substantial discretion exists here, too, though it is somewhat more canalized than it is in Georgia. Why these types of discretion are regarded by the plurality as constitutionally permissible, while that which may occur in the North Carolina system is not, is no support whatever to the principle that the Constitution requires individualized consideration. . . .

IV

. . . The plurality also relies upon the indisputable proposition that "death is different" for the result which it reaches in Part III-C. But the respects in which death is "different" from other punishment which may be imposed upon convicted criminals do not seem to me to establish the proposition that the Constitution requires individualized sentencing.

One of the principal reasons why death is different is because it is irreversible; an executed defendant cannot be brought back to life. This aspect of the difference between death and other penalties would undoubtedly support statutory provisions for specially careful review of the fairness of the trial, the accuracy of the fact-finding process, and the fairness of the sentencing procedure where the death penalty is imposed. But none of those aspects of the death sentence is at issue here. Petitioners were found guilty of the crime of first-degree murder in a trial the constitutional validity of which is unquestioned here. And since the punishment of death is conceded by the plurality not to be a cruel and unusual punishment for such a crime, the irreversible aspect of the death penalty has no connection whatever with any requirement for individualized consideration of the sentence.

The second aspect of the death penalty which makes it "different" from other penalties is the fact that it is indeed an ultimate penalty, which ends a human life rather than simply requiring that a living human being be confined for a given period of time in a penal institution. This aspect of the difference may enter into the decision of whether or not it is a "cruel and unusual" penalty for a given offense. But since in this case the offense was first-degree murder, that particular inquiry need proceed no further.

The plurality's insistence on individualized consideration of the sentencing, therefore, does not depend upon any traditional application of the prohibition against cruel and unusual punishment contained in the Eighth Amendment. The punishment here is concededly not cruel and unusual, and that determination has traditionally ended judicial inquiry in our cases construing the Cruel and Unusual Punishments Clause. *Trop v. Dulles*; *Robinson v. California*; *Louisiana ex rel. Francis v. Resweber*; *Wilkerson v. Utah*. What the plurality opinion has actually done is to import into the Due Process Clause of the Fourteenth Amendment what it conceives to be desirable procedural guarantees where the punishment of death, concededly not cruel and unusual for the crime of which the defendant was convicted, is to be imposed. This is squarely contrary to *McGautha*, and unsupported by any other decision of this Court.

I agree with the conclusion of the plurality, and with that of Mr. Justice White, that death is not a cruel and unusual punishment for the offense of which these petitioners were convicted. Since no member of the Court suggests that the trial which led to those convictions in any way fell short of the standards mandated by the Constitution, the judgments of conviction should be affirmed. The Fourteenth Amendment, giving the fullest scope to its "majestic generalities," . . . is conscripted rather than interpreted when used to permit one but not another system for imposition of the death penalty.

Chapter 7

"Mandatory" Death Statutes—
Blystone v. Pennsylvania
(1990)

Blystone v. Pennsylvania, 494 U.S. 299, 110 S. Ct. 1078, 108 L. Ed.2d
255 (1990) (5–4, statute providing mandatory death penalty where the
jury finds one aggravating circumstance and no mitigating circumstances
does not violate the Eighth Amendment).

❖　❖　❖

OPINION OF CHIEF JUSTICE REHNQUIST FOR THE COURT

. . . Petitioner was charged with and convicted of first-degree murder, robbery,
criminal conspiracy to commit homicide, and criminal conspiracy to commit
robbery. The same jury that convicted petitioner found as an aggravating
circumstance that petitioner "committed a killing while in the perpetration of a
felony." . . . The jury found that no mitigating circumstances existed, and accordingly sentenced petitioner to death pursuant to the Pennsylvania death penalty
statute which provides that "[t]he verdict must be a sentence of death if the jury
unanimously finds at least one aggravating circumstance . . . and no mitigating
circumstance or if the jury unanimously finds one or more aggravating circumstances or if the jury unanimously finds one or more aggravating circumstances
which outweight any mitigating circumstances." On direct appeal to the Supreme
Court of Pennsylvania, petitioner argued that the death penalty statute was
unconstitutional because it mandated a sentence of death based on the outcome
of the weighing process. The court summarily rejected this argument. . . . We
granted certiorari to decide whether the mandatory aspect of the Pennsylvania
death penalty statute renders the penalty imposed upon petitioner unconstitutional because it improperly limited the discretion of the jury in deciding the
appropriate penalty for his crime. We now affirm. . . .

We think that the Pennsylvania death penalty statute satisfies the requirement that a capital sentencing jury be allowed to consider and give effect to all relevant mitigating evidence. [It] does not limit the types of mitigating evidence which may be considered, and [it] provides a jury with a nonexclusive list of mitigating factors which may be taken into account—including a "catchall" category providing for the consideration of "[a]ny other evidence of mitigation concerning the character and record of the defendant and the circumstances of his offense." . . . Nor is the statute impermissibly "mandatory" as that term was understood in *Woodson* or *Roberts*. Death is not automatically imposed upon conviction for certain types of murder. It is imposed only after a determination that the aggravating circumstances outweigh the mitigating circumstances present in the particular crime committed by the particular defendant, or that there are no such mitigating circumstances. This is sufficient under *Lockett* and *Penry*.[a]

Petitioner challenges the statute as it was applied in his particular case. This challenge essentially consists of a claim that his sentencing proceeding was rendered "unreliable" by the mandatory aspect [there]of for two reasons. See *Woodson*, 428 U.S., at 305 (there is a "need for reliability in the determination that death is the appropriate punishment in a specific case") (plurality opinion). First, petitioner asserts that the mandatory feature of his jury instructions—derived, of course, from the statute—precluded the jury from evaluating the weight of the particular aggravating circumstance found in his case. Second, petitioner contends that the mandatory feature of the sentencing instructions unconstitutionally limited the jury's consideration of unenumerated mitigating circumstances. We address these arguments in turn.

At sentencing, petitioner's jury found one aggravating circumstance present in this case—that petitioner committed a killing while in the perpetration of a robbery. No mitigating circumstances were found. Petitioner contends that the mandatory imposition of death in this situation violates the Eighth Amendment requirement of individualized sentencing since the jury was precluded from considering whether the severity of his aggravating circumstance warranted the death sentence. We reject this argument. The presence of aggravating circumstances serves the purpose of limiting the class of death-eligible defendants, and the Eighth Amendment does not require that these aggravating circumstances be further refined or weighed by a jury. . . . The requirement of individualized sentencing in capital cases is satisfied by allowing the jury to consider all relevant mitigating evidence. In petitioner's case the jury was specifically instructed to consider, as mitigating evidence, any "matter concerning the character or record of the defendant, or the circumstances of his offense." . . . This was sufficient to satisfy the dictates of the Eighth Amendment.

---

[a] Editor's note: *Lockett v. Ohio*, 438 U.S. 586 (1978) held that a defendant has an Eighth Amendment right to present, in the penalty phase of a capital trial, any mitigating evidence he wishes regarding his character or the circumstances of the crime. *Penry v. Lynaugh*, 492 U.S. 302 (1989) held that it does not violate the Eighth Amendment to execute someone who is mentally retarded. Both cases are reprinted in this book.

Next, petitioner maintains that the mandatory aspect of his sentencing instructions foreclosed the jury's consideration of certain mitigating circumstances. The trial judge gave the jury examples of mitigating circumstances that it was entitled to consider, essentially the list of factors contained in ... [the statute]. Among these, the judge stated that the jury was allowed to consider whether petitioner was affected by an "extreme" mental or emotional disturbance, whether petitioner was "substantially" impaired from appreciating his conduct, or whether petitioner acted under "extreme" duress. Petitioner argues that these instructions impermissibly precluded the jury's consideration of lesser degrees of disturbance, impairment, or duress. This claim bears scant relation to the mandatory aspect of Pennsylvania's statute, but in any event we reject it. The judge at petitioner's trial made clear to the jury that these were merely items it could consider, and that it was also entitled to consider "any other mitigating matter concerning the character or record of the defendant, or the circumstances of his offense." ... This instruction fully complied with the requirements of *Lockett* and *Penry*. ...

The fact that other States have enacted different forms of death penalty statutes which also satisfy constitutional requirements casts no doubt on Pennsylvania's choice. Within the constitutional limits defined by our cases, the States enjoy their traditional latitude to prescribe the method by which those who commit murder shall be punished. Affirmed.

DISSENTING OPINION OF JUSTICE BRENNAN, JOINED BY JUSTICES MARSHALL, BLACKMUN, AND STEVENS

... Today, for the first time, the Court upholds a statute containing a mandatory provision that gives the legislature rather than the jury the ultimate decision whether the death penalty is appropriate in a particular set of circumstances. Such a statute deprives the defendant of the type of individualized sentencing hearing required by the Eighth Amendment. I respectfully dissent.

II-B

... The nature of the individualized determination required by *Woodson* is derived from this Court's recognition that the decision to impose the death penalty must reflect a reasoned moral judgment about the defendant's actions and character in light of all the circumstances of the offense and the defendant's background. ... Just as a jury must be free to consider and weigh mitigating circumstances as independently relevant to the defendant's moral culpability, ... a jury must also be able to consider and weigh the severity of each aggravating circumstance. The weight of an aggravating circumstance depends on the seriousness of the crime—a significant aspect of the defendant's moral culpability. Thus, a reasoned moral response to the defendant's conduct requires the consideration of the significance of both aggravating and mitigating factors. "[I]n the end it is the jury that must make the difficult, *individualized* judgment as to whether the defendant deserves the sentence of death." ...

... This Court has never held that a legislature may mandate the death sentence for any category of murderers. Instead, a legislature's role must be limited to the definition of the class of death-*eligible* defendants. A legislature does not, and indeed cannot, consider every possible fact pattern that technically will fall within an aggravating circumstance. Hence, the definition of an aggravating circumstance provides a basis for distinguishing crimes only on a *general* level; it does not embody the type of reasoned moral judgment required to justify the imposition of the death penalty. See *Sumner v. Shuman*, 483 U.S., at 78 (legislative judgment does not "provide an adequate basis on which to determine whether the death sentence is the appropriate sanction in any *particular* case") (emphasis added). The Pennsylvania statute provides a stark example of this constitutional flaw. It permits the jury to find an aggravating circumstance if the killing was committed in the course of a felony. ... A variety of murders fit under this aggravating circumstance. Since the Pennsylvania Supreme Court has interpreted this aggravating circumstance to include nonviolent felonies, ... the aggravating circumstance covers a very wide range of cases. A jury, however, likely would draw a different inference about the culpability of the defendant—and therefore the propriety of the death sentence—if the murder were committed during a rape rather than (as here) during a $13 robbery. The majority today allows the legislature to preclude a jury from considering such factors in deciding whether to impose death.

Such a conclusion flies in the face of our reasoning in *Sumner v. Shuman*. In *Sumner*, we invalidated a statute that mandated death for a prisoner who committed murder while already serving a life term. Although the Court acknowledged the legislature's power to determine that the crime was sufficiently serious to make the defendants *eligible* for the death penalty, the Court held that the legislature had no power to conclude that the sole fact that the defendant was serving a life sentence justified the death penalty in every such case. ...

The majority dismisses *Sumner* as inapposite because the sentencing scheme in that case did not allow for the consideration of mitigating evidence. ... In *Sumner*, [however,] the Court invalidated the statute because it precluded the jury from considering mitigating factors *and* because it prevented the jury from determining whether certain crimes were serious enough to require the death penalty. ...

III

The Court's refusal to recognize that the "mandatory aspect" of the Pennsylvania statute deprives the defendant of an individualized sentencing hearing is contrary to reason. Rather than address the merits of petitioner's claim, the majority summarily concludes that the Eighth Amendment is "satisfied" because the jury may consider mitigating evidence. Although our cases clearly hold that the ability to consider mitigating evidence is a constitutional requirement, it does not follow that this ability satisfies the constitutional demand for an individualized sentencing hearing. The "weight" of an aggravating circumstance is just as relevant to the propriety of the death penalty as the "weight" of any mitigating circumstances. The Court's unarticulated assumption that the legislature may define a group of crimes for which the death penalty is required in certain situations represents a marked departure from our previous cases. The Court's failure to provide any reasoning to reject a claim well grounded in our case law is always disturbing. An unexplained departure from fundamental principles in the death penalty context is inexcusable. I respectfully dissent. . . .

Chapter 8

Vague Aggravating Factors—
Godfrey v. Georgia (1980)

Godfrey v. Georgia, 446 U.S. 420, 100 S. Ct. 1759, 64 L. Ed.2d 398 (1980) (6–3, the death penalty may not be imposed where the aggravating factor is too broad and vague).

Editor's comment: Before the jury deliberates on a verdict in any criminal case and before it decides on the sentence in a capital case, the judge must instruct that jury on the meaning of the law. This instruction is especially important where the language of the law is unclear. If the judge fails to properly clarify matters, an appeals court might reverse the conviction on the ground that the jury probably misunderstood the law it was supposed to apply. Appeals courts will usually clarify the meaning of the law themselves when asked to do so on appeal. Ultimately, the state court of last resort is responsible for providing the authoritative meaning of the law of that state.

In the *Godfrey* case, the U.S. Supreme Court found the aggravating factor—that the murder was "outrageously or wantonly vile, horrible and inhuman"—to be too vague. It also found that the trial judge did not explain its meaning to the jury, and that the state supreme court did not apply a clarifying interpretation of the meaning that it had developed in earlier cases. Consequently, it reversed the death sentence. In effect, the Supreme Court equated a vague aggravating circumstance with having no aggravating circumstance at all, which meant that the jury's discretion was not limited as required by *Furman*.

By contrast, in a later case to come before the U.S. Supreme Court— *Walton v. Arizona*, 497 U.S. 639 (1990)—the Court upheld a death sentence where the aggravating factor was that the murder was "especially heinous, cruel or depraved." In *Walton*, unlike *Godfrey*, the state high court did an adequate job of clarifying the meaning of the aggravator and independently applying it to the facts of the case.

❖   ❖   ❖

OPINION OF JUSTICE STEWART, JOINED BY JUSTICES BLACKMUN, POWELL, AND STEVENS

I

On a day in early September in 1977, the petitioner and his wife of 28 years had a heated argument in their home. During the course of this altercation, the petitioner, who had consumed several cans of beer, threatened his wife with a knife and damaged some of her clothing. At this point, the petitioner's wife declared that she was going to leave him, and departed to stay with relatives.

That afternoon she went to a Justice of the Peace and secured a warrant charging the petitioner with aggravated assault. A few days later, while still living away from home, she filed suit for divorce. Summons was served on the petitioner, and a court hearing was set on a date some two weeks later. Before the date of the hearing, the petitioner on several occasions asked his wife to return to their home. Each time his efforts were rebuffed. At some point during this period, his wife moved in with her mother. The petitioner believed that his mother-in-law was actively instigating his wife's determination not to consider a possible reconciliation.

In the early evening of September 20, according to the petitioner, his wife telephoned him at home. Once again they argued. She asserted that reconciliation was impossible and allegedly demanded all the proceeds from the planned sale of their house. The conversation was terminated after she said that she would call back later. This she did in an hour or so. The ensuing conversation was, according to the petitioner's account, even more heated than the first. His wife reiterated her stand that reconciliation was out of the question, said that she still wanted all proceeds from the sale of their house, and mentioned that her mother was supporting her position. Stating that she saw no further use in talking or arguing, she hung up.

At this juncture, the petitioner got out his shotgun and walked with it down the hill from his home to the trailer where his mother-in-law lived. Peering through a window, he observed his wife, his mother-in-law, and his 11-year-old daughter playing a card game. He pointed the shotgun at his wife through the window and pulled the trigger. The charge from the gun struck his wife in the forehead and killed her instantly. He proceeded into the trailer, striking and injuring his fleeing daughter with the barrel of the gun. He then fired the gun at his mother-in-law, striking her in the head and killing her instantly.

The petitioner then called the local sheriff's office, identified himself, said where he was, explained that he had just killed his wife and mother-in-law, and asked that the sheriff come and pick him up. Upon arriving at the trailer, the law enforcement officers found the petitioner seated on a chair in open view near the driveway. He told one of the officers that "they're dead, I killed them" and directed the officer to the place where he had put the murder weapon. Later the petitioner told a police officer: "I've done a hideous crime, . . . but I have been thinking about it for eight years . . . I'd do it again."

The petitioner was subsequently indicted on two counts of murder and one count of aggravated assault. He pleaded not guilty and relied primarily on a defense of temporary insanity at his trial. The jury returned verdicts of guilty on all three counts.

The sentencing phase of the trial was held before the same jury. No further evidence was tendered, but counsel for each side made arguments to the jury. Three times during the course of his argument, the prosecutor stated that the case involved no allegation of "torture" or of an "aggravated battery." When counsel had completed their arguments, the trial judge instructed the jury orally and in writing on the standards that must guide them in imposing sentence. Both orally and in writing, the judge quoted to the jury the statutory language of the § (b)(7) aggravating circumstance in its entirety.[a]

The jury imposed sentences of death on both of the murder convictions. As to each, the jury specified that the aggravating circumstance they had found beyond a reasonable doubt was "that the offense of murder was outrageously or wantonly vile, horrible and inhuman."

In accord with Georgia law in capital cases, the trial judge prepared a report in the form of answers to a questionnaire for use on appellate review. One question on the form asked whether or not the victim had been "physically harmed or tortured." The trial judge's response was "No, as to both victims, excluding the actual murdering of the two victims."

The Georgia Supreme Court affirmed the judgments of the trial court in all respects. With regard to the imposition of the death sentence for each of the two murder convictions, the court rejected the petitioner's contention that § (b)(7) is unconstitutionally vague. The court noted that Georgia's death penalty legislation had been upheld in *Gregg v. Georgia*, and cited its prior decisions upholding § (b)(7) in the face of similar vagueness challenges. As to the petitioner's argument that the jury's phraseology was, as a matter of law, an inadequate statement of § (b)(7), the court responded by simply observing that the language "was not objectionable." The court found no evidence that the sentence had been "imposed under the influence of passion, prejudice, or any other arbitrary factor," held that the sentence was neither excessive nor disproportionate to the penalty imposed in similar cases, and stated that the evidence supported the jury's finding of the § (b)(7) statutory aggravating circumstance. Two justices dissented.

In *Gregg v. Georgia* the Court held that this statutory aggravating circumstance (§ (b)(7) is not unconstitutional on its face. Responding to the argument that the language of the provision is "so broad that capital punishment could be imposed in any murder case," the joint opinion said:

---

[a] Editor's note: In its entirety, the statutory aggravator reads as follows: "The offense of murder, rape, armed robbery, or kidnapping was outrageously or wantonly vile, horrible or inhuman in that it involved torture, depravity of mind, or an aggravated battery to the victim."

It is, of course, arguable that any murder involves depravity of mind or an aggravated battery. But this language need not be construed in this way, and there is no reason to assume that the Supreme Court of Georgia will adopt such an open-ended construction. . . .

Nearly four years have passed since the *Gregg* decision, and during that time many death sentences based in whole or in part on § (b)(7) have been affirmed by the Supreme Court of Georgia. The issue now before us is whether, in affirming the imposition of the sentences of death in the present case, the Georgia Supreme Court has adopted such a broad and vague construction of the § (b)(7) aggravating circumstance as to violate the Eighth and Fourteenth Amendments to the United States Constitution.

II

In *Furman v. Georgia*, the Court held that the penalty of death may not be imposed under sentencing procedures that create a substantial risk that the punishment will be inflicted in an arbitrary and capricious manner. *Gregg v. Georgia* reaffirmed this holding:

> [W]here discretion is afforded a sentencing body on a matter so grave as the determination of whether a human life should be taken or spared, that discretion must be suitably directed and limited so as to minimize the risk of wholly arbitrary and capricious action. . . .

A capital sentencing scheme must, in short, provide a " 'meaningful basis for distinguishing the few cases in which [the penalty] is imposed from the many cases in which it is not.' " . . .

This means that if a State wishes to authorize capital punishment it has a constitutional responsibility to tailor and apply its law in a manner that avoids the arbitrary and capricious infliction of the death penalty. Part of a State's responsibility in this regard is to define the crimes for which death may be the sentence in a way that obviates "standardless [sentencing] discretion." *Gregg.* . . . It must channel the sentencer's discretion by "clear and objective standards" that provide "specific and detailed guidance," and that "make rationally reviewable the process for imposing a sentence of death." As was made clear in *Gregg*, a death penalty "system could have standards so vague that they would fail adequately to channel the sentencing decision patterns of juries with the result that a pattern of arbitrary and capricious sentencing like that found unconstitutional in *Furman* could occur." . . .

In the case before us the Georgia Supreme Court has affirmed a sentence of death based upon no more than a finding that the offense was "outrageously or wantonly vile, horrible and inhuman." There is nothing in these few words, standing alone, that implies any inherent restraint on the arbitrary and capricious infliction of the death sentence. A person of ordinary sensibility could fairly characterize almost every murder as "outrageously or wantonly vile, horrible and inhuman." Such a view may, in fact, have been one to which the members of the jury in this case subscribed. If so, their preconceptions were not dispelled by the trial judge's sentencing instructions. These gave the jury no guidance concerning the meaning of any of § (b)(7)'s terms. In fact, the jury's interpretation of § (b)(7) can only be the subject of sheer speculation.

The standardless and unchanneled imposition of death sentences in the uncontrolled discretion of a basically uninstructed jury in this case was in no way cured by the affirmance of those sentences by the Georgia Supreme Court. Under state law that court may not affirm a judgment of death until it has independently assessed the evidence of record and determined that such evidence supports the trial judge's or jury's finding of an aggravating circumstance.

In past cases the State Supreme Court has apparently understood this obligation as carrying with it the responsibility to keep § (b)(7) within constitutional bounds. . . .

The . . . Georgia Supreme Court had by 1977 reached three separate but consistent conclusions respecting the § (b)(7) aggravating circumstance. The first was that the evidence that the offense was "outrageously or wantonly vile, horrible or inhuman" had to demonstrate "torture, depravity of mind, or an aggravated battery to the victim." The second was that the phrase, "depravity of mind," comprehended only the kind of mental state that led the murderer to torture or to commit an aggravated battery before killing his victim. The third, . . . was that the word, "torture," must be construed in pari materia with "aggravated battery" so as to require evidence of serious physical abuse of the victim before death.[b] The Georgia courts did not, however, so limit § (b)(7) in the present case. No claim was made, and nothing in the record before us suggests, that the petitioner committed an aggravated battery upon his wife or mother-in-law or, in fact, caused either of them to suffer any physical injury preceding their deaths. Moreover, in the trial court, the prosecutor repeatedly told the jury—and the trial judge wrote in his sentencing report—that the murders did not involve "torture." Nothing said on appeal by the Georgia Supreme Court indicates that it took a different view of the evidence. The circumstances of this case, therefore, do not satisfy the criteria laid out by the Georgia Supreme Court itself. . . . In holding that the evidence supported the jury's § (b)(7) finding, the State Supreme Court simply asserted that the verdict was "factually substantiated."

Thus, the validity of the petitioner's death sentences turns on whether, in light of the facts and circumstances of the murders that he was convicted of committing, the Georgia Supreme Court can be said to have applied a constitutional construction of the phrase "outrageously or wantonly vile, horrible or inhuman in that [they] involved . . . depravity of mind. . . ."

---

[b] Editor's note: That is, *torture* and *aggravated battery* both require "evidence of serious physical abuse of the victim before death."

We conclude that the answer must be no. The petitioner's crimes cannot be said to have reflected a consciousness materially more "depraved" than that of any person guilty of murder. His victims were killed instantaneously. They were members of his family who were causing him extreme emotional trauma. Shortly after the killings, he acknowledged his responsibility and the heinous nature of his crimes. These factors certainly did not remove the criminality from the petitioner's acts. But, . . . it "is of vital importance to the defendant and to the community that any decision to impose the death sentence be, and appear to be, based on reason rather than caprice or emotion."

That cannot be said here. There is no principled way to distinguish this case, in which the death penalty was imposed, from the many cases in which it was not. Accordingly, the judgment of the Georgia Supreme Court insofar as it leaves standing the petitioner's death sentences is reversed, and the case is remanded to that court for further proceedings.

[The concurring opinions of Justices Brennan and Marshall and the dissenting opinion of Chief Justice Burger are omitted.]

DISSENTING OPINION OF JUSTICE WHITE, JOINED BY JUSTICE REHNQUIST

IV

The question remains whether the facts of this case bear sufficient relation to § (b)(7) to conclude that the Georgia Supreme Court responsibly and constitutionally discharged its review function. I believe that they do.

As described earlier, petitioner, in a cold blooded executioner's style, murdered his wife and his mother-in-law and, in passing, struck his young daughter on the head with the barrel of his gun. The weapon, a shotgun, is hardly known for the surgical precision with which it perforates its target. The murder scene, in consequence, can only be described in the most unpleasant terms. Petitioner's wife lay prone on the floor. Mrs. Godfrey's head had a hole described as "[a]pproximately the size of a silver dollar" on the side where the shot entered, and much less decipherable and more extensive damage on the side where the shot exited. Pellets that had passed through Mrs. Godfrey's head were found embedded in the kitchen cabinet.

It will be remembered that after petitioner inflicted this much damage, he took out time not only to strike his daughter on the head, but also to reload his single-shot shotgun and to enter the house. Only then did he get around to shooting his mother-in-law, Mrs. Wilkerson whose last several moments as a sentient being must have been as terrifying as the human mind can imagine. The police eventually found her facedown on the floor with a substantial portion of her head missing and her brain, no longer cabined by her skull, protruding for some distance onto the floor. Blood not only covered the floor and table, but dripped from the ceiling as well.

The Georgia Supreme Court held that these facts supported the jury's finding of the existence of statutory aggravating circumstance § (b)(7). A majority of this Court disagrees. But this disagreement, founded as it is on the notion that the lower court's construction of the provision was overly broad, in fact reveals a conception of this Court's role in back-stopping the Georgia Supreme Court that is itself overly broad. Our role is to correct genuine errors of constitutional significance resulting from the application of Georgia's capital sentencing procedures; our role is not to peer majestically over the lower court's shoulder so that we might second-guess its interpretation of facts that quite reasonably—perhaps even quite plainly—fit within the statutory language.

Who is to say that the murders of Mrs. Godfrey and Mrs. Wilkerson were not "vile," or "inhuman," or "horrible"? In performing his murderous chore, petitioner employed a weapon known for its disfiguring effects on targets, human or other, and he succeeded in creating a scene so macabre and revolting that, if anything, "vile," "horrible," and "inhuman" are descriptively inadequate.

And who among us can honestly say that Mrs. Wilkerson did not feel "torture" in her last sentient moments. Her daughter, an instant ago a living being sitting across the table from Mrs. Wilkerson, lay prone on the floor, a bloodied and mutilated corpse. The seconds ticked by; enough time for her son-in-law to reload his gun, to enter the home, and to take a gratuitous swipe at his daughter. What terror must have run through her veins as she first witnessed her daughter's hideous demise and then came to terms with the imminence of her own. Was this not torture? And if this was not torture, can it honestly be said that petitioner did not exhibit a "depravity of mind" in carrying out this cruel drama to its mischievous and murderous conclusion? I should have thought, moreover, that the Georgia court could reasonably have deemed the scene awaiting the investigating policemen as involving "an aggravated battery to the victim[s]." . . .

The point is not that, in my view, petitioner's crimes were definitively vile, horrible, or inhuman, or that, as I assay the evidence, they beyond any doubt involved torture, depravity of mind, or an aggravated battery to the victims. Rather, the lesson is a much more elementary one, an instruction that, I should have thought, this Court would have taken to heart long ago. Our mandate does not extend to interfering with fact finders in state criminal proceedings or with state courts that are responsibly and consistently interpreting state law, unless that interference is predicated on a violation of the Constitution. No convincing showing of such a violation is made here, for, as Mr. Justice Stewart has written in another place the issue here is not what our verdict would have been, but whether "any rational fact finder" could have found the existence of aggravating circumstance § (b)(7). . . .

V

Under the present statutory regime, adopted in response to *Furman*, the Georgia Supreme Court has responsibly and consistently performed its review function pursuant to the Georgia capital-sentencing procedures. The State reports that, at the time its brief was written, the Georgia Supreme Court had reviewed some 99 cases in which the death penalty has been imposed. Of these, 66 had been affirmed; 5 had been reversed for errors in the guilt phase; and 22 had been reversed for errors in the sentencing phase. . . . This reversal rate of over 27 percent is not substantially lower than the historic reversal rate of state supreme courts. See Courting Reversal: The Supervisory Role of State Supreme Courts, 87 Yale L. J. 1191, 1198, 1209 (1978), where it is indicated that 16 state supreme courts over a 100-year period, in deciding 5,133 cases, had a reversal rate of 38.5 percent; for criminal cases, the reversal rate was 35.6 percent. To the extent that the reversal rate is lower than the historic level, it doubtless can be attributed to the great and admirable extent to which discretion and uncertainty have been removed from Georgia's capital-sentencing procedures since our decision in *Furman* and to the fact that review is mandatory. . . .

VI

In the circumstances of this case, the majority today endorses the argument that I thought we had rejected in *Gregg*: namely, "that no matter how effective the death penalty may be as a punishment, government, created and run as it must be by humans, is inevitably incompetent to administer it." 428 U.S., at 226 (opinion of White, J.). The Georgia Supreme Court, faced with a seemingly endless train of macabre scenes, has endeavored in a responsible, rational, and consistent fashion to effectuate its statutory mandate as illuminated by our judgment in *Gregg*. Today, a majority of this Court, its arguments shredded by its own illogic, informs the Georgia Supreme Court that, to some extent, its efforts have been outside the Constitution. I reject this as an unwarranted invasion into the realm of state law, for, as in *Gregg*, "I decline to interfere with the manner in which Georgia has chosen to enforce [its] laws" until a genuine error of constitutional magnitude surfaces. [*Ibid.*] I would affirm the judgment of the Supreme Court of Georgia.

Chapter 9

Mitigating Evidence— *Lockett v. Ohio* (1978)

Lockett v. Ohio, 438 U.S. 586, 98 S. Ct. 2954, 57 L. Ed.2d 973 (1978) (6–2, defendant has an Eighth Amendment right to present, in the penalty phase of a capital trial, any mitigating evidence relevant to his character or the circumstances of the crime).

Editor's comment: *Woodson v. North Carolina*, 428 U.S. 280 (1976), held that the sentencer (usually the jury) in a capital trial must consider the character and record of the defendant and the circumstances of the crime before imposing sentence. This virtually required the consideration of mitigating evidence, evidence that would support a less harsh punishment. The issue resolved by the *Lockett* case was whether the state could limit jury consideration to a list of possible mitigators written into the death penalty statute. The Court's negative answer contrasts with its rule regarding aggravating factors: these must be enumerated in the statute, and the jury must find that at least one of the statutory aggravators exists if the death penalty is to be imposed. The *Lockett* dissenters considered these two rules to be inconsistent. For an elaboration of this position, see Justice Scalia's concurring opinion in *Walton v. Arizona*, 497 U.S. 639 (1990).

❖   ❖   ❖

OPINION OF CHIEF JUSTICE BURGER, JOINED BY JUSTICES STEWART, POWELL, AND STEVENS

. . . Lockett challenges the constitutionality of Ohio's death penalty statute on a number of grounds. We find it necessary to consider only her contention that her death sentence is invalid because the statute under which it was imposed did not permit the sentencing judge to consider, as mitigating factors, her character, prior record, age, lack of specific intent to cause death, and her relatively minor part in the crime. . . .

Essentially she contends that the Eighth and Fourteenth Amendments require that the sentencer be given a full opportunity to consider mitigating circumstances in capital cases and that the Ohio statute does not comply with that requirement. . . .

We begin by recognizing that the concept of individualized sentencing in criminal cases generally, although not constitutionally required, has long been accepted in this country. Consistent with that concept, sentencing judges traditionally have taken a wide range of factors into account. That States have authority to make aiders and abettors equally responsible, as a matter of law, with principals, or to enact felony-murder statutes is beyond constitutional challenge. But the definition of crimes generally has not been thought automatically to dictate what should be the proper penalty. And where sentencing discretion is granted, it generally has been agreed that the sentencing judge's "possession of the fullest information possible concerning the defendant's life and characteristics" is "[h]ighly relevant—*if not essential*—[to the] selection of an appropriate sentence. . . ."

The opinions of this Court going back many years in dealing with sentencing in capital cases have noted the strength of the basis for individualized sentencing. . . .

Although legislatures remain free to decide how much discretion in sentencing should be reposed in the judge or jury in noncapital cases, the plurality opinion in *Woodson*, after reviewing the historical repudiation of mandatory sentencing in capital cases, concluded that

> in capital cases the fundamental respect for humanity underlying the Eighth
> Amendment . . . requires consideration of the character and record of the
> individual offender and the circumstances of the particular offense as a
> constitutionally indispensable part of the process of inflicting the penalty
> of death.

That declaration rested "on the predicate that the penalty of death is qualitatively different" from any other sentence. We are satisfied that this qualitative difference between death and other penalties calls for a greater degree of reliability when the death sentence is imposed. The mandatory death penalty statute in *Woodson* was held invalid because it permitted *no* consideration of "relevant facets of the character and record of the individual offender or the circumstances of the particular offense." The plurality did not attempt to indicate, however, which facets of an offender or his offense it deemed "relevant" in capital sentencing or what degree of consideration of "relevant facets" it would require.

We are now faced with those questions and we conclude that the Eighth and Fourteenth Amendments require that the sentencer, in all but the rarest kind of capital case, not be precluded from considering *as a mitigating factor*, any aspect of a defendant's character or record and any of the circumstances of the offense that the defendant proffers as a basis for a sentence less than death.[12] We recog-

---

[12] Nothing in this opinion limits the traditional authority of a court to exclude, as irrelevant, evidence not bearing on the defendant's character, prior record, or the circumstances of his offense.

nize that, in noncapital cases, the established practice of individualized sentences rests not on constitutional commands, but on public policy enacted into statutes.

The considerations that account for the wide acceptance of individualization of sentences in noncapital cases surely cannot be thought less important in capital cases. Given that the imposition of death by public authority is so profoundly different from all other penalties, we cannot avoid the conclusion that an individualized decision is essential in capital cases. The need for treating each defendant in a capital case with that degree of respect due the uniqueness of the individual is far more important than in noncapital cases. A variety of flexible techniques— probation, parole, work furloughs, to name a few—and various postconviction remedies may be available to modify an initial sentence of confinement in noncapital cases. The nonavailability of corrective or modifying mechanisms with respect to an executed capital sentence underscores the need for individualized consideration as a constitutional requirement in imposing the death sentence.

There is no perfect procedure for deciding in which cases governmental authority should be used to impose death. But a statute that prevents the sentencer in all capital cases from giving independent mitigating weight to aspects of the defendant's character and record and to circumstances of the offense proffered in mitigation creates the risk that the death penalty will be imposed in spite of factors which may call for a less severe penalty. When the choice is between life and death, that risk is unacceptable and incompatible with the commands of the Eighth and Fourteenth Amendments.

The Ohio death penalty statute does not permit the type of individualized consideration of mitigating factors we now hold to be required by the Eighth and Fourteenth Amendments in capital cases. Its constitutional infirmities can best be understood by comparing it with the statutes upheld in *Gregg, Proffitt*, and *Jurek*.[a] . . . None of the statutes we sustained in *Gregg* and the companion cases clearly operated at that time to prevent the sentencer from considering any aspect of the defendant's character and record or any circumstances of his offense as an independently mitigating factor.

In this regard the statute now before us is significantly different. Once a defendant is found guilty of aggravated murder with at least one of seven specified aggravating circumstances, the death penalty must be imposed unless, considering "the nature and circumstances of the offense and the history, character, and condition of the offender," the sentencing judge determines that at least one of the following mitigating circumstances is established by a preponderance of the evidence:

(1) The victim of the offense induced or facilitated it.

(2) It is unlikely that the offense would have been committed, but for the fact that the offender was under duress, coercion, or strong provocation.

---

[a] Editor's note: *Proffitt v. Florida*, 428 U.S. 242 (1976), and *Jurek v. Texas*, 428 U.S. 262 (1976) were companion cases to *Gregg*, in which the Florida and Texas death penalty statutes, respectively, were upheld.

(3) The offense was primarily the product of the offender's psychosis or mental deficiency, though such condition is insufficient to establish the defense of insanity.

The Ohio Supreme Court has concluded that there is no constitutional distinction between the statute approved in *Proffitt*, and Ohio's statute, because the mitigating circumstances in Ohio's statute are "liberally construed in favor of the accused," and because the sentencing judge or judges may consider factors such as the age and criminal record of the defendant in determining whether any of the mitigating circumstances is established. But even under the Ohio court's construction of the statute, only the three factors specified in the statute can be considered in mitigation of the defendant's sentence. We see, therefore, that once it is determined that the victim did not induce or facilitate the offense, that the defendant did not act under duress or coercion, and that the offense was not primarily the product of the defendant's mental deficiency, the Ohio statute mandates the sentence of death. The absence of direct proof that the defendant intended to cause the death of the victim is relevant for mitigating purposes only if it is determined that it sheds some light on one of the three statutory mitigating factors. Similarly, consideration of a defendant's comparatively minor role in the offense, or age, would generally not be permitted, as such, to affect the sentencing decision.

The limited range of mitigating circumstances which may be considered by the sentencer under the Ohio statute is incompatible with the Eighth and Fourteenth Amendments. To meet constitutional requirements, a death penalty statute must not preclude consideration of relevant mitigating factors. . . .

DISSENTING OPINION OF JUSTICE WHITE

. . . The Court has now completed its about-face since *Furman v. Georgia. Furman* held that as a result of permitting the sentencer to exercise unfettered discretion to impose or not to impose the death penalty for murder, the penalty was then being imposed discriminatorily, wantonly and freakishly, and so infrequently that any given death sentence was cruel and unusual. The Court began its retreat in *Woodson v. North Carolina* and *Roberts (Stanislaus) v. Louisiana*, 428 U.S. 325 (1976), where a plurality held that statutes which imposed mandatory death sentences even for first-degree murders were constitutionally invalid because the Eighth Amendment required that consideration be given by the sentencer to aspects of character of the individual offender and the circumstances of the particular offense in deciding whether to impose the punishment of death. Today it is held, again through a plurality, that the sentencer may constitutionally impose the death penalty only as an exercise of his unguided discretion after being presented with all circumstances which the defendant might believe to be conceivably relevant to the appropriateness of the penalty for the individual offender.

With all due respect, I dissent. I continue to be of the view, for the reasons set forth in my dissenting opinion in *Roberts*, that it does not violate the Eighth Amendment for a State to impose the death penalty on a mandatory basis when the defendant has been found guilty beyond a reasonable doubt of committing a deliberate, unjustified killing. Moreover, I greatly fear that the effect of the Court's decision today will be to compel constitutionally a restoration of the state of affairs at the time *Furman* was decided, where the death penalty is imposed so erratically and the threat of execution is so attenuated for even the most atrocious murders that "its imposition would then be the pointless and needless extinction of life with only marginal contributions to any discernible social or public purposes." *Furman*, [408 U.S.,] at 312 (White, J., concurring). By requiring as a matter of constitutional law that sentencing authorities be permitted to consider and in their discretion to act upon any and all mitigating circumstances, the Court permits them to refuse to impose the death penalty no matter what the circumstances of the crime. This invites a return to the pre-*Furman* days when the death penalty was generally reserved for those very few for whom society has least consideration. I decline to extend *Woodson* and *Roberts* in this respect. . . .

DISSENTING OPINION OF JUSTICE REHNQUIST

. . . As a practical matter, I doubt that today's opinion will make a great deal of difference in the manner in which trials in capital cases are conducted, since I would suspect that it has been the practice of most trial judges to permit a defendant to offer virtually any sort of evidence in his own defense as he wished. But as my Brother White points out in his dissent, the theme of today's opinion, far from supporting those views expressed in *Furman* which did appear to be carried over to the *Woodson* cases, tends to undercut those views. If a defendant as a matter of constitutional law is to be permitted to offer as evidence in the sentencing hearing any fact, however bizarre, which he wishes, even though the most sympathetically disposed trial judge could conceive of no basis upon which the jury might take it into account in imposing a sentence, the new constitutional doctrine will not eliminate arbitrariness or freakishness in the imposition of sentences, but will codify and institutionalize it. By encouraging defendants in capital cases, and presumably sentencing judges and juries, to take into consideration anything under the sun as a "mitigating circumstance," it will not guide sentencing discretion but will totally unleash it. . . .

[Justice Brennan took no part in the case. The opinions of Justices Blackmun, concurring in part and concurring in the judgment, and Marshall, concurring in the judgment, were omitted.]

Chapter 10

Jury Unanimity on Mitigating Evidence—*McKoy v. North Carolina* (1990)

McKoy v. North Carolina, 494 U.S. 433, 110 S. Ct. 1227, 108 L. Ed.2d 369 (1990) (6–3, the Eighth Amendment prohibits a requirement that the jurors unanimously agree on the existence of mitigating circumstances).

Editor's comment: Generally, the states that impose capital punishment require that the capital trial jury be unanimous as to the verdict and as to the existence of any aggravating factor. *McKoy v. North Carolina*, excerpted here, examines whether a state may also require jury unanimity regarding the existence of a mitigating factor. In *Mills v. Maryland*, 486 U.S. 367 (1988), which is referred to in *McKoy*, the Supreme Court had answered the question in the negative, but because much of *Mills* was taken up with a discussion of the meaning of the ambiguous Maryland law, the unanimity issue arose again in *McKoy*.

❖   ❖   ❖

OPINION OF JUSTICE MARSHALL FOR THE COURT

In this case we address the constitutionality of the unanimity requirement in North Carolina's capital sentencing scheme. That requirement prevents the jury from considering, in deciding whether to impose the death penalty, any mitigating factor that the jury does not unanimously find. We hold that under our decision in *Mills v. Maryland*, 486 U.S. 367, 108 S.Ct. 1860, 100 L. Ed.2d 384 (1988), North Carolina's unanimity requirement violates the Constitution by preventing the sentencer from considering all mitigating evidence. We therefore vacate petitioner's death sentence and remand for resentencing.

I

Petitioner Dock McKoy, Jr., was convicted in Stanly County, North Carolina, of first-degree murder. During the sentencing phase of McKoy's trial, the trial court instructed the jury, both orally and in a written verdict form, to answer four questions in determining its sentence. Issue One asked: "Do you unanimously find from the evidence, beyond a reasonable doubt, the existence of one or more of the following aggravating circumstances?" The jury found two statutory aggravating circumstances: that McKoy "had been previously convicted of a felony involving the use or threat of violence to the person" and that the murder was committed against a deputy sheriff who was "engaged in the performance of his official duties." The jury therefore answered "Yes" to Issue One and was instructed to proceed to the next Issue. Issue Two asked: "Do you unanimously find from the evidence the existence of one or more of the following mitigating circumstances?" The judge submitted to the jury eight possible mitigating circumstances. With respect to each circumstance, the judge orally instructed the jury as follows: "If you do not unanimously find this mitigating circumstance by a preponderance of the evidence, so indicate by having your foreman write, 'No,' in that space" on the verdict form. The verdict form reiterated the unanimity requirement: "In the space after each mitigating circumstance, write 'Yes,' if you unanimously find that mitigating circumstance by a preponderance of the evidence. Write, 'No,' if you do not unanimously find that mitigating circumstance by a preponderance of the evidence."

The jury unanimously found the statutory mitigating circumstance that McKoy's capacity "to appreciate the criminality of his conduct or to conform his conduct to the requirements of law was impaired." It also unanimously found the nonstatutory mitigating circumstance that McKoy had a "borderline intellectual functioning with a IQ test score of 74." The jury did not, however, unanimously find the statutory mitigating circumstances that McKoy committed the crime while "under the influence of mental or emotional disturbance" or that McKoy's age at the time of the crime, 65, was a mitigating factor. The jury also failed to find unanimously four nonstatutory mitigating circumstances: that for several decades McKoy exhibited signs of mental or emotional disturbance or defect that went untreated; that McKoy's mental and emotional disturbance was aggravated by his poor physical health; that McKoy's ability to remember the events of the day of the murder was actually impaired; and that there was any other circumstance arising from the evidence that had mitigating value.

Because the jury found the existence of mitigating circumstances, it was instructed to answer Issue Three, which asked: "Do you unanimously find beyond a reasonable doubt that the mitigating circumstance or circumstances found by you is, or are, insufficient to outweigh the aggravating circumstance or circumstances found by you?" The jury answered this issue "Yes," and so proceeded to the final issue. Issue Four asked: "Do you unanimously find beyond a reasonable doubt that the aggravating circumstance or circumstances found by you is, or are, sufficiently substantial to call for the imposition of the death penalty when considered with the mitigating circumstance or circumstances found by you?" The jury again responded "Yes." Pursuant to the verdict form and the court's instructions, the jury therefore made a binding recommendation of death.

During the pendency of petitioner's direct appeal to the North Carolina Supreme Court, this Court decided *Mills v. Maryland.* There, we reversed a death sentence imposed under Maryland's capital punishment scheme because the jury instructions and verdict form created "a substantial probability that reasonable jurors . . . well may have thought they were precluded from considering any mitigating evidence unless all 12 jurors agreed on the existence of a particular such circumstance." We reasoned that allowing a "holdout" juror to prevent the other jurors from considering mitigating evidence violated the principle established in *Lockett v. Ohio*, that a sentencer may not be precluded from giving effect to all mitigating evidence.

Petitioner challenged his sentence on the basis of *Mills.* The North Carolina Supreme Court, in a split decision, purported to distinguish *Mills* on two grounds and therefore denied relief. First, it noted that "Maryland's procedure required the jury to impose the death penalty if it 'found' at least one aggravating circumstance and did not 'find' any mitigating circumstances" or "if it unanimously found that the mitigating circumstances did not outweigh the aggravating circumstances." In contrast, the court stated, Issue Four in North Carolina's scheme allows the jury to recommend life imprisonment "if it feels that the aggravating circumstances are not sufficiently substantial to call for the death penalty, even if it has found several aggravating circumstances and no mitigating circumstances."

Second, the court asserted that whereas in Maryland's scheme evidence remained "legally relevant" as long as one or more jurors found the presence of a mitigating circumstance supported by that evidence, "in North Carolina evidence in effect becomes legally irrelevant to prove mitigation if the defendant fails to prove to the satisfaction of all the jurors that such evidence supports the finding of a mitigating factor." The North Carolina Supreme Court believed that we had found the "relevance" of the evidence in *Mills* a significant factor because we had stated in a footnote that "[n]o one has argued here, nor did the Maryland Court of Appeals suggest, that mitigating evidence can be rendered legally 'irrelevant' by one holdout vote." The court thus interpreted *Mills* as allowing States to define as "irrelevant" and to exclude from jurors' consideration any evidence introduced to support a mitigating circumstance that the jury did not unanimously find. Accordingly, the State Supreme Court upheld McKoy's death sentence.

II

Despite the state court's inventive attempts to distinguish *Mills*, our decision there clearly governs this case. First, North Carolina's Issue Four does not ameliorate the constitutional infirmity created by the unanimity requirement. Issue

Four, like Issue Three, allows the jury to consider only mitigating factors that it unanimously finds under Issue Two. Although the jury may opt for life imprisonment even where it fails unanimously to find any mitigating circumstances, the fact remains that the jury is required to make its decision based only on those circumstances it unanimously finds. The unanimity requirement thus allows one holdout juror to prevent the others from giving effect to evidence that they believe calls for a "sentence less than death." Moreover, even if all 12 jurors agree that there are some mitigating circumstances, North Carolina's scheme prevents them from giving effect to evidence supporting any of those circumstances in their deliberations under Issues Three and Four unless they unanimously find the existence of the same circumstance. This is the precise defect that compelled us to strike down the Maryland scheme in *Mills*. Our decision in *Mills* was not limited to cases in which the jury is required to impose the death penalty if it finds that aggravating circumstances outweigh mitigating circumstances or that no mitigating circumstances exist at all. Rather, we held that it would be the "height of arbitrariness to allow or require the imposition of the death penalty" where 1 juror was able to prevent the other 11 from giving effect to mitigating evidence.

Second, the State Supreme Court's holding that mitigating evidence is "relevant" only if the jury unanimously finds that it proves the existence of a mitigating circumstance distorts the concept of relevance.

. . .

Furthermore, . . . the mere declaration that evidence is "legally irrelevant" to mitigation cannot bar the consideration of that evidence if the sentencer could reasonably find that it warrants a sentence less than death.

. . .

Nor can the State save the unanimity requirement by characterizing it as a standard of proof intended to ensure the reliability of mitigating evidence. The State's reliance on *Patterson v. New York*, 432 U.S. 197 (1977), is misplaced. In that case, this Court rejected a due process challenge to a New York law requiring a defendant charged with second-degree murder to prove by a preponderance of the evidence the affirmative defense of extreme emotional disturbance in order to reduce the crime to manslaughter. The Court reasoned that a State is not constitutionally required to provide that affirmative defense. But if a State "nevertheless chooses to recognize a factor that mitigates the degree of criminality or punishment, . . . the State may assure itself that the fact has been established with reasonable certainty." *Id.*, at 209. *Patterson*, however, did not involve the validity of a capital sentencing procedure under the Eighth Amendment. The Constitution requires States to allow consideration of mitigating evidence in capital cases. Any barrier to such consideration must therefore fall. As we stated in *Mills*:

> Under our decisions, it is not relevant whether the barrier to the sentencer's consideration of all mitigating evidence is interposed by statute; by the sentencing court; or by an evidentiary ruling. The same must be true with

respect to a single juror's holdout vote against finding the presence of a mitigating circumstance. Whatever the cause, . . . the conclusion would necessarily be the same: "Because the [sentencer's] failure to consider all of the mitigating evidence risks erroneous imposition of the death sentence, in plain violation of *Lockett*, it is our duty to remand this case for resentencing."
. . .

It is no answer, of course, that the jury is permitted to "consider" mitigating evidence when it decides collectively, under Issue Two, whether any mitigating circumstances exist. Rather, *Mills* requires that each juror be permitted to consider and give effect to mitigating evidence when deciding the ultimate question whether to vote for a sentence of death. This requirement means that, in North Carolina's system, each juror must be allowed to consider all mitigating evidence in deciding Issues Three and Four: whether aggravating circumstances outweigh mitigating circumstances, and whether the aggravating circumstances, when considered with any mitigating circumstances, are sufficiently substantial to justify a sentence of death. Under *Mills*, such consideration of mitigating evidence may not be foreclosed by one or more jurors' failure to find a mitigating circumstance under Issue Two.

Finally, we reject the State's contention that requiring unanimity on mitigating circumstances is constitutional because the State also requires unanimity on aggravating circumstances. The Maryland scheme in *Mills* also required unanimity on both mitigating and aggravating circumstances. Such consistent treatment did not, however, save the unanimity requirement for mitigating circumstances in that case. A State may not limit a sentencer's consideration of mitigating evidence merely because it places the same limitation on consideration of aggravating circumstances. As the Court stated in *Penry v. Lynaugh*:

> "In contrast to the carefully defined standards that must narrow a sentencer's discretion to *impose* the death sentence, the Constitution limits a State's ability to narrow a sentencer's discretion to consider relevant evidence that might cause it to *decline to impose* the death sentence." *McCleskey v. Kemp*. Indeed, it is precisely because the punishment should be directly related to the personal culpability of the defendant that the jury must be allowed to consider and give effect to mitigating evidence relevant to a defendant's character or record or the circumstances of the offense.

III

We conclude that North Carolina's unanimity requirement impermissibly limits jurors' consideration of mitigating evidence and hence is contrary to our decision in *Mills*. We therefore vacate the petitioner's death sentence and remand this case to the North Carolina Supreme Court for further proceedings not inconsistent with this opinion.

DISSENTING OPINION OF JUSTICE SCALIA, JOINED BY CHIEF JUSTICE REHNQUIST AND JUSTICE O'CONNOR

Today the Court holds that the Eighth Amendment prohibits a State from structuring its capital sentencing scheme to channel jury discretion by requiring that mitigating circumstances be found unanimously. Because I believe that holding is without support in either the Eighth Amendment or our previous decisions, I dissent.

I

. . .

I think this scheme, taken as a whole, satisfies the due process and Eighth Amendment concerns enunciated by this Court. By requiring that the jury find at least one statutory aggravating circumstance, North Carolina has adequately narrowed the class of death-eligible murderers. On the other hand, by permitting the jury to consider evidence of, and find, any mitigating circumstance offered by the defendant, North Carolina has ensured that the jury will "be able to consider and give effect to that evidence in imposing sentence." *Penry v. Lynaugh.* By requiring both aggravating circumstances to be found unanimously (beyond a reasonable doubt) and mitigating circumstances to be found unanimously (by only a preponderance of the evidence), North Carolina has "reduc[ed] the likelihood that [the jury] will impose a sentence that fairly can be called capricious or arbitrary." *Gregg v. Georgia.* Finally, by requiring the jury unanimously to find beyond a reasonable doubt not only that the aggravating circumstances outweigh the mitigating circumstances, but also that they are sufficiently substantial in light of the mitigating circumstances to justify the death penalty, North Carolina has provided even an extra measure of assurance that death will not be lightly or mechanically imposed.

. . .

III

The constitutional issue conceded in *Mills* is both presented and contested in the present case. North Carolina's capital sentencing statute unambiguously provides that mitigating circumstances must be found by the jury unanimously. The Court finds this scheme constitutionally defective because it prevents individual jurors "from giving effect to evidence that they believe calls for a sentence less than death." This is so because each juror's answers to the ultimately dispositive Issues Three and Four can take account of only those mitigating circumstances found by the jury unanimously under Issue Two. Thus, any juror who concludes that the defendant has proved additional mitigating circumstances is precluded by his colleagues' disagreement from giving that conclusion effect. The Court several times refers to the prospect that 1 " 'holdout' juror" will prevent the other 11 from reaching the decision they wish, but the reader should not be misled: The constitutional principle appealed to is not majority rule but just the opposite. According to the Court, North Carolina's system in which one juror can prevent the others from giving effect to a mitigating circumstance is invalid only because the Constitution *requires*, in the context of the North Carolina statute, a system in which one juror can prevent the others from *denying effect* to a mitigating circumstance. The " 'holdout' juror" scenario provides attractive atmosphere, but the alleged constitutional principle upon which the decision rests is that "*each juror* [must] be permitted to consider *and give effect* to mitigating evidence when deciding the ultimate question whether to vote for a sentence of death," and "may not be foreclosed by one *or more* jurors' failure," to find that those mitigating facts existed, or that those existing facts were mitigating. Such a scheme, under which (at least where the statute requires the jury's recommendation of death to be unanimous) a single juror's finding regarding the existence of mitigation must control, is asserted to be demanded by "the principle established in *Lockett v. Ohio*, that a sentencer may not be precluded from giving effect to all mitigating evidence."

With respect, "the principle established in *Lockett*" does not remotely support that conclusion. In *Lockett*, the Court vacated a death sentence imposed under a statute that limited the sentencing judge's consideration of mitigating factors to three statutory circumstances. A plurality of the Court reasoned that "the Eighth and Fourteenth Amendments require that the sentencer, in all but the rarest kind of capital case, not be precluded from considering, as a mitigating factor, any aspect of a defendant's character or record and any of the circumstances of the offense that the defendant proffers as a basis for a sentence less than death." Similarly, in *Eddings [v. Oklahoma]*, also relied upon by the Court, we vacated a death sentence because the sentencing judge refused to consider evidence proffered by the defendant of his unhappy upbringing. We reasoned: "Just as the State may not by statute preclude the sentencer from considering any mitigating factor, neither may the sentencer refuse to consider, *as a matter of law*, any relevant mitigating evidence." Accord, *Penry v. Lynaugh*, 492 U.S. 302 (1989) (failure to instruct Texas jury that it could consider and give effect to mitigating evidence beyond the scope of three statutory special issues inconsistent with *Lockett* and *Eddings*); *Hitchcock v. Dugger*, 481 U.S. 393 (1987) (trial judge's belief that Florida law prohibited consideration of nonstatutory mitigating circumstances and corresponding instruction to the jury contravened *Lockett*); *Skipper v. South Carolina*, 476 U.S. 1 (1986) (trial judge's failure to permit jury to consider evidence of defendant's good behavior in prison inconsistent with *Lockett* and *Eddings*).

The principle established by these cases is that a State may not preclude the sentencer from considering and giving effect to evidence of any relevant mitigating circumstance proffered by the defendant. . . . The sentencer in this case was the North Carolina jury, which has not been precluded from considering and giving effect to all mitigating circumstances.

What petitioner complains of here is not a limitation upon *what* the sentencer was allowed to give effect to, but rather a limitation upon the *manner* in which it was allowed to do so—viz., only unanimously. As the Court observes today, that is a crucial distinction. "There is a simple and logical difference between rules that govern *what* factors the jury must be permitted to consider in making the sentencing decision and rules that govern *how* the State may guide the jury in considering and weighing those factors in reaching a decision." *Saffle v. Parks*, 494 U.S. 484, 490 (1990) (emphasis added). . . . In short, *Lockett* and *Eddings* are quite simply irrelevant to the question before us, and cannot be pressed into service by describing them as establishing that "*a* sentencer [by which the reader is invited to understand an individual member of the jury] may not be precluded from giving effect to all mitigating evidence."

IV

Nothing in our prior cases, then, supports the rule the Court has announced; and since the Court does not even purport to rely upon constitutional text or traditional practice, nothing remains to support the result. There are, moreover, some affirmative indications in prior cases that what North Carolina has done is constitutional. Those indications are not compelling—for the perverse reason that the less support exists for a constitutional claim, the less likely it is that the claim has been raised or taken seriously before, and hence the less likely that this Court has previously rejected it. If petitioner should seek reversal of his sentence because two jurors were wearing green shirts, it would be impossible to say anything against the claim except that there is nothing to be said *for* it—neither in text, tradition, nor jurisprudence. That is the point I have already made here, and that alone suffices.

With the caution, however, that it is entirely superfluous, I may mention several aspects of our jurisprudence that appear to contradict the Court's result. To begin with, not only have we never before invalidated a jury-unanimity requirement, but we have approved schemes imposing such a requirement in contexts of great importance to the criminal defendant—for example, as a condition to establishing the defense of self-defense in a capital murder case, . . . as a condition to establishing the defense of extreme emotional disturbance in a second-degree murder case, . . . and as a condition to establishing the defense of insanity in a second-degree murder case. . . .

Of course the Court's holding today—and its underlying thesis that each individual juror must be empowered to "give effect" to his own view—invalidates not just a requirement of *unanimity* for the defendant to benefit from a mitigating factor, but a requirement of *any* number of jurors more than one. Thus it is also in tension with *Leland v. Oregon*, 343 U.S. 790 (1952), which upheld, in a capital case, a requirement that the defense of insanity be proved (beyond a reasonable doubt) to the satisfaction of at least 10 of the 12-member jury. Even with respect to proof of the substantive offense, as opposed to an affirmative defense, we have approved verdicts by less than a unanimous jury. See *Apodaca v. Oregon,* 406 U.S. 404 (1972) (upholding state statute providing for conviction by 10-to-2 vote). We have, to be sure, found that a criminal verdict by less than all of a six-person jury is unconstitutional—not, however, because of any inherent vice in nonunanimity, but because a 5-to-1 verdict, no less than a 5-to-0 verdict ... "presents a ... threat to preservation of the substance of the jury trial guarantee." *Burch v. Louisiana,* 441 U.S. 130, 138 (1979).

The Court discusses briefly one of the above cases (*Patterson*), in which we said that if a State "chooses to recognize a factor that mitigates the degree of criminality or punishment, ... the State may assure itself that the fact has been established with reasonable certainty." It distinguishes that case, and presumably would distinguish the rest I have cited, as follows: "The Constitution requires States to allow consideration of mitigating evidence in capital cases. Any barrier to such consideration must therefore fall." But surely the Constitution also requires States to allow consideration of all evidence bearing upon the substantive criminal offense and consideration of all evidence bearing upon the substantive criminal offense and consideration of all evidence bearing upon affirmative defenses. If, in those contexts, it is not regarded as a "barrier" to such consideration to require unanimity before any single juror's evaluation of the evidence can be "given effect" to the defendant's advantage, I do not understand why a comparable requirement constitutes a "barrier" to consideration of mitigation. Or why, in the latter context, assuring "reasonable certainty" is no longer a legitimate objective.

Likewise incompatible with the Court's theory is the principle of guided discretion that we have previously held to be essential to the validity of capital sentencing. States, we have said, "must channel the sentencer's discretion by 'clear and objective standards' that provide 'specific and detailed guidance' and that 'make rationally reviewable the process for imposing a sentence of death.'" *Godfrey v. Georgia.* There is little guidance in a system that requires each individual juror to bring to the ultimate decision his own idiosyncratic notion of what facts are mitigating, untempered by the discipline of group deliberation and agreement. Until today, I would have thought that North Carolina's scheme was a model of guided discretion. The requirement that the jury determine four specific issues operates like a special verdict—a device long recognized as enhancing the reliability and rationality of jury determinations. Moreover, by enabling the reviewing court to examine the specific findings underlying the verdict it facilitates appellate review, which we have described as "an important additional safeguard against arbitrariness and caprice." *Gregg v. Georgia.* "Where the sentencing authority is required to specify the factors it relied upon in reaching its decision, the further safeguard of meaningful appellate review is available to ensure that death sentences are not imposed capriciously or in a freakish manner." *Id.*

The Court strikes down this eminently reasonable scheme. The quality of what it substitutes is conveniently evaluated by considering how future North Carolina juries will behave under the Court's own doomsday hypothetical, in which all jurors believe the defendant has proved one mitigating circumstance, but each believes a different one. A jury, of course, is not a collection of individuals who are asked separately about their independent views, but a body designed to deliberate and decide collectively. See *Williams v. Florida*, 399 U.S. 78 (1970) (Sixth Amendment requires a jury "large enough to promote group deliberation"); *Ballew v. Georgia*, 435 U.S. 223 (1978) (five-person jury too small); *id.*, at 232–234 (opinion of Blackmun, J.) (small juries impede group deliberation). But after today's decision, in the hypothetical the Court has posed, it will be quite impossible for North Carolina sentencing juries to "deliberate" on the dispositive questions (Issues Three and Four—whether the aggravating circumstances out-weigh the mitigating circumstances, and whether in light of the mitigating circumstances the aggravating circumstances justify death), because no two jurors agree on the identity of the "mitigating circumstances." Each juror must presumably decide in splendid isolation, on the basis of his uniquely determined mitigating circumstance, whether death should be imposed. What was supposed to be jury trial has degenerated into a poll. It seems to me inconceivable that such a system should be—not just tolerated under the Constitution—but constitutionally prescribed.[5]

In sum, the constitutional prohibition asserted by the petitioner was not decided in *Mills* and is not supported by *Lockett* and *Eddings*. Since nothing else is adduced to support it, there is no basis for believing that it exists. It is, moreover, contrary to the constitutional principles governing jury trial in other contexts, contrary to the principle of guided discretion that launched our modern incursion into the field of capital sentencing, and destructive of sound jury deliberation. When we abandon text and tradition, and in addition do not restrict prior cases to their holdings, knowing and observing the law of the land becomes impossible. State officials sworn to uphold the Constitution we expound rush to comply with one of our newly designed precepts, only to be told that by complying they have violated another one that points in the opposite direction. Compare *Furman v.* Georgia (invalidating discretionary death penalty), with *Woodson v. North Carolina* (invalidating mandatory death penalty enacted in light of *Furman*). I dissent from today's decision, and from the unpredictable jurisprudence of capital sentencing that it represents.

---

[5] Justice Blackmun believes that this grotesque distortion of normal jury deliberations cannot be blamed upon the rule the Court today announces, but is rather North Carolina's own fault, because the scheme it has adopted represents "an extraordinary departure from the way in which juries customarily operate." Typically, he points out, juries "are ... called upon to render unanimous verdicts on the ultimate issues of a given case," with "no general requirement that the jury reach agreement on the preliminary factual issues which underlie the verdict." This is the sort of argument that causes state legislators to pull their hair. A general verdict is of course the usual practice. *But it is this Court that has pushed the States to special verdicts in the capital sentencing field.* We have intimated that requiring "the sentencing authority ... to specify the factors it relied upon in reaching its decision" may be necessary to ensure, through "meaningful appellate review[,] that death sentences are not imposed capriciously or in a freakish manner." *Gregg v. Georgia.* Disparaging a practice we have at least encouraged, if not indeed coerced, gives new substance to the charge that we have been administering a "bait and switch" capital sentencing jurisprudence.

Chapter 11

Murder Defendants Who Did Not Kill (I)— *Enmund v. Florida* (1982)

Enmund v. Florida, 458 U.S. 782, 102 S. Ct. 3368, 73 L. Ed.2d 1140 (1982) (5–4, the participant in a felony-murder who does not kill or intend to kill may not be executed).

Editor's comment: As detailed in Chapter 1 in the discussion of homicide statutes, felony-murder is a murder for which the prosecutor need not prove mens rea (culpable mental state). The defendant may not have intended to kill the victim, and may not even have directly caused the death, but he is nonetheless guilty of murder—in many states, first degree murder—because he committed a specified felony that caused someone's death. The issue is this: How blameworthy is the felony-murderer? Does he deserve capital punishment even though he did not intend to kill and, as in Enmund's case, did not actually do the killing? Or is his participation in an armed robbery where shooting and death are foreseeable sufficient for culpability for the death that occurs? The *Enmund* ruling seems to say "No" to both questions, but the next case in this book, *Tison v. Arizona*, 481 U.S. 137 (1987), clarifies and modifies *Enmund*. Note that Justice O'Connor, dissenting here, writes the opinion of the Court in *Tison*.

❖   ❖   ❖

OPINION OF JUSTICE WHITE FOR THE COURT

I

The facts of this case, taken principally from the opinion of the Florida Supreme Court, are as follows. On April 1, 1975, at approximately 7:45 A.M., Thomas and

Eunice Kersey, aged 86 and 74, were robbed and fatally shot at their farmhouse in central Florida. The evidence showed that Sampson and Jeanette Armstrong had gone to the back door of the Kersey house and asked for water for an over-heated car. When Mr. Kersey came out of the house, Sampson Armstrong grabbed him, pointed a gun at him, and told Jeanette Armstrong to take his money. Mr. Kersey cried for help, and his wife came out of the house with a gun and shot Jeanette Armstrong, wounding her. Sampson Armstrong, and perhaps Jeanette Armstrong, then shot and killed both of the Kerseys, dragged them into the kitchen, and took their money and fled.

Two witnesses testified that they drove past the Kersey house between 7:30 and 7:40 A.M. and saw a large cream- or yellow-colored car parked beside the road about 200 yards from the house and that a man was sitting in the car. Another witness testified that at approximately 6:45 A.M. he saw Ida Jean Shaw, petitioner's common-law wife and Jeanette Armstrong's mother, driving a yellow Buick with a vinyl top which belonged to her and petitioner Earl Enmund. Enmund was a passenger in the car along with an unidentified woman. At about 8 A.M. the same witness saw the car return at a high rate of speed. Enmund was driving, Ida Jean Shaw was in the front seat, and one of the other two people in the car was lying down across the back seat.

Enmund, Sampson Armstrong, and Jeanette Armstrong were indicted for the first-degree murder and robbery of the Kerseys. Enmund and Sampson Armstrong were tried together. The prosecutor maintained in his closing argument that "Sampson Armstrong killed the old people." The judge instructed the jury that "[t]he killing of a human being while engaged in the perpetration of or in the attempt to perpetrate the offense of robbery is murder in the first degree even though there is no premeditated design or intent to kill." [Defendant was convicted of murder in the first degree and robbery, and was sentenced to death.]
. . .

II

As recounted above, the Florida Supreme Court held that the record supported no more than the inference that Enmund was the person in the car by the side of the road at the time of the killings, waiting to help the robbers escape. This was enough under Florida law to make Enmund a constructive aider and abettor and hence a principal in first-degree murder upon whom the death penalty could be imposed. It was thus irrelevant to Enmund's challenge to the death sentence that he did not himself kill and was not present at the killings; also beside the point was whether he intended that the Kerseys be killed or anticipated that lethal force would or might be used if necessary to effectuate the robbery or a safe escape. We have concluded that imposition of the death penalty in these circumstances is inconsistent with the Eighth and Fourteenth Amendments.

. . . Thirty-six state and federal jurisdictions presently authorize the death penalty. Of these, only eight jurisdictions authorize imposition of the death penalty solely for participation in a robbery in which another robber takes life. Of the remaining 28 jurisdictions, in 4 felony murder is not a capital crime. Eleven States require some culpable mental state with respect to the homicide as a prerequisite to conviction of a crime for which the death penalty is authorized. Of these 11 States, 8 make knowing, intentional, purposeful, or premeditated killing an element of capital murder. Three other States require proof of a culpable mental state short of intent, such as recklessness or extreme indifference to human life, before the death penalty may be imposed. In these 11 States, therefore, the actors in a felony murder are not subject to the death penalty without proof of their mental state, proof which was not required with respect to Enmund either under the trial court's instructions or under the law announced by the Florida Supreme Court. Four additional jurisdictions do not permit a defendant such as Enmund to be put to death. Of these, one State flatly prohibits capital punishment in cases where the defendant did not actually commit murder. Two jurisdictions preclude the death penalty in cases such as this one where the defendant "was a principal in the offense, which was committed by another, but his participation was relatively minor, although not so minor as to constitute a defense to prosecution." One other State limits the death penalty in felony murders to narrow circumstances not involved here.

Nine of the remaining States deal with the imposition of the death penalty for a vicarious felony murder in their capital sentencing statutes. In each of these States, a defendant may not be executed solely for participating in a felony in which a person was killed if the defendant did not actually cause the victim's death. For a defendant to be executed in these States, typically the statutory aggravating circumstances which are present must outweigh mitigating factors. To be sure, a vicarious felony murderer may be sentenced to death in these jurisdictions absent an intent to kill if sufficient aggravating circumstances are present. However, six of these nine States make it a statutory mitigating circumstance that the defendant was an accomplice in a capital felony committed by another person and his participation was relatively minor. By making minimal participation in a capital felony committed by another person a mitigating circumstance, these sentencing statutes reduce the likelihood that a person will be executed for vicarious felony murder. The remaining three jurisdictions exclude felony murder from their lists of aggravating circumstances that will support a death sentence. In each of these nine States, a nontriggerman guilty of felony murder cannot be sentenced to death for the felony murder absent aggravating circumstances above and beyond the felony murder itself.

Thus only a small minority of jurisdictions—eight—allow the death penalty to be imposed solely because the defendant somehow participated in a robbery in the course of which a murder was committed. Even if the nine States are included where such a defendant could be executed for an unintended felony murder if sufficient aggravating circumstances are present to outweigh mitigating circumstances—which often include the defendant's minimal participation in the murder—only about a third of American jurisdictions would ever permit a defendant who somehow participated in a robbery where a murder occurred to be sentenced to die. Moreover, of the eight States which have enacted new death penalty statutes since 1978, none authorize capital punishment in such circumstances. While the current legislative judgment with respect to imposition of the death penalty where a defendant did not take life, attempt to take it, or intend to take life is neither "wholly unanimous among state legislatures," nor as compelling as the legislative judgments considered in *Coker*, it nevertheless weighs on the side of rejecting capital punishment for the crime at issue.

Society's rejection of the death penalty for accomplice liability in felony murders is also indicated by the sentencing decisions that juries have made. As we have previously observed, " '[t]he jury . . . is a significant and reliable objective index of contemporary values because it is so directly involved.' " . . . The evidence is overwhelming that American juries have repudiated imposition of the death penalty for crimes such as petitioner's. First, according to the petitioner, a search of all reported appellate court decisions since 1954 in cases where a defendant was executed for homicide shows that of the 362 executions, in 339 the person executed personally committed a homicidal assault. In 2 cases the person executed had another person commit the homicide for him, and in 16 cases the facts were not reported in sufficient detail to determine whether the person executed committed the homicide. The survey revealed only 6 cases out of 362 where a nontriggerman felony murderer was executed. All six executions took place in 1955. By contrast, there were 72 executions for rape in this country between 1955 and this Court's decision in *Coker v. Georgia* in 1977.

That juries have rejected the death penalty in cases such as this one where the defendant did not commit the homicide, was not present when the killing took place, and did not participate in a plot or scheme to murder is also shown by petitioner's survey of the Nation's death-row population. As of October 1, 1981, there were 796 inmates under sentences of death for homicide. Of the 739 for whom sufficient data are available, only 41 did not participate in the fatal assault on the victim. Of the 40 among the 41 for whom sufficient information was available, only 16 were not physically present when the fatal assault was committed. These 16 prisoners included only 3, including petitioner, who were sentenced to die absent a finding that they hired or solicited someone else to kill the victim or participated in a scheme designed to kill the victim. The figures for Florida are similar.

The dissent criticizes these statistics on the ground that they do not reveal the percentage of homicides that were charged as felony murders or the percentage of cases where the State sought the death penalty for an accomplice guilty of felony murder. We doubt whether it is possible to gather such information, and at any rate, it would be relevant if prosecutors rarely sought the death penalty for accomplice felony murder, for it would tend to indicate that prosecutors, who represent society's interest in punishing crime, consider the death penalty excessive for accomplice felony murder. The fact remains that we are not aware of a single person convicted of felony murder over the past quarter century who did not kill or attempt to kill, and did not intend the death of the victim, who has been executed, and that only three persons in that category are presently sentenced to die. Nor can these figures be discounted by attributing to petitioner the argument that "death is an unconstitutional penalty absent an intent to kill," and observing that the statistics are incomplete with respect to intent. Petitioner's argument is that because he did not kill, attempt to kill, and he did not intend to kill, the death penalty is disproportionate as applied to him, and the statistics he cites are adequately tailored to demonstrate that juries—and perhaps prosecutors as well—consider death a disproportionate penalty for those who fall within his category.

III

Although the judgments of legislatures, juries, and prosecutors weigh heavily in the balance, it is for us ultimately to judge whether the Eighth Amendment permits imposition of the death penalty on one such as Enmund who aids and abets a felony in the course of which a murder is committed by others but who does not himself kill, attempt to kill, or intend that a killing take place or that lethal force will be employed. We have concluded, along with most legislatures and juries, that it does not.

We have no doubt that robbery is a serious crime deserving serious punishment. It is not, however, a crime "so grievous an affront to humanity that the only adequate response may be the penalty of death." *Gregg.* "[I]t does not compare with murder, which does involve the unjustified taking of human life. Although it may be accompanied by another crime, [robbery] by definition does not include the death of or even the serious injury to another person. The murderer kills; the [robber], if no more than that, does not. Life is over for the victim of the murderer; for the [robbery] victim, life . . . is not over and normally is not beyond repair." *Coker.* As was said of the crime of rape in *Coker,* we have the abiding conviction that the death penalty, which is "unique in its severity and irrevocability," is an excessive penalty for the robber who, as such, does not take human life.

Here the robbers did commit murder; but they were subjected to the death penalty only because they killed as well as robbed. The question before us is not the disproportionality of death as a penalty for murder, but rather the validity of capital punishment for Enmund's own conduct. The focus must be on his culpability, not on that of those who committed the robbery and shot the victims, for we insist on "individualized consideration as a constitutional requirement in imposing the death sentence," which means that we must focus on "relevant facets of the character and record of the individual offender."

Enmund himself did not kill or attempt to kill; and, as construed by the Florida Supreme Court, the record before us does not warrant a finding that Enmund had any intention of participating in or facilitating a murder. Yet under Florida law death was an authorized penalty because Enmund aided and abetted a robbery in the course of which murder was committed. It is fundamental that "causing harm intentionally must be punished more severely than causing the same harm unintentionally." H. Hart, Punishment and Responsibility 162 (1968). Enmund did not kill or intend to kill and thus his culpability is plainly different from that of the robbers who killed; yet the State treated them alike and attributed to Enmund the culpability of those who killed the Kerseys. This was impermissible under the Eighth Amendment.

In *Gregg v. Georgia* the opinion announcing the judgment observed that "[t]he death penalty is said to serve two principal social purposes: retribution and deterrence of capital crimes by prospective offenders." Unless the death penalty when applied to those in Enmund's position measurably contributes to one or both of these goals, it "is nothing more than the purposeless and needless imposition of pain and suffering," and hence an unconstitutional punishment.

We are quite unconvinced, however, that the threat that the death penalty will be imposed for murder will measurably deter one who does not kill and has no intention or purpose that life will be taken. Instead, it seems likely that "capital punishment can serve as a deterrent only when murder is the result of premeditation and deliberation," for if a person does not intend that life be taken or contemplate that lethal force will be employed by others, the possibility that the death penalty will be imposed for vicarious felony murder will not "enter into the cold calculus that precedes the decision to act."

It would be very different if the likelihood of a killing in the course of a robbery were so substantial that one should share the blame for the killing if he somehow participated in the felony. But competent observers have concluded that there is no basis in experience for the notion that death so frequently occurs in the course of a felony for which killing is not an essential ingredient that the death penalty should be considered as a justifiable deterrent to the felony itself. Model Penal Code §210.2, Comment. This conclusion was based on three comparisons of robbery statistics, each of which showed that only about one-half of 1 percent of robberies resulted in homicide. The most recent national crime statistics strongly support this conclusion. In addition to the evidence that killings only rarely occur during robberies is the fact, already noted, that however often death occurs in the course of a felony such as robbery, the death penalty is rarely imposed on one only vicariously guilty of the murder, a fact which further attenuates its possible utility as an effective deterrence.

As for retribution as a justification for executing Enmund, we think this very much depends on the degree of Enmund's culpability—what Enmund's intentions, expectations, and actions were. American criminal law has long considered a defendant's intention—and therefore his moral guilt—to be critical to "the degree of [his] criminal culpability," and the Court has found criminal penalties to be unconstitutionally excessive in the absence of intentional wrongdoing.

For purposes of imposing the death penalty, Enmund's criminal culpability must be limited to his participation in the robbery, and his punishment must be tailored to his personal responsibility and moral guilt. Putting Enmund to death to avenge two killings that he did not commit and had no intention of committing or causing does not measurably contribute to the retributive end of ensuring that the criminal gets his just deserts. This is the judgment of most of the legislatures that have recently addressed the matter, and we have no reason to disagree with that judgment for purposes of construing and applying the Eighth Amendment.

IV

Because the Florida Supreme Court affirmed the death penalty in this case in the absence of proof that Enmund killed or attempted to kill, and regardless of whether Enmund intended or contemplated that life would be taken, we reverse the judgment upholding the death penalty and remand for further proceedings not inconsistent with this opinion.

DISSENTING OPINION OF JUSTICE O'CONNOR, JOINED BY CHIEF JUSTICE BURGER AND JUSTICES POWELL AND REHNQUIST

. . . The evidence at trial showed that at approximately 7:30 A.M. on April 1, 1975, Sampson and Jeanette Armstrong approached the backdoor of Thomas and Eunice Kersey's farmhouse on the pretext of obtaining water for their overheated car. When Thomas Kersey retrieved a water jug to help the Armstrongs, Sampson Armstrong grabbed him, held a gun to him, and told Jeanette Armstrong to take his wallet. Hearing her husband's cries for help, Eunice Kersey came around the side of the house with a gun and shot Jeanette Armstrong. Sampson Armstrong, and perhaps Jeanette Armstrong, returned the fire, killing both of the Kerseys. The Armstrongs dragged the bodies into the kitchen, took Thomas Kersey's money, and fled to a nearby car, where the petitioner, Earl Enmund, was waiting to help the Armstrongs escape. . . .

In his closing argument, the prosecutor did not argue that Earl Enmund had killed the Kerseys. Instead, he maintained that the petitioner had initiated and planned the armed robbery, and was in the car during the killings. According to the prosecutor, "Sampson Armstrong killed the old people." . . .

Most notably, the [trial] court concluded that the evidence clearly showed that the petitioner was an accomplice to the capital felony and that his participation had not been "relatively minor," but had been major in that he "planned the capital felony and actively participated in an attempt to avoid detection by disposing of the murder weapons." . . .

Earl Enmund's claim in this Court is that the death sentence imposed by the Florida trial court, and affirmed by the Florida Supreme Court, is unconstitutionally disproportionate to the role he played in the robbery and murders of the Kerseys. In particular, he contends that because he had no actual intent to kill the victims—in effect, because his behavior and intent were no more blameworthy than that of any robber—capital punishment is too extreme a penalty. . . .

In sum, in considering the petitioner's challenge, the Court should decide not only whether the petitioner's sentence of death offends contemporary standards as reflected in the responses of legislatures and juries, but also whether it is disproportionate to the harm that the petitioner caused and to the petitioner's involvement in the crime, as well as whether the procedures under which the petitioner was sentenced satisfied the constitutional requirement of individualized consideration set forth in *Lockett*. . . .

The Court's curious method of counting the States that authorize imposition of the death penalty for felony murder cannot hide the fact that 23 States permit a sentencer to impose the death penalty even though the felony murderer has neither killed nor intended to kill his victim. While the Court acknowledges that 8 state statutes follow the Florida death penalty scheme, it also concedes that 15 other statutes permit imposition of the death penalty where the defendant neither intended to kill or [nor?] actually killed the victims. Not all of the statutes list the same aggravating circumstances. Nevertheless, the question before the Court is not whether a particular species of death penalty statute is unconstitutional, but whether a scheme that permits imposition of the death penalty, absent a finding that the defendant either killed or intended to kill the victims, is unconstitutional. In short, the Court's peculiar statutory analysis cannot withstand closer scrutiny.

Thus, in nearly half of the States, and in two-thirds of the States that permit the death penalty for murder, a defendant who neither killed the victim nor specifically intended that the victim die may be sentenced to death for his participation in the robbery-murder. Far from "weigh[ing] very heavily on the side of rejecting capital punishment as a suitable penalty for" felony murder, these legislative judgments indicate that our "evolving standards of decency" still embrace capital punishment for this crime. For this reason, I conclude that the petitioner has failed to meet the standards in *Coker* and *Woodson* that the "two crucial indicators of evolving standards of decency . . .—jury determinations and legislative enactments—*both point conclusively* to the repudiation" of capital punishment for felony murder. In short, the death penalty for felony murder does not fall short of our national "standards of decency."

As I noted earlier, the Eighth Amendment concept of proportionality involves more than merely a measurement of contemporary standards of decency. It requires in addition that the penalty imposed in a capital case be proportional to the harm caused and the defendant's blameworthiness. Critical to the holding in *Coker*, for example, was that "in terms of moral depravity and of the injury to the person and to the public, [rape] does not compare with murder, which . . . involve[s] the unjustified taking of human life."

Although the Court disingenuously seeks to characterize Enmund as only a "robber," it cannot be disputed that he is responsible, along with Sampson and Jeanette Armstrong, for the murders of the Kerseys. There is no dispute that their lives were unjustifiably taken, and that the petitioner, as one who aided and abetted the armed robbery, is legally liable for their deaths.[40] Quite unlike the defendant in *Coker*, the petitioner cannot claim that the penalty imposed is "grossly out of proportion" to the harm for which he admittedly is at least partly responsible.

The Court's holding today is especially disturbing because it makes intent a matter of federal constitutional law, requiring this Court both to review highly subjective definitional problems customarily left to state criminal law and to develop an Eighth Amendment meaning of intent. As Justice Blackmun pointed out in his concurring opinion in *Lockett*, the Court's holding substantially "interfere[s] with the States' individual statutory categories for assessing legal guilt." ...

Although the Court's opinion suggests that intent can be ascertained as if it were some historical fact, in fact it is a legal concept, not easily defined. Thus, while proportionality requires a nexus between the punishment imposed and the defendant's blameworthiness, the Court fails to explain why the Eighth Amendment concept of proportionality requires rejection of standards of blameworthiness based on other levels of intent, such as, for example, the intent to commit an armed robbery coupled with the knowledge that armed robberies involve substantial risk of death or serious injury to other persons. Moreover, the intent-to-kill requirement is crudely crafted; it fails to take into account the complex picture of the defendant's knowledge of his accomplice's intent and whether he was armed, the defendant's contribution to the planning and success of the crime, and the defendant's actual participation during the commission of the crime. Under the circumstances, the determination of the degree of blameworthiness is best left to the sentencer, who can sift through the facts unique to each case. Consequently, while the type of mens rea of the defendant must be considered carefully in assessing the proper penalty, it is not so critical a factor in determining blameworthiness as to require a finding of intent to kill in order to impose the death penalty for felony murder.

In sum, the petitioner and the Court have failed to show that contemporary standards, as reflected in both jury determinations and legislative enactments, preclude imposition of the death penalty for accomplice felony murder. Moreover, examination of the qualitative factors underlying the concept of proportionality do not show that the death penalty is disproportionate as applied to Earl

---

[40] The Court's attempt to downplay the significance of Enmund's role in the murders, does not square with the facts of this case. The trial court expressly found that because Enmund had planned the robbery, his role was not minor, and that therefore no statutory mitigating circumstances applied. The Florida Supreme Court affirmed the finding of no mitigating circumstances, thereby affirming the underlying factual predicate—Enmund had planned the armed robbery. Moreover, even Enmund's trial counsel conceded at the sentencing hearing that Enmund initiated the armed robbery and drove the getaway car.

The Court misreads the opinion below in suggesting that the State Supreme Court deduced from the *sentencing hearing* that Enmund's only participation was as the getaway driver. In fact, the court made that statement with respect to the *guilt* phase of the trial. As I mentioned above, Enmund's counsel conceded at the sentencing hearing that Enmund had initiated the armed robbery.

Enmund. In contrast to the crime in *Coker*, the petitioner's crime involves the very type of harm that this Court has held justifies the death penalty. Finally, because of the unique and complex mixture of facts involving a defendant's actions, knowledge, motives, and participation during the commission of a felony murder, I believe that the factfinder is best able to assess the defendant's blameworthiness. Accordingly, I conclude that the death penalty is not disproportionate to the crime of felony murder, even though the defendant did not actually kill or intend to kill his victims.

Chapter 12

Murder Defendants
Who Did Not Kill (II)—
Tison v. Arizona (1987)

Tison v. Arizona, 481 U.S. 137, 107 S. Ct. 1676, 95 L. Ed.2d 127 (1987)
(5–4, the major participant in a felony-murder who does not kill or intend
to kill but has a mental state of "reckless indifference" to human life may
be sentenced to death).

Editor's comment: Two key points distinguish this case, in which the Court
upheld the death penalty for a felony-murder, and *Enmund*, which held
to the contrary. The first involves the criminal law concept of mens rea,
or the culpable mental state of the defendant at the time of the crime. To
put it simply, in a murder case, mens rea concerns whether or not, at the
time of the homicide, the defendant intended the victim's death, was
aware of the risk of death (this is the mens rea of "recklessness"), or
should have been aware of the risk of death ("negligence"). Most people
would agree that the criminal who intends the death is more blameworthy than the one who was merely negligent (unaware of the risk). The
reckless offender who is indifferent to the victim's plight (sometimes
referred to as *depraved indifference*) often is considered somewhere in
between in terms of blameworthiness. The *Tison* case stands for the
proposition that the "reckless" felony-murder defendant has a mens rea
sufficient to justify the death penalty.
    The second point of difference concerns the degree of a defendant's
involvement in the murder, such as whether or not he was active in the
events leading up to the killing or whether or not he was at the murder
scene. In *Tison*, the Court held that the defendants were much more
involved in the homicide than Enmund had been (although in her
Enmund dissent, Justice O'Connor had disputed the majority's claim that
Enmund was a mere lookout).

In short, the Supreme Court held that someone found guilty of felony-murder may be executed, so long as his mens rea and involvement in the killing were sufficient.

❖ ❖ ❖

OPINION OF JUSTICE O'CONNOR FOR THE COURT

The question presented is whether the petitioners' participation in the events leading up to and following the murder of four members of a family makes the sentences of death imposed by the Arizona courts constitutionally permissible although neither petitioner specifically intended to kill the victims and neither inflicted the fatal gunshot wounds. We hold that the Arizona Supreme Court applied an erroneous standard in making the findings required by *Enmund v. Florida*, and, therefore, vacate the judgments below and remand the case for further proceedings not inconsistent with this opinion.

I

Gary Tison was sentenced to life imprisonment as the result of a prison escape during the course of which he had killed a guard. After he had been in prison a number of years, Gary Tison's wife, their three sons Donald, Ricky, and Raymond, Gary's brother Joseph, and other relatives made plans to help Gary Tison escape again. The Tison family assembled a large arsenal of weapons for this purpose. Plans for escape were discussed with Gary Tison, who insisted that his cellmate, Randy Greenawalt, also a convicted murderer, be included in the prison break. The following facts are largely evidenced by petitioners' detailed confessions given as part of a plea bargain according to the terms of which the State agreed not to seek the death sentence. The Arizona courts interpreted the plea agreement to require that petitioners testify to the planning stages of the breakout. When they refused to do so, the bargain was rescinded and they were tried, convicted, and sentenced to death.

On July 30, 1978, the three Tison brothers entered the Arizona State Prison at Florence carrying a large ice chest filled with guns. The Tisons armed Greenawalt and their father, and the group, brandishing their weapons, locked the prison guards and visitors present in a storage closet. The five men fled the prison grounds in the Tisons' Ford Galaxy automobile. No shots were fired at the prison.

After leaving the prison, the men abandoned the Ford automobile and proceeded on to an isolated house in a white Lincoln automobile that the brothers had parked at a hospital near the prison. At the house, the Lincoln automobile had a flat tire; the only spare tire was pressed into service. After two nights at the house, the group drove toward Flagstaff. As the group traveled on back roads and secondary highways through the desert, another tire blew out. The group decided to flag down a passing motorist and steal a car. Raymond stood out in front of the Lincoln; the other four armed themselves and lay in wait by the side of the road. One car passed by without stopping, but a second car, a Mazda occupied by John Lyons, his wife Donnelda, his 2-year-old son Christopher, and his 15-year-old niece, Theresa Tyson, pulled over to render aid.

As Raymond showed John Lyons the flat tire on the Lincoln, the other Tisons and Greenawalt emerged. The Lyons family was forced into the backseat of the Lincoln. Raymond and Donald drove the Lincoln down a dirt road off the highway and then down a gas line service road farther into the desert; Gary Tison, Ricky Tison, and Randy Greenawalt followed in the Lyons' Mazda. The two cars were parked trunk to trunk and the Lyons family was ordered to stand in front of the Lincoln's headlights. The Tisons transferred their belongings from the Lincoln into the Mazda. They discovered guns and money in the Mazda which they kept, and they put the rest of the Lyons' possessions in the Lincoln.

Gary Tison then told Raymond to drive the Lincoln still farther into the desert. Raymond did so, and, while the others guarded the Lyons and Theresa Tyson, Gary fired his shotgun into the radiator, presumably to completely disable the vehicle. The Lyons and Theresa Tyson were then escorted to the Lincoln and again ordered to stand in its headlights. Ricky Tison reported that John Lyons begged, in comments "more or less directed at everybody," "Jesus, don't kill me." Gary Tison said he was "thinking about it." John Lyons asked the Tisons and Greenawalt to "[g]ive us some water . . . just leave us out here, and you all go home." Gary Tison then told his sons to go back to the Mazda and get some water. Raymond later explained that his father "was like in conflict with himself. . . . What it was, I think it was the baby being there and all this, and he wasn't sure about what to do."

The petitioners' statements diverge to some extent, but it appears that both of them went back towards the Mazda, along with Donald, while Randy Greenawalt and Gary Tison stayed at the Lincoln guarding the victims. Raymond recalled being at the Mazda filling the water jug "when we started hearing the shots." Ricky said that the brothers gave the water jug to Gary Tison who then, with Randy Greenawalt, went behind the Lincoln, where they spoke briefly, then raised the shotguns and started firing. In any event, petitioners agree they saw Greenawalt and their father brutally murdered their four captives with repeated blasts from their shotguns. Neither made an effort to help the victims, though both later stated they were surprised by the shooting. The Tisons got into the Mazda and drove away, continuing their flight. Physical evidence suggested that Theresa Tyson managed to crawl away from the bloodbath, severely injured. She died in the desert after the Tisons left.

Several days later the Tisons and Greenawalt were apprehended after a shoot-out at a police roadblock. Donald Tison was killed. Gary Tison escaped into the desert where he subsequently died of exposure. Raymond and Ricky Tison and Randy Greenawalt were captured and tried jointly for the crimes associated with the prison break itself and the shoot-out at the roadblock; each was convicted and sentenced.

The State then individually tried each of the petitioners for capital murder of the four victims as well as for the associated crimes of armed robbery, kidnapping, and car theft. The capital murder charges were based on Arizona felony-murder law providing that a killing occurring during the perpetration of robbery or kidnapping is capital murder, and that each participant in the kidnapping or robbery is legally responsible for the acts of his accomplices. Each of the petitioners was convicted of the four murders under these accomplice liability and felony-murder statutes.

Arizona law also provided for a capital sentencing proceeding, to be conducted without a jury, to determine whether the crime was sufficiently aggravated to warrant the death sentence. The statute set out six aggravating and four mitigating factors. The judge found three statutory aggravating factors:

(1) the Tisons had created a grave risk of death to others (not the victims);
(2) the murders had been committed for pecuniary gain;
(3) the murders were especially heinous.

The judge found no statutory mitigating factor. Importantly, the judge specifically found that the crime was not mitigated by the fact that each of the petitioner's "participation was relatively minor." Rather, he found that the "participation of each [petitioner] in the crimes giving rise to the application of the felony murder rule in this case was very substantial." The trial judge also specifically found that each "could reasonably have foreseen that his conduct ... would cause or create a grave risk of ... death." He did find, however, three nonstatutory mitigating factors:

(1) the petitioners' youth—Ricky was 20 and Raymond was 19;
(2) neither had prior felony records;
(3) each had been convicted of the murders under the felony-murder rule.

Nevertheless, the judge sentenced both petitioners to death. On direct appeal, the Arizona Supreme Court affirmed. . . .

II

. . . *Enmund [v. Florida]* explicitly dealt with two distinct subsets of all felony murders in assessing whether Enmund's sentence was disproportional under the Eighth Amendment. At one pole was Enmund himself: the minor actor in an armed robbery, not on the scene, who neither intended to kill nor was found to have had any culpable mental state. Only a small minority of States even authorized the death penalty in such circumstances and even within those jurisdictions the death penalty was almost never exacted for such a crime. The Court held that capital punishment was disproportional in these cases. *Enmund* also clearly dealt with the other polar case: the felony murderer who actually killed, attempted to kill, or intended to kill. The Court clearly held that the equally small minority of jurisdictions that limited the death penalty to these circumstances could continue to exact it in accordance with local law when the circumstances warranted. The Tison brothers' cases fall into neither of these neat categories.

Petitioners argue strenuously that they did not "intend to kill" as that concept has been generally understood in the common law. We accept this as true. Traditionally, "one intends certain consequences when he desires that his acts cause those consequences or knows that those consequences are substantially certain to result from his acts." W. LaFave and A. Scott, Criminal Law §28, p. 196 (1972). As petitioners point out, there is no evidence that either Ricky or Raymond Tison took any act which he desired to, or was substantially certain would, cause death.

The Arizona Supreme Court did not attempt to argue that the facts of this case supported an inference of "intent" in the traditional sense. Instead, the Arizona Supreme Court attempted to reformulate "intent to kill" as a species of foreseeability. The Arizona Supreme Court wrote:

Intend [sic] to kill includes the situation in which the defendant intended, contemplated, or anticipated that lethal force would or might be used or that life would or might be taken in accomplishing the underlying felony.

This definition of intent is broader than that described by the *Enmund* Court. Participants in violent felonies like armed robberies can frequently "anticipat[e] that lethal force ... might be used ... in accomplishing the underlying felony." *Enmund* himself may well have so anticipated. Indeed, the possibility of bloodshed is inherent in the commission of any violent felony and this possibility is generally foreseeable and foreseen; it is one principal reason that felons arm themselves. The Arizona Supreme Court's attempted reformulation of intent to kill amounts to little more than a restatement of the felony-murder rule itself. Petitioners do not fall within the "intent to kill" category of felony murderers for which *Enmund* explicitly finds the death penalty permissible under the Eighth Amendment.

On the other hand, it is equally clear that petitioners also fall outside the category of felony murderers for whom Enmund explicitly held the death penalty disproportional: their degree of participation in the crimes was major rather than minor, and the record would support a finding of the culpable mental state of reckless indifference to human life. We take the facts as the Arizona Supreme Court has given them to us.

Raymond Tison brought an arsenal of lethal weapons into the Arizona State Prison which he then handed over to two convicted murderers, one of whom he knew had killed a prison guard in the course of a previous escape attempt. By his own admission he was prepared to kill in furtherance of the prison break. He performed the crucial role of flagging down a passing car occupied by an innocent family whose fate was then entrusted to the known killers he had previously armed. He robbed these people at their direction and then guarded the victims at gunpoint while they considered what next to do. He stood by and watched the killing, making no effort to assist the victims before, during, or after the shooting. Instead, he chose to assist the killers in their continuing criminal endeavors, ending in a gun battle with the police in the final showdown.

Ricky Tison's behavior differs in slight details only. Like Raymond, he intentionally brought the guns into the prison to arm the murderers. He could have foreseen that lethal force might be used, particularly since he knew that his father's previous escape attempt had resulted in murder. He, too, participated fully in the kidnapping and robbery and watched the killing after which he chose to aid those whom he had placed in the position to kill rather than their victims.

These facts not only indicate that the Tison brothers' participation in the crime was anything but minor; they also would clearly support a finding that they both subjectively appreciated that their acts were likely to result in the taking of innocent life. The issue raised by this case is whether the Eighth Amendment prohibits the death penalty in the intermediate case of the defendant whose participation is major and whose mental state is one of reckless indifference to the value of human life. *Enmund* does not specifically address this point. We now take up the task of determining whether the Eighth Amendment proportionality requirement bars the death penalty under these circumstances.

Like the *Enmund* Court, we find the state legislatures' judgment as to proportionality in these circumstances relevant to this constitutional inquiry. The largest number of States still fall into the two intermediate categories discussed in *Enmund*. Four States authorize the death penalty in felony-murder cases upon a showing of culpable mental state such as recklessness or extreme indifference to human life. Two jurisdictions require that the defendant's participation be substantial and the statutes of at least six more, including Arizona, take minor participation in the felony expressly into account in mitigation of the murder. These requirements significantly overlap both in this case and in general, for the greater the defendant's participation in the felony murder, the more likely that he acted with reckless indifference to human life. At a minimum, however, it can be said that all these jurisdictions, as well as six States which *Enmund* classified along with Florida as permitting capital punishment for felony murder simpliciter, and the three States which simply require some additional aggravation before imposing the death penalty upon a felony murderer, specifically authorize the death penalty in a felony-murder case where, though the defendant's mental state fell short of intent to kill, the defendant was a major actor in a felony in which he knew death was highly likely to occur. On the other hand, even after *Enmund*, only 11 States authorizing capital punishment forbid imposition of the death penalty even though the defendant's participation in the felony murder is major and the likelihood of killing is so substantial as to raise an inference of extreme recklessness. This substantial and recent legislative authorization of the death penalty for the crime of felony murder regardless of the absence of a finding of an intent to kill powerfully suggests that our society does not reject the death penalty as grossly excessive under these circumstances.

Moreover, a number of state courts have interpreted *Enmund* to permit the imposition of the death penalty in such aggravated felony murders. We do not approve or disapprove the judgments as to proportionality reached on the particular facts of these cases, but we note the apparent consensus that substantial participation in a violent felony under circumstances likely to result in the loss of innocent human life may justify the death penalty even absent an "intent to kill."

Against this backdrop, we now consider the proportionality of the death penalty in these midrange felony-murder cases for which the majority of American jurisdictions clearly authorize capital punishment and for which American courts have not been nearly so reluctant to impose death as they are in the case of felony murder simpliciter.

A critical facet of the individualized determination of culpability required in capital cases is the mental state with which the defendant commits the crime. Deeply ingrained in our legal tradition is the idea that the more purposeful is the criminal conduct, the more serious is the offense, and, therefore, the more severely it ought to be punished. The ancient concept of malice aforethought was an early attempt to focus on mental state in order to distinguish those who deserved death from those who through "Benefit of . . . Clergy" would be spared.[a] Over time, malice aforethought came to be inferred from the mere act of killing in a variety of circumstances; in reaction, Pennsylvania became the first American jurisdiction to distinguish between degrees of murder, reserving capital punishment to "willful, deliberate and premeditated" killings and felony murders. More recently, in *Lockett v. Ohio*, the plurality opinion made clear that the defendant's mental state was critical to weighing a defendant's culpability under a system of guided discretion, vacating a death sentence imposed under an Ohio statute that did not permit the sentencing authority to take into account "[t]he absence of direct proof that the defendant intended to cause the death of the victim." In *Enmund v. Florida*, the Court recognized again the importance of mental state, explicitly permitting the death penalty in at least those cases where the felony murderer intended to kill and forbidding it in the case of a minor actor not shown to have had any culpable mental state.

A narrow focus on the question of whether or not a given defendant "intended to kill," however, is a highly unsatisfactory means of definitively distinguishing the most culpable and dangerous of murderers. Many who intend to, and do, kill are not criminally liable at all—those who act in self-defense or with other justification or excuse. Other intentional homicides, though criminal, are often felt undeserving of the death penalty—those that are the result of provocation. On the other hand, some nonintentional murderers may be among the

---

[a] Editor's note: "Benefit of Clergy" began as an immunity for English clergymen from secular court jurisdiction. It then became a death penalty exemption, and was eventually extended to anyone working for the church, and then to anyone who could read. Benefit of Clergy was used to soften the harshness of the British common law with respect to the death penalty. Benefit of Clergy was, along with the common law, exported to America, where it was subject to such abuse that Congress banned it for federal capital crimes in 1790. Today it no longer exists.

most dangerous and inhumane of all—the person who tortures another not caring whether the victim lives or dies, or the robber who shoots someone in the course of the robbery, utterly indifferent to the fact that the desire to rob may have the unintended consequence of killing the victim as well as taking the victim's property.

This reckless indifference to the value of human life may be every bit as shocking to the moral sense as an "intent to kill." Indeed it is for this very reason that the common law and modern criminal codes alike have classified behavior such as occurred in this case along with intentional murders. *Enmund* held that when "intent to kill" results in its logical though not inevitable consequence— the taking of human life—the Eighth Amendment permits the State to exact the death penalty after a careful weighing of the aggravating and mitigating circumstances. Similarly, we hold that the reckless disregard for human life implicit in knowingly engaging in criminal activities known to carry a grave risk of death represents a highly culpable mental state, a mental state that may be taken into account in making a capital sentencing judgment when that conduct causes its natural, though also not inevitable, lethal result.

The petitioners' own personal involvement in the crimes was not minor, but rather, as specifically found by the trial court, "substantial." Far from merely sitting in a car away from the actual scene of the murders acting as the getaway driver to a robbery, each petitioner was actively involved in every element of the kidnapping-robbery and was physically present during the entire sequence of criminal activity culminating in the murder of the Lyons family and the subsequent flight. The Tisons' high level of participation in these crimes further implicates them in the resulting deaths. Accordingly, they fall well within the overlapping second intermediate position which focuses on the defendant's degree of participation in the felony.

Only a small minority of those jurisdictions imposing capital punishment for felony murder have rejected the possibility of a capital sentence absent an intent to kill, and we do not find this minority position constitutionally required. We will not attempt to precisely delineate the particular types of conduct and states of mind warranting imposition of the death penalty here.

Rather, we simply hold that major participation in the felony committed, combined with reckless indifference to human life, is sufficient to satisfy the *Enmund* culpability requirement. The Arizona courts have clearly found that the former exists; we now vacate the judgments below and remand for determination of the latter in further proceedings not inconsistent with this opinion.

DISSENTING OPINION OF JUSTICE BRENNAN, JOINED BY JUSTICES MARSHALL, BLACKMUN, AND STEVENS

The murders that Gary Tison and Randy Greenawalt committed revolt and grieve all who learn of them. When the deaths of the Lyons family and Theresa Tyson were first reported, many in Arizona erupted "in a towering yell" for retribution and justice. Yet Gary Tison, the central figure in this tragedy, the man who had his family arrange his and Greenawalt's escape from prison, and the man who chose, with Greenawalt, to murder this family while his sons stood by, died of exposure in the desert before society could arrest him and bring him to trial. The question this case presents is what punishment Arizona may constitutionally exact from two of Gary Tison's sons for their role in these events. Because our precedents and our Constitution compel a different answer than the one the Court reaches today, I dissent.

I

Under the felony-murder doctrine, a person who commits a felony is liable for any murder that occurs during the commission of that felony, regardless of whether he or she commits, attempts to commit, or intended to commit that murder. The doctrine thus imposes liability on felons for killings committed by cofelons during a felony. This curious doctrine is a living fossil from a legal era in which all felonies were punishable by death; in those circumstances, the state of mind of the felon with respect to the murder was understandably superfluous, because he or she could be executed simply for intentionally committing the felony. Today, in most American jurisdictions and in virtually all European and Commonwealth countries, a felon cannot be executed for a murder that he or she did not commit or specifically intend or attempt to commit. In some American jurisdictions, however, the authority to impose death in such circumstances still persists. Arizona is such a jurisdiction. . . .

The Court has chosen . . . to announce a new substantive standard for capital liability: a defendant's "major participation in the felony committed, combined with reckless indifference to human life, is sufficient to satisfy the Enmund culpability requirement." . . .

I join no part of this. First, the Court's dictum that its new category of mens rea is applicable to these petitioners is not supported by the record. Second, even assuming petitioners may be so categorized, objective evidence and this Court's Eighth Amendment jurisprudence demonstrate that the death penalty is disproportionate punishment for this category of defendants. Finally, the fact that the Court reaches a different conclusion is illustrative of the profound problems that continue to plague capital sentencing.

II

The facts on which the Court relies are not sufficient, in my view, to support the Court's conclusion that petitioners acted with reckless disregard for human life. But even if they were, the Court's decision to restrict its vision to the limited set of facts that "the Arizona Supreme Court has given . . . to us," is improper . . .

The evidence in the record overlooked today regarding petitioners' mental states with respect to the shootings is not trivial. For example, while the Court has found that petitioners made no effort prior to the shooting to assist the victims, the uncontradicted statements of both petitioners are that just prior to the shootings they were attempting to find a jug of water to give to the family. While the Court states that petitioners were on the scene during the shooting and that they watched it occur, Raymond stated that he and Ricky were still engaged in repacking the Mazda after finding the water jug when the shootings occurred. Ricky stated that they had returned with the water, but were still some distance ("farther than this room") from the Lincoln when the shootings started, and that the brothers then turned away from the scene and went back to the Mazda. Neither stated that they anticipated that the shootings would occur, or that they could have done anything to prevent them or to help the victims afterward. Both, however, expressed feelings of surprise, helplessness, and regret. This statement of Raymond's is illustrative:

> Well, I just think you should know when we first came into this we had an agreement with my dad that nobody would get hurt because we [the brothers] wanted no one hurt. And when this [killing of the kidnap victims] came about we were not expecting it. And it took us by surprise as much as it took the family [the victims] by surprise because we were not expecting this to happen. And I feel bad about it happening. I wish we could [have done] something to stop it, but by the time it happened it was too late to stop it. And it's just something we are going to live with the rest of our lives. It will always be there.

III

Notwithstanding the Court's unwarranted observations on the applicability of its new standard to this case, the basic flaw in today's decision is the Court's failure to conduct the sort of proportionality analysis that the Constitution and past cases require. Creation of a new category of culpability is not enough to distinguish this case from *Enmund*. The Court must also establish that death is a proportionate punishment for individuals in this category. In other words, the Court must demonstrate that major participation in a felony with a state of mind of reckless indifference to human life deserves the same punishment as intending to commit a murder or actually committing a murder. The Court does not attempt to conduct a proportionality review of the kind performed in past cases raising a proportionality question, *e.g.*, *Solem v. Helm*, 463 U.S. 277 (1983); *Enmund*; *Coker*, but instead offers two reasons in support of its view.

A. One reason the Court offers for its conclusion that death is proportionate punishment for persons falling within its new category is that limiting the death penalty to those who intend to kill "is a highly unsatisfactory means of definitively distinguishing the most culpable and dangerous of murderers." To illustrate that intention cannot be dispositive, the Court offers as examples "the person who tortures another not caring whether the victim lives or dies, or the robber who shoots someone in the course of the robbery, utterly indifferent to the fact that the desire to rob may have the unintended consequence of killing the victim as well as taking the victim's property." Influential commentators and some States have approved the use of the death penalty for persons, like those given in the Court's examples, *who kill* others in circumstances manifesting an extreme indifference to the value of human life. Thus an exception to the requirement that only intentional murders be punished with death might be made for persons who actually commit an act of homicide; *Enmund*, by distinguishing from the accomplice case "those who kill," clearly reserved that question. But the constitutionality of the death penalty for those individuals is no more relevant to this case than it was to *Enmund*, because this case, like *Enmund*, involves accomplices who did not kill. Thus, although some of the "most culpable and dangerous of murderers" may be those who killed without specifically intending to kill, it is considerably more difficult to apply that rubric convincingly to those who not only did not intend to kill, but who also have not killed.

It is precisely in this context—where the defendant has not killed—that a finding that he or she nevertheless intended to kill seems indispensable to establishing capital culpability. It is important first to note that such a defendant has not committed an act for which he or she could be sentenced to death. The applicability of the death penalty therefore turns entirely on the defendant's mental state with regard to an act committed by another. Factors such as the defendant's major participation in the events surrounding the killing or the defendant's presence at the scene are relevant insofar as they illuminate the defendant's mental state with regard to the killings. They cannot serve, however, as independent grounds for imposing the death penalty.

Second, when evaluating such a defendant's mental state, a determination that the defendant acted with intent is qualitatively different from a determination that the defendant acted with reckless indifference to human life. The difference lies in the nature of the choice each has made. The reckless actor has not *chosen* to bring about the killing in the way the intentional actor has. The person who chooses to act recklessly and is indifferent to the possibility of fatal consequences often deserves serious punishment. But because that person has not *chosen* to kill, his or her moral and criminal culpability is of a different degree than that of one who killed or intended to kill.

The importance of distinguishing between these different choices is rooted in our belief in the "freedom of the human will and a consequent ability and duty of the normal individual to choose between good and evil." *Morissette v. United States*, 342 U.S. 246, 250 (1952). To be faithful to this belief, which is "universal and persistent in mature systems of law," *ibid.*, the criminal law must ensure that the punishment an individual receives conforms to the choices that individual has made. Differential punishment of reckless and intentional actions is therefore essential if we are to retain "the relation between criminal liability and moral cul-

pability" on which criminal justice depends. . . . The State's ultimate sanction—if it is ever to be used—must be reserved for those whose culpability is greatest.
. . .

Distinguishing intentional from reckless action in assessing culpability is particularly important in felony-murder cases. . . . In *Enmund*, the Court explained at length the reasons a finding of intent is a necessary prerequisite to the imposition of the death penalty. In any given case, the Court said, the death penalty must "measurably contribut[e]" to one or both of the two "social purposes"—deterrence and retribution—which this Court has accepted as justifications for the death penalty. . . . If it does not so contribute, it " 'is nothing more than the purposeless and needless imposition of pain and suffering' and hence an unconstitutional punishment." . . . Enmund's lack of intent to commit the murder—rather than the lack of evidence as to his mental state—was the decisive factor in the Court's decision that the death penalty served neither of the two purposes. With regard to deterrence, the Court was

> quite unconvinced . . . that the threat that the death penalty will be imposed for murder will measurably deter one who does not kill and has no intention or purpose that life will be taken. Instead, it seems likely that 'capital punishment can serve as a deterrent only when murder is the result of premeditation and deliberation'. . . .

As for retribution, the Court again found that Enmund's lack of intent, together with the fact that he did not kill the victims, was decisive. "American criminal law has long considered a defendant's intention—and therefore his moral guilt—to be critical to the 'degree of [his] criminal culpability.' " . . . The Court concluded that "[p]utting Enmund to death to avenge two killings that he did not commit and had no intention of committing or causing does not measurably contribute to the retributive end of ensuring that the criminal gets his just deserts." . . . Thus, in *Enmund* the Court established that a finding of an intent to kill was a constitutional prerequisite for the imposition of the death penalty on an accomplice who did not kill. The Court has since reiterated that "*Enmund* . . . imposes a categorical rule: a person who has not in fact killed, attempted to kill, or intended that a killing take place or that lethal force be used may not be sentenced to death." *Cabana v. Bullock*, 474 U.S. [376], at 386 [1986]. The Court's decision today to approve the death penalty for accomplices who lack this mental state is inconsistent with *Enmund* and with the only justifications this Court has put forth for imposing the death penalty in any case.

B. The Court's second reason for abandoning the intent requirement is based on its survey of state statutes authorizing the death penalty for felony murder, and on a handful of state cases. On this basis, the Court concludes that "[o]nly a small minority *of those jurisdictions imposing capital punishment for felony murder* have rejected the possibility of a capital sentence absent an intent to kill, and we do not find this minority position constitutionally required." The Court would thus have us believe that "the majority of American jurisdictions clearly authorize capital punishment" in cases such as this. This is not the case. First, the Court excludes from its survey those jurisdictions that have abolished the death penalty and those that have authorized it only in circumstances different from those presented here. When these jurisdictions are included, and are considered with those jurisdictions that require a finding of intent to kill in order to impose the death sentence for felony murder, one discovers that approximately three-fifths of American jurisdictions do not authorize the death penalty for a non-triggerman absent a finding that he intended to kill. Thus, contrary to the Court's implication that its view is consonant with that of "the majority of American jurisdictions," the Court's view is itself distinctly the minority position.

Second, it is critical to examine not simply those jurisdictions that authorize the death penalty in a given circumstance, but those that actually *impose* it. Evidence that a penalty is imposed only infrequently suggests not only that jurisdictions are reluctant to apply it but also that, when it is applied, its imposition is arbitrary and therefore unconstitutional. *Furman.* Thus, the Court in *Enmund* examined the relevant statistics on the imposition of the death penalty for accomplices in a felony murder. The Court found that of all executions between 1954 and 1982, there were *"only 6 cases out of 362 where a nontriggerman felony murderer was executed. All six executions took place in 1955."* This evidence obviously militates against imposing the death penalty on petitioners as powerfully as it did against imposing it on Enmund.

The Court in *Enmund* also looked at the imposition of the death penalty for felony murder within Florida, the State that had sentenced Enmund. Of the 45 murderers then on death row, 36 had been found to have "intended" to take life, and 8 of the 9 for which there was no finding of intent had been the triggerman. Thus in only one case—*Enmund*—had someone (such as the Tisons) who had neither killed nor intended to kill received the death sentence. Finally, the Court noted that in no Commonwealth or European country could Enmund have been executed, since all have either abolished or never employed a felony-murder doctrine.

The Court today neither reviews nor updates this evidence. Had it done so, it would have discovered that, even including the 65 executions since *Enmund*, "[t]he fact remains that we are not aware of a single person convicted of felony murder over the past quarter century who did not kill or attempt to kill, and did not intend the death of the victim, who has been executed. . . . " Of the 64 persons on death row in Arizona, all of those who have raised and lost an *Enmund* challenge in the Arizona Supreme Court have been found either to have killed or to have specifically intended to kill. Thus, like *Enmund*, the Tisons' sentence appears to be an aberration within Arizona itself as well as nationally and internationally. The Court's objective evidence that the statutes of roughly 20 States appear to authorize the death penalty for defendants in the Court's new category is therefore an inadequate substitute for a proper proportionality analysis, and is not persuasive evidence that the punishment that was unconstitutional for Enmund is constitutional for the Tisons.

C. The Court's failure to examine the full range of relevant evidence is troubling not simply because of what that examination would have revealed, but because until today such an examination has been treated as constitutionally required whenever the Court undertakes to determine whether a given punishment is disproportionate to the severity of a given crime. *Enmund* is only one of a series of cases that have framed the proportionality inquiry in this way. See, *e.g.*, *Coker*. In the most recent such case, *Solem v. Helm*, 463 U.S. 277, 292 (1983), the Court summarized the essence of the inquiry:

> In sum, a court's proportionality analysis under the Eighth Amendment should be guided by objective criteria, including (i) the gravity of the offense and the harshness of the penalty; (ii) the sentences *imposed* on other criminals in the same jurisdiction; and (iii) the sentences *imposed* for commission of the same crime in other jurisdictions (emphasis added).

By addressing at best only the first of these criteria, the Court has ignored most of the guidance this Court has developed for evaluating the proportionality of punishment.

Such guidance is essential in determining the constitutional limits on the State's power to punish. These limits must be defined with care, not simply because the death penalty is involved, but because the social purposes that the Court has said justify the death penalty—retribution and deterrence—are justifications that possess inadequate self-limiting principles. As Professor Packer observed, under a theory of deterrence the state may justify such punishments as "boiling people in oil; a slow and painful death may be thought more of a deterrent to crime than a quick and painless one." Packer, Making the Punishment Fit the Crime, 77 Harv. L. Rev. 1071, 1076 (1964). Retribution, which has as its core logic the crude proportionality of "an eye for an eye," has been regarded as a constitutionally valid basis for punishment only when the punishment is consistent with an "individualized consideration" of the defendant's culpability, *Lockett*, and when "the administration of criminal justice" works to "channe[l]" society's "instinct for retribution." *Furman* (Stewart, J., concurring). Without such channeling, a State could impose a judgment of execution by torture as appropriate retribution for murder by torture. Thus, under a simple theory either of deterrence or retribution, unfettered by the Constitution, results disturbing to civil sensibilities and inconsistent with "the evolving standards of decency" in our society become rationally defensible. . . .

The Framers provided in the Eighth Amendment the limiting principles otherwise absent in the prevailing theories of punishment. One such principle is that the States may not impose punishment that is disproportionate to the severity of the offense or to the individual's own conduct and culpability.

Because the proportionality inquiry in this case overlooked evidence and considerations essential to such an inquiry, it is not surprising that the result appears incongruous. Ricky and Raymond Tison are similarly situated with Earl Enmund in every respect that mattered to the decision in *Enmund*. Like

Enmund, the Tisons neither killed nor attempted or intended to kill anyone. Like Enmund, the Tisons have been sentenced to death for the intentional acts of others which the Tisons did not expect, which were not essential to the felony, and over which they had no control. Unlike Enmund, however, the Tisons will be the first individuals in over 30 years to be executed for such behavior.

I conclude that the proportionality analysis and result in this case cannot be reconciled with the analyses and results of previous cases. On this ground alone, I would dissent. But the fact that this Court's death penalty jurisprudence can validate different results in analytically indistinguishable cases suggests that something more profoundly disturbing than faithlessness to precedent is at work in capital sentencing.

IV

... What makes this a difficult case is the challenge of giving substantive content to the concept of criminal culpability. Our Constitution demands that the sentencing decision itself, and not merely the procedures that produce it, respond to the reasonable goals of punishment. But the decision to execute these petitioners, ... like other decisions to kill, appears responsive less to reason than to other, more visceral, demands. The urge to employ the felony-murder doctrine against accomplices is undoubtedly strong when the killings stir public passion and the actual murderer is beyond human grasp. And an intuition that sons and daughters must sometimes be punished for the sins of the father may be deeply rooted in our consciousness. Yet punishment that conforms more closely to such retributive instincts than to the Eighth Amendment is tragically anachronistic in a society governed by our Constitution. . . .

Chapter 13

Jurors Opposed to Capital Punishment— *Witherspoon v. Illinois* (1968)

Witherspoon v. Illinois, 391 U.S. 510, 88 S. Ct. 1770, 20 L. Ed.2d 776 (1968) (6–3, during the jury selection, a prospective juror may not be removed from the panel "for cause" simply because he voiced general objections to the death penalty or expressed conscientious or religious scruples against its infliction).

Editor's comment: In most states providing capital punishment the jury has the burden of deciding on guilt or innocence and imposing sentence. Jury selection, therefore, becomes even more significant than usual. That selection process is at issue in the *Witherspoon* case. Potential jurors, called a *venire* (pronounced ven-EYE-ree), are drawn from residents in the county of the crime. They are questioned by the prosecutor and defense attorney (or sometimes by the judge) to determine their suitability to serve as jurors. This questioning is called the *voir dire.* A venireman considered unsuitable by either attorney may be challenged or stricken from the venire and excused. These challenges are of two types: for cause or peremptory. Challenges for cause are for disqualifying conditions listed in state law, such as blood relationship to the litigants, or a financial interest in the case. Such challenges are unlimited in number. Peremptory challenges need not be explained,[a] but they are limited in number, for example, 20 for each side.

The issue in *Witherspoon* was whether a state could permit excusal for cause because of scruples about the death penalty. The defendant contended that juries stripped of those with misgivings about the death penalty were biased in two ways. First, they were more likely to find the

---

[a] There are exceptions to the no-explanation rule. Most notably, in *Batson v. Kentucky,* 476 U.S. 79 (1986), the Supreme Court said that the prosecutor must explain peremptory challenges that appear to have been made on the basis of race.

accused guilty. This argument assumes that favorable attitudes toward capital punishment predispose one toward a guilty verdict. Second, Witherspoon argued that such a jury was biased in favor of death as a sentence. The Court agreed with the second claim, but note that it also seemed to suggest that a state could still excuse for cause veniremen who were so opposed to the death penalty that they would be unable to consider it as a sentencing option. The issue was resolved in the *Lockhart* case (Chapter 14). And, of course, the prosecutor may still use peremptories, which need not be explained, to strike scrupled jurors. As for jurors who would *always* impose the death penalty upon conviction, *Morgan v. Illinois*, 504 U.S. 719 (1992), held that the accused has a right to have any potential juror asked whether he holds such a view—and to excuse him for cause if he does.

❖   ❖   ❖

OPINION OF JUSTICE STEWART FOR THE COURT

The petitioner was brought to trial in 1960 in Cook County, Illinois, upon a charge of murder. The jury found him guilty and fixed his penalty at death. At the time of his trial an Illinois statute provided:

> In trials for murder it shall be a cause for challenge of any juror who shall, on being examined, state that he has conscientious scruples against capital punishment, or that he is opposed to the same.

Through this provision the State of Illinois armed the prosecution with unlimited challenges for cause in order to exclude those jurors who, in the words of the State's highest court, "might hesitate to return a verdict inflicting [death]." At the petitioner's trial, the prosecution eliminated nearly half the venire of prospective jurors by challenging, under the authority of this statute, any venireman who expressed qualms about capital punishment. From those who remained were chosen the jurors who ultimately found the petitioner guilty and sentenced him to death. The Supreme Court of Illinois denied post-conviction relief, and we granted certiorari to decide whether the Constitution permits a State to execute a man pursuant to the verdict of a jury so composed.

I

The issue before us is a narrow one. It does not involve the right of the prosecution to challenge for cause those prospective jurors who state that their reservations about capital punishment would prevent them from making an impartial decision as to the defendant's guilt. Nor does it involve the State's assertion of a right to exclude from the jury in a capital case those who say that they could never vote to impose the death penalty or that they would refuse even to consider its imposition in the case before them. For the State of Illinois did not stop there, but authorized the prosecution to exclude as well all who said that they were opposed to capital punishment and all who indicated that they had conscientious scruples against inflicting it.

In the present case the tone was set when the trial judge said early in the voir dire, "Let's get these conscientious objectors out of the way, without wasting any time on them." In rapid succession, 47 veniremen were successfully challenged for cause on the basis of their attitudes toward the death penalty. Only 5 of the 47 explicitly stated that under no circumstances would they vote to impose capital punishment. Six said that they did not "believe in the death penalty" and were excused without any attempt to determine whether they could nonetheless return a verdict of death. Thirty-nine veniremen, including four of the six who indicated that they did not believe in capital punishment, acknowledged having "conscientious or religious scruples against the infliction of the death penalty" or against its infliction "in a proper case" and were excluded without any effort to find out whether their scruples would invariably compel them to vote against capital punishment. . . .

II

The petitioner contends that a State cannot confer upon a jury selected in this matter the power to determine guilt. He maintains that such a jury, unlike one chosen at random from a cross-section of the community, must necessarily be biased in favor of conviction, for the kind of juror who would be unperturbed by the prospect of sending a man to his death, he contends, is the kind of juror who would too readily ignore the presumption of the defendant's innocence, accept the prosecution's version of the facts, and return a verdict of guilt. To support this view, the petitioner refers to what he describes as "competent scientific evidence that death-qualified jurors are partial to the prosecution on the issue of guilt or innocence."[10]

The data adduced by the petitioner, however, are too tentative and fragmentary to establish that jurors not opposed to the death penalty tend to favor

---

[10] In his brief, the petitioner cites two surveys, one involving 187 college students, W. C. Wilson, Belief in Capital Punishment and Jury Performance (Unpublished Manuscript, University of Texas, 1964), and the other involving 200 college students, F. J. Goldberg, Attitude Toward Capital Punishment and Behavior as a Juror in Simulated Capital Cases (Unpublished Manuscript, Morehouse College, undated). In his petition for certiorari, he cited a study based upon interviews with 1,248 jurors in New York and Chicago. A preliminary, unpublished summary of the results of that study stated that "a jury consisting only of jurors who have no scruples against the death penalty is likely to be more prosecution prone than a jury on which objectors to the death penalty sit," and that "the defendant's chances of acquittal are somewhat reduced if the objectors are excluded from the jury." H. Zeisel, Some Insights into the Operation of Criminal Juries 42 (Confidential First Draft, University of Chicago, November 1957).

the prosecution in the determination of guilt. We simply cannot conclude, either on the basis of the record now before us or as a matter of judicial notice, that the exclusion of jurors opposed to capital punishment results in an unrepresentative jury on the issue of guilt or substantially increases the risk of conviction. In light of the presently available information, we are not prepared to announce a *per se* constitutional rule requiring the reversal of every conviction returned by a jury selected as this one was.

III

It does not follow, however, that the petitioner is entitled to no relief. For in this case the jury was entrusted with two distinct responsibilities: first, to determine whether the petitioner was innocent or guilty; and second, if guilty, to determine whether his sentence should be imprisonment or death. It has not been shown that this jury was biased with respect to the petitioner's guilt. But it is self-evident that, in its role as arbiter of the punishment to be imposed, this jury fell woefully short of that impartiality to which the petitioner was entitled under the Sixth and Fourteenth Amendments.

The only justification the State has offered for the jury-selection technique it employed here is that individuals who express serious reservations about capital punishment cannot be relied upon to vote for it even when the laws of the State and the instructions of the trial judge would make death the proper penalty. But in Illinois, as in other States, the jury is given broad discretion to decide whether or not death is "the proper penalty" in a given case, and a juror's general views about capital punishment play an inevitable role in any such decision.

A man who opposes the death penalty, no less than one who favors it, can make the discretionary judgment entrusted to him by the State and can thus obey the oath he takes as a juror. But a jury from which all such men have been excluded cannot perform the task demanded of it. Guided by neither rule nor standard, "free to select or reject as it [sees] fit," a jury that must choose between life imprisonment and capital punishment can do little more—and must do nothing less—than express the conscience of the community on the ultimate question of life or death. Yet, in a nation less than half of whose people believe in the death penalty, a jury composed exclusively of such people cannot speak for the community. Culled of all who harbor doubts about the wisdom of capital punishment—of all who would be reluctant to pronounce the extreme penalty—such a jury can speak only for a distinct and dwindling minority.

If the State had excluded only those prospective jurors who stated in advance of trial that they would not even consider returning a verdict of death, it could argue that the resulting jury was simply "neutral" with respect to penalty. But when it swept from the jury all who expressed conscientious or religious scruples against capital punishment and all who opposed it in principle, the State crossed the line of neutrality. In its quest for a jury capable of imposing the death penalty, the State produced a jury uncommonly willing to condemn a man to die.

It is, of course, settled that a State may not entrust the determination of whether a man is innocent or guilty to a tribunal "organized to convict." It requires but a short step from that principle to hold, as we do today, that a State may not entrust the determination of whether a man should live or die to a tribunal organized to return a verdict of death. Specifically, we hold that a sentence of death cannot be carried out if the jury that imposed or recommended it was chosen by excluding veniremen for cause simply because they voiced general objections to the death penalty or expressed conscientious or religious scruples against its infliction.[21] No defendant can constitutionally be put to death at the hands of a tribunal so selected.

Whatever else might be said of capital punishment, it is at least clear that its imposition by a hanging jury cannot be squared with the Constitution. The State of Illinois has stacked the deck against the petitioner. To execute this death sentence would deprive him of his life without due process of law. Reversed.

DISSENTING OPINION OF JUSTICE BLACK, JOINED BY JUSTICES HARLAN AND WHITE

... As I see the issue in this case, it is a question of plain bias. A person who has conscientious or religious scruples against capital punishment will seldom if ever vote to impose the death penalty. This is just human nature, and no amount of semantic camouflage can cover it up. In the same manner, I would not dream of foisting on a criminal defendant a juror who admitted that he had conscientious or religious scruples against not inflicting the death sentence on any person convicted of murder (a juror who claims, for example, that he adheres literally to the Biblical admonition of "an eye for an eye"). Yet the logical result of the majority's holding is that such persons must be allowed so that the "conscience of the community" will be fully represented when it decides "the ultimate question of

---

[21] Just as veniremen cannot be excluded for cause on the ground that they hold such views, so too they cannot be excluded for cause simply because they indicate that there are some kinds of cases in which they would refuse to recommend capital punishment. And a prospective juror cannot be expected to say in advance of trial whether he would in fact vote for the extreme penalty in the case before him. The most that can be demanded of a venireman in this regard is that he be willing to consider all of the penalties provided by state law, and that he not be irrevocably committed, before the trial has begun, to vote against the penalty of death regardless of the facts and circumstances that might emerge in the course of the proceedings. If the voir dire testimony in a given case indicates that veniremen were excluded on any broader basis than this, the death sentence cannot be carried out even if applicable statutory or case law in the relevant jurisdiction would appear to support only a narrower ground of exclusion.

We repeat, however, that nothing we say today bears upon the power of a State to execute a defendant sentenced to death by a jury from which the only veniremen who were in fact excluded for cause were those who made unmistakably clear (1) that they would automatically vote against the imposition of capital punishment without regard to any evidence that might be developed at the trial of the case before them, or (2) that their attitude toward the death penalty would prevent them from making an impartial decision as to the defendant's guilt. Nor does the decision in this case affect the validity of any sentence other than one of death. Nor, finally, does today's holding render invalid the conviction, as oppose to the sentence, in this or any other case.

life or death." While I have always advocated that the jury be as fully representative of the community as possible, I would never carry this so far as to require
that those biased against one of the critical issues in a trial should be represented
on a jury. . . .

The majority opinion attempts to equate those who have conscientious or
religious scruples against the death penalty with those who do not in such a way
as to balance the allegedly conflicting viewpoints in order that a truly representative jury can be established to exercise the community's discretion in deciding
on punishment. But for this purpose I do not believe that those who have conscientious or religious scruples against the death penalty and those who have no
feelings either way are in any sense comparable. Scruples against the death
penalty are commonly the result of a deep religious conviction or a profound
philosophical commitment developed after much soul-searching. The holders of
such scruples must necessarily recoil from the prospect of making possible what
they regard as immoral. On the other hand, I cannot accept the proposition that
persons who do not have conscientious scruples against the death penalty are
"prosecution prone." With regard to this group, I would agree with the following
statement of the Court of Appeals for the District of Columbia Circuit:

> No proof is available, so far as we know, and we can imagine none, to indicate
> that, generally speaking, persons not opposed to capital punishment are so
> bent in their hostility to criminals as to be incapable of rendering impartial
> verdicts on the law and the evidence in a capital case. Being not opposed to
> capital punishment is not synonymous with favoring it. Individuals may indeed
> be so prejudiced in respect to serious crimes that they cannot be impartial
> arbiters, but that extreme is not indicated by mere lack of opposition to capital
> punishment. The two antipathies can readily coexist; contrariwise either can
> exist without the other; and, indeed, neither may exist in a person. It seems
> clear enough to us that a person or a group of persons may not be opposed to
> capital punishment and at the same time may have no particular bias against
> any one criminal or, indeed, against criminals as a class; people, it seems to us,
> may be completely without a controlling conviction one way or the other on
> either subject. . . . *Turberville v. United States*, 112 U.S. App. D.C. 400, 409–410,
> 303 F.2d 411, 420–421 (1962).

It seems to me that the Court's opinion today must be read as holding just
the opposite from what has been stated above. For no matter how the Court
might try to hide it, the implication is inevitably in its opinion that people who
do not have conscientious scruples against the death penalty are somehow callous
to suffering and are, as some of the commentators cited by the Court called them,
"prosecution prone." This conclusion represents a psychological foray into the
human mind that I have considerable doubt about my ability to make, and I must
confess that the two or three so-called "studies" cited by the Court on this subject
are not persuasive to me.

Finally, I want to point out that the *real* holding in this case is, at least to me,
very ambiguous. If we are to take the opinion literally, then I submit the Court

today has decided nothing of substance, but has merely indulged itself in a semantic exercise. For as I read the opinion, the new requirement placed upon the States is that they cease asking prospective jurors whether they have "conscientious or religious scruples against the infliction of the death penalty," but instead ask whether "they would *automatically* vote against the imposition of capital punishment without regard to any evidence that might be developed at the trial of the case before them." ... I believe that this fine line the Court attempts to draw is based on a semantic illusion and that the practical effect of the Court's new formulation of the question to be asked state juries will not produce a significantly different kind of jury from the one chosen in this case. And I might add that the States will have been put to a great deal of trouble for nothing. Yet, as I stated above, it is not clear that this is all the Court is holding. For the majority opinion goes out of its way to state that in some future case a defendant might well establish that a jury selected in the way the Illinois statute here provides is "less than neutral with respect to *guilt*." ... This seems to me to be but a thinly veiled warning to the States that they had better change their jury selection procedures or face a decision by this Court that their murder convictions have been obtained unconstitutionally....

I shall not contribute in any way to the destruction of our ancient judicial and constitutional concept of trial by an impartial jury by forcing the States through "constitutional doctrine" laid down by this Court to accept jurors who are bound to be biased. For this reason I dissent.

Chapter 14

Selecting the "Death-Qualified" Jury— *Lockhart v. McCree* (1986)

Lockhart v. McCree, 476 U.S. 162, 106 S. Ct. 1758, 90 L. Ed.2d 137 (1986) (6–3, a prospective juror may be excused "for cause" if his opposition to the death penalty would impair his performance in the sentencing phase of a capital case).

Editor's comment: The *Witherspoon* case (Chapter 13) was decided in 1968, well before the Court endorsed, in *Gregg v. Georgia* (1976), bifurcated trials for capital cases. Thus, *Witherspoon* left unanswered the question resolved in *Lockhart v. McCree*: May a potential juror be removed for cause if his opposition to the death penalty would impair his performance in the sentencing phase of a capital case? *Witherspoon* also left uncertain exactly how much opposition to the death penalty was required for a juror to be removed. The process of determining whether or not veniremen were qualified to serve on a capital jury or could be removed ("*Witherspoon* excludables") has come to be known as *death qualification*.

In *Adams v. Texas*, 448 U.S. 38 (1980), the Court held that the mere refusal to take an oath that a "mandatory penalty of death or imprisonment for life will not affect his deliberations" was not a sufficient basis for excusal. But in *Wainwright v. Witt*, 469 U.S. 412 (1985), the Court approved a removal where the juror did not express an unequivocal refusal to impose the death penalty, but voiced enough opposition to leave the impression that his attitude will "prevent or substantially impair the performance of his duties as a juror in accordance with his instructions and his oath."

McCree's twofold constitutional claims were both based on the Sixth Amendment, which states, in part: "In all criminal prosecutions, the accused shall enjoy the right to a speedy and public trial, by an impartial jury of the State and district wherein the crime shall have been committed." First, *McCree* argued that the jury was not drawn from a fair cross-section of the community because a distinctive group—*Witherspoon* excludables—was kept off. Second, he claimed that the jury was not "impartial" because a death-qualified panel is more predisposed to convict.

❖   ❖   ❖

OPINION OF JUSTICE REHNQUIST FOR THE COURT

In this case we address the question left open by our decision nearly 18 years ago in *Witherspoon v. Illinois*: Does the Constitution prohibit the removal for cause, prior to the guilt phase of a bifurcated capital trial, of prospective jurors whose opposition to the death penalty is so strong that it would prevent or substantially impair the performance of their duties as jurors at the sentencing phase of the trial? We hold that it does not. . . .

Before turning to the legal issues in the case, we are constrained to point out what we believe to be several serious flaws in the evidence upon which the courts below reached the conclusion that "death qualification" produces "conviction-prone" juries. McCree introduced into evidence some 15 social science studies in support of his constitutional claims, but only 6 of the studies even purported to measure the potential effects on the guilt-innocence determination of the removal from the jury of "*Witherspoon*-excludables." Eight of the remaining nine studies dealt solely with generalized attitudes and beliefs about the death penalty and other aspects of the criminal justice system, and were thus, at best, only marginally relevant to the constitutionality of McCree's conviction. . . .

Of the six studies introduced by McCree that at least purported to deal with the central issue in this case, namely, the potential effects on the determination of guilt or innocence of excluding "*Witherspoon*-excludables" from the jury, three were also before this Court when it decided *Witherspoon*. . . .

It goes almost without saying that if these studies were "too tentative and fragmentary" to make out a claim of constitutional error in 1968, the same studies, unchanged but for having aged some 18 years, are still insufficient to make out such a claim in this case.

Nor do the three post-*Witherspoon* studies introduced by McCree on the "death qualification" issue provide substantial support for the "*per se* constitutional rule" McCree asks this Court to adopt. All three of the "new" studies were based on the responses of individuals randomly selected from some segment of the population, but who were not actual jurors sworn under oath to apply the law to the facts of an actual case involving the fate of an actual capital defendant. We have serious doubts about the value of these studies in predicting the behavior of actual jurors. In addition, two of the three "new" studies did not even attempt to simulate the process of jury deliberation, and none of the "new" studies was able to predict to what extent, if any, the presence of one or more

"*Witherspoon*-excludables" on a guilt-phase jury would have altered the outcome of the guilt determination.

Finally, and most importantly, only one of the six "death qualification" studies introduced by McCree even attempted to identify and account for the presence of so-called "nullifiers," or individuals who, because of their deep-seated opposition to the death penalty, would be unable to decide a capital defendant's guilt or innocence fairly and impartially. McCree concedes, as he must, that "nullifiers" may properly be excluded from the guilt-phase jury, and studies that fail to take into account the presence of such "nullifiers" thus are fatally flawed. Surely a "*per se* constitutional rule" as far reaching as the one McCree proposes should not be based on the results of the lone study that avoids this fundamental flaw.

Having identified some of the more serious problems with McCree's studies, however, we will assume for purposes of this opinion that the studies are both methodologically valid and adequate to establish that "death qualification" in fact produces juries somewhat more "conviction-prone" than "nondeath-qualified" juries. We hold, nonetheless, that the Constitution does not prohibit the States from "death qualifying" juries in capital cases.

The Eighth Circuit ruled that "death qualification" violated McCree's right under the Sixth Amendment, as applied to the States via incorporation through the Fourteenth Amendment, ... to a jury selected from a representative cross section of the community. But we do not believe that the fair-cross-section requirement can, or should, be applied as broadly as that court attempted to apply it. We have never invoked the fair-cross-section principle to invalidate the use of either for-cause or peremptory challenges to prospective jurors, or to require petit juries, as opposed to jury panels or venires, to reflect the composition of the community at large. ... The limited scope of the fair-cross-section requirement is a direct and inevitable consequence of the practical impossibility of providing each criminal defendant with a truly "representative" petit jury. ... We remain convinced that an extension of the fair-cross-section requirement to petit juries would be unworkable and unsound, and we decline McCree's invitation to adopt such an extension.

But even if we were willing to extend the fair-cross-section requirement to petit juries, we would still reject the Eighth Circuit's conclusion that "death qualification" violates that requirement. The essence of a "fair-cross-section" claim is the systematic exclusion of "a 'distinctive' group in the community." In our view, groups defined solely in terms of shared attitudes that would prevent or substantially impair members of the group from performing one of their duties as jurors, such as the "*Witherspoon*-excludables" at issue here, are not "distinctive groups" for fair-cross-section purposes. ...

Our prior jury-representativeness cases, whether based on the fair-cross-section component of the Sixth Amendment or the Equal Protection Clause of the Fourteenth Amendment, have involved such groups as blacks, ... women, ... and Mexican-Americans. ... Because these groups were excluded for reasons completely unrelated to the ability of members of the group to serve as jurors in a particular case, the exclusion raised at least the possibility that the composition of juries would be arbitrarily skewed in such a way as to deny criminal defendants the benefit of the common-sense judgment of the community. In addition, the exclusion from jury service of large groups of individuals not on the basis of their inability to serve as jurors, but on the basis of some immutable characteristic such as race, gender, or ethnic background, undeniably gave rise to an "appearance of unfairness." Finally, such exclusion improperly deprived members of these often historically disadvantaged groups of their right as citizens to serve on juries in criminal cases.

The group of "*Witherspoon*-excludables" involved in the case at bar differs significantly from the groups we have previously recognized as "distinctive." "Death qualification," unlike the wholesale exclusion of blacks, women, or Mexican-Americans from jury service, is carefully designed to serve the State's concededly legitimate interest in obtaining a single jury that can properly and impartially apply the law to the facts of the case at both the guilt and sentencing phases of a capital trial. There is very little danger, therefore, and McCree does not even argue, that "death qualification" was instituted as a means for the State to arbitrarily skew the composition of capital-case juries.

Furthermore, unlike blacks, women, and Mexican-Americans, "*Witherspoon*-excludables" are singled out for exclusion in capital cases on the basis of an attribute that is within the individual's control. It is important to remember that not all who oppose the death penalty are subject to removal for cause in capital cases; those who firmly believe that the death penalty is unjust may nevertheless serve as jurors in capital cases so long as they state clearly that they are willing to temporarily set aside their own beliefs in deference to the rule of law. Because the group of "*Witherspoon*-excludables" includes only those who cannot and will not conscientiously obey the law with respect to one of the issues in a capital case, "death qualification" hardly can be said to create an "appearance of unfairness."

Finally, the removal for cause of "*Witherspoon*-excludables" in capital cases does not prevent them from serving as jurors in other criminal cases, and thus leads to no substantial deprivation of their basic rights of citizenship. They are treated no differently than any juror who expresses the view that he would be unable to follow the law in a particular case.

In sum, "*Witherspoon*-excludables," or for that matter any other group defined solely in terms of shared attitudes that render members of the group unable to serve as jurors in a particular case, may be excluded from jury service without contravening any of the basic objectives of the fair-cross-section requirement. It is for this reason that we conclude that "*Witherspoon*-excludables" do not constitute a "distinctive group" for fair-cross-section purposes, and hold that "death qualification" does not violate the fair-cross-section requirement.

McCree argues that, even if we reject the Eighth Circuit's fair-cross-section holding, we should affirm the judgment below on the alternative ground, adopted by the District Court, that "death qualification" violated his constitutional right to an impartial jury. . . . McCree does not claim that his conviction was tainted by any of the kinds of jury bias or partiality that we have previously recognized as violative of the Constitution. Instead, McCree argues that his jury lacked impartiality because the absence of *"Witherspoon*-excludables" "slanted" the jury in favor of conviction.

We do not agree. McCree's "impartiality" argument apparently is based on the theory that, because all individual jurors are to some extent predisposed towards one result or another, a constitutionally impartial *jury* can be constructed only by "balancing" the various predispositions of the individual *jurors*. Thus, according to McCree, when the State "tips the scales" by excluding prospective jurors with a particular viewpoint, an impermissibly partial jury results. We have consistently rejected this view of jury impartiality, including as recently as last Term when we squarely held that an impartial *jury* consists of nothing more than *"jurors* who will conscientiously apply the law and find the facts." *Wainwright v. Witt,* 469 U.S. 412, 423 (1985). . . .

The view of jury impartiality urged upon us by McCree is both illogical and hopelessly impractical. McCree characterizes the jury that convicted him as "slanted" by the process of "death qualification." But McCree admits that exactly the same 12 individuals could have ended up on his jury through the "luck of the draw," without in any way violating the constitutional guarantee of impartiality. Even accepting McCree's position that we should focus on the *jury* rather than the individual *jurors*, it is hard for us to understand the logic of the argument that a given jury is unconstitutionally partial when it results from a state-ordained process, yet impartial when exactly the same jury results from mere chance. On a more practical level, if it were true that the Constitution required a certain mix of individual viewpoints on the jury, then trial judges would be required to undertake the Sisyphean task of "balancing" juries, making sure that each contains the proper number of Democrats and Republicans, young persons and old persons, white-collar executives and blue-collar laborers, and so on. Adopting McCree's concept of jury impartiality would also likely require the elimination of peremptory challenges, which are commonly used by both the State and the defendant to attempt to produce a jury favorable to the challenger.

McCree argues, however, that this Court's decisions in *Witherspoon* and *Adams v. Texas,* 448 U.S. 38 (1980), stand for the proposition that a State violates the Constitution whenever it "slants" the jury by excluding a group of individuals more likely than the population at large to favor the criminal defendant. We think McCree overlooks two fundamental differences between *Witherspoon* and *Adams* and the instant case, and therefore misconceives the import and scope of those two decisions.

First, the Court in *Witherspoon* viewed the Illinois system as having been deliberately slanted for the purpose of making the imposition of the death penalty more likely. . . .

Here, on the other hand, the removal for cause of *"Witherspoon*-excludables" serves the State's entirely proper interest in obtaining a single jury that could impartially decide all of the issues in McCree's case. Arkansas by legislative enactment and judicial decision provides for the use of a unitary jury in capital cases. We have upheld against constitutional attack the Georgia capital sentencing plan which provided that the same jury must sit in both phases of a bifurcated capital murder trial, *Gregg v. Georgia.* . . .

Unlike the Illinois system criticized by the Court in *Witherspoon*, and the Texas system at issue in *Adams*, the Arkansas system excludes from the jury only those who may properly be excluded from the penalty phase of the deliberations under *Witherspoon, Adams* and *Wainwright v. Witt*, 469 U.S. 412 (1985). That State's reasons for adhering to its preference for a single jury to decide both the guilt and penalty phases of a capital trial are sufficient to negate the inference which the Court drew in *Witherspoon* concerning the lack of any neutral justification for the Illinois rule on jury challenges.

Second, and more importantly, both *Witherspoon* and *Adams* dealt with the special context of capital sentencing, where the range of jury discretion necessarily gave rise to far greater concern over the possible effects of an "imbalanced" jury. . . . Because capital sentencing under the Illinois statute involved such an exercise of essentially unfettered discretion, we held that the State violated the Constitution when it "crossed the line of neutrality" and "produced a jury uncommonly willing to condemn a man to die." . . .

In the case at bar, by contrast, we deal not with capital sentencing, but with the jury's more traditional role of finding the facts and determining the guilt or innocence of a criminal defendant, where jury discretion is more channeled.

We reject McCree's suggestion that *Witherspoon* and *Adams* have broad applicability outside the special context of capital sentencing, and conclude that those two decisions do not support the result reached by the Eighth Circuit here.

In our view, it is simply not possible to define jury impartiality, for constitutional purposes, by reference to some hypothetical mix of individual viewpoints. Prospective jurors come from many different backgrounds, and have many different attitudes and predispositions. But the Constitution presupposes that a jury selected from a fair cross section of the community is impartial, regardless of the mix of individual viewpoints actually represented on the jury, so long as the jurors can conscientiously and properly carry out their sworn duty to apply the law to the facts of the particular case. We hold that McCree's jury satisfied both aspects of this constitutional standard. The judgment of the Court of Appeals is therefore reversed.

DISSENTING OPINION OF JUSTICE MARSHALL, JOINED BY JUSTICES BRENNAN AND STEVENS

. . . Respondent contends here that the "death-qualified" jury that convicted him, from which the State, as authorized by *Witherspoon*, had excluded all venirepersons unwilling to consider imposing the death penalty, was in effect "organized to return a verdict" of guilty. In support of this claim, he has presented overwhelming evidence that death-qualified juries are substantially more likely to

Chapter 15

Selecting an Unbiased Jury—
Turner v. Murray (1986)

Turner v. Murray, 476 U.S. 28, 106 S. Ct. 1683, 90 L. Ed.2d 27 (1986) (7–2, defendant in an interracial murder case has a right to question prospective jurors about racial prejudice).

Editor's comment: Another voir dire issue is raised by this case: Is the judge required (by the Impartial Jury Clause of the Sixth Amendment) to permit questions to determine if veniremen harbor racial prejudice simply because the murder was interracial? Previous Supreme Court cases gave mixed signals. *Ham v. South Carolina*, 409 U.S. 524 (1973), established a right to inquire about prejudice where the facts of the case suggested that bias might be a problem. (Ham was a civil rights activist who claimed that marijuana possession charges against him were a frame-up.) But *Ristaino v. Ross*, 424 U.S. 589 (1976), which, significantly, was not a death penalty case, held that there was no constitutional right to ask bias questions whenever the defendant and victim were of different races. *Rosales-Lopez v. United States*, 451 U.S. 182 (1981) was contrary to *Ristaino*, but the right (to ask about anti-Mexican bias) was based on the Supreme Court's authority to supervise lower federal courts, and did not apply to state courts. *Turner*, reprinted here, creates an exception to *Ristaino*, illustrating the Supreme Court's preference for special trial procedures in capital cases.

❖ ❖ ❖

OPINION OF JUSTICE WHITE FOR THE COURT

Because of the range of discretion entrusted to a jury in a capital sentencing hearing, there is a unique opportunity for racial prejudice to operate but remain undetected. On the facts of this case, a juror who believes that blacks are vio-

lence prone or morally inferior might well be influenced by that belief in deciding whether petitioner's crime involved the aggravating factors specified under
Virginia law. Such a juror might also be less favorably inclined toward petitioner's
evidence of mental disturbance as a mitigating circumstance. More subtle, less
consciously held racial attitudes could also influence a juror's decision in this case.
Fear of blacks, which could easily be stirred up by the violent facts of petitioner's
crime, might incline a juror to favor the death penalty.

The risk of racial prejudice infecting a capital sentencing proceeding is especially serious in light of the complete finality of the death sentence. "The Court,
as well as the separate opinions of a majority of the individual Justices, has recognized that the qualitative difference of death from all other punishments
requires a correspondingly greater degree of scrutiny of the capital sentencing
determination." . . . We have struck down capital sentences when we found that
the circumstances under which they were imposed "created an unacceptable risk
that 'the death penalty [may have been] meted out arbitrarily or capriciously' or
through 'whim . . . or mistake.' " . . . In the present case, we find the risk that racial
prejudice may have infected petitioner's capital sentencing unacceptable in light
of the ease with which that risk could have been minimized. By refusing to question prospective jurors on racial prejudice, the trial judge failed to adequately
protect petitioner's constitutional right to an impartial jury. . . .

III

We hold that a capital defendant accused of an interracial crime is entitled to
have prospective jurors informed of the race of the victim and questioned on the
issue of racial bias. The rule we propose is minimally intrusive; as in other cases
involving "special circumstances," the trial judge retains discretion as to the form
and number of questions on the subject, including the decision whether to question the venire individually or collectively. . . . Also, a defendant cannot complain
of a judge's failure to question the venire on racial prejudice unless the defendant has specifically requested such an inquiry.

IV

The inadequacy of voir dire in this case requires that petitioner's death sentence
be vacated. It is not necessary, however, that he be retried on the issue of guilt.
Our judgment in this case is that there was an unacceptable risk of racial prejudice infecting the capital sentencing proceeding. This judgment is based on a con-
junction of three factors: the fact that the crime charged involved interracial
violence, the broad discretion given the jury at the death-penalty hearing, and
the special seriousness of the risk of improper sentencing in a capital case. At the
guilt phase of petitioner's trial, the jury had no greater discretion than it would
have had if the crime charged had been noncapital murder. Thus, with respect to

the guilt phase of petitioner's trial, we find this case to be indistinguishable from *Ristaino*, to which we continue to adhere.

DISSENTING OPINION OF JUSTICE POWELL, JOINED BY JUSTICE REHNQUIST

... In effect, the Court recognizes a presumption that jurors who have sworn to decide the case impartially nevertheless are racially biased. Such a presumption is flatly contrary to our decisions in *Ristaino v. Ross* [424 U.S. 589 (1976)] and *Rosales-Lopez v. United States*, 451 U.S. 182, 190 (1981).[2] The facts of this case demonstrate why it is unnecessary and unwise for this Court to rule, as a matter of constitutional law, that a trial judge always must inquire into racial bias in a capital case involving an interracial murder, rather than leaving that decision to be made on a case-by-case basis. Before today the facts that a defendant is black and his victim was white were insufficient to raise "a constitutionally significant likelihood that, absent questioning about racial prejudice," an impartial jury would not be seated. *Ristaino v. Ross, supra*, at 596.

I

Nothing in this record suggests that racial bias played any role in the jurors' deliberations. The relevant circumstances merit emphasis because they demonstrate that the fact of an interracial murder, by itself, does not create a substantial likelihood that racial issues can be expected to distort capital sentencing trials. Without further evidence that race can be expected to be a factor in such trials, there is no justification for departing from the rule of *Ham* and *Ristaino*.

Petitioner committed murder in the course of an armed robbery of a jewelry store in Franklin, Virginia. The murder was brutal. Petitioner shot the store's proprietor three times. The first shot did not kill, but caused the victim to fall helplessly to the floor, bleeding from a scalp wound. A police officer, who had arrived in answer to a silent alarm, pleaded with petitioner not to shoot again. But petitioner fired two more shots into his victim's chest, causing his death. The officer then managed to subdue and arrest petitioner. At trial, the evidence of peti-

---

[2] "Although *Ristaino* involved an alleged criminal confrontation between a black assailant and a white victim, that fact pattern alone did not create a need of 'constitutional dimensions' to question the jury concerning racial prejudice.... There is no constitutional presumption of juror bias for or against members of any particular racial or ethnic groups. As *Ristaino* demonstrates, there is no *per se* constitutional rule in such circumstances requiring inquiry as to racial prejudice. Only when there are more substantial indications of the likelihood of racial or ethnic prejudice affecting the jurors in a particular case does the trial court's denial of a defendant's request to examine the jurors' ability to deal impartially with this subject amount to an unconstitutional abuse of discretion." *Rosales-Lopez v. United States*, 451 U.S., at 190 (plurality opinion). Although Justice White's opinion in *Rosales-Lopez* was for a plurality, Justice Rehnquist's opinion concurring in the result was entirely consistent with the foregoing language.

tioner's guilt was conclusive. Because the local media gave the murder extensive publicity, petitioner requested and was granted a change of venue from Southampton County to Northampton County, across the Chesapeake Bay some 80 miles away from the location of the murder. No member of the jury empaneled had read or heard about the murder.

Virginia law vests the trial judge with the responsibility to conduct voir dire examination of prospective jurors. Ordinarily, the judge, rather than counsel, questions members of the venire to provide a basis for the exercise of challenges. In this case, in accordance with state practice, the judge permitted the parties to propose questions to be asked during voir dire. Counsel for petitioner submitted 15 questions. As the 10th question on his list, counsel requested the following:

> "The defendant, Willie Lloyd Turner, is a member of the Negro race. The
> victim, W. Jack Smith, Jr., was a white Caucasian. Will those facts prejudice you
> against Willie Lloyd Turner or affect your ability to render a fair and impartial
> verdict based solely on the evidence?"

As support for this proposed question, petitioner's counsel referred only to certain studies that were subsequently placed in the record. The studies purported to show that a black defendant who murders a white person is more likely to receive the death penalty than other capital defendants, but the studies included no statistics concerning administration of the death penalty in Virginia. Counsel then discussed their proposed questions with the judge. The prosecutor pointed out that the case presented no racial issues beyond the fact that petitioner and his victim were of different races.

The trial judge declined to ask the proposed question, but he did ask general questions designed to uncover bias. For example, the prospective jurors were asked, "Do any of you know any reason whatsoever why you cannot render a fair and impartial verdict in this case, either for the defendant or for the Commonwealth of Virginia?" Each juror responded negatively. The jury of 12 persons ultimately empaneled included 4 black citizens, and a black juror was selected to act as foreman.

There is nothing in the record of this trial that reflects racial overtones of any kind. From voir dire through the close of trial, no circumstance suggests that the trial judge's refusal to inquire particularly into racial bias posed "an impermissible threat to the fair trial guaranteed by due process." *Ristaino v. Ross*, 424 U.S., at 595. The Court does not purport to identify any such circumstance, or to explain why the facts that a capital defendant is of one race and his victim of another now create a significant likelihood that racial issues will distort the jurors' consideration of the issues in the trial. *Id.*, at 597. This case illustrates that it is unnecessary for the Court to adopt a *per se* rule that constitutionalizes the unjustifiable presumption that jurors are racially biased.

Chapter 16

Victim Impact Evidence—
Payne v. Tennessee (1991)

Payne v. Tennessee, 501 U.S. 808, 111 S. Ct. 2597, 115 L. Ed.2d 720 (1991) (6–3, the Eighth Amendment does not prohibit victim impact evidence at a capital sentencing procedure).

Editor's comment: In noncapital cases most states permit the sentencing judge to take into consideration statements of the victims of the crime. The question is whether, in a capital case, the sentencing jury or judge may be permitted to hear evidence of the impact of a murder on the victim's survivors. At first, the Supreme Court, in *Booth v. Maryland*, 482 U.S. 496 (1987), held, 5–4, that the introduction of a victim impact statement at the sentencing phase of a capital murder trial violated the Eighth Amendment. Likewise, *South Carolina v. Gathers*, 490 U.S. 805 (1989), prohibited statements made by a prosecutor to the capital sentencing jury regarding the personal qualities of the victim. Both of these decisions were overruled by *Payne*. An issue not resolved by *Payne* is the admissibility of testimony by family members characterizing the crime and the defendant, and recommending a sentence. For example, there were statements by the deceased's son in *Booth* that his parents were "butchered like animals" and that he "doesn't think anyone should be able to do something like that and get away with it." *Booth* had barred such evidence.

❖ ❖ ❖

OPINION OF CHIEF JUSTICE REHNQUIST FOR THE COURT

In this case we reconsider our holdings in *Booth v. Maryland*, 482 U.S. 496 (1987), and *South Carolina v. Gathers*, 490 U.S. 805 (1989), that the Eighth Amendment bars the admission of victim impact evidence during the penalty phase of a capital trial.

Petitioner, Pervis Tyrone Payne, was convicted by a jury on two counts of first-degree murder and one count of assault with intent to commit murder in the first degree. He was sentenced to death for each of the murders and to 30 years in prison for the assault.

The victims of Payne's offenses were 28-year-old Charisse Christopher, her 2-year-old daughter Lacie, and her 3-year-old son Nicholas. The three lived together in an apartment in Millington, Tennessee, across the hall from Payne's girlfriend, Bobbie Thomas. . . .

During the sentencing phase of the trial, Payne presented the testimony of four witnesses: his mother and father, Bobbie Thomas, and Dr. John T. Hutson, a clinical psychologist specializing in criminal court evaluation work. Bobbie Thomas testified that she met Payne at church, during a time when she was being abused by her husband. She stated that Payne was a very caring person, and that he devoted much time and attention to her three children, who were being affected by her marital difficulties. She said that the children had come to love him very much and would miss him, and that he "behaved just like a father that loved his kids." She asserted that he did not drink, nor did he use drugs, and that it was generally inconsistent with Payne's character to have committed these crimes.

Dr. Hutson testified that based on Payne's low score on an IQ test, Payne was "mentally handicapped." Hutson also said that Payne was neither psychotic nor schizophrenic, and that Payne was the most polite prisoner he had ever met. Payne's parents testified that their son had no prior criminal record and had never been arrested. They also stated that Payne had no history of alcohol or drug abuse, he worked with his father as a painter, he was good with children, and he was a good son.

The State presented the testimony of Charisse's mother, Mary Zvolanek. When asked how Nicholas had been affected by the murders of his mother and sister, she responded:

> He cries for his mom. He doesn't seem to understand why she doesn't come home. And he cries for his sister Lacie. He comes to me many times during the week and asks me, Grandmama, do you miss my Lacie. And I tell him yes. He says, I'm worried about my Lacie.

In arguing for the death penalty during closing argument, the prosecutor commented on the continuing effects of Nicholas' experience, stating:

> But we do know that Nicholas was alive. And Nicholas was in the same room. Nicholas was still conscious. His eyes were open. He responded to the paramedics. He was able to follow their directions. He was able to hold his intestines in as he was carried to the ambulance. So he knew what happened to his mother and baby sister.
>
> There is nothing you can do to ease the pain of any of the families involved in this case. There is nothing you can do to ease the pain of Bernice or Carl

Payne, and that's a tragedy. There is nothing you can do basically to ease the pain of Mr. and Mrs. Zvolanek, and that's a tragedy. They will have to live with it the rest of their lives. There is obviously nothing you can do for Charisse and Lacie Jo. But there is something that you can do for Nicholas.

Somewhere down the road Nicholas is going to grow up, hopefully. He's going to want to know what happened. And he is going to know what happened to his baby sister and his mother. He is going to want to know what type of justice was done. He is going to want to know what happened. With your verdict, you will provide the answer.

. . .

In the rebuttal to Payne's closing argument, the prosecutor stated:

You saw the videotape this morning. You saw what Nicholas Christopher will carry in his mind forever. When you talk about cruel, when you talk about atrocious, and when you talk about heinous, that picture will always come into your mind, probably throughout the rest of your lives. . . .

No one will ever know about Lacie Jo because she never had the chance to grow up. Her life was taken from her at the age of two years old. So, no there won't be a high school principal to talk about Lacie Jo Christopher, and there won't be anybody to take her to her high school prom. And there won't be anybody there—there won't be her mother there or Nicholas' mother there to kiss him at night. His mother will never kiss him good night or pat him as he goes off to bed, or hold him and sing him a lullaby.

[Petitioner's attorney] wants you to think about a good reputation, people who love the defendant and things about him. He doesn't want you to think about the people who love Charisse Christopher, her mother and daddy who loved her. The people who loved little Lacie Jo, the grandparents who are still here. The brother who mourns for her every single day and wants to know where his best little playmate is. He doesn't have anybody to watch cartoons with him, a little one. These are the things that go into why it is especially cruel, heinous, and atrocious, the burden that that child will carry forever.

The jury sentenced Payne to death on each of the murder counts.

The Supreme Court of Tennessee affirmed the conviction and sentence. The court rejected Payne's contention that the admission of the grandmother's testimony and the State's closing argument constituted prejudicial violations of his rights under the Eighth Amendment as applied in *Booth v. Maryland* and *South Carolina v. Gathers.* The court characterized the grandmother's testimony as "technically irrelevant," but concluded that it "did not create a constitutionally unacceptable risk of an arbitrary imposition of the death penalty and was harmless beyond a reasonable doubt."

The court determined that the prosecutor's comments during closing argument were "relevant to [Payne's] personal responsibility and moral guilt." The court explained that "[w]hen a person deliberately picks a butcher knife out of a kitchen drawer and proceeds to stab to death a 28-year-old mother, her $2\frac{1}{2}$-year-old daughter and her $3\frac{1}{2}$-year-old son, in the same room, the physical and mental condition of the boy he left for dead is surely relevant in determining his 'blame-worthiness.' " The court concluded that any violation of Payne's rights under *Booth* and *Gathers* "was harmless beyond a reasonable doubt."

We granted certiorari to reconsider our holdings in *Booth* and *Gathers* that the Eighth Amendment prohibits a capital sentencing jury from considering "victim impact" evidence relating to the personal characteristics of the victim and the emotional impact of the crimes on the victim's family.

In *Booth*, the defendant robbed and murdered an elderly couple. As required by a state statute, a victim impact statement was prepared based on interviews with the victims' son, daughter, son-in-law, and granddaughter. The statement, which described the personal characteristics of the victims, the emotional impact of the crimes on the family, and set forth the family members' opinions and characterizations of the crimes and the defendant, was submitted to the jury at sentencing. The jury imposed the death penalty. The conviction and sentence were affirmed on appeal by the State's highest court.

This Court held by a 5-to-4 vote that the Eighth Amendment prohibits a jury from considering a victim impact statement at the sentencing phase of a capital trial. The Court made clear that the admissibility of victim impact evidence was not to be determined on a case-by-case basis, but that such evidence was *per se* inadmissible in the sentencing phase of a capital case except to the extent that it "relate[d] directly to the circumstances of the crime." In *Gathers*, decided two years later, the Court extended the rule announced in *Booth* to statements made by a prosecutor to the sentencing jury regarding the personal qualities of the victim.

The *Booth* Court began its analysis with the observation that the capital defendant must be treated as a "uniquely individual human bein[g]," and therefore the Constitution requires the jury to make an individualized determination as to whether the defendant should be executed based on the "character of the individual and the circumstances of the crime." The Court concluded that while no prior decision of this Court had mandated that only the defendant's character and immediate characteristics of the crime may constitutionally be considered, other factors are irrelevant to the capital sentencing decision unless they have "some bearing on the defendant's 'personal responsibility and moral guilt.' " To the extent that victim impact evidence presents "factors about which the defendant was unaware, and that were irrelevant to the decision to kill," the Court concluded, it has nothing to do with the "blameworthiness of a particular defendant." Evidence of the victim's character, the Court observed, "could well distract the sentencing jury from its constitutionally required task [of] determining whether the death penalty is appropriate in light of the background and record of the accused and the particular circumstances of the crime." The Court concluded that, except to the extent that victim impact evidence relates "directly to the circumstances of the crime," the prosecution may not introduce such evidence at a capital sentencing hearing because "it creates an impermissible risk that the capital sentencing decision will be made in an arbitrary manner."

Booth and *Gathers* were based on two premises: that evidence relating to a particular victim or to the harm that a capital defendant causes a victim's family do not in general reflect on the defendant's "blameworthiness," and that only evidence relating to "blameworthiness" is relevant to the capital sentencing decision. However, the assessment of harm caused by the defendant as a result of the crime charged has understandably been an important concern of the criminal law, both in determining the elements of the offense and in determining the appropriate punishment. Thus, two equally blameworthy criminal defendants may be guilty of different offenses solely because their acts cause differing amounts of harm. "If a bank robber aims his gun at a guard, pulls the trigger, and kills his target, he may be put to death. If the gun unexpectedly misfires, he may not. His moral guilt in both cases is identical, but his responsibility in the former is greater." *Booth*, 482 U.S., at 519 (Scalia, J., dissenting). The same is true with respect to two defendants, each of whom participates in a robbery, and each of whom acts with reckless disregard for human life; if the robbery in which the first defendant participated results in the death of a victim, he may be subjected to the death penalty, but if the robbery in which the second defendant participates does not result in the death of a victim, the death penalty may not be imposed. *Tison v. Arizona.*

The principles which have guided criminal sentencing—as opposed to criminal liability—have varied with the times. The book of Exodus prescribes the Lex talionis, "An eye for an eye, a tooth for a tooth." Exodus 21:22–23. In England and on the continent of Europe, as recently as the 18th century, crimes which would be regarded as quite minor today were capital offenses. Writing in the 18th century, the Italian criminologist Cesare Beccaria advocated the idea that "the punishment should fit the crime." He said that "[w]e have seen that the true measure of crimes is the injury done to society."

Gradually the list of crimes punishable by death diminished, and legislatures began grading the severity of crimes in accordance with the harm done by the criminal. The sentence for a given offense, rather than being precisely fixed by the legislature, was prescribed in terms of a minimum and a maximum, with the actual sentence to be decided by the judge. With the increasing importance of probation, as opposed to imprisonment, as a part of the penological process, some States such as California developed the "indeterminate sentence," where the time of incarceration was left almost entirely to the penological authorities rather than to the courts. But more recently the pendulum has swung back. The Federal Sentencing Guidelines, which went into effect in 1987, provided for very precise calibration of sentences, depending upon a number of factors. These factors relate both to the subjective guilt of the defendant and to the harm caused by his acts.

Wherever judges in recent years have had discretion to impose sentence, the consideration of the harm caused by the crime has been an important factor in the exercise of that discretion:

The first significance of harm in Anglo-American jurisprudence is, then, as a prerequisite to the criminal sanction. The second significance of harm—one no less important to judges—is as a measure of the seriousness of the offense and therefore as a standard for determining the severity of the sentence that will be meted out. S. Wheeler, K. Mann, and A. Sarat, Sitting in Judgment: The Sentencing of White-Collar Criminals 56 (1988).

Whatever the prevailing sentencing philosophy, the sentencing authority has always been free to consider a wide range of relevant material. In the federal system, we observed that "a judge may appropriately conduct an inquiry broad in scope, largely unlimited either as to the kind of information he may consider, or the source from which it may come." Even in the context of capital sentencing, prior to *Booth* the joint opinion of Justices Stewart, Powell, and Stevens in *Gregg v. Georgia* had rejected petitioner's attack on the Georgia statute because of the "wide scope of evidence and argument allowed at presentence hearings." The joint opinion stated:

> We think that the Georgia court wisely has chosen not to impose unnecessary restrictions on the evidence that can be offered at such a hearing and to approve open and far-ranging argument. . . . So long as the evidence introduced and the arguments made at the presentence hearing do not prejudice a defendant, it is preferable not to impose restrictions. We think it desirable for the jury to have as much information before it as possible when it makes the sentencing decision.

The Maryland statute involved in *Booth* required that the presentence report in all felony cases include a "victim impact statement" which would describe the effect of the crime on the victim and his family. Congress and most of the States have, in recent years, enacted similar legislation to enable the sentencing authority to consider information about the harm caused by the crime committed by the defendant. The evidence involved in the present case was not admitted pursuant to any such enactment, but its purpose and effect were much the same as if it had been. While the admission of this particular kind of evidence—designed to portray for the sentencing authority the actual harm caused by a particular crime—is of recent origin, this fact hardly renders it unconstitutional. . . .

We have held that a State cannot preclude the sentencer from considering "any relevant mitigating evidence" that the defendant proffers in support of a sentence less than death. *Eddings v. Oklahoma.*[a] Thus we have, as the Court observed in *Booth*, required that the capital defendant be treated as a "uniquely individual human bein[g]." But it was never held or even suggested in any of our cases preceding *Booth* that the defendant, entitled as he was to individualized consideration, was to receive that consideration wholly apart from the crime which he had committed. The language quoted from *Woodson* in the *Booth* opinion was not intended to describe a class of evidence that *could not* be

---

[a] Editor's note: In *Eddings v. Oklahoma*, 455 U.S. 104 (1982), the Court held that there was a right to present as mitigating evidence proof of a capital defendant's emotional disturbance.

received, but a class of evidence which *must* be received. Any doubt on the matter is dispelled by comparing the language in *Woodson* with the language from *Gregg v. Georgia*, quoted above, which was handed down the same day as *Woodson*. This misreading of precedent in *Booth* has, we think, unfairly weighted the scales in a capital trial; while virtually no limits are placed on the relevant mitigating evidence a capital defendant may introduce concerning his own circumstances, the State is barred from either offering "a quick glimpse of the life" which a defendant "chose to extinguish," *Mills v. Maryland*, 486 U.S., 367, [397] (1988) (Rehnquist, C. J., dissenting), or demonstrating the loss to the victim's family and to society which has resulted from the defendant's homicide.

The *Booth* Court reasoned that victim impact evidence must be excluded because it would be difficult, if not impossible, for the defendant to rebut such evidence without shifting the focus of the sentencing hearing away from the defendant, thus creating a "'mini-trial' on the victim's character." In many cases the evidence relating to the victim is already before the jury at least in part because of its relevance at the guilt phase of the trial. But even as to additional evidence admitted at the sentencing phase, the mere fact that for tactical reasons it might not be prudent for the defense to rebut victim impact evidence makes the case no different than others in which a party is faced with this sort of a dilemma. As we explained in rejecting the contention that expert testimony on future dangerousness should be excluded from capital trials, "the rules of evidence generally extant at the federal and state levels anticipate that relevant, unprivileged evidence should be admitted and its weight left to the factfinder, who would have the benefit of cross-examination and contrary evidence by the opposing party."

Payne echoes the concern voiced in Booth's case that the admission of victim impact evidence permits a jury to find that defendants whose victims were assets to their community are more deserving of punishment than those whose victims are perceived to be less worthy. As a general matter, however, victim impact evidence is not offered to encourage comparative judgments of this kind—for instance, that the killer of a hardworking, devoted parent deserves the death penalty, but that the murderer of a reprobate does not. It is designed to show instead each victim's "uniqueness as an individual human being," whatever the jury might think the loss to the community resulting from his death might be. The facts of Gathers are an excellent illustration of this: The evidence showed that the victim was an out of work, mentally handicapped individual, perhaps not, in the eyes of most, a significant contributor to society, but nonetheless a murdered human being.

Under our constitutional system, the primary responsibility for defining crimes against state law, fixing punishments for the commission of these crimes, and establishing procedures for criminal trials rests with the States. The state laws respecting crimes, punishments, and criminal procedure are, of course, subject to the overriding provisions of the United States Constitution. Where the State imposes the death penalty for a particular crime, we have held that the Eighth Amendment imposes special limitations upon that process. . . .

"Within the constitutional limitations defined by our cases, the States enjoy their traditional latitude to prescribe the method by which those who commit murder shall be punished." *Blystone v. Pennsylvania.* The States remain free, in capital cases, as well as others, to devise new procedures and new remedies to meet felt needs. Victim impact evidence is simply another form or method of informing the sentencing authority about the specific harm caused by the crime in question, evidence of a general type long considered by sentencing authorities. We think the *Booth* Court was wrong in stating that this kind of evidence leads to the arbitrary imposition of the death penalty. In the majority of cases, and in this case, victim impact evidence serves entirely legitimate purposes. In the event that evidence is introduced that is so unduly prejudicial that it renders the trial fundamentally unfair, the Due Process Clause of the Fourteenth Amendment provides a mechanism for relief. Courts have always taken into consideration the harm done by the defendant in imposing sentence, and the evidence adduced in this case was illustrative of the harm caused by Payne's double murder.

We are now of the view that a State may properly conclude that for the jury to assess meaningfully the defendant's moral culpability and blameworthiness, it should have before it at the sentencing phase evidence of the specific harm caused by the defendant. "[T]he State has a legitimate interest in counteracting the mitigating evidence which the defendant is entitled to put in, by reminding the sentences that just as the murderer should be considered as an individual, so too the victim is an individual whose death represents a unique loss to society and in particular to his family." *Booth*, 482 U.S., at 517 (White, J., dissenting). By turning the victim into a "faceless stranger at the penalty phase of a capital trial," *Gathers*, 490 U.S., at 821 (O'Connor, J., dissenting), *Booth* deprives the State of the full moral force of its evidence and may prevent the jury from having before it all the information necessary to determine the proper punishment for a first-degree murder.

The present case is an example of the potential for such unfairness. The capital sentencing jury heard testimony from Payne's girlfriend that they met at church; that he was affectionate, caring, and kind to her children; that he was not an abuser of drugs or alcohol; and that it was inconsistent with his character to have committed the murders. Payne's parents testified that he was a good son, and a clinical psychologist testified that Payne was an extremely polite prisoner and suffered from a low IQ. None of this testimony was related to the circumstances of Payne's brutal crimes. In contrast, the only evidence of the impact of Payne's offenses during the sentencing phase was Nicholas' grandmother's description—in response to a single question—that the child misses his mother and baby sister. Payne argues that the Eighth Amendment commands that the jury's death sentence must be set aside because the jury heard this testimony. But the testimony illustrated quite poignantly some of the harm that Payne's killing had caused; there is nothing unfair about allowing the jury to bear in mind that harm at the same time as it considers the mitigating evidence introduced by the defendant. The Supreme Court of Tennessee in this case obviously felt the unfairness of the rule pronounced by *Booth* when it said: "It is an affront to the civilized members of the human race to say that at sentencing in a capital case, a parade of witnesses may praise the background, character and good deeds of Defendant (as was done in this case), without limitation as to relevancy, but nothing may be said that bears upon the character of, or the harm imposed, upon the victims."

In *Gathers*, as indicated above, we extended the holding of *Booth* barring victim impact evidence to the prosecutor's argument to the jury. Human nature being what it is, capable lawyers trying cases to juries try to convey to the jurors that the people involved in the underlying events are, or were, living human beings, with something to be gained or lost from the jury's verdict. Under the aegis of the Eighth Amendment, we have given the broadest latitude to the defendant to introduce relevant mitigating evidence reflecting on his individual personality, and the defendant's attorney may argue that evidence to the jury. Petitioner's attorney in this case did just that. For the reasons discussed above, we now reject the view—expressed in *Gathers*—that a State may not permit the prosecutor to similarly argue to the jury the human cost of the crime of which the defendant stands convicted. We reaffirm the view expressed by Justice Cardozo in *Snyder v. Massachusetts*, 291 U.S. 97, 122 (1934): "[J]ustice, though due to the accused, is due to the accuser also. The concept of fairness must not be strained till it is narrowed to a filament. We are to keep the balance true."

We thus hold that if the State chooses to permit the admission of victim impact evidence and prosecutorial argument on that subject, the Eighth Amendment erects no *per se* bar. A State may legitimately conclude that evidence about the victim and about the impact of the murder on the victim's family is relevant to the jury's decision as to whether or not the death penalty should be imposed. There is no reason to treat such evidence differently than other relevant evidence is treated. . . .

[The concurring opinions of Justices O'Connor, Scalia and Souter are omitted.]

DISSENTING OPINION OF JUSTICE MARSHALL, JOINED BY JUSTICE BLACKMUN

. . . As the majorities in *Booth* and *Gathers* recognized, the core principle of this Court's capital jurisprudence is that the sentence of death must reflect an "*individualized* determination" of the defendant's "personal responsibility and moral guilt" and must be based upon factors that channel the jury's discretion "so as to minimize the risk of wholly arbitrary and capricious action." . . . The State's introduction of victim-impact evidence, Justice Powell and Justice Brennan explained, violates this fundamental principle. Where, as is ordinarily the case, the defendant was unaware of the personal circumstances of his victim, admitting evidence of the victim's character and the impact of the murder upon the victim's family predicates the sentencing determination on "factors . . . wholly unrelated to the blameworthiness of [the] particular defendant." . . . And even where the defendant *was* in a position to foresee the likely impact of his conduct, admission of victim-impact evidence creates an unacceptable risk of sentencing arbitrariness. As Justice Powell explained in *Booth*, the probative value of such evidence is always outweighed by its prejudicial effect because of its inherent capacity to draw the jury's attention away from the character of the defendant and the circumstances of the crime to such illicit considerations as the eloquence with which family members express their grief and the status of the victim in the community. . . . I continue to find these considerations wholly persuasive, and I see no purpose in trying to improve upon Justice Powell's and Justice Brennan's exposition of them.

There is nothing new in the majority's discussion of the supposed deficiencies in *Booth* and *Gathers*. Every one of the arguments made by the majority can be found in the dissenting opinions filed in those two cases, and, as I show in the margin, each argument was convincingly answered by Justice Powell and Justice Brennan.[1] . . .

---

[1] The majority's primary argument is that punishment in criminal law is frequently based on an "assessment of [the] harm caused by the defendant as a result of the crime charged." Nothing in *Booth* or *Gathers*, however, conflicts with this unremarkable observation. These cases stand merely for the proposition that the State may not put on evidence of one particular species of harm—namely, that associated with the victim's personal characteristics independent of the circumstances of the offense—in the course of *a capital murder proceeding*. . . . It may be the case that such a rule departs from the latitude of sentencers in criminal law generally "[to] tak[e] into consideration the harm done by the defendant." But as the *Booth* Court pointed out, because this Court's capital-sentencing jurisprudence is founded on the premise that "death is a 'punishment different from all other sanctions,'" it is completely unavailing to attempt to infer from sentencing considerations in noncapital settings the proper treatment of any particular sentencing issue in a capital case. . . .

The majority also discounts Justice Powell's concern with the inherently prejudicial quality of victim-impact evidence. "[T]he mere fact that for tactical reasons it might not be prudent for the defense to rebut victim impact evidence," the majority protests, "makes the case no different than others in which a party is faced with this sort of a dilemma." Unsurprisingly, this tautology is completely unresponsive to Justice Powell's argument. The *Booth* Court established a rule excluding introduction of victim-impact evidence not merely because it is difficult to rebut—a feature of victim-impact evidence that may be "no different" from that of many varieties of relevant, legitimate evidence—but because the effect of this evidence in the sentencing proceeding is *unfairly prejudicial*: "The prospect of a 'mini-trial' on the victim's character is more than simply unappealing; it could well distract the sentencing jury from its constitutionally required task—determining whether the death penalty is appropriate in light of the background and record of the accused and the particular circumstances of the crime." . . . The law is replete with *per se* prohibitions of types of evidence the probative effect of which is generally outweighed by its unfair prejudice. . . . There is nothing anomalous in the notion that the Eighth Amendment would similarly exclude evidence that has an undue capacity to undermine the regime of individualized sentencing that our capital jurisprudence demands.

Finally, the majority contends that the exclusion of victim-impact evidence "deprives the State of the full moral force of its evidence and may prevent the jury from having before it all the information necessary to determine the proper punishment for a first-degree murder." The majority's recycled contention . . . begs the question. Before it is possible to conclude that the exclusion of victim-impact evidence prevents the State from making its case or the jury from considering relevant evidence, it is necessary to determine whether victim-impact evidence is consistent with the substantive standards that define the scope of permissible sentencing determinations under the Eighth Amendment. The majority offers no persuasive answer to Justice Powell and Justice Brennan's conclusion that victim-impact evidence is frequently *irrelevant* to any permissible sentencing consideration and that such evidence risks exerting *illegitimate* "moral force" by directing the jury's attention on illicit considerations such as the victim's standing in the community.

DISSENTING OPINION OF JUSTICE STEVENS, JOINED BY JUSTICE BLACKMUN

The novel rule that the Court announces today represents a dramatic departure for the principles that have governed our capital sentencing jurisprudence for decades. . . . Our cases provide no support whatsoever for the majority's conclusion that the prosecutor may introduce evidence that sheds no light on the defendant's guilt or moral culpability, and thus serves no purpose other than to encourage jurors to decide in favor of death rather than life on the basis of their emotions rather than their reason.

Until today our capital punishment jurisprudence has required that any decision to impose the death penalty be based solely on evidence that tends to inform the jury about the character of the offense and the character of the defendant. Evidence that serves no purpose other than to appeal to the sympathies or emotions of the jurors has never been considered admissible. Thus, if a defendant, who had murdered a convenience store clerk in cold blood in the course of an armed robbery, offered evidence unknown to him at the time of the crime about the immoral character of his victim, all would recognize immediately that the evidence was irrelevant and inadmissible. Evenhanded justice requires that the same constraint be imposed on the advocate of the death penalty. . . .

II

Today's majority has obviously been moved by an argument that has strong political appeal but no proper place in a reasoned judicial opinion. Because our decision in *Lockett* recognizes the defendant's right to introduce all mitigating evidence that may inform the jury about his character, the Court suggests that fairness requires that the State be allowed to respond with similar evidence about the victim. This argument is a classic non sequitur: The victim is not on trial; her character, whether good or bad, cannot therefore constitute either an aggravating or a mitigating circumstance.

Even if introduction of evidence about the victim could be equated with introduction of evidence about the defendant, the argument would remain flawed in both its premise and its conclusion. The conclusion that exclusion of victim impact evidence results in a significantly imbalanced sentencing procedure is simply inaccurate. Just as the defendant is entitled to introduce any relevant mitigating evidence, so the State may rebut that evidence and may designate any relevant conduct to be an aggravating factor provided that the factor is sufficiently well defined and consistently applied to cabin the sentencer's discretion.

The premise that a criminal prosecution requires an even-handed balance between the State and the defendant is also incorrect. The Constitution grants certain rights to the criminal defendant and imposes special limitations on the State designed to protect the individual from overreaching by the disproportionately powerful State. Thus, the State must prove a defendant's guilt beyond a reasonable doubt. See *In re Winship*, 397 U.S. 358 (1970). Rules of evidence are also weighted in the defendant's favor. For example, the prosecution generally cannot introduce evidence of the defendant's character to prove his propensity to commit a crime, but the defendant can introduce such reputation evidence to show his law-abiding nature. . . . Even if balance were required or desirable, today's decision, by permitting both the defendant and the State to introduce irrelevant evidence for the sentencer's consideration without any guidance, surely does nothing to enhance parity in the sentencing process.

III

Victim impact evidence, as used in this case, has two flaws, both related to the Eighth Amendment's command that the punishment of death may not be meted out arbitrarily or capriciously. First, aspects of the character of the victim unforeseeable to the defendant at the time of his crime are irrelevant to the defendant's "personal responsibility and moral guilt" and therefore cannot justify a death sentence. See *Enmund v. Florida; Tison v. Arizona; California v. Brown*, 479 U.S. 538, 545 (1987) (O'Connor, J., concurring).

Second, the quantity and quality of victim impact evidence sufficient to turn a verdict of life in prison into a verdict of death is not defined until after the crime has been committed and therefore cannot possibly be applied consistently in different cases. The sentencer's unguided consideration of victim impact evidence thus conflicts with the principle central to our capital punishment jurisprudence that, "where discretion is afforded a sentencing body on a matter so grave as the determination of whether a human life should be taken or spared, that discretion must be suitably directed and limited so as to minimize the risk of wholly arbitrary and capricious action." *Gregg.* Open-ended reliance by a capital sentencer on victim impact evidence simply does not provide a "principled way to distinguish [cases], in which the death penalty [i]s imposed, from the many cases in which it [i]s not." *Godfrey v. Georgia*, 446 U.S. 420, 433.

The majority attempts to justify the admission of victim impact evidence by arguing that "consideration of the harm caused by the crime has been an important factor in the exercise of [sentencing] discretion." This statement is misleading and inaccurate. It is misleading because it is not limited to harm that is foreseeable. It is inaccurate because it fails to differentiate between legislative determinations and judicial sentencing. It is true that an evaluation of the harm caused by different kinds of wrongful conduct is a critical aspect in legislative definitions of offenses and determinations concerning sentencing guidelines. There is a rational correlation between moral culpability and the foreseeable harm caused by criminal conduct. Moreover, in the capital sentencing area, legislative identification of the special aggravating factors that may justify the imposition of the death penalty is entirely appropriate. But the majority cites no authority for the suggestion that unforeseeable and indirect harms to a victim's family are properly considered as aggravating evidence on a case-by-case basis.

The dissents in *Booth* and *Gathers* and the majority today offer only the recent decision in *Tison v. Arizona* and two legislative examples to support their contention that harm to the victim has traditionally influenced sentencing discretion. *Tison* held that the death penalty may be imposed on a felon who acts with reckless disregard for human life if a death occurs in the course of the felony, even though capital punishment cannot be imposed if no one dies as a result of the crime. The first legislative example is that attempted murder and murder are classified as two different offenses subject to different punishments. The second legislative example is that a person who drives while intoxicated is guilty of vehicular homicide if his actions result in a death but is not guilty of this offense if he has the good fortune to make it home without killing anyone.

These three scenarios, however, are fully consistent with the Eighth Amendment jurisprudence reflected in *Booth* and *Gathers* and do not demonstrate that harm to the victim may be considered by a capital sentencer in the ad hoc and post hoc manner authorized by today's majority. The majority's examples demonstrate only that harm to the victim may justify enhanced punishment if the harm is both foreseeable to the defendant and clearly identified in advance of the crime by the legislature as a class of harm that should in every case result in more severe punishment.

In each scenario, the defendants could reasonably foresee that their acts might result in loss of human life. In addition, in each, the decision that the defendants should be treated differently was made prior to the crime by the legislature, the decision of which is subject to scrutiny for basic rationality. Finally, in each scenario, every defendant who causes the well-defined harm of destroying a human life will be subject to the determination that his conduct should be punished more severely. The majority's scenarios therefore provide no support for its holding, which permits a jury to sentence a defendant to death because of harm to the victim and his family that the defendant could not foresee, which was not even identified until after the crime had been committed, and which may be deemed by the jury, without any rational explanation, to justify a death sentence in one case but not in another. Unlike the rule elucidated by the scenarios on which the majority relies, the majority's holding offends the Eighth Amendment because it permits the sentencer to rely on irrelevant evidence in an arbitrary and capricious manner.

The majority's argument that "the sentencing authority has always been free to consider a wide range of *relevant* material," thus cannot justify consideration of victim impact evidence that is *irrelevant* because it details harms that the defendant could not have foreseen. Nor does the majority's citation of *Gregg v. Georgia* concerning the "wide scope of evidence and argument allowed at presentence hearings," support today's holding. The *Gregg* joint opinion endorsed the sentencer's consideration of a wide range of evidence "[s]o long as the evidence introduced and the arguments made at the presentence hearing do not prejudice a defendant." . . . Irrelevant victim impact evidence that distracts the sentencer from the proper focus of sentencing and encourages reliance on emotion and other arbitrary factors necessarily prejudices the defendant.

The majority's apparent inability to understand this fact is highlighted by its misunderstanding of Justice Powell's argument in *Booth* that admission of victim impact evidence is undesirable because it risks shifting the focus of the sentencing hearing away from the defendant and the circumstances of the crime and creating a "'mini-trial' on the victim's character." *Booth* found this risk insupportable not, as today's majority suggests, because it creates a "tactical" "dilemma" for the defendant, but because it allows the possibility that the jury will be so distracted by prejudicial and irrelevant considerations that it will base its life-or-death decision on whim or caprice.

IV

The majority thus does far more than validate a State's judgment that "the jury should see 'a quick glimpse of the life petitioner chose to extinguish,'" *Mills v. Maryland*, 486 U.S. 367, 397 (Rehnquist, C.J., dissenting). Instead, it allows a jury to hold a defendant responsible for a whole array of harms that he could not foresee and for which he is therefore not blameworthy. Justice Souter argues that these harms are sufficiently foreseeable to hold the defendant accountable because "[e]very defendant knows, if endowed with the mental competence for criminal responsibility, that the life he will take by his homicidal behavior is that of a unique person, like himself, and that the person to be killed probably has close associates, 'survivors,' who will suffer harms and deprivations from the victim's death." But every juror and trial judge knows this much as well. Evidence about who those survivors are and what harms and deprivations they have suffered is therefore not necessary to apprise the sentencer of any information that was actually foreseeable to the defendant. Its only function can be to "divert the jury's attention away from the defendant's background and record, and the circumstances of the crime." . . .

Arguing in the alternative, Justice Souter correctly points out that victim impact evidence will sometimes come to the attention of the jury during the guilt phase of the trial. He reasons that the ideal of basing sentencing determinations entirely on the moral culpability of the defendant is therefore unattainable unless a different jury is empaneled for the sentencing hearing. Thus, to justify overruling *Booth*, he assumes that the decision must otherwise be extended far beyond its actual holding.

Justice Souter's assumption is entirely unwarranted. For as long as the contours of relevance at sentencing hearings have been limited to evidence concerning the character of the offense and the character of the offender, the law has also recognized that evidence that is admissible for a proper purpose may not be excluded because it is inadmissible for other purposes and may indirectly prejudice the jury. . . . In the case before us today, much of what might be characterized as victim impact evidence was properly admitted during the guilt phase of the trial and, given the horrible character of this crime, may have been sufficient to justify the Tennessee Supreme Court's conclusion that the error was harmless because the jury would necessarily have imposed the death sentence even absent the error. The fact that a good deal of such evidence is routinely and properly brought to the attention of the jury merely indicates that the rule of *Booth* may not affect the outcome of many cases.

In reaching our decision today, however, we should not be concerned with the cases in which victim impact evidence will not make a difference. We should be concerned instead with the cases in which it will make a difference. In those cases, defendants will be sentenced arbitrarily to death on the basis of evidence that would not otherwise be admissible because it is irrelevant to the defendants' moral culpability. The Constitution's proscription against the arbitrary imposition of the death penalty must necessarily proscribe the admission of evidence that serves no purpose other than to result in such arbitrary sentences.

V

The notion that the inability to produce an ideal system of justice in which every punishment is precisely married to the defendant's blameworthiness somehow justifies a rule that completely divorces some capital sentencing determinations from moral culpability is incomprehensible to me. Also incomprehensible is the argument that such a rule is required for the jury to take into account that each murder victim is a "unique" human being. . . . The fact that each of us is unique is a proposition so obvious that it surely requires no evidentiary support. What is not obvious, however, is the way in which the character or reputation in one case may differ from that of other possible victims. Evidence offered to prove such differences can only be intended to identify some victims as more worthy of protection than others. Such proof risks decisions based on the same invidious motives as a prosecutor's decision to seek the death penalty if a victim is white but to accept a plea bargain if the victim is black. See *McCleskey v. Kemp*, 481 U.S. 279, 366 (1987) (Stevens, J., dissenting).

Given the current popularity of capital punishment in a crime-ridden society, the political appeal of arguments that assume that increasing the severity of sentences is the best cure for the cancer of crime, and the political strength of the "victims' rights" movement, I recognize that today's decision will be greeted with enthusiasm by a large number of concerned and thoughtful citizens. The great tragedy of the decision, however, is the danger that the "hydraulic pressure" of public opinion that Justice Holmes once described—and that properly influences the deliberations of democratic legislatures—has played a role not only in the Court's decision to hear this case, and in its decision to reach the constitutional question without pausing to consider affirming on the basis of the Tennessee Supreme Court's rationale, but even in its resolution of the constitutional issue involved. Today is a sad day for a great institution.

Chapter 17

Jury Instructions on Parole Ineligibility—*Simmons v. South Carolina* (1994)

Simmons v. South Carolina, 512 U.S. 154, 114 S. Ct. 2187, 129 L. Ed.2d 133 (1994) (7-2, where the defendant's future dangerousness is at issue and state law prohibits his release on parole, due process requires that the sentencing jury be informed that the defendant is parole ineligible).

Editor's comment: Some commentators believe that jurors vote for death in capital cases because they think that otherwise, dangerous defendants will be prematurely released from prison.[a] Moreover, jurors may adhere to these beliefs even where they may not be true, for instance, where the alternative to death is imprisonment for life without parole (LWOP). The *Simmons* case indicated that (as of 1994) 26 states provided life without parole as an alternative to capital punishment. In 17 of these states, the jury was expressly informed of the defendant's ineligibility for parole. South Carolina was one of three states with an LWOP alternative that did not permit the capital jury to be informed about that sentencing option. Of course, even an LWOP-sentenced defendant may be dangerous to prison personnel and inmates and may gain release by executive clemency, retroactive liberalization of the sentencing laws, or escape. It is difficult to obtain accurate data on the actual time served by life-sentenced convicts.

    Simmons did not require that all capital juries be told about the defendant's ineligibility for parole. Rather, it held that in states in which

---

[a] See, *e.g.*, Bowers and Steiner, "Death by Default: An Empirical Demonstration of False and Forced Choices in Capital Sentencing," 77 Tex. L. Rev. 605 (1999).

LWOP is an alternative and the prosecution argues that the defendant poses a future danger to society (and therefore ought to be put to death), due process entitles the defense to have the jury informed of defendant's parole-ineligibility.

❖   ❖   ❖

OPINION OF JUSTICE BLACKMUN, JOINED BY JUSTICE STEVENS, SOUTER, AND GINSBURG

This case presents the question whether the Due Process Clause of the Fourteenth Amendment was violated by the refusal of a state trial court to instruct the jury in the penalty phase of a capital trial that under state law the defendant was ineligible for parole. We hold that where the defendant's future dangerousness is at issue, and state law prohibits the defendant's release on parole, due process requires that the sentencing jury be informed that the defendant is parole ineligible.

I

A.   In July 1990, petitioner beat to death an elderly woman, Josie Lamb, in her home in Columbia, South Carolina. The week before petitioner's capital murder trial was scheduled to begin, he pleaded guilty to first-degree burglary and two counts of criminal sexual conduct in connection with two prior assaults on elderly women. Petitioner's guilty pleas resulted in convictions for violent offenses, and those convictions rendered petitioner ineligible for parole if convicted of any subsequent violent-crime offense.

Prior to jury selection, the prosecution advised the trial judge that the State "[o]bviously [was] going to ask you to exclude any mention of parole throughout this trial." Over defense counsel's objection, the trial court granted the prosecution's motion for an order barring the defense from asking any question during voir dire regarding parole. Under the court's order, defense counsel was forbidden even to mention the subject of parole, and expressly was prohibited from questioning prospective jurors as to whether they understood the meaning of a "life" sentence under South Carolina law. After a three-day trial, petitioner was convicted of the murder of Ms. Lamb.

During the penalty phase, the defense brought forward mitigating evidence tending to show that petitioner's violent behavior reflected serious mental disorders that stemmed from years of neglect and extreme sexual and physical abuse petitioner endured as an adolescent. While there was some disagreement among witnesses regarding the extent to which petitioner's mental condition properly could be deemed a "disorder," witnesses for both the defense and the prosecution agreed that petitioner posed a continuing danger to elderly women.

In its closing argument the prosecution argued that petitioner's future dangerousness was a factor for the jury to consider when fixing the appropriate punishment. The question for the jury, said the prosecution, was "what to do with [petitioner] now that he is in our midst." The prosecution further urged that a verdict for death would be "a response of society to someone who is a threat. Your verdict will be an act of self-defense."

Petitioner sought to rebut the prosecution's generalized argument of future dangerousness by presenting evidence that, due to his unique psychological problems, his dangerousness was limited to elderly women, and that there was no reason to expect further acts of violence once he was isolated in a prison setting. In support of his argument, petitioner introduced testimony from a female medical assistant and from two supervising officers at the Richland County jail where petitioner had been held prior to trial.

All three testified that petitioner had adapted well to prison life during his pretrial confinement and had not behaved in a violent manner toward any of the other inmates or staff. Petitioner also offered expert opinion testimony from Richard L. Boyle, a clinical social worker and former correctional employee, who had reviewed and observed petitioner's institutional adjustment. Mr. Boyle expressed the view that, based on petitioner's background and his current functioning, petitioner would successfully adapt to prison if he was sentenced to life imprisonment.

Concerned that the jury might not understand that "life imprisonment" did not carry with it the possibility of parole in petitioner's case, defense counsel asked the trial judge to clarify this point by defining the term "life imprisonment" for the jury. . . . To buttress his request, petitioner proffered, outside the presence of the jury, evidence conclusively establishing his parole ineligibility. On petitioner's behalf, attorneys for the South Carolina Department of Corrections and the Department of Probation, Parole, and Pardons testified that any offender in petitioner's position was in fact ineligible for parole under South Carolina law. The prosecution did not challenge or question petitioner's parole ineligibility. Instead, it sought to elicit admissions from the witnesses that, notwithstanding petitioner's parole ineligibility, petitioner might receive holiday furloughs or other forms of early release. Even this effort was unsuccessful, however, as the cross-examination revealed that Department of Corrections regulations prohibit petitioner's release under early release programs such as work-release or supervised furloughs, and that no convicted murderer serving life without parole ever had been furloughed or otherwise released for any reason.

Petitioner then offered into evidence, without objection, the results of a statewide public-opinion survey conducted by the University of South Carolina's Institute for Public Affairs. The survey had been conducted a few days before petitioner's trial, and showed that only 7.1 percent of all jury-eligible adults who were questioned firmly believed that an inmate sentenced to life imprisonment in South Carolina actually would be required to spend the rest of his life in prison. Almost half of those surveyed believed that a convicted murderer might be paroled within 20 years; nearly three-quarters thought that release certainly would occur in less than 30 years. More than 75 percent of those surveyed indicated that if they were called upon to make a capital sentencing decision as jurors, the amount of time the convicted murderer actually would have to spend in prison would be an "extremely important" or a "very important" factor in choosing between life and death.

Petitioner argued that, in view of the public's apparent misunderstanding about the meaning of "life imprisonment" in South Carolina, there was a reasonable likelihood that the jurors would vote for death simply because they believed, mistakenly, that petitioner eventually would be released on parole.

The prosecution opposed the proposed instruction, urging the court "not to allow . . . any argument by state or defense about parole and not charge the jury on anything concerning parole." Citing the South Carolina Supreme Court's opinion in *State v. Torrence*, 305 S.C. 45, 406 S.E.2d 315 (1991), the trial court refused petitioner's requested instruction.

Petitioner then asked alternatively for the following instruction:

> "I charge you that these sentences mean what they say. That is, if you recommend that the defendant Jonathan Simmons be sentenced to death, he actually will be sentenced to death and executed. If, on the other hand, you recommend that he be sentenced to life imprisonment, he actually will be sentenced to imprisonment in the state penitentiary for the balance of his natural life.
>
> "In your deliberations, you are not to speculate that these sentences mean anything other than what I have just told you, for what I have told you is exactly what will happen to the defendant, depending on what your sentencing decision is."

The trial judge also refused to give this instruction, but indicated that he might give a similar instruction if the jury inquired about parole eligibility.

After deliberating on petitioner's sentence for 90 minutes, the jury sent a note to the judge asking a single question: "Does the imposition of a life sentence carry with it the possibility of parole?" Over petitioner's objection, the trial judge gave the following instruction:

> "You are instructed not to consider parole or parole eligibility in reaching your verdict. Do not consider parole or parole eligibility. That is not a proper issue for your consideration. The terms life imprisonment and death sentence are to be understood in their plan [sic] and ordinary meaning."

Twenty-five minutes after receiving this response from the court, the jury returned to the courtroom with a sentence of death.

On appeal to the South Carolina Supreme Court, petitioner argued that the trial judge's refusal to provide the jury accurate information regarding his parole ineligibility violated the Eighth Amendment and the Due Process Clause of the Fourteenth Amendment. The South Carolina Supreme Court declined to reach the merits of petitioner's challenges. . . .

II

The Due Process Clause does not allow the execution of a person "on the basis of information which he had no opportunity to deny or explain." *Gardner v. Florida*, 430 U.S. 349 (1977). In this case, the jury reasonably may have believed that petitioner could be released on parole if he were not executed. To the extent this misunderstanding pervaded the jury's deliberations, it had the effect of creating a false choice between sentencing petitioner to death and sentencing him to a limited period of incarceration. This grievous misperception was encouraged by the trial court's refusal to provide the jury with accurate information regarding petitioner's parole ineligibility, and by the State's repeated suggestion that petitioner would pose a future danger to society if he were not executed. Three times petitioner asked to inform the jury that in fact he was ineligible for parole under state law; three times his request was denied. The State thus succeeded in securing a death sentence on the ground, at least in part, of petitioner's future dangerousness, while at the same time concealing from the sentencing jury the true meaning of its noncapital sentencing alternative, namely, that life imprisonment meant life without parole. We think it is clear that the State denied petitioner due process.[4]

A. This Court has approved the jury's consideration of future dangerousness during the penalty phase of a capital trial, recognizing that a defendant's future dangerousness bears on all sentencing determinations made in our criminal justice system.

Although South Carolina statutes do not mandate consideration of the defendant's future dangerousness in capital sentencing, the State's evidence in aggravation is not limited to evidence relating to statutory aggravating circumstances. . . . Thus, prosecutors in South Carolina, like those in other States that impose the death penalty, frequently emphasize a defendant's future dangerousness in their evidence and argument at the sentencing phase; they urge the jury to sentence the defendant to death so that he will not be a danger to the public if released from prison.

Arguments relating to a defendant's future dangerousness ordinarily would be inappropriate at the guilt phase of a trial, as the jury is not free to convict a defendant simply because he poses a future danger; nor is a defendant's future dangerousness likely relevant to the question whether each element of an alleged offense has been proved beyond a reasonable doubt. But where the jury has sentencing responsibilities in a capital trial, many issues that are irrelevant to the guilt-innocence determination step into the foreground and require consideration at the sentencing phase. The defendant's character, prior criminal history, mental capacity, background, and age are just a few of the many factors, in addition to future dangerousness, that a jury may consider in fixing appropriate punishment.

---

[4] We express no opinion on the question whether the result we reach today is also compelled by the Eighth Amendment.

In assessing future dangerousness, the actual duration of the defendant's prison sentence is indisputably relevant. Holding all other factors constant, it is entirely reasonable for a sentencing jury to view a defendant who is eligible for parole as a greater threat to society than a defendant who is not. Indeed, there may be no greater assurance of a defendant's future nondangerousness to the public than the fact that he never will be released on parole. The trial court's refusal to apprise the jury of information so crucial to its sentencing determination, particularly when the prosecution alluded to the defendant's future dangerousness in its argument to the jury, cannot be reconciled with our well-established precedents interpreting the Due Process Clause.

B. In *Skipper v. South Carolina*, 476 U.S. 1 (1986), this Court held that a defendant was denied due process by the refusal of the state trial court to admit evidence of the defendant's good behavior in prison in the penalty phase of his capital trial. Although the majority opinion stressed that the defendant's good behavior in prison was "relevant evidence in mitigation of punishment," and thus admissible under the Eighth Amendment, the *Skipper* opinion expressly noted that the Court's conclusion also was compelled by the Due Process Clause. The Court explained that where the prosecution relies on a prediction of future dangerousness in requesting the death penalty, elemental due process principles operate to require admission of the defendant's relevant evidence in rebuttal. 476 U.S., at 5, n. 1. See also *id.*, 476 U.S., at 9 (Powell, J., opinion concurring in judgment) ("[B]ecause petitioner was not allowed to rebut evidence and argument used against him," the defendant clearly was denied due process).

The Court reached a similar conclusion in *Gardner v. Florida*, 430 U.S. 349 (1977). In that case, a defendant was sentenced to death on the basis of a presentence report which was not made available to him and which he therefore could not rebut. A plurality of the Court explained that sending a man to his death "on the basis of information which he had no opportunity to deny or explain" violated fundamental notions of due process. The principle announced in *Gardner* was reaffirmed in *Skipper*, and it compels our decision today. See also *Crane v. Kentucky*, 476 U.S. 683, 690 (1986) (due process entitles a defendant to "a meaningful opportunity to present a complete defense"); *Ake v. Oklahoma*, 470 U.S. 68, 83–87 (1985) (where the State presents psychiatric evidence of a defendant's future dangerousness at a capital sentencing proceeding, due process entitles an indigent defendant to the assistance of a psychiatrist for the development of his defense).

Like the defendants in *Skipper* and *Gardner*, petitioner was prevented from rebutting information that the sentencing authority considered, and upon which it may have relied, in imposing the sentence of death. The State raised the specter of petitioner's future dangerousness generally, but then thwarted all efforts by petitioner to demonstrate that, contrary to the prosecutor's intimations, he never would be released on parole and thus, in his view, would not pose a future danger to society. The logic and effectiveness of petitioner's argument naturally depended on the fact that he was legally ineligible for parole and thus would remain in prison if afforded a life sentence. Petitioner's efforts to focus the jury's attention on the question whether, in prison, he would be a future danger were futile, as he repeatedly was denied any opportunity to inform the jury that he never would be released on parole. The jury was left to speculate about petitioner's parole eligibility when evaluating petitioner's future dangerousness, and was denied a straight answer about petitioner's parole eligibility even when it was requested.

C.   The State and its amici contend that petitioner was not entitled to an instruction informing the jury that petitioner is ineligible for parole because such information is inherently misleading.[6] Essentially, they argue that because future exigencies such as legislative reform, commutation, clemency, and escape might allow petitioner to be released into society, petitioner was not entitled to inform the jury that he is parole ineligible. Insofar as this argument is targeted at the specific wording of the instruction petitioner requested, the argument is misplaced. Petitioner's requested instruction ("If . . . you recommend that [the defendant] be sentenced to life imprisonment, he actually will be sentenced to imprisonment in the state penitentiary for the balance of his natural life,") was proposed only after the trial court ruled that South Carolina law prohibited a plain-language instruction that petitioner was ineligible for parole under state law. To the extent that the State opposes even a simple parole-ineligibility instruction because of hypothetical future developments, the argument has little force. Respondent admits that an instruction informing the jury that petitioner is ineligible for parole is legally accurate. Certainly, such an instruction is more accurate than no instruction at all, which leaves the jury to speculate whether "life imprisonment" means life without parole or something else.

The State's asserted accuracy concerns are further undermined by the fact that a large majority of States which provide for life imprisonment without parole as an alternative to capital punishment inform the sentencing authority of the defendant's parole ineligibility.[7] The few States that do not provide capital sentencing juries with any information regarding parole ineligibility seem to rely, as South Carolina does here, on the proposition that *California v. Ramos*, 463 U.S. 992 (1983) held that such determinations are purely matters of state law.[8]

---

[6] In this regard, the State emphasizes that no statute prohibits petitioner's eventual release into society. While this technically may be true, state regulations unambiguously prohibit work-release and virtually all other furloughs for inmates who are ineligible for parole. As for pardons, the statute itself provides that they are available only in "the most extraordinary circumstances."

[7] At present, there are 26 States that both employ juries in capital sentencing and provide for life imprisonment without parole as an alternative to capital punishment. In 17 of these, the jury expressly is informed of the defendant's ineligibility for parole. Nine States simply identify the jury's sentencing alternatives as death and life without parole. Eight States allow the jury to specify whether the defendant should or should not be eligible for parole. In three States, statutory or decisional law requires that the sentencing jury be instructed, where accurate, that the defendant will be ineligible for parole. . . .

[8] Only two States other than South Carolina have a life-without-parole sentencing alternative to capital punishment for some or all convicted murderers but refuse to inform sentencing juries of this fact. [Citing Pennsylvania and Virginia.]

Justice Scalia points out that two additional States, Texas and North Carolina, traditionally have kept information about a capital defendant's parole ineligibility from the sentencing jury. Neither of these States, however, has a life-without-parole sentencing alternative to capital punishment. It is also worthy of note that, pursuant to recently enacted legislation, North Carolina now requires trial courts to instruct capital sentencing juries concerning parole eligibility.

It is true that *Ramos* stands for the broad proposition that we generally will defer to a State's determination as to what a jury should and should not be told about sentencing. In a State in which parole is available, how the jury's knowledge of parole availability will affect the decision whether or not to impose the death penalty is speculative, and we shall not lightly second-guess a decision whether or not to inform a jury of information regarding parole. States reasonably may conclude that truthful information regarding the availability of commutation, pardon, and the like should be kept from the jury in order to provide "greater protection in [the States'] criminal justice system than the Federal Constitution requires." *Id.*, 463 U.S., at 1014. Concomitantly, nothing in the Constitution prohibits the prosecution from arguing any truthful information relating to parole or other forms of early release.

But if the State rests its case for imposing the death penalty at least in part on the premise that the defendant will be dangerous in the future, the fact that the alternative sentence to death is life without parole will necessarily undercut the State's argument regarding the threat the defendant poses to society. Because truthful information of parole ineligibility allows the defendant to "deny or explain" the showing of future dangerousness, due process plainly requires that he be allowed to bring it to the jury's attention by way of argument by defense counsel or an instruction from the court.

III

There remains to be considered whether the South Carolina Supreme Court was correct in concluding that the trial court "satisfie[d] in substance [petitioner's] request for a charge on parole ineligibility," when it responded to the jury's query by stating that life imprisonment was to be understood in its "plain and ordinary meaning."

In the court's view, petitioner basically received the parole-ineligibility instruction he requested. We disagree.

It can hardly be questioned that most juries lack accurate information about the precise meaning of "life imprisonment" as defined by the States. For much of our country's history, parole was a mainstay of state and federal sentencing regimes, and every term (whether a term of life or a term of years) in practice was understood to be shorter than the stated term. Increasingly, legislatures have enacted mandatory sentencing laws with severe penalty provisions, yet the precise contours of these penal laws vary from State to State. Justice Chandler of the South Carolina Supreme Court observed that it is impossible to ignore "the reality, known to the 'reasonable juror,' that, historically, life-term defendants have been eligible for parole." *State v. Smith*, 298 S.C. 482, 489–490, 381 S.E.2d 724, 728 (1989) (opinion concurring and dissenting).

An instruction directing juries that life imprisonment should be understood in its "plain and ordinary" meaning does nothing to dispel the misunderstanding reasonable jurors may have about the way in which any particular State defines "life imprisonment." *See Boyde v. California*, 494 U.S. 370 (1990) (where there is a "reasonable likelihood that the jury has applied the challenged instruction in a way that prevents the consideration of constitutionally relevant evidence," the defendant is denied due process).

It is true, as the State points out, that the trial court admonished the jury that "you are instructed not to consider parole" and that parole "is not a proper issue for your consideration." Far from ensuring that the jury was not misled, however, this instruction actually suggested that parole was available but that the jury, for some unstated reason, should be blind to this fact. Undoubtedly, the instruction was confusing and frustrating to the jury, given the arguments by both the prosecution and the defense relating to petitioner's future dangerousness, and the obvious relevance of petitioner's parole ineligibility to the jury's formidable sentencing task. While juries ordinarily are presumed to follow the court's instructions, we have recognized that in some circumstances "the risk that the jury will not, or cannot, follow instructions is so great, and the consequences of failure so vital to the defendant, that the practical and human limitations of the jury system cannot be ignored." *Bruton v. United States*, 391 U.S. 123, 135 (1968). . . .

But even if the trial court's instruction successfully prevented the jury from considering parole, petitioner's due process rights still were not honored. Because petitioner's future dangerousness was at issue, he was entitled to inform the jury of his parole ineligibility. An instruction directing the jury not to consider the defendant's likely conduct in prison would not have satisfied due process in *Skipper*, and, for the same reasons, the instruction issued by the trial court in this case does not satisfy due process.

IV

The State may not create a false dilemma by advancing generalized arguments regarding the defendant's future dangerousness while, at the same time, preventing the jury from learning that the defendant never will be released on parole. The judgment of the South Carolina Supreme Court accordingly is reversed, and the case is remanded for further proceedings.

It is so ordered.

CONCURRING OPINION OF JUSTICE SOUTER, JOINED BY JUSTICE STEVENS

I join in Justice Blackmun's opinion that, at least when future dangerousness is an issue in a capital sentencing determination, the defendant has a due process right to require that his sentencing jury be informed of his ineligibility for parole. I write separately because I believe an additional, related principle also compels today's decision, regardless of whether future dangerousness is an issue at sentencing.

The Eighth Amendment entitles a defendant to a jury capable of a reasoned moral judgment about whether death, rather than some lesser sentence, ought to be imposed. The Court has explained that the Amendment imposes a heightened standard "for reliability in the determination that death is the appropriate punishment in a specific case," *Woodson*. Thus, it requires provision of "accurate sentencing information [as] an indispensable prerequisite to a reasoned determination of whether a defendant shall live or die," *Gregg*, and invalidates "procedural rules that ten[d] to diminish the reliability of the sentencing determination," *Beck v. Alabama*, 447 U.S. 625, 638 (1980).

That same need for heightened reliability also mandates recognition of a capital defendant's right to require instructions on the meaning of the legal terms used to describe the sentences (or sentencing recommendations) a jury is required to consider, in making the reasoned moral choice between sentencing alternatives. Thus, whenever there is a reasonable likelihood that a juror will misunderstand a sentencing term, a defendant may demand instruction on its meaning, and a death sentence following the refusal of such a request should be vacated as having been "arbitrarily or discriminatorily" and "wantonly and . . . freakishly imposed." *Furman*.

While I join the other Members of the Court's majority in holding that, at least, counsel ought to be permitted to inform the jury of the law that it must apply, I also accept the general rule that, on matters of law, arguments of counsel do not effectively substitute for statements by the court.

"[A]rguments of counsel generally carry less weight with a jury than do instructions from the court. The former are usually billed in advance to the jury as matters of argument, not evidence, and are likely viewed as the statements of advocates; the latter, we have often recognized, are viewed as definitive and binding statements of the law." *Boyde v. California*, 494 U.S. 370, 384 (1990). I would thus impose that straightforward duty on the court.

Because Justice Blackmun persuasively demonstrates that juries in general are likely to misunderstand the meaning of the term "life imprisonment" in a given context, the judge must tell the jury what the term means, when the defendant so requests. It is, moreover, clear that at least one of these particular jurors did not understand the meaning of the term, since the jury sent a note to the judge asking,: "Does the imposition of a life sentence carry with it the possibility of parole?" The answer here was easy and controlled by state statute. The judge should have said no.

Justice Blackmun shows that the instruction actually given was at best a confusing, "equivocal direction to the jury on a basic issue," *Bollenbach v. United States*, 326 U.S. 607, 613 (1946), and that "there is a reasonable likelihood that the jury has applied the challenged instruction in a way" that violated petitioner's rights. *Boyde*, 494 U.S. at 380. By effectively withholding from the jury the life-without-parole alternative, the trial court diminished the reliability of the jury's decision that death, rather than that alternative, was the appropriate penalty in this case.

While States are, of course, free to provide more protection for the accused than the Constitution requires, they may not provide less. South Carolina did so here. For these reasons, as well as those set forth by Justice Blackmun, whose opinion I join, the judgment of the Supreme Court of South Carolina must be reversed.

CONCURRING OPINION OF JUSTICE GINSBURG

This case is most readily resolved under a core requirement of due process, the right to be heard. *Crane v. Kentucky*, 476 U.S. 683, 690 (1986). When the prosecution urges a defendant's future dangerousness as cause for the death sentence, the defendant's right to be heard means that he must be afforded an opportunity to rebut the argument. *See Skipper v. South Carolina*, 476 U.S. 1, 5, n. 1 (1986). To be full and fair, that opportunity must include the right to inform the jury, if it is indeed the case, that the defendant is ineligible for parole. Justice Blackmun's opinion is in accord with Justice O'Connor's on this essential point.

As a subsidiary matter, Justice O'Connor's opinion clarifies that the due process requirement is met if the relevant information is intelligently conveyed to the jury; due process does not dictate that the judge herself, rather than defense counsel, provide the instruction. I do not read Justice Blackmun's opinion to say otherwise. And I note that the trial court here not only refused to instruct the jury that in this case life means "life without parole"; the court also ordered petitioner's counsel to refrain from saying anything to the jury about parole ineligibility.

On these understandings, I concur in Justice Blackmun's opinion.

CONCURRING OPINION OF JUSTICE O'CONNOR, JOINED BY CHIEF JUSTICE REHNQUIST AND JUSTICE KENNEDY

"Capital sentencing proceedings must of course satisfy the dictates of the Due Process Clause," *Clemons v. Mississippi*, 494 U.S. 738, 746 (1990), and one of the hallmarks of due process in our adversary system is the defendant's ability to meet the State's case against him. *Cf. Crane v. Kentucky*, 476 U.S. 683, 690 (1986). In capital cases, we have held that the defendant's future dangerousness is a consideration on which the State may rely in seeking the death penalty. See *California v. Ramos*, 463 U.S. 992, 1002-1003 (1983). But "[w]here the prosecution specifically relies on a prediction of future dangerousness in asking for the death penalty, ... the elemental due process requirement that a defendant not be sentenced to death 'on the basis of information which he had no opportunity to deny or explain' [requires that the defendant be afforded an opportunity to introduce evidence on this point]." *Skipper v. South Carolina*, 476 U.S. 1, 5, n. 1 (1986), quoting *Gardner v. Florida*, 430 U.S. 349, 362 (1977) (plurality opinion).

In this case, petitioner physically and sexually assaulted three elderly women—one of them his own grandmother—before killing a fourth. At the capital sentencing proceeding, the State sought to show that petitioner is a vicious predator who would pose a continuing threat to the community. The prosecutor argued that the jury's role was to decide "what to do with [petitioner] now that he is in our midst," and told the jury: "Your verdict should be a response of society to someone who is a threat. Your verdict will be an act of self-defense." Petitioner's response was that he only preyed on elderly women, a class of victims he would not encounter behind bars. This argument stood a chance of succeeding, if at all, only if the jury were convinced that petitioner would stay in prison. Although the only available alternative sentence to death in petitioner's case was life imprisonment without possibility of parole, the trial court precluded the jury from learning that petitioner would never be released from prison.

Unlike in *Skipper*, where the defendant sought to introduce factual evidence tending to disprove the State's showing of future dangerousness, petitioner sought to rely on the operation of South Carolina's sentencing law in arguing that he would not pose a threat to the community if he were sentenced to life imprisonment. We have previously noted with approval, however, that "[m]any state courts have held it improper for the jury to consider or to be informed—through argument or instruction—of the possibility of commutation, pardon, or parole." *California v. Ramos*, 463 U.S., at 1013, n. 30. The decision whether or not to inform the jury of the possibility of early release is generally left to the States. In a State in which parole is available, the Constitution does not require (or preclude) jury consideration of that fact. Likewise, if the prosecution does not argue future dangerousness, the State may appropriately decide that parole is not a proper issue for the jury's consideration even if the only alternative sentence to death is life imprisonment without possibility of parole.

When the State seeks to show the defendant's future dangerousness, however, the fact that he will never be released from prison will often be the only way that a violent criminal can successfully rebut the State's case. I agree with the Court that in such a case the defendant should be allowed to bring his parole ineligibility to the jury's attention—by way of argument by defense counsel or an instruction from the court—as a means of responding to the State's showing of future dangerousness. And despite our general deference to state decisions regarding what the jury should be told about sentencing, I agree that due process requires that the defendant be allowed to do so in cases in which the only available alternative sentence to death is life imprisonment without possibility of parole and the prosecution argues that the defendant will pose a threat to society in the future. Of course, in such cases the prosecution is free to argue that the defendant would be dangerous in prison; the State may also (though it need not) inform the jury of any truthful information regarding the availability of commutation, pardon, and the like.

The prosecutor in this case put petitioner's future dangerousness in issue, but petitioner was not permitted to argue parole ineligibility to the capital sentencing jury. Although the trial judge instructed the jurors that "[t]he terms life imprisonment and death sentence are to be understood in their pla[i]n and ordinary meaning," I cannot agree with the court below that this instruction "satisfie[d] in substance [petitioner's] request for a charge on parole ineligibility." The rejection of parole by many States (and the Federal Government) is a recent development that displaces the longstanding practice of parole availability, and common sense tells us that many jurors might not know whether a life sentence carries with it the possibility of parole. While it may come to pass that the "plain and ordinary meaning" of a life sentence is life without parole, that the jury in this case felt compelled to ask whether parole was available shows that the jurors did not know whether or not a life-sentenced defendant will be released from prison. Moreover, the prosecutor, by referring to a verdict of death as an act of "self-defense," strongly implied that petitioner would be let out eventually if the jury did not recommend a death sentence.

Where the State puts the defendant's future dangerousness in issue, and the only available alternative sentence to death is life imprisonment without possibility of parole, due process entitles the defendant to inform the capital sentencing jury—by either argument or instruction—that he is parole ineligible. In this case, the prosecution argued at the capital sentencing proceeding that petitioner would be dangerous in the future. Although the only alternative sentence to death under state law was life imprisonment without possibility of parole, petitioner was not allowed to argue to the jury that he would never be released from prison, and the trial judge's instruction did not communicate this information to the jury. I therefore concur in the Court's judgment that petitioner was denied the due process of law to which he is constitutionally entitled.

DISSENTING OPINION OF JUSTICE SCALIA, JOINED BY JUSTICE THOMAS

Today's judgment certainly seems reasonable enough as a determination of what a capital sentencing jury should be permitted to consider. That is not, however, what it purports to be. It purports to be a determination that any capital sentencing scheme that does not permit jury consideration of such material is so incompatible with our national traditions of criminal procedure that it violates the Due Process Clause of the Constitution of the United States. There is really no basis for such a pronouncement, neither in any near uniform practice of our people, nor in the jurisprudence of this Court.

With respect to the former I shall discuss only current practice, since the parties and amici have addressed only that, and since traditional practice may be relatively uninformative with regard to the new schemes of capital sentencing imposed upon the States by this Court's recent jurisprudence. The overwhelming majority of the 32 States that permit juries to impose or recommend capital sentences do not allow specific information regarding parole to be given to the jury. To be sure, in many of these States the sentencing choices specifically include "life without parole," so that the jury charge itself conveys the information whether parole is available. In at least eight of those States, however, the jury's choice is not merely between "life without parole" and "death," but among some variation of (parole eligible) "life," "life without parole," and "death"[1] —so that the precise date of availability of parole is relevant to the jury's choice. Moreover, even among those States that permit the jury to choose only between "life" (unspecified) and "death," South Carolina is not alone in keeping parole information from the jury. Four other States in widely separated parts of the country follow that same course,[2] and there are other States that lack any clear practice.[3] By contrast, the parties and their amici point to only 10 States that arguably employ the procedure which, according to today's opinions, the Constitution requires.[4] This picture of national practice falls far short of demonstrating a principle so widely shared that it is part of even a current and temporary American consensus.

As for our prior jurisprudence: The opinions of Justice Blackmun and Justice O'Connor rely on the Fourteenth Amendment's guarantee of due process, rather than on the Eighth Amendment's "cruel and unusual punishments" prohibition, as applied to the States by the Fourteenth Amendment. . . . The prior law applicable to that subject indicates that petitioner's due process rights would be violated if he was "sentenced to death 'on the basis of information which he had no opportunity to deny or explain.' " *Skipper v. South Carolina*, 476 U.S. 1, 5, n. 1 (1986), quoting *Gardner v. Florida*, 430 U.S. 349, 362 (1977). Both opinions try to bring this case within that description, but it does not fit.

The opinions paint a picture of a prosecutor who repeatedly stressed that petitioner would pose a threat to society upon his release. The record tells a different story. Rather than emphasizing future dangerousness as a crucial factor, the prosecutor stressed the nature of petitioner's crimes: the crime that was the subject of the prosecution, the brutal murder of a 79-year-old woman in her home, and three prior crimes confessed to by petitioner, all rapes and beatings of elderly women, one of them his grandmother. I am sure it was the sheer depravity of those crimes, rather than any specific fear for the future, which induced the South Carolina jury to conclude that the death penalty was justice.

---

[1] The eight States are Georgia, Indiana, Maryland, Nevada, Oklahoma, Oregon, Tennessee, and Utah.

[2] The four States are Pennsylvania, Texas, Virginia, and North Carolina, which will alter its practice effective January 1, 1995.

[3] The States that allow the jury to choose between "life without parole" and "death" and have not squarely decided whether the jury should receive information about parole include South Dakota and Wyoming.

[4] The 10 States identified by the parties and their amici are Colorado, Florida, Illinois, Maryland, Mississippi, New Jersey, New Mexico, Nevada, Oklahoma, and Oregon.

Not only, moreover, was future dangerousness not emphasized, but future dangerousness outside of prison was not even mentioned. The trial judge undertook specifically to prevent that, in response to the broader request of petitioner's counsel that the prosecutor be prevented from arguing future dangerousness at all:

> "Obviously, I will listen carefully to the argument of the solicitor to see if it contravenes the actual factual circumstance. Certainly, I recognize the right of the State to argue concerning the defendant's dangerous propensity. I will not allow the solicitor, for example, to say to the jury anything that would indicate that the defendant is not going to be jailed for the period of time that is encompassed within the actual law. The fact that we do not submit the parole eligibility to the jury does not negate the fact that the solicitor must stay within the trial record."

As I read the record, the prosecutor followed this admonition—and the Due Process Clause requires nothing more.

Both Justice Blackmun and Justice O'Connor focus on two portions of the prosecutor's final argument to the jury in the sentencing phase. First, they stress that the prosecutor asked the jury to answer the question of "what to do with [petitioner] now that he is in our midst." That statement, however, was not made (as they imply) in the course of an argument about future dangerousness, but was a response to petitioner's mitigating evidence. Read in context, the statement is not even relevant to the issue in this case:

> "The defense in this case as to sentence . . . [is] a diversion. It's putting the blame on society, on his father, on his grandmother, on whoever else he can, spreading it out to avoid that personal responsibility. That he came from a deprived background. That he didn't have all of the breaks in life and certainly that helps shape someone. But we are not concerned about how he got shaped. We are concerned about what to do with him now that he is in our midst."

Both opinions also seize upon the prosecutor's comment that the jury's verdict would be "an act of self-defense." That statement came at the end of admonition of the jury to avoid emotional responses and enter a rational verdict:

> "Your verdict shouldn't be returned in anger. Your verdict shouldn't be an emotional catharsis. Your verdict shouldn't be . . . a response to that eight-year-old kid [testifying in mitigation] and really shouldn't be a response to the gruesome grotesque handiwork of [petitioner]. Your verdict should be a response of society to someone who is a threat. Your verdict will be an act of self-defense."

This reference to "self-defense" obviously alluded neither to defense of the jurors' own persons, nor specifically to defense of persons outside the prison walls, but to defense of all members of society against this individual, wherever he or they might be. Thus, as I read the record (and bear in mind that the trial judge was on the lookout with respect to this point), the prosecutor did not invite the jury to believe that petitioner would be eligible for parole—he did not mislead the jury.

The rule the majority adopts in order to overturn this sentence therefore goes well beyond what would be necessary to counteract prosecutorial misconduct (a disposition with which I might agree). It is a rule at least as sweeping as this: that the Due Process Clause overrides state law limiting the admissibility of information concerning parole whenever the prosecution argues future dangerousness. Justice Blackmun appears to go even further, requiring the admission of parole ineligibility even when the prosecutor does not argue future dangerousness. . . . I do not understand the basis for this broad prescription. As a general matter, the Court leaves it to the States to strike what they consider the appropriate balance among the many factors—probative value, prejudice, reliability, potential for confusion, among others—that determine whether evidence ought to be admissible. Even in the capital punishment context, the Court has noted that "the wisdom of the decision to permit juror consideration of [postsentencing contingencies] is best left to the States." *California v. Ramos*, 463 U.S. 992, 1014 (1983). "[T]he States, and not this Court, retain 'the traditional authority' to determine what particular evidence . . . is relevant." *Skipper v. South Carolina*, 476 U.S., at 11 (Powell, J., concurring in judgment). One reason for leaving it that way is that a sensible code of evidence cannot be invented piecemeal. Each item cannot be considered in isolation, but must be given its place within the whole. Preventing the defense from introducing evidence regarding parolability is only half of the rule that prevents the prosecution from introducing it as well. If the rule is changed for defendants, many will think that evenhandedness demands a change for prosecutors as well. State's attorneys ought to be able to say that if, ladies and gentlemen of the jury, you do not impose capital punishment upon this defendant (or if you impose anything less than life without parole) he may be walking the streets again in eight years! Many would not favor the admission of such an argument—but would prefer it to a state scheme in which defendants can call attention to the unavailability of parole, but prosecutors cannot note its availability. This Court should not force state legislators into such a difficult choice unless the isolated state evidentiary rule that the Court has before it is not merely less than ideal, but beyond a high threshold of unconstitutionality.

The low threshold the Court constructs today is difficult to reconcile with our almost simultaneous decision in *Romano v. Oklahoma*, 512 U.S. 1 (1994). There, the Court holds that the proper inquiry when evidence is admitted in contravention of a state law is "whether the admission of evidence . . . so infected the sentencing proceeding with unfairness as to render the jury's imposition of the death penalty a denial of due process." *Id.*, 512 U.S., at 12. I do not see why the unconstitutionality criterion for excluding evidence in accordance with state law should be any less demanding than the unconstitutionality criterion *Romano* recites for admitting evidence in violation of state law: "fundamental unfairness."

And "fundamentally unfair" the South Carolina rule is assuredly not. The notion that the South Carolina jury imposed the death penalty "just in case" Simmons might be released on parole seems to me quite farfetched. And the notion that the decision taken on such grounds would have been altered by information on the current state of the law concerning parole (which could of course be amended) is even more farfetched. And the scenario achieves the ultimate in farfetchedness when there is added the fact that, according to uncontroverted testimony of prison officials in this case, even current South Carolina law (as opposed to discretionary prison regulations) does not prohibit furloughs and work-release programs for life-without-parole inmates.

When the prosecution has not specifically suggested parolability, I see no more reason why the United States Constitution should compel the admission of evidence showing that, under the State's current law, the defendant would be non-parolable, than that it should compel the admission of evidence showing that parolable life-sentence murderers are in fact almost never paroled, or are paroled only after age 70; or evidence to the effect that escapes of life-without-parole inmates are rare; or evidence showing that, though under current law the defendant will be parolable in 20 years, the recidivism rate for elderly prisoners released after long incarceration is negligible. All of this evidence may be thought relevant to whether the death penalty should be imposed, and a petition raising the last of these claims has already arrived.

As I said at the outset, the regime imposed by today's judgment is undoubtedly reasonable as a matter of policy, but I see nothing to indicate that the Constitution requires it to be followed coast to coast. I fear we have read today the first page of a whole new chapter in the "death-is-different" jurisprudence which this Court is in the apparently continuous process of composing. It adds to our insistence that state courts admit "all relevant mitigating evidence," see, *e.g.*, *Eddings*; *Lockett*, a requirement that they adhere to distinctive rules, more demanding than what the Due Process Clause normally requires, for admitting evidence of other sorts—Federal Rules of Death Penalty Evidence, so to speak, which this Court will presumably craft (at great expense to the swiftness and predictability of justice) year by year. The heavily outnumbered opponents of capital punishment have successfully opened yet another front in their guerilla war to make this unquestionably constitutional sentence a practical impossibility.

I dissent.

Chapter 18

The Right to Effective Counsel—*Burger v. Kemp* (1987)

Burger v. Kemp, 483 U.S. 776, 107 S. Ct. 3114, 97 L. Ed.2d 638 (1987) (5-4, failure of counsel's investigation to develop any mitigating evidence was not ineffective assistance of counsel in violation of the Sixth Amendment).

Editor's comment: The Sixth Amendment guarantees the accused "the Assistance of Counsel for his defense," and the Supreme Court has said that this means effective counsel. The need for a competent lawyer is especially great in a capital case, where the stakes are high, the trial procedures are different, and each phase of the trial requires especially careful attention. Ineffective counsel is a frequent claim on appeal in death penalty cases.

In *Strickland v. Washington*, 466 U.S. 668 (1984), the Supreme Court established a two-part standard for such appeals. It is a difficult standard to meet, because the Court did not want to encourage appeals judges to routinely second-guess trial lawyers, as this would flood the courts with ineffective assistance appeals and retrials where such appeals succeeded. The *Strickland* standard is also known as the *performance and prejudice* test. First, the defendant has the burden of proving that his trial lawyer's performance was deficient. This requires showing serious specific errors of a type that a reasonably competent professional would not make. Second, the defendant must show that the deficient performance prejudiced the defense; in other words, that counsel's errors were so serious that defendant was deprived of a fair trial. In *Burger v. Kemp*, the Court considered a claim that counsel was ineffective because his investigation of defendant's background was deficient.

❖   ❖   ❖

OPINION OF JUSTICE STEVENS FOR THE COURT

A jury in the Superior Court of Wayne County, Georgia, found petitioner Christopher Burger guilty of murder and sentenced him to death on January 25, 1978. In this habeas corpus proceeding, he contends that he was denied his constitutional right to the effective assistance of counsel because his lawyer [Leaphart] . . . failed to make an adequate investigation of the possibly mitigating circumstances of his offense. After a full evidentiary hearing, the District Court rejected the claim. We are persuaded, as was the Court of Appeals, that the judgment of the District Court must be affirmed. . . .

The District Court expressed much more concern about petitioner's argument that Leaphart had failed to develop and present mitigating evidence at either of the two sentencing hearings [than about defendant's other claim].[a] At both hearings Leaphart offered no mitigating evidence at all. A capital sentencing proceeding "is sufficiently like a trial in its adversarial format and in the existence of standards for decision" that counsel's role in the two proceedings is comparable—it is "to ensure that the adversarial testing process works to produce a just result under the standards governing that decision." *Strickland v. Washington*, 466 U.S. 668, 686, 687 (1984). We therefore must determine whether Leaphart's performance in evaluating the mitigating evidence available to him, and in deciding not to pursue further mitigating evidence, undermines confidence in the adversarial process of this case. In embarking on our review of the District Court's conclusions, we are guided by our most recent admonition on this subject:

> Judicial scrutiny of counsel's performance must be highly deferential. It is all too tempting for a defendant to second-guess counsel's assistance after conviction or adverse sentence, and it is all too easy for a court, examining counsel's defense after it has proved unsuccessful, to conclude that a particular act or omission of counsel was unreasonable. A fair assessment of attorney performance requires that every effort be made to eliminate the distorting effects of hindsight, to reconstruct the circumstances of counsel's challenged conduct, and to evaluate the conduct from counsel's perspective at the time. *Strickland*, 466 U.S., at 689.

The evidence that might have been presented would have disclosed that petitioner had an exceptionally unhappy and unstable childhood. Most of this evidence was described by petitioner's mother, who testified at length at the habeas corpus hearing. At the age of 14 she married Burger's father, who was 16. She was divorced from petitioner's father when petitioner was nine years old. She remarried twice, and neither of petitioner's stepfathers wanted petitioner in the home; one of them beat his mother in petitioner's presence when he was 11 and

---

[a] Editor's note: Burger also argued that his attorney had a conflict of interest, another Sixth Amendment claim, because Leaphart's law partner represented Burger's codefendant. The Court held that this did not impair Burger's defense. This portion of the case is not reprinted here.

the other apparently "got him involved with marijuana, and that was the whole point of his life, where the next bag was coming from, or the next bottle of beer. And, this was the kind of influence that he had.". . . When his mother moved from Indiana to Florida, petitioner ran away from his father and hitchhiked to Tampa. After he became involved in an auto accident, she returned him to Indiana where he was placed in a juvenile detention home until he was released to his father's custody. Except for one incident of shoplifting, being absent from school without permission, and being held in juvenile detention—none of which was brought to the jury's attention—petitioner apparently had no criminal record before entering the Army.

Leaphart was aware of some, but not all, of this family history prior to petitioner's trial. He talked with petitioner's mother on several occasions, an attorney in Indiana who had befriended petitioner and his mother, and a psychologist whom Leaphart had employed to conduct an examination of petitioner in preparation for trial. He reviewed psychologists' reports that were obtained with the help of petitioner's mother. He also interviewed [codefendant] Stevens and other men at Fort Stewart. Based on these interviews, Leaphart made the reasonable decision that his client's interest would not be served by presenting this type of evidence.

His own meetings with petitioner, as well as the testimony of the psychologist at the hearing on the admissibility of petitioner's confession, convinced Leaphart that it would be unwise to put petitioner himself on the witness stand. The record indicates that petitioner never expressed any remorse about his crime, and the psychologist's testimony indicates that he might even have bragged about it on the witness stand. Leaphart formed the opinion that Burger enjoyed talking about the crimes; he was worried that the jury might regard Burger's attitude on the witness stand as indifferent or worse. Quite obviously, as the District Court concluded, an experienced trial lawyer could properly have decided not to put either petitioner or the psychologist who had thus evaluated him in a position where he would be subjected to cross-examination that might be literally fatal.

The other two witnesses that Leaphart considered using were petitioner's mother and the Indiana lawyer who had acted as petitioner's "big brother." Leaphart talked with the mother on several occasions and concluded that her testimony would not be helpful and might have been counterproductive. As the record stood, there was absolutely no evidence that petitioner had any prior criminal record of any kind. Her testimony indicates that petitioner had committed at least one petty offense. The District Judge who heard all of the testimony that she would have given on direct examination at the sentencing hearing was not convinced that it would have aided petitioner's case; it was surely not unreasonable for Leaphart to have concluded that cross-examination might well have revealed matters of historical fact that would have harmed his client's chances for a life sentence.

The Indiana lawyer was willing to travel to Georgia to testify on petitioner's behalf, but nothing in the record describes the content of the testimony he might have given. Although Leaphart was unable to recall the details of the background information that he received from the Indiana lawyer, he testified that the information was not helpful to petitioner, and the Indiana lawyer apparently agreed with that assessment. Consistently with that conclusion, petitioner's present counsel—even with the benefit of hindsight—has submitted no affidavit from that lawyer establishing that he would have offered substantial mitigating evidence if he had testified. Accordingly, while Leaphart's judgment may have been erroneous, the record surely does not permit us to reach that conclusion.

Finally, petitioner submitted several affidavits to the court to describe the evidence that Leaphart might have used if he had conducted a more thorough investigation. These affidavits present information about petitioner's troubled family background that could have affected the jury adversely by introducing facts not disclosed by his clean adult criminal record. The affidavits indicate that the affiants, had they testified, might well have referred on direct examination or cross-examination to his encounters with law enforcement authorities. For example, a former neighbor, Phyllis Russell, stated that petitioner's father did not want to associate with him when he "got into trouble and was on juvenile probation." Petitioner's uncle, Earnest Holtsclaw, narrated that petitioner "got involved with drugs" while in Florida. Cathy Russell Ray, petitioner's friend in junior high school, stated that "Chris's father was supposed to go with him to juvenile court to get a release so that he could join the service [Army]."

Even apart from their references to damaging facts, the papers are by no means uniformly helpful to petitioner because they suggest violent tendencies that are at odds with the defense's strategy of portraying petitioner's actions on the night of the murder as the result of Stevens' strong influence upon his will. For example, the District Judge pointed out:

> In an affidavit submitted to this Court, petitioner's uncle attests that
> petitioner came from a broken home and that he was unwanted by his parents.
> He opined that Burger had a split personality. "Sometimes [Burger] would be
> a nice, normal guy, then at times he would flip out and would get violent over
> nothing." Affidavit of Earnest R. Holtcsclaw [sic]; see also Affidavit of Cathy
> Russell Ray ("He had a hairtrigger temper. He would get mad and punch the
> walls. Once he broke his knuckles he got so ma[d].").
>
> On one hand, a jury could react with sympathy over the tragic childhood
> Burger endured. On the other hand, since Burger's sanity was not in issue in
> this case, the prosecution could use this same testimony, after pointing out that
> petitioner was nevertheless responsible for his acts, to emphasize that it was
> this same unpredictable propensity for violence which played a prominent role
> in the death of Burger's victim. "[M]itigation . . . ," after all, "[m]ay be in the
> eye of the beholder."

The record at the habeas corpus hearing does suggest that Leaphart could well have made a more thorough investigation than he did. Nevertheless, in considering claims of ineffective assistance of counsel, "[w]e address not what is prudent or appropriate, but only what is constitutionally compelled." We have decided that "strategic choices made after less than complete investigation are reasonable precisely to the extent that reasonable professional judgments support the limitations on investigation." Strickland, 466 U.S., at 690–691. Applying this standard, we agree with the courts below that counsel's decision not to mount an all-out investigation into petitioner's background in search of mitigating circumstances was supported by reasonable professional judgment. It appears that he did interview all potential witnesses who had been called to his attention and that there was a reasonable basis for his strategic decision that an explanation of petitioner's history would not have minimized the risk of the death penalty. Having made this judgment, he reasonably determined that he need not undertake further investigation to locate witnesses who would make statements about Burger's past. We hold that the Court of Appeals complied with the directives of *Strickland*:

> In any ineffectiveness case, a particular decision not to investigate must be directly assessed for reasonableness in all the circumstances, applying a heavy measure of deference to counsel's judgments.
>
> The reasonableness of counsel's actions may be determined or substantially influenced by the defendant's own statements or actions. Counsel's actions are usually based, quite properly, on informed strategic choices made by the defendant and on information supplied by the defendant. In particular, what investigation decisions are reasonable depends critically on such information. For example, when the facts that support a certain potential line of defense are generally known to counsel because of what the defendant has said, the need for further investigation may be considerably diminished or eliminated altogether. And when a defendant has given counsel reason to believe that pursuing certain investigations would be fruitless or even harmful, counsel's failure to pursue those investigations may not later be challenged as unreasonable. *Id.*, at 691.

Petitioner has not established that "in light of all the circumstances, the identified acts or omissions [of counsel] were outside the wide range of professionally competent assistance." *Id.*, at 690. He "has made no showing that the justice of his sentence was rendered unreliable by a breakdown in the adversary process caused by deficiencies in counsel's assistance." *Id.*, at 700.

Accordingly, the judgment of the Court of Appeals is Affirmed.

DISSENTING OPINION OF JUSTICE BLACKMUN, JOINED BY JUSTICES BRENNAN, MARSHALL, AND POWELL

. . . Even if no conflict of interest existed in this case, I would still dissent from the Court's denial of relief because petitioner was deprived of the effective assistance of counsel in connection with his capital-sentencing proceeding. His counsel failed to investigate mitigating evidence and failed to present any evidence at the sentencing hearing despite the fact that petitioner was an adolescent with psychological problems and apparent diminished mental capabilities. I agree with the Court that the adversarial nature of Georgia's capital-sentencing proceedings is sufficiently similar to a trial that petitioner's claim is governed by the same standards that apply to general claims of ineffective assistance of counsel at trial. [S]ee *Strickland v. Washington*, 466 U.S., at 686–687. It is also important to "keep in mind that counsel's function, as elaborated in prevailing professional norms, is to make the adversarial testing process work in the particular case." *Id.*, at 690. Applying that standard to petitioner's claim in light of the record of this case yields a finding that the inaction by petitioner's lawyer was "outside the wide range of professionally competent assistance" and was prejudicial to petitioner. *Id.*, at 690, 692.

In *Strickland*, this Court specifically addressed counsel's duty to investigate. It explained:

> [S]trategic choices made after thorough investigation of law and facts relevant to plausible options are virtually unchallengeable; and strategic choices made after less than complete investigation are reasonable precisely to the extent that reasonable professional judgments support the limitations on investigation. In other words, counsel has a duty to make reasonable investigations or to make a reasonable decision that makes particular investigations unnecessary. In any ineffectiveness case, a particular decision not to investigate must be directly assessed for reasonableness in all the circumstances, applying a heavy measure of deference to counsel's judgments. *Id.*, at 690–691. . . .

The limitation counsel placed on his investigation of the evidence of petitioner's mental capabilities and psychological makeup despite the indications that petitioner had problems in these respects was not supported by reasonable professional judgment.

Counsel stated that he based his decision not to move the court for a complete psychological examination of petitioner on his prior experience with the mental hospital where, he assumed, petitioner would be sent for the examination. He stated that "the results I've had with personnel at Central Hospital as far as the defense is concerned . . . hasn't been good at all." He added that he thought that any further examinations would yield the same psychopathic diagnosis reached by the psychologist who had examined petitioner once briefly and primarily to administer an IQ test for purposes of the hearing on whether petitioner's confession was admissible.

Counsel's failure to request an examination because of what he considered to be a biased procedure constituted a breakdown in the adversarial process. If in fact the procedure for psychological examinations of an indigent criminal defendant in that jurisdiction was biased, the role of petitioner's counsel at least was to seek an alternative examination process or to challenge the biased procedure. Counsel's decision to forgo the psychological examination imperiled petitioner's ability to counter the prosecutor's argument that he deserved to be executed for his role in the murder and therefore undermined the reliability of the sentencing proceeding. Moreover, such a decision to proceed without the examination in a case in which an adolescent with indications of significant psychological problems and diminished mental capabilities faces the death penalty is contrary to professional norms of competent assistance. The usefulness of a thorough evaluation in a case where there are indications that the capital defendant has problems of that kind is obvious. See *Eddings v. Oklahoma*, 455 U.S. 104, 116 (1982); cf. *Ake v. Oklahoma*, 470 U.S. 68 (1985).[b]

Counsel's decision not to investigate petitioner's family or childhood background also was not within the range of professionally reasonable judgment. Viewed as of the time he decided not to get in touch with any family member or to investigate any place where petitioner had lived, counsel provided inadequate assistance. He relied on petitioner to suggest possible witnesses or mitigating evidence. But his question to petitioner whether he could produce evidence of "anything good about him," hardly could be expected to yield information about petitioner's childhood and broken home. It is unlikely that in response to that question a defendant would volunteer the facts that his father threw him out of the house, that his mother did the same, that his stepfathers beat him and his mother, or that one stepfather involved him in drugs and alcohol at age 11. All this is mitigating evidence that could be highly relevant. See *Eddings v. Oklahoma*, 455 U.S., at 107. Furthermore, counsel testified that he spoke with petitioner perhaps "half a dozen times," the longest being "[p]robably about an hour." These bare six hours provided counsel little time to discuss possible mitigating evidence for the sentencing proceeding because counsel surely also had to discuss in detail the circumstances surrounding petitioner's confession which he was challenging and all the other features of the guilt/innocence phase of the trial. Moreover, after petitioner's death sentence was vacated on appeal and the case was remanded, counsel did not perform any further investigation whatsoever during the nine-month period before the second hearing. He simply proceeded in the same manner that had resulted in petitioner's being sentenced to death at the first hearing.

The only reason counsel spoke to petitioner's mother at all was because she sought him out after learning elsewhere that her son was charged with murder. Even after petitioner's mother initiated the contact, counsel's conduct was inexplicable. He testified that he never explained the penalty phase of the trial to petitioner's mother or what evidence then could be presented. The Court finds reasonable counsel's decision not to have petitioner's mother testify because he concluded that her testimony might be counterproductive in that it might reveal a petty offense petitioner had committed. That decision is a prime example, however, of a strategic choice made after less-than-adequate investigation, which therefore is not supported by informed professional judgment. Counsel could not reasonably determine whether presenting character witnesses would pose a risk

---

[b] Editor's note: In *Eddings*, the Court held that there was a right to present as mitigating evidence proof of a capital defendant's emotional disturbance. *Ake* established a right to a psychiatric examination at state expense for indigent defendants who offer an insanity defense.

of disclosing past criminal behavior by petitioner without first determining whether there was any such criminal behavior. Although there is a reference in the record to an incident of shoplifting a candy bar, and another reference to an automobile accident, there is no indication that counsel ever determined whether petitioner in fact had a prior criminal record. The account provided by petitioner's mother of petitioner's hitchhiking to Florida to be with her after having been thrown out of his father's house and having to sell his shoes during the trip to get food, may well have outweighed the relevance of any earlier petty theft.

I also find troubling the fact that defense counsel rejected the assistance of another lawyer (who had known petitioner) merely on the basis that the lawyer was black. The lawyer offered to come to Georgia at his own expense to provide what assistance he could. Counsel thought his assistance might have "an ill effect," however, on the trial of petitioner who is white. Counsel testified that he and the lawyer agreed that because of his race it was not wise to have the lawyer testify. I question whether this is a reasonable professional decision. The adversarial duty of petitioner's counsel was to pursue a means by which to present testimony from such a witness while doing his best to safeguard the trial from racial prejudice. Counsel apparently made no effort to investigate possible racial bias of petitioner's jury. Like counsel's abandonment of the psychological investigation because of the suspected unfairness of the examination procedure, his surrender to the perceived risk of racial discrimination without any effort to eliminate that risk is inconsistent with his adversarial role and his responsibility to further the reliability of the court proceeding.

Acceptance of the unpleasant likelihood of racial prejudice in such a trial, however, does not justify counsel's failure to accept assistance from the lawyer in any number of ways, such as investigating petitioner's childhood background in Indianapolis where the lawyer had known petitioner. Testimony by petitioner's mother at the federal habeas corpus hearing revealed that when the lawyer was in law school he had worked in a volunteer "big brother" organization for men who spent time with children who did not have a father-son relationship or a big brother. He was undoubtedly familiar with some of petitioner's friends and family members there. The affidavits submitted at the federal hearing indicate that many of those persons still reside in Indianapolis but were never approached by counsel. In sum, I reluctantly conclude that counsel fell short in his "duty to make reasonable investigations or to make a reasonable decision that makes particular investigations unnecessary." *Strickland v. Washington,* 466 U.S., at 691. Application of the *Strickland* standard to this case convinces me that further investigation was compelled constitutionally because there was inadequate information on which a reasonable professional judgment to limit the investigation could have been made.

Having concluded that the conduct of petitioner's lawyer in failing to pursue an investigation into petitioner's psychological problems or into his family and childhood background was professionally unreasonable, given the circumstances known to counsel at the time, I must also address the question whether this inadequate performance prejudiced petitioner. In my view, if more information about this adolescent's psychological problems, troubled childhood, and unfortunate family history had been available, "there is a reasonable probability that . . . the sentencer—including an appellate court, to the extent it independently reweighs the evidence—would have concluded that the balance of aggravating and mitigating circumstances did not warrant death." *Strickland v. Washington*, 466 U.S., at 695.

Chapter 19

Capital Sentencing by Judges—*Spaziano v. Florida* (1984)

Spaziano v. Florida, 468 U.S. 447, 104 S. Ct. 3154, 82 L. Ed.2d 340 (1984) (6-3, death penalty law permitting the judge to override a jury recommendation of life imprisonment is not unconstitutional).

Editor's comment: Most states require the sentence in a capital case to be imposed by the same jury that determined defendant's guilt. Some states, however, authorize the judge to determine the sentence, and a few, such as Florida, permit an override by the judge of the jury's sentence recommendation. Studies indicate that most of the overrides involve judges imposing death sentences after the jury recommended life imprisonment.

In *Walton v. Arizona*, 497 U.S. 639 (1990), the Supreme Court upheld a capital sentencing scheme in which the judge determines the existence of aggravating and mitigating factors and imposes the sentence. *Walton* was overruled by *Ring v. Arizona*, 122 S. Ct. 2428 (2002), which held that it violates the Sixth Amendment right to a jury trial for the trial judge to determine the presence or absence of aggravating factors. *Ring* did not involve the determination of mitigating factors by the judge, nor did it require that a jury make the ultimate determination whether to impose the death penalty.

❖   ❖   ❖

OPINION OF JUSTICE BLACKMUN FOR THE COURT

. . . Petitioner's . . . challenge concerns the trial judge's imposition of a sentence of death after the jury had recommended life imprisonment. Petitioner urges that allowing a judge to override a jury's recommendation of life violates the Eighth Amendment's proscription against "cruel and unusual punishments.". . .

Petitioner's primary argument is that the laws and practice in most of the States indicate a nearly unanimous recognition that juries, not judges, are better equipped to make reliable capital-sentencing decisions and that a jury's decision for life should be inviolate. The reason for that recognition, petitioner urges, is that the nature of the decision whether a defendant should live or die sets capital sentencing apart and requires that a jury have the ultimate word. Noncapital sentences are imposed for various reasons, including rehabilitation, incapacitation, and deterrence. In contrast, the primary justification for the death penalty is retribution. As has been recognized, "the decision that capital punishment may be the appropriate sanction in extreme cases is an expression of the community's belief that certain crimes are themselves so grievous an affront to humanity that the only adequate response may be the penalty of death." *Gregg.* The imposition of the death penalty, in other words, is an expression of community outrage. Since the jury serves as the voice of the community, the jury is in the best position to decide whether a particular crime is so heinous that the community's response must be death. If the answer is no, that decision should be final.

Petitioner's argument obviously has some appeal. But it has two fundamental flaws. First, the distinctions between capital and noncapital sentences are not so clear as petitioner suggests. Petitioner acknowledges, for example, that deterrence may be a justification for capital as well as for noncapital sentences. He suggests only that deterrence is not a proper consideration for particular sentencers who are deciding whether the penalty should be imposed in a given case. The same is true, however, in noncapital cases. Whatever the sentence, its deterrent function is primarily a consideration for the legislature. *Gregg.* Similar points can be made about the other purposes of capital and noncapital punishment. Although incapacitation has never been embraced as a sufficient justification for the death penalty, it is a legitimate consideration in a capital sentencing proceeding. While retribution clearly plays a more prominent role in a capital case, retribution is an element of all punishments society imposes, and there is no suggestion as to any of these that the sentence may not be imposed by a judge.

Second, even accepting petitioner's premise that the retributive purpose behind the death penalty is the element that sets the penalty apart, it does not follow that the sentence must be imposed by a jury. Imposing the sentence in individual cases is not the sole or even the primary vehicle through which the community's voice can be expressed. This Court's decisions indicate that the discretion of the sentencing authority, whether judge or jury, must be limited and reviewable. The sentencer is responsible for weighing the specific aggravating and mitigating circumstances the legislature has determined are necessary touchstones in determining whether death is the appropriate penalty. Thus, even if it is a jury that imposes the sentence, the "community's voice" is not given free rein. The community's voice is heard at least as clearly in the legislature when the death penalty is authorized and the particular circumstances in which death is appropriate are defined.

We do not denigrate the significance of the jury's role as a link between the community and the penal system and as a bulwark between the accused and the

State. The point is simply that the purpose of the death penalty is not frustrated by, or inconsistent with, a scheme in which the imposition of the penalty in individual cases is determined by a judge.

We also acknowledge the presence of the majority view that capital sentencing, unlike other sentencing, should be performed by a jury. As petitioner points out, 30 out of 37 jurisdictions with a capital sentencing statute give the life-or-death decision to the jury, with only 3 of the remaining 7 allowing a judge to override a jury's recommendation of life.

The fact that a majority of jurisdictions have adopted a different practice, however, does not establish that contemporary standards of decency are offended by the jury override. The Eighth Amendment is not violated every time a State reaches a conclusion different from a majority of its sisters over how best to administer its criminal laws. "Although the judgments of legislatures, juries, and prosecutors weigh heavily in the balance, it is for us ultimately to judge whether the Eighth Amendment" is violated by a challenged practice. In light of the facts that the Sixth Amendment does not require jury sentencing, that the demands of fairness and reliability in capital cases do not require it, and that neither the nature of, nor the purpose behind, the death penalty requires jury sentencing, we cannot conclude that placing responsibility on the trial judge to impose the sentence in a capital case is unconstitutional.

As the Court several times has made clear, we are unwilling to say that there is any one right way for a State to set up its capital sentencing scheme. The Court twice has concluded that Florida has struck a reasonable balance between sensitivity to the individual and his circumstances and ensuring that the penalty is not imposed arbitrarily or discriminatorily. . . . We are not persuaded that placing the responsibility on a trial judge to impose the sentence in a capital case is so fundamentally at odds with contemporary standards of fairness and decency that Florida must be required to alter its scheme and give final authority to the jury to make the life-or-death decision. . . .

OPINION OF JUSTICE STEVENS, CONCURRING IN PART AND DISSENTING IN PART, JOINED BY JUSTICES BRENNAN AND MARSHALL

In this case, as in 82 others arising under the capital punishment statute enacted by Florida in 1972, the trial judge sentenced the defendant to death after a jury had recommended a sentence of life imprisonment. The question presented is whether the Constitution of the United States permits petitioner's execution when the prosecution has been unable to persuade a jury of his peers that the death penalty is the appropriate punishment for his crime. . . .

Because it is the one punishment that cannot be prescribed by a rule of law as judges normally understand such rules, but rather is ultimately understood only as an expression of the community's outrage—its sense that an individual has lost his moral entitlement to live—I am convinced that the danger of an excessive response can only be avoided if the decision to impose the death penalty is made by a jury rather than by a single governmental official. This conviction is consistent with the judgment of history and the current consensus of opinion that juries are better equipped than judges to make capital sentencing decisions. The basic explanation for that consensus lies in the fact that the question whether a sentence of death is excessive in the particular circumstances of any case is one that must be answered by the decision maker that is best able to "express the conscience of the community on the ultimate question of life or death." *Witherspoon v. Illinois*, 391 U.S. 510, 519 (1968) (footnote omitted). . . .

IV

The Court correctly notes that sentencing has traditionally been a question with which the jury is not concerned. Deciding upon the appropriate sentence for a person who has been convicted of a crime is the routine work of judges. By reason of this experience, as well as their training, judges presumably perform this function well. But, precisely because the death penalty is unique, the normal presumption that a judge is the appropriate sentencing authority does not apply in the capital context. The decision whether or not an individual must die is not one that has traditionally been entrusted to judges. This tradition, which has marked a sharp distinction between the usual evaluations of judicial competence with respect to capital and noncapital sentencing, not only eliminates the general presumption that judicial sentencing is appropriate in the capital context, but also in itself provides reason to question whether assigning this role to governmental officials and not juries is consistent with the community's moral sense.

While tradition and contemporary practice in most American jurisdictions indicate that capital sentencing by judges offends a moral sense that this unique kind of judgment must be made by a more authentic voice of the community, nevertheless the Court is correct to insist that these factors cannot be conclusive, or the Eighth Amendment would prevent any innovation or variation in the administration of the criminal law. Therefore, a more focused inquiry into the Eighth Amendment implications of the decision to put an accused to death, and the jury's relationship to those implications, is essential.

V

Punishment may be "cruel and unusual" because of its barbarity or because it is "excessive" or "disproportionate" to the offense. In order to evaluate a claim that a punishment is excessive, one must first identify the reasons for imposing it.

In general, punishment may rationally be imposed for four reasons: (1) to rehabilitate the offender; (2) to incapacitate him from committing offenses in the future; (3) to deter others from committing offenses; or (4) to assuage the victim's or the community's desire for revenge or retribution. The first of these purposes is obviously inapplicable to the death sentence. The second would be served by execution, but in view of the availability of imprisonment as an alternative means of preventing the defendant from violating the law in the future, the death sentence would clearly be an excessive response to this concern. We are thus left with deterrence and retribution as the justifications for capital punishment.

A majority of the Court has concluded that the general deterrence rationale adequately justifies the imposition of capital punishment at least for certain classes of offenses for which the legislature may reasonably conclude that the death penalty has a deterrent effect. However, in reaching this conclusion we have stated that this is a judgment peculiarly within the competence of legislatures and not the judiciary. Thus, the deterrence rationale cannot be used to support the use of judicial as opposed to jury discretion in capital sentencing, at least absent some finding, which the Florida Legislature has not purported to make, that judges are better at gauging the general deterrent effect of a capital sentence than are juries.

Moreover, the deterrence rationale in itself argues only for ensuring that the death sentence be imposed in a significant number of cases and remain as a potential social response to the defined conduct. Since the decision whether to employ jury sentencing does not change the number of cases for which death is a possible punishment, the use of judicial sentencing cannot have sufficient impact on the deterrent effect of the statute to justify its use; a murderer's calculus will not be affected by whether the death penalty is imposed by a judge or jury.

Finally, even though the deterrence rationale may provide a basis for identifying the defendants eligible for the death penalty, our cases establish that the decision whether to condemn a man to death in a given case may not be the product of deterrence considerations alone. Despite the fact that a legislature may rationally conclude that mandatory capital punishment will have a deterrent effect for a given class of aggravated crimes significantly greater than would discretionary capital sentencing, we have invalidated mandatory capital punishment statutes, as well as statutes that do not permit the trier of fact to consider any mitigating circumstance, even if unrelated to or perhaps inconsistent with the deterrent purposes of the penalty. It is now well settled that the trier of fact in a capital case must be permitted to weigh any consideration—indeed any aspect of the defendant's crime or character—relevant to the question whether death is an excessive punishment for the offense. Thus, particular capital sentencing decisions cannot rest entirely on deterrent considerations.

In the context of capital felony cases, therefore, the question whether the death sentence is an appropriate, nonexcessive response to the particular facts of the case will depend on the retribution justification. The nature of that justification was described in *Gregg*:

> In part, capital punishment is an expression of society's moral outrage at
> particularly offensive conduct. This function may be unappealing to many, but
> it is essential in an ordered society that asks its citizens to rely on legal

processes rather than self-help to vindicate their wrongs. 428 U.S., at 183–184 (opinion of Stewart, Powell, and Stevens, JJ).

Thus, in the final analysis, capital punishment rests on not a legal but an ethical judgment—an assessment of what we called in *Enmund* the "moral guilt" of the defendant. And if the decision that capital punishment is the appropriate sanction in extreme cases is justified because it expresses the community's moral sensibility—its demand that a given affront to humanity requires retribution—it follows, I believe, that a representative cross section of the community must be given the responsibility for making that decision. In no other way can an unjustifiable risk of an excessive response be avoided. . . .

VII

. . . That the jury provides a better link to community values than does a single judge is supported not only by our cases, but also by common sense. Juries— comprised as they are of a fair cross section of the community—are more representative institutions than is the judiciary; they reflect more accurately the composition and experiences of the community as a whole, and inevitably make decisions based on community values more reliably, than can that segment of the community that is selected for service on the bench. Indeed, as the preceding discussion demonstrates, the belief that juries more accurately reflect the conscience of the community than can a single judge is the central reason that the jury right has been recognized at the guilt stage in our jurisprudence. This same belief firmly supports the use of juries in capital sentencing, in order to address the Eighth Amendment's concern that capital punishment be administered consistently with community values. In fact, the available empirical evidence indicates that judges and juries do make sentencing decisions in capital cases in significantly different ways, thus supporting the conclusion that entrusting the capital decision to a single judge creates an unacceptable risk that the decision will not be consistent with community values. . . .

Chapter 20

Proportional Sentencing Review—*Pulley v. Harris* (1984)

Pulley v. Harris, 465 U.S. 37, 104 S. Ct. 871, 79 L. Ed.2d 29 (1984) (7–2, the Eighth Amendment does not require appeals courts to determine if a death sentence is consistent with the punishment imposed in similar cases).

Editor's comment: In *Furman v. Georgia* (Chapter 2), a plurality of the Supreme Court criticized the uneven distribution of death sentences. They pointed out that equally blameworthy offenders were not treated alike: some got the death penalty, while others did not. Subsequently, in *Gregg v. Georgia* (Chapter 3), the Court upheld a capital punishment law that required appellate review of death sentences to determine if they were disproportionate to the punishments imposed in similar cases. Such comparative proportionality review—the type sought by defendant Harris in this case—asks whether the death penalty is imposed on offenders of comparable blameworthiness, taking into account the nature of the offense and the characteristics of the offender. It is different from traditional proportionality analysis, which asks whether the punishment is inappropriately harsh for a particular offense or offender. *Coker v. Georgia* (Chapter 5), in which the Court held that the death penalty was "grossly excessive" punishment for rape, illustrates the traditional approach.

❖ ❖ ❖

OPINION OF JUSTICE WHITE FOR THE COURT

Respondent Harris was convicted of a capital crime in a California court and was sentenced to death. Along with many other challenges to the conviction and sentence, Harris claimed on appeal that the California capital punishment statute

221

was invalid under the United States Constitution because it failed to require the California Supreme Court to compare Harris's sentence with the sentences imposed in similar capital cases and thereby to determine whether they were proportionate. . . .

II

At the outset, we should more clearly identify the issue before us. Traditionally, "proportionality" has been used with reference to an abstract evaluation of the appropriateness of a sentence for a particular crime. Looking to the gravity of the offense and the severity of the penalty, to sentences imposed for other crimes, and to sentencing practices in other jurisdictions, this Court has occasionally struck down punishments as inherently disproportionate, and therefore cruel and unusual, when imposed for a particular crime or category of crime. See, *e.g.*, *Solem v. Helm; Enmund v. Florida; Coker v. Georgia.* The death penalty is not in all cases a disproportionate penalty in this sense. *Gregg.*

The proportionality review sought by Harris, required by the Court of Appeals, and provided for in numerous state statutes is of a different sort. This sort of proportionality review presumes that the death sentence is not disproportionate to the crime in the traditional sense. It purports to inquire instead whether the penalty is nonetheless unacceptable in a particular case because it is disproportionate to the punishment imposed on others convicted of the same crime. The issue in this case, therefore, is whether the Eighth Amendment, applicable to the States through the Fourteenth Amendment, requires a state appellate court, before it affirms a death sentence, to compare the sentence in the case before it with the penalties imposed in similar cases if requested to do so by the prisoner. Harris insists that it does and that this is the invariable rule in every case. Apparently, the Court of Appeals was of the same view. We do not agree. . . .

III

Harris's submission is rooted in *Furman v. Georgia*. In *Furman*, the Court concluded that capital punishment, as then administered under statutes vesting unguided sentencing discretion in juries and trial judges, had become unconstitutionally cruel and unusual punishment. The death penalty was being imposed so discriminatorily (Douglas, J., concurring), so wantonly and freakishly (Stewart, J., concurring), and so infrequently (White, J., concurring), that any given death sentence was cruel and unusual. In response to that decision, roughly two-thirds of the States promptly redrafted their capital sentencing statutes in an effort to limit jury discretion and avoid arbitrary and inconsistent results. All of the new statutes provide for automatic appeal of death sentences. Most, such as Georgia's, require the reviewing court, to some extent at least, to determine whether, considering both the crime and the defendant, the sentence is disproportionate to that imposed in similar cases. Not every State has adopted such a procedure. In some States, such as Florida, the appellate court performs proportionality review despite the absence of a statutory requirement; in others, such as California and Texas, it does not.

Four years after *Furman*, this Court examined several of the new state statutes. We upheld one of each of the three sorts mentioned above. See *Gregg v. Georgia*; *Proffitt v. Florida*, 428 U.S. 242 (1976); *Jurek v. Texas*. Needless to say, that some schemes providing proportionality review are constitutional does not mean that such review is indispensable. We take statutes as we find them. To endorse the statute as a whole is not to say that anything different is unacceptable. As was said in *Gregg*, "[w]e do not intend to suggest that only the above-described procedures would be permissible under *Furman* or that any sentencing system constructed along these general lines would inevitably satisfy the concerns of *Furman*, for each distinct system must be examined on an individual basis." Examination of our 1976 cases makes clear that they do not establish proportionality review as a constitutional requirement.

In *Gregg*, six Justices concluded that the Georgia system adequately directed and limited the jury's discretion. The bifurcated proceedings, the limited number of capital crimes, the requirement that at least one aggravating circumstance be present, and the consideration of mitigating circumstances minimized the risk of wholly arbitrary, capricious, or freakish sentences. In the opinion announcing the judgment of the Court, three Justices concluded that sentencing discretion under the statute was sufficiently controlled by clear and objective standards. In a separate concurrence, three other Justices found sufficient reason to expect that the death penalty would not be imposed so wantonly, freakishly, or infrequently as to be invalid under *Furman*.

Both opinions made much of the statutorily-required comparative proportionality review. This was considered an additional safeguard against arbitrary or capricious sentencing. While the opinion of Justices Stewart, Powell and Stevens suggested that some form of meaningful appellate review is required, those Justices did not declare that comparative review was so critical that without it the Georgia statute would not have passed constitutional muster. Indeed, in summarizing the components of an adequate capital sentencing scheme, Justices Stewart, Powell, and Stevens did not mention comparative review:

> "[T]he concerns expressed in *Furman* . . . can be met by a carefully drafted statute that ensures that the sentencing authority be given adequate information and guidance. As a general proposition, these concerns are best met by a system that provides for a bifurcated proceeding at which the sentencing authority is apprised of the information relevant to the imposition of sentence and provided with standards to guide its use of the information."

In short, the Court of Appeals erred in concluding that *Gregg* required proportionality review. There is even less basis for reliance on *Proffitt v. Florida*. The

Florida statute provides for a bifurcated procedure and forecloses the death penalty unless the sentencing authority finds that at least one of eight statutory aggravating circumstances is present and is not outweighed by any mitigating circumstances. The joint opinion of Justices Stewart, Powell, and Stevens observed that the Florida scheme, like its Georgia counterpart, requires the sentencer to focus on the individual circumstances of each homicide and each defendant. Also, by vesting ultimate sentencing authority in the judge rather than the jury, the statute was expected to yield more consistent sentencing at the trial court level. Only after concluding that trial judges are given specific and detailed guidance to assist them in deciding whether to impose the death penalty did the opinion observe that death sentences are reviewed to ensure that they are consistent with the sentences imposed in similar cases. The concurring opinion filed by three other Justices approved the Florida statute without even mentioning appellate review.

That *Gregg* and *Proffitt* did not establish a constitutional requirement of proportionality review is made clearer by *Jurek v. Texas*, decided the same day. In *Jurek* we upheld a death sentence even though neither the statute, as in Georgia, nor state case-law, as in Florida, provided for comparative proportionality review. . . .

That the three [*Jurek* plurality] Justices considered such appellate review as Texas provided "a means to promote the evenhanded, rational, and consistent imposition of death sentences," is revealing. First, it makes plain that, at least in light of the other safeguards in the Texas statute, proportionality review would have been constitutionally superfluous. Second, it suggests that the similarly-worded references to appellate review in *Gregg* and *Proffitt* were focused not on proportionality review as such, but only on the provision of some sort of prompt and automatic appellate review. The concurring opinion expressing the views of three other Justices sustained the Texas statute by focusing solely on the limitations on the jury's discretion, without even mentioning appellate review. In view of *Jurek*, we are quite sure that at that juncture the Court had not mandated comparative proportionality review whenever a death sentence was imposed.

There is thus no basis in our cases for holding that comparative proportionality review by an appellate court is required in every case in which the death penalty is imposed and the defendant requests it. Indeed, to so hold would effectively overrule *Jurek* and would substantially depart from the sense of *Gregg* and *Proffitt*. We are not persuaded that the Eighth Amendment requires us to take that course.

IV

Assuming that there could be a capital sentencing system so lacking in other checks on arbitrariness that it would not pass constitutional muster without comparative proportionality review, the 1977 California statute is not of that sort. Under this scheme, a person convicted of first degree murder is sentenced to life imprisonment unless one or more "special circumstances" are found, in which case the punishment is either death or life imprisonment without parole. Special circumstances are alleged in the charging paper and tried with the issue of guilt at the initial phase of the trial. At the close of evidence, the jury decides guilt or innocence and determines whether the special circumstances alleged are present. Each special circumstance must be proved beyond a reasonable doubt. If the jury finds the defendant guilty of first degree murder and finds at least one special circumstance, the trial proceeds to a second phase to determine the appropriate penalty. Additional evidence may be offered and the jury is given a list of relevant factors. . . .

By requiring the jury to find at least one special circumstance beyond a reasonable doubt, the statute limits the death sentence to a small sub-class of capital-eligible cases. The statutory list of relevant factors, applied to defendants within this sub-class, "provide[s] jury guidance and lessen[s] the chance of arbitrary application of the death penalty, guarantee[ing] that the jury's discretion will be guided and its consideration deliberate." The jury's "discretion is suitably directed and limited so as to minimize the risk of wholly arbitrary and capricious action." *Gregg.* Its decision is reviewed by the trial judge and the State Supreme Court. On its face, this system, without any requirement or practice of comparative proportionality review, cannot be successfully challenged under *Furman* and our subsequent cases.

Any capital sentencing scheme may occasionally produce aberrational outcomes. Such inconsistencies are a far cry from the major systemic defects identified in *Furman.* As we have acknowledged in the past, "there can be 'no perfect procedure for deciding in which cases governmental authority should be used to impose death.'" *Lockett.* As we are presently informed, we cannot say that the California procedures provided Harris inadequate protection against the evil identified in *Furman.* The Court of Appeals therefore erred in ordering the writ of habeas corpus to issue. Its judgment is reversed and the case remanded for further proceedings consistent with this opinion.

CONCURRING OPINION OF JUSTICE STEVENS

While I agree with the basic conclusion of part III of the Court's opinion—our case law does not establish a constitutional requirement that comparative proportionality review be conducted by an appellate court in every case in which the death penalty is imposed—my understanding of our decisions in *Gregg; Proffitt; Jurek;* and *Zant v. Stephens,* 462 U.S. 862 (1983)[a] is sufficiently different from that reflected in part III to prevent me from joining that portion of the opinion.

---

[a] Editor's note: *Zant v. Stephens* relied in part on the Georgia appellate process, including proportionality review, in upholding a death sentence. (The sentence was based on three aggravating factors, one of which had been held invalid after the trial.)

While the cases relied upon by respondent do not establish that comparative proportionality review is a constitutionally required element of a capital sentencing system, I believe the case law does establish that appellate review plays an essential role in eliminating the systemic arbitrariness and capriciousness which infected death penalty schemes invalidated by *Furman*, and hence that some form of meaningful appellate review is constitutionally required.

The systemic arbitrariness and capriciousness in the imposition of capital punishment under statutory schemes invalidated by *Furman* resulted from two basic defects in those schemes. First, the systems were permitting the imposition of capital punishment in broad classes of offenses for which the penalty would always constitute cruel and unusual punishment. Second, even among those types of homicides for which the death penalty could be constitutionally imposed as punishment, the schemes vested essentially unfettered discretion in juries and trial judges to impose the death sentence. Given these defects, arbitrariness and capriciousness in the imposition of the punishment was inevitable, and given the extreme nature of the punishment, constitutionally intolerable. The statutes we have approved in *Gregg*, *Proffitt*, and *Jurek* were designed to eliminate each of these defects. Each scheme provided an effective mechanism for categorically narrowing the class of offenses for which the death penalty could be imposed and provided special procedural safeguards including appellate review of the sentencing authority's decision to impose the death penalty. . . .

DISSENTING OPINION OF JUSTICE BRENNAN, JOINED BY JUSTICE MARSHALL

. . . II

The question directly presented by this case is whether the Federal Constitution requires a court of statewide jurisdiction to undertake comparative proportionality review before a death sentence may be carried out. The results obtained by many states that undertake such proportionality review, pursuant to either state statute or judicial decision, convince me that this form of appellate review serves to eliminate some, if only a small part, of the irrationality that infects the current imposition of death sentences throughout the various States. To this extent, I believe that comparative proportionality review is mandated by the Constitution.

A. Some forms of irrationality that infect the administration of the death penalty—unlike discrimination by race, gender, socioeconomic status, or geographic location within a State—cannot be measured in any comprehensive way. That does not mean, however, that the process under which death sentences are currently being imposed is otherwise rational or acceptable. Rather, for any individual defendant the process is filled with so much unpredictability that "it smacks of little more than a lottery system," *Furman v. Georgia*, 408 U.S., at 293

(Brennan, J., concurring), under which being chosen for a death sentence remains as random as "being struck by lightning," *id.*, at 309 (Stewart, J., concurring).

Chief among the reasons for this unpredictability is the fact that similarly situated defendants, charged and convicted for similar crimes within the same State, often receive vastly different sentences. Professor John Kaplan of the Stanford Law School has summarized the dilemma:

> The problem [of error in imposing capital punishment] is much more serious if we consider the chances of error in the system to be more than the execution of someone who is completely innocent—the ultimate horror case. Though examples of victims of mistaken identity are sometimes found on death row, the far more common cases fall into two types. In one, the recipient of the death penalty is guilty of a crime, but of a lesser offense, for which capital punishment is not in theory available. . . .
>
> The second type of error in capital punishment occurs when we execute someone whose crime does not seem so aggravated when compared to those of many who escaped the death penalty. It is in this kind of case—which is extremely common—that we must worry whether, first, we have designed procedures which are appropriate to the decision between life and death and, second, whether we have followed those procedures. Kaplan, The Problem of Capital Punishment, 1983 U. Ill. L. Rev. 555, 576.

Comparative proportionality review is aimed at eliminating this second type of error.

B. Disproportionality among sentences given different defendants can only be eliminated after sentencing disparities are identified. And the most logical way to identify such sentencing disparities is for a court of statewide jurisdiction to conduct comparisons between death sentences imposed by different judges or juries within the State. This is what the Court labels comparative proportionality review. Although clearly no panacea, such review often serves to identify the most extreme examples of disproportionality among similarly situated defendants. At least to this extent, this form of appellate review serves to eliminate some of the irrationality that currently surrounds imposition of a death sentence. If only to further this limited purpose, therefore, I believe that the Constitution's prohibition on the irrational imposition of the death penalty requires that this procedural safeguard be provided.

Indeed, despite the Court's insistence that such review is not compelled by the Federal Constitution, over 30 States now require, either by statute or judicial decision, some form of comparative proportionality review before any death sentence may be carried out. By itself, this should weigh heavily on the side of requiring such appellate review. In addition, these current practices establish beyond dispute that such review can be administered without much difficulty by a court of statewide jurisdiction in each State.

Perhaps the best evidence of the value of proportionality review can be gathered by examining the actual results obtained in those States which now require such review. For example, since 1973, the statute controlling appellate review of death sentences in the State of Georgia has required that the Supreme Court of Georgia determine "[w]hether the sentence of death is excessive or disproportionate to the penalty imposed in similar cases, considering both the crime and the defendant."... Pursuant to this statutory mandate, the Georgia Supreme Court has vacated at least seven death sentences because it was convinced that they were comparatively disproportionate. See, *e.g., High v. State,* 276 S.E.2d 5 (1981) (death sentence disproportionate for armed robbery and kidnapping); *Hall v. State,* 244 S.E.2d 833 (1978) (death sentence disproportionate for felony murder when co-defendant received life sentence in subsequent jury trial); *Ward v. State,* 236 S.E.2d 365 (1977) (death sentence disproportionate for murder when defendant had received life sentence for same crime in previous trial); *Jarrell v. State,* 216 S.E.2d 258 (1975) (death sentence disproportionate for armed robbery); *Floyd v. State,* 210 S.E.2d 810 (1974) (same); *Gregg v. State,* 210 S.E.2d 659 (1974) (same); *Coley v. State,* 204 S.E.2d 612 (1974) (death sentence disproportionate for rape). Cf. *Hill v. State,* 229 S.E.2d 737 (1976) (death sentence not disproportionate even though unclear which defendant actually committed murder; sentence later commuted to life imprisonment by Board of Pardons and Paroles).

... What these cases clearly demonstrate, in my view, is that comparative proportionality review serves to eliminate some, if only a small part, of the irrationality that currently infects imposition of the death penalty by the various States. Before any execution is carried out, therefore, a State should be required under the Eighth and Fourteenth Amendments to conduct such appellate review. The Court's decision in *Furman,* and the Court's continuing emphasis on meaningful appellate review ... require no less.... I dissent.

Chapter 21

Death Sentences and Double Jeopardy—*Arizona v. Rumsey* (1984)

Arizona v. Rumsey, 467 U.S. 203, 104 S. Ct. 2305, 81 L. Ed.2d 164 (1984) (7–2, Double Jeopardy Clause of Fifth Amendment prohibits a death sentence after defendant, sentenced to life imprisonment, won a reversal on appeal).

Editor's comment: The interpretation of the Fifth Amendment's rather straightforward language—"nor shall any person be subject for the same offense to be twice put in jeopardy of life or limb"—is marked by great confusion. To properly understand the Court's thinking in the *Rumsey* case, some background on double jeopardy law is necessary. The double jeopardy principles that follow apply to all cases, not just capital cases.

A defendant who is acquitted may not be retried, but a defendant who is convicted and appeals successfully may ordinarily be tried again. *United States v. Ball*, 163 U.S. 662 (1896). If the accused faces multiple charges, is convicted of some and acquitted of others, he may be retried only on the convicted charges. Indeed, even an "implied acquittal" of certain charges serves as a bar to retrial of those charges. *Green v. United States*, 355 U.S. 184 (1957). For instance, if the jury at a defendant's initial trial was instructed that it could convict of either a greater charge or a lesser included offense—such as first-degree murder or second-degree murder—and it convicted defendant of the lesser offense, the defendant would be implicitly acquitted of the greater offense. Consequently, such a defendant who appealed the second-degree murder conviction could not be retried for first-degree murder. The implied acquittal doctrine generally does not apply to sentencing, however. The imposition of a particular sentence is not considered an "acquittal" of a higher sentence. Therefore, following an appeal and a second conviction, a higher sentence may be imposed. *North Carolina v. Pearce*, 395 U.S. 711 (1969).

This brings us to double jeopardy in the death sentence context. If, in a capital case, the sentencer chooses the life imprisonment option, and the defendant appeals this conviction and wins, may he be sentenced to death if again convicted of the capital offense? The *Pearce* rule, just noted, suggests that he could, but in *Bullington v. Missouri*, 451 U.S. 430 (1981), the Supreme Court created an exception for death penalty cases: the selection of a life sentence is an "implied acquittal" of the ultimate punishment. The same issue was reconsidered in *Arizona v. Rumsey*, the main difference being that Arizona provided for sentencing by the trial judge instead of a jury. The effect of the Court's rule is that a capital defendant sentenced to life will not have to face a death sentence again for the same crime. Because the *Rumsey* dissent relies heavily on Justice Powell's dissenting opinion in *Bullington*, the latter is also reprinted here.

❖   ❖   ❖

OPINION OF JUSTICE O'CONNOR FOR THE COURT

. . . In *Bullington v. Missouri* this Court held that the Double Jeopardy Clause applies to Missouri's capital sentencing proceeding and thus bars imposition of the death penalty upon reconviction after an initial conviction, set aside on appeal, has resulted in rejection of the death sentence. The Court identified several characteristics of Missouri's sentencing proceeding that make it comparable to a trial for double jeopardy purposes. The discretion of the sentencer— the jury in Missouri—is restricted to precisely two options: death, and life imprisonment without possibility of release for 50 years. In addition, the sentencer is to make its decision guided by substantive standards and based on evidence introduced in a separate proceeding that formally resembles a trial. Finally, the prosecution has to prove certain statutorily defined facts beyond a reasonable doubt in order to support a sentence of death. For these reasons, when the Missouri sentencer imposes a sentence of life imprisonment in a capital sentencing proceeding, it has determined that the prosecution has failed to prove its case. Because the Court believed that the anxiety and ordeal suffered by a defendant in Missouri's capital sentencing proceeding are the equal of those suffered in a trial on the issue of guilt, the Court concluded that the Double Jeopardy Clause prohibits the State from resentencing the defendant to death after the sentencer has in effect acquitted the defendant of that penalty.

The capital sentencing proceeding in Arizona shares the characteristics of the Missouri proceeding that make it resemble a trial for purposes of the Double Jeopardy Clause. The sentencer—the trial judge in Arizona—is required to choose between two options: death, and life imprisonment without possibility of parole for 25 years. The sentencer must make the decision guided by detailed statutory standards defining aggravating and mitigating circumstances; in particular, death may not be imposed unless at least one aggravating circumstance is found, whereas death must be imposed if there is one aggravating circumstance and no mitigating circumstance sufficiently substantial to call for leniency. The sentencer must make findings with respect to each of the statutory aggravating and mitigating circumstances, and the sentencing hearing involves the submission of evidence and the presentation of argument. The usual rules of evidence govern the admission of evidence of aggravating circumstances, and the State must prove the existence of aggravating circumstances beyond a reasonable doubt. As the Supreme Court of Arizona held, these characteristics make the Arizona capital sentencing proceeding indistinguishable for double jeopardy purposes from the capital sentencing proceeding in Missouri.

That the sentencer in Arizona is the trial judge rather than the jury does not render the sentencing proceeding any less like a trial. Nor does the availability of appellate review, including reweighing of aggravating and mitigating circumstances, make the appellate process part of a single continuing sentencing proceeding. The Supreme Court of Arizona noted that its role is strictly that of an appellate court, not a trial court. Indeed, no appeal need be taken if life imprisonment is imposed, and the appellate reweighing can work only to the defendant's advantage. In short, a sentence imposed after a completed Arizona capital sentencing hearing is a judgment like the sentence at issue in *Bullington v. Missouri,* which this Court held triggers the protections of the Double Jeopardy Clause.

The double jeopardy principle relevant to respondent's case is the same as that invoked in *Bullington*: an acquittal on the merits by the sole decision maker in the proceeding is final and bars retrial on the same charge. Application of the *Bullington* principle renders respondent's death sentence a violation of the Double Jeopardy Clause because respondent's initial sentence of life imprisonment was undoubtedly an acquittal on the merits of the central issue in the proceeding—whether death was the appropriate punishment for respondent's offense. The trial court entered findings denying the existence of each of the seven statutory aggravating circumstances, and as required by state law, the court then entered judgment in respondent's favor on the issue of death. That judgment, based on findings sufficient to establish legal entitlement to the life sentence, amounts to an acquittal on the merits and, as such, bars any retrial of the appropriateness of the death penalty. . . .

Bullington v. Missouri held that double jeopardy protections attach to Missouri's capital sentencing proceeding because that proceeding is like a trial. The capital sentencing proceeding in Arizona is indistinguishable for double jeopardy purposes from the proceeding in Missouri. Under *Bullington,* therefore, respondent's initial sentence of life imprisonment constitutes an acquittal of the death penalty, and the State of Arizona cannot now sentence respondent to death on his conviction for first degree murder. . . .

DISSENTING OPINION OF JUSTICE REHNQUIST, JOINED BY JUSTICE WHITE

. . . I continue to believe that *Bullington* was wrongly decided for the reasons expressed in Justice Powell's dissent in that case. But even apart from those views,

I do not believe that the reasoning underlying *Bullington* applies to this remand for resentencing to correct a legal error. Accordingly, I dissent.

The central premise of the Court's holding today is that the trial court's first finding—that there were no aggravating and no mitigating circumstances and therefore only a life sentence could be imposed—amounted to an "implied acquittal" on the merits of respondent's eligibility for the death sentence, thereby barring the possibility of an enhanced sentence upon resentencing by virtue of the Double Jeopardy Clause. But the Court's continued reliance on the "implied acquittal" rationale of *Bullington* is simply inapt. Unlike the jury's decision in *Bullington*, where the jury had broad discretion to decide whether capital punishment was appropriate, the trial judge's discretion in this case was carefully confined and directed to determining whether certain specified aggravating factors ✨ existed. . . . It is obvious from the record that the State established at the first hearing that respondent murdered his victim in the course of an armed robbery, a fact which was undisputed at sentencing. In no sense can it be meaningfully argued that the State failed to "prove" its case—the existence of at least one aggravating circumstance. It is hard to see how there has been an "implied acquittal" of a statutory aggravating circumstance when the record explicitly establishes the factual basis that such an aggravating circumstance existed. But for the trial judge's erroneous construction of governing state law, the judge would have been required to impose the death penalty.

If, as a matter of state law, the Arizona Supreme Court had simply corrected the erroneous sentence itself without remanding, there could be no argument that *Bullington* would prevent the imposition of the death sentence. . . .

The fact that in this case the legal error was ultimately corrected by the trial court did not mean that the State sought to marshal the same or additional evidence against a capital defendant which had proved insufficient to prove the State's "case" against him the first time. There is no logical reason for a different result here simply because the Arizona Supreme Court remanded the case to the trial court for the purpose of correcting the legal error, particularly when the resentencing did not constitute the kind of "retrial" which the *Bullington* Court condemned. Accordingly, I would reverse the decision of the Arizona Supreme Court in this case.

DISSENTING OPINION OF JUSTICE POWELL, JOINED BY CHIEF JUSTICE BURGER AND JUSTICES WHITE AND REHNQUIST, IN *BULLINGTON V. MISSOURI*, 451 U.S. 430 (1981)

. . . This is the first time the Court has held that the Double Jeopardy Clause applies equally to sentencing and to determinations of guilt or innocence. It heretofore has been thought that there is a fundamental difference between the two. . . . I would adhere to these precedents, and think they control this case.

Underlying the question of guilt or innocence is an objective truth: the defendant, in fact, did or did not commit the acts constituting the crime charged. From the time an accused is first suspected to the time the decision on guilt or inno-cence is made, our criminal justice system is designed to enable the trier of fact to discover that truth according to law. But triers of fact can err, and an innocent person can be pronounced guilty. In contrast, the law provides only limited stan-dards for assessing the validity of a sentencing decision. The sentencer's function is not to discover a fact, but to mete out just deserts as he sees them. Absent a mandatory sentence, there is no objective measure by which the sentencer's deci-sion can be deemed correct or erroneous if it is duly made within the authority conferred by the legislature.

In light of this difference in the nature of the decisions, the question in this case is not—as the Court would frame it—whether the procedures by which a sentencing decision is made are similar to the procedures by which a decision on guilt or innocence is made. Rather, the question is whether the reasons for con-sidering an acquittal on guilt or innocence as absolutely final apply equally to a sentencing decision imposing less than the most severe sentence authorized by law. I would have thought that the pertinence of this question was clear, and that the answer consistently given in the past could not have escaped the Court. Earlier this Term, in *United States v. DiFrancesco*, we stated that "[t]here are ... fundamental distinctions between a sentence and an acquittal, and to fail to rec-ognize them is to ignore the particular significance of an acquittal." 449 U.S. [117], at 133.

The reasons for considering an acquittal on guilt or innocence as absolutely final do not apply equally to a sentencing decision for less than the most severe sentence authorized by law. A retrial of a defendant once found to have been innocent "enhanc[es] the possibility that even though innocent he may be found guilty." *Green v. United States*, 355 U.S. [184], at 188. But in *Chaffin v. Stynch-combe*, 412 U.S. [17], at 25, we held that "[t]he possibility of a higher sentence was recognized and accepted [in *Pearce*] as a legitimate concomitant of the retrial process." The possibility of a higher sentence is acceptable under the Double Jeopardy Clause, whereas the possibility of error as to guilt or innocence is not, because the second jury's sentencing decision is as "correct" as the first jury's. Similarly, a defendant once found to have been innocent cannot be forced a second time through the ordeal of trial. But when a defendant is found guilty, he must bear the ordeal of being sentenced just as he does the ordeal of serving sentence.

In sum, I find wholly unpersuasive the Court's justification for applying the implicit-acquittal principle to sentencing. The Court does not purport to justify its conclusion with the argument that facing the death sentence a second time is more of an ordeal in the legal sense than facing any other sentence a second time. The death sentence, of course, is unlike any other punishment. For that reason, this Court has read the Eighth Amendment and the Due Process Clause of the Fourteenth Amendment to require that States prescribe unique procedural safe-guards to protect against capricious or discriminatory impositions of the death sentence. *Furman; Gregg*. But a death sentence imposed in accord with the strictures of the Eighth Amendment and the Fourteenth Amendment is a lawful sentence, and Missouri provides the requisite procedures. I find no basis under the Double Jeopardy Clause for the Court to single out a sentence which is statutorily authorized, and otherwise may be imposed constitutionally, as nonetheless one that a guilty defendant may not be required to face twice. . . .

Chapter 22

Juveniles May Be Executed—
Stanford v. Kentucky (1989)

Stanford v. Kentucky, 492 U.S. 361, 109 S. Ct. 2969, 106 L. Ed.2d 306 (1989) (5–4, the Eighth Amendment does not prohibit the death penalty for a defendant who was 16 or 17 years old when he committed the crime).

Editor's comment: One year before *Stanford v. Kentucky* was decided, the Supreme Court ruled in *Thompson v. Oklahoma*, 487 U.S. 815 (1988), that a defendant who was 15 years old at the time of the murder could not be executed. The vote was 5–3, Justice Kennedy not participating, and the fifth vote was cast by Justice O'Connor, who concurred because Oklahoma capital punishment law specified no minimum age and she could not discern a clear national consensus on capital punishment for crimes committed by 15-year-olds. In *Stanford*, O'Connor and Kennedy supported the death penalty for defendants who were 16 or 17 years old at the time of the crime, and the four justices who had written the lead opinion in *Thompson* dissented.

❖   ❖   ❖

OPINION OF JUSTICE SCALIA FOR THE COURT, EXCEPT FOR PARTS IV-B AND V, WHICH WERE JOINED BY CHIEF JUSTICE REHNQUIST AND JUSTICES WHITE AND KENNEDY

These two consolidated cases require us to decide whether the imposition of capital punishment on an individual for a crime committed at 16 or 17 years of age constitutes cruel and unusual punishment under the Eighth Amendment.

I

The first case involves the shooting death of 20-year-old Barbel Poore in Jefferson County, Kentucky. Petitioner Kevin Stanford committed the murder on January 7, 1981, when he was approximately 17 years and 4 months of age. Stanford and his accomplice repeatedly raped and sodomized Poore during and after their commission of a robbery at a gas station where she worked as an attendant. They then drove her to a secluded area near the station, where Stanford shot her pointblank in the face and then in the back of her head. The proceeds from the robbery were roughly 300 cartons of cigarettes, two gallons of fuel, and a small amount of cash. A corrections officer testified that petitioner explained the murder as follows: " '[H]e said, I had to shoot her, [she] lived next door to me and she would recognize me. . . . I guess we could have tied her up or something or beat [her up] . . . and tell her if she tells, we would kill her. . . . Then after he said that he started laughing.' "

After Stanford's arrest, a Kentucky juvenile court . . . found certification for trial as an adult to be in the best interest of petitioner and the community. Stanford was convicted of murder, first-degree sodomy, first-degree robbery, and receiving stolen property, and was sentenced to death and 45 years in prison. The Kentucky Supreme Court affirmed the death sentence. . . .

The second case before us today involves the stabbing death of Nancy Allen, a 26-year-old mother of two who was working behind the sales counter of the convenience store she and David Allen owned and operated in Avondale, Missouri. Petitioner Heath Wilkins committed the murder on July 27, 1985, when he was approximately 16 years and 6 months of age. The record reflects that Wilkins' plan was to rob the store and murder "whoever was behind the counter" because "a dead person can't talk." While Wilkins' accomplice, Patrick Stevens, held Allen, Wilkins stabbed her, causing her to fall to the floor. When Stevens had trouble operating the cash register, Allen spoke up to assist him, leading Wilkins to stab her three more times in her chest. Two of these wounds penetrated the victim's heart. When Allen began to beg for her life, Wilkins stabbed her four more times in the neck, opening her carotid artery. After helping themselves to liquor, cigarettes, rolling papers, and approximately $450 in cash and checks, Wilkins and Stevens left Allen to die on the floor.

Because he was roughly six months short of the age of majority for purposes of criminal prosecution, Wilkins could not automatically be tried as an adult under Missouri law. Before that could happen, the juvenile court was required to terminate juvenile court jurisdiction and certify Wilkins for trial as an adult. Relying on the "viciousness, force and violence" of the alleged crime, petitioner's maturity, and the failure of the juvenile justice system to rehabilitate him after previous delinquent acts, the juvenile court made the necessary certification.

Wilkins was charged with first-degree murder, armed criminal action, and carrying a concealed weapon. After the court found him competent, petitioner entered guilty pleas to all charges. A punishment hearing was held, at which both the State and petitioner himself urged imposition of the death sentence. [He was convicted to first-degree murder and sentenced to death, and he appealed. The Supreme Court of Missouri affirmed.]

II

The thrust of both Wilkins' and Stanford's arguments is that imposition of the death penalty on those who were juveniles when they committed their crimes falls within the Eighth Amendment's prohibition against "cruel and unusual punishments." Wilkins would have us define juveniles as individuals 16 years of age and under; Stanford would draw the line at 17.

Neither petitioner asserts that his sentence constitutes one of "those modes or acts of punishment that had been considered cruel and unusual at the time that the Bill of Rights was adopted." Nor could they support such a contention. At that time, the common law set the rebuttable presumption of incapacity to commit any felony at the age of 14, and theoretically permitted capital punishment to be imposed on anyone over the age of 7. See 4 W. Blackstone, Commentaries 23–24; 1 M. Hale, Pleas of the Crown 24–29 (1800). ... In accordance with the standards of this common-law tradition, at least 281 offenders under the age of 18 have been executed in this country, and at least 126 under the age of 17. See V. Streib, Death Penalty for Juveniles 57 (1987).

Thus petitioners are left to argue that their punishment is contrary to the "evolving standards of decency that mark the progress of a maturing society." They are correct in asserting that this Court has "not confined the prohibition embodied in the Eighth Amendment to 'barbarous' methods that were generally outlawed in the 18th century," but instead has interpreted the Amendment "in a flexible and dynamic manner." *Gregg.* In determining what standards have "evolved," however, we have looked not to our own conceptions of decency, but to those of modern American society as a whole.[1] As we have said, "Eighth Amendment judgments should not be, or appear to be, merely the subjective views of individual Justices; judgment should be informed by objective factors to the maximum possible extent." This approach is dictated both by the language of the Amendment—which proscribes only those punishments that are both "cruel and *unusual*"—and by the "deference we owe to the decisions of the state legislatures under our federal system," *Gregg.*

---

[1] We emphasize that it is *American* conceptions of decency that are dispositive, rejecting the contention of petitioners ... that the sentencing practices of other countries are relevant. While "[t]he practices of other nations, particularly other democracies, can be relevant to determining whether a practice uniform among our people is not merely a historical accident, but rather so 'implicit in the concept of ordered liberty' that it occupies a place not merely in our mores, but, text permitting, in our Constitution as well," ... they cannot serve to establish the first Eighth Amendment prerequisite, that the practice is accepted among our people.

III

"[F]irst" among the "objective indicia that reflect the public attitude toward a given sanction" are statutes passed by society's elected representatives. Of the 37 States whose laws permit capital punishment, 15 decline to impose it upon 16-year-old offenders and 12 decline to impose it on 17-year-old offenders. This does not establish the degree of national consensus this Court has previously thought sufficient to label a particular punishment cruel and unusual. . . .

Since a majority of the States that permit capital punishment authorize it for crimes committed at age 16 or above,[3] petitioners' cases are more analogous to *Tison v. Arizona.* . . . In *Tison*, which upheld Arizona's imposition of the death penalty for major participation in a felony with reckless indifference to human life, we noted that only 11 of those jurisdictions imposing capital punishment rejected its use in such circumstances. As we noted earlier, here the number is 15 for offenders under 17, and 12 for offenders under 18. We think the same conclusion as in *Tison* is required in these cases.

Petitioners make much of the recently enacted federal statute providing capital punishment for certain drug-related offenses, but limiting that punishment to offenders 18 and over. The Anti-Drug Abuse Act of 1988. That reliance is entirely misplaced. To begin with, the statute in question does not embody a judgment by the Federal Legislature that no murder is heinous enough to warrant the execution of such a youthful offender, but merely that the narrow class of offense it defines is not. The congressional judgment on the broader question, if apparent at all, is to be found in the law that permits 16- and 17-year-olds (after appropriate findings) to be tried and punished as adults for *all* federal offenses, including those bearing a capital penalty that is not limited to 18-year-olds. Moreover, even if it were true that no federal statute permitted the execution of persons under 18, that would not remotely establish—in the face of a substantial number of state statutes to the contrary—a national consensus that such punishment is inhumane, any more than the absence of a federal lottery establishes a national consensus that lotteries are socially harmful. To be sure, the absence of a federal death penalty for 16- or 17-year-olds (if it existed) might be evidence that there is no national consensus *in favor* of such punishment. It is not the burden of Kentucky and Missouri, however, to establish a national consensus approving what their citizens have voted to do; rather, it is the "heavy burden" of petitioners to establish a national consensus against it. As far as the primary and most reliable indication of consensus is concerned—the pattern of enacted laws—petitioners have failed to carry that burden.

---

[3] The dissent again works its statistical magic by refusing to count among the States that authorize capital punishment of 16- and 17-year-old offenders those 19 States that set no minimum age in their death penalty statute, and specifically permit 16- and 17-year-olds to be sentenced as adults. We think that describing this position is adequate response.

IV–A

Wilkins and Stanford argue, however, that even if the laws themselves do not establish a settled consensus, the application of the laws does. That contemporary society views capital punishment of 16- and 17-year-old offenders as inappropriate is demonstrated, they say, by the reluctance of juries to impose, and prosecutors to seek, such sentences. Petitioners are quite correct that a far smaller number of offenders under 18 than over 18 have been sentenced to death in this country. From 1982 through 1988, for example, out of 2,106 total death sentences, only 15 were imposed on individuals who were 16 or under when they committed their crimes, and only 30 on individuals who were 17 at the time of the crime. ... And it appears that actual executions for crimes committed under age 18 accounted for only about 2 percent of the total number of executions that occurred between 1642 and 1986. ... As Wilkins points out, the last execution of a person who committed a crime under 17 years of age occurred in 1959. These statistics, however, carry little significance. Given the undisputed fact that a far smaller percentage of capital crimes are committed by persons under 18 than over 18, the discrepancy in treatment is much less than might seem. Granted, however, that a substantial discrepancy exists, that does not establish the requisite proposition that the death sentence for offenders under 18 is categorically unacceptable to prosecutors and juries. To the contrary, it is not only possible, but overwhelmingly probable, that the very considerations which induce petitioners and their supporters to believe that death should *never* be imposed on offenders under 18 cause prosecutors and juries to believe that it should *rarely* be imposed.

IV–B

This last point suggests why there is also no relevance to the laws cited by petitioners and their amici which set 18 or more as the legal age for engaging in various activities, ranging from driving to drinking alcoholic beverages to voting. It is, to begin with, absurd to think that one must be mature enough to drive carefully, to drink responsibly, or to vote intelligently, in order to be mature enough to understand that murdering another human being is profoundly wrong, and to conform one's conduct to that most minimal of all civilized standards. But even if the requisite degrees of maturity were comparable, the age statutes in question would still not be relevant. They do not represent a social judgment that all persons under the designated ages are not responsible enough to drive, to drink, or to vote, but at most a judgment that the vast majority are not. These laws set the appropriate ages for the operation of a system that makes its determinations in gross, and that does not conduct individualized maturity tests for each driver, drinker, or voter. The criminal justice system, however, does provide individualized testing. In the realm of capital punishment in particular, "individualized consideration [is] a constitutional requirement," and one of the individualized mitigating factors that sentencers must be permitted to consider is the defendant's age. Twenty-nine States, including both Kentucky and Missouri, have codified this constitutional requirement in laws specifically designating the defendant's age as a mitigating factor in capital cases. Moreover, the determinations required by juvenile transfer statutes to certify a juvenile for trial as an adult ensure individualized consideration of the maturity and moral responsibility of 16- and 17-year-old offenders before they are even held to stand trial as adults. The application of this particularized system to the petitioners can be declared constitutionally inadequate only if there is a consensus, not that 17 or 18 is the age at which most persons, or even almost all persons, achieve sufficient maturity to be held fully responsible for murder; but that 17 or 18 is the age before which no one can reasonably be held fully responsible. What displays society's views on this latter point are not the ages set forth in the generalized system of driving, drinking, and voting laws cited by petitioners and their amici, but the ages at which the States permit their particularized capital punishment systems to be applied.

V

Having failed to establish a consensus against capital punishment for 16- and 17-year-old offenders through state and federal statutes and the behavior of prosecutors and juries, petitioners seek to demonstrate it through other indicia, including public opinion polls, the views of interest groups, and the positions adopted by various professional associations. We decline the invitation to rest constitutional law upon such uncertain foundations. A revised national consensus so broad, so clear, and so enduring as to justify a permanent prohibition upon all units of democratic government must appear in the operative acts (laws and the application of laws) that the people have approved.

We also reject petitioners' argument that we should invalidate capital punishment of 16- and 17-year-old offenders on the ground that it fails to serve the legitimate goals of penology. According to petitioners, it fails to deter because juveniles, possessing less developed cognitive skills than adults, are less likely to fear death; and it fails to exact just retribution because juveniles, being less mature and responsible, are also less morally blameworthy. In support of these claims, petitioners and their supporting amici marshal an array of socioscientific evidence concerning the psychological and emotional development of 16- and 17-year-olds.

If such evidence could conclusively establish the entire lack of deterrent effect and moral responsibility, resort to the Cruel and Unusual Punishments Clause would be unnecessary; the Equal Protection Clause of the Fourteenth Amendment would invalidate these laws for lack of rational basis. But as the adjective "socioscientific" suggests (and insofar as evaluation of moral responsibility is concerned perhaps the adjective "ethicoscientific" would be more apt), it is not demonstrable that no 16-year-old is "adequately responsible" or significantly deterred. It is rational, even if mistaken, to think the contrary. The battle must be fought, then, on the field of the Eighth Amendment; and in that struggle socioscientific, ethicoscientific, or even purely scientific evidence is not an available weapon. The punishment is either "cruel *and* unusual" (*i.e.*, society has set its face against it) or it is not. The audience for these arguments, in other words, is not this Court but the citizenry of the United States. It is they, not we, who must be persuaded. For as we stated earlier, our job is to *identify* the "evolving standards of decency"; to determine, not what they *should* be, but what they *are*. We have no power under the Eighth Amendment to substitute our belief in the scientific evidence for the society's apparent skepticism. In short, we emphatically reject petitioner's suggestion that the issues in this case permit us to apply our "own informed judgment," regarding the desirability of permitting the death penalty for crimes by 16- and 17-year-olds. . . .

We discern neither a historical nor a modern societal consensus forbidding the imposition of capital punishment on any person who murders at 16 or 17 years of age. Accordingly, we conclude that such punishment does not offend the Eighth Amendment's prohibition against cruel and unusual punishment.

The judgments of the Supreme Court of Kentucky and the Supreme Court of Missouri are therefore affirmed.

CONCURRING OPINION OF JUSTICE O'CONNOR

Last Term, in *Thompson v. Oklahoma*, I expressed the view that a criminal defendant who would have been tried as a juvenile under state law, but for the granting of a petition waiving juvenile court jurisdiction, may only be executed for a capital offense if the State's capital punishment statute specifies a minimum age at which the commission of a capital crime can lead to an offender's execution and the defendant had reached that minimum age at the time the crime was committed. As a threshold matter, I indicated that such specificity is not necessary to avoid constitutional problems if it is clear that no national consensus forbids the imposition of capital punishment for crimes committed at such an age. Applying this two-part standard in *Thompson*, I concluded that Oklahoma's imposition of a death sentence on an individual who was 15 years old at the time he committed a capital offense should be set aside. Applying the same standard today, I conclude that the death sentences for capital murder imposed by Missouri and Kentucky on petitioners Wilkins and Stanford respectively should not be set aside because it is sufficiently clear that no national consensus forbids the imposition of capital punishment on 16- or 17-year-old capital murderers. . . .

The day may come when there is such general legislative rejection of the execution of 16- or 17-year-old capital murderers that a clear national consensus can be said to have developed. Because I do not believe that day has yet arrived, I concur in Parts I, II, III, and IV-A of the Court's opinion, and I concur in its judgment.

I am unable, however, to join the remainder of the plurality's opinion for reasons I stated in *Thompson*. Part V of the plurality's opinion "emphatically reject[s]," the suggestion that, beyond an assessment of the specific enactments of American legislatures, there remains a constitutional obligation imposed upon this Court to judge whether the "nexus between the punishment imposed and the defendant's blameworthiness" is proportional. Part IV-B of the plurality's opinion specifically rejects as irrelevant to Eighth Amendment considerations state statutes that distinguish juveniles from adults for a variety of other purposes. In my view, this Court does have a constitutional obligation to conduct proportionality analysis. In *Thompson* I specifically identified age-based statutory classifications as "relevant to Eighth Amendment proportionality analysis." Thus, although I do not believe that these particular cases can be resolved through proportionality analysis, I reject the suggestion that the use of such analysis is improper as a matter of Eighth Amendment jurisprudence. Accordingly, I join all but Parts IV-B and V of Justice Scalia's opinion.

DISSENTING OPINION OF JUSTICE BRENNAN, JOINED BY JUSTICES MARSHALL, BLACKMUN, AND STEVENS

I believe that to take the life of a person as punishment for a crime committed when below the age of 18 is cruel and unusual and hence is prohibited by the Eighth Amendment. . . .

I–D

Together, the rejection of the death penalty for juveniles by a majority of the States, the rarity of the sentence for juveniles, both as an absolute and a comparative matter, the decisions of respected organizations in relevant fields that this punishment is unacceptable, and its rejection generally throughout the world, provide to my mind a strong grounding for the view that it is not constitutionally tolerable that certain States persist in authorizing the execution of adolescent offenders. It is unnecessary, however, to rest a view that the Eighth Amendment prohibits the execution of minors solely upon a judgment as to the meaning to be attached to the evidence of contemporary values outlined above, for the execution of juveniles fails to satisfy two well-established and independent Eighth Amendment requirements—that a punishment not be disproportionate, and that it make a contribution to acceptable goals of punishment. . . .

III

There can be no doubt at this point in our constitutional history that the Eighth Amendment forbids punishment that is wholly disproportionate to the blameworthiness of the offender. "The constitutional principle of proportionality has been recognized explicitly in this Court for almost a century." *Solem v. Helm,* 463 U.S. 277, 286 (1983). Usually formulated as a requirement that sentences not be "disproportionate to the crime committed," the proportionality principle takes account not only of the "injury to the person and to the public" caused by a crime, but also of the "moral depravity" of the offender. *Coker.* The offender's culpability for his criminal acts—"the degree of the defendant's blameworthiness"— is thus of central importance to the constitutionality of the sentence imposed. Indeed, this focus on a defendant's blameworthiness runs throughout our constitutional jurisprudence relating to capital sentencing. See, *e.g., Booth v. Maryland; California v. Brown,* 479 U.S. 538 (1987).

Proportionality analysis requires that we compare "the gravity of the offense," understood to include not only the injury caused, but also the defendant's culpability, with "the harshness of the penalty." *Solem.* In my view, juveniles so generally lack the degree of responsibility for their crimes that is a predicate for the constitutional imposition of the death penalty that the Eighth Amendment forbids that they receive that punishment.

III–A

Legislative determinations distinguishing juveniles from adults abound. These age-based classifications reveal much about how our society regards juveniles as a class, and about societal beliefs regarding adolescent levels of responsibility. See *Thompson,* 487 U.S., at 823–825 (plurality opinion).

The participation of juveniles in a substantial number of activities open to adults is either barred completely or significantly restricted by legislation. All States but two have a uniform age of majority, and have set that age at 18 or above. No State has lowered its voting age below 18. Nor does any State permit a person under 18 to serve on a jury. Only four States ever permit persons below 18 to marry without parental consent. Thirty-seven States have specific enactments requiring that a patient have attained 18 before she may validly consent to medical treatment. Thirty-four States require parental consent before a person below 18 may drive a motor car. Legislation in 42 States prohibits those under 18 from purchasing pornographic materials. Where gambling is legal, adolescents under 18 are generally not permitted to participate in it, in some or all of its forms. In these and a host of other ways, minors are treated differently from adults in our laws, which reflects the simple truth derived from communal experience that juveniles as a class have not the level of maturation and responsibility that we presume in adults and consider desirable for full participation in the rights and duties of modern life. . . .

III–B

There may be exceptional individuals who mature more quickly than their peers, and who might be considered fully responsible for their actions prior to the age of 18, despite their lack of the experience upon which judgment depends. In my view, however, it is not sufficient to accommodate the facts about juveniles that an individual youth's culpability may be taken into account in the decision to transfer him or her from the juvenile to the adult court system for trial, or that a capital sentencing jury is instructed to consider youth and other mitigating factors. I believe that the Eighth Amendment requires that a person who lacks that full degree of responsibility for his or her actions associated with adulthood not be sentenced to death. Hence it is constitutionally inadequate that a juvenile offender's level of responsibility be taken into account only along with a host of other factors that the court or jury may decide outweigh that want of responsibility. . . .

III–C

Juveniles very generally lack that degree of blameworthiness that is, in my view, a constitutional prerequisite for the imposition of capital punishment under our precedents concerning the Eighth Amendment proportionality principle. The individualized consideration of an offender's youth and culpability at the transfer stage and at sentencing has not operated to ensure that the only offenders under 18 singled out for the ultimate penalty are exceptional individuals whose level of responsibility is more developed than that of their peers. In that circumstance, I believe that the same categorical assumption that juveniles as a class are insufficiently mature to be regarded as fully responsible that we make in so many other areas is appropriately made in determining whether minors may be subjected to the death penalty. As we noted in *Thompson*, it would be ironic if the assumptions we so readily make about minors as a class were suddenly unavailable in conducting proportionality analysis. I would hold that the Eighth Amendment prohibits the execution of any person for a crime committed below the age of 18.

IV

Under a second strand of Eighth Amendment inquiry into whether a particular sentence is excessive and hence unconstitutional, we ask whether the sentence makes a measurable contribution to acceptable goals of punishment. *Thompson; Enmund v. Florida; Coker v. Georgia; Gregg v. Georgia.* The two "principal social purposes" of capital punishment are said to be "retribution and the deterrence of capital crimes by prospective offenders." . . . Unless the death penalty applied to persons for offenses committed under 18 measurably contributes to one of these goals, the Eighth Amendment prohibits it.

"[R]etribution as a justification for executing [offenders] very much depends on the degree of [their] culpability." . . . I have explained in Part III, supra, why I believe juveniles lack the culpability that makes a crime so extreme that it may warrant, according to this Court's cases, the death penalty; and why we should treat juveniles as a class as exempt from the ultimate penalty. These same considerations persuade me that executing juveniles "does not measurably contribute to the retributive end of ensuring that the criminal gets his just deserts." ...A punishment that fails the Eighth Amendment test of proportionality because disproportionate to the offender's blameworthiness by definition is not justly deserved.

Nor does the execution of juvenile offenders measurably contribute to the goal of deterrence. Excluding juveniles from the class of persons eligible to receive the death penalty will have little effect on any deterrent value capital punishment may have for potential offenders who are over 18: these adult offenders may of course remain eligible for a death sentence. The potential deterrent effect of juvenile executions on adolescent offenders is also insignificant. The deterrent value of capital punishment rests "on the assumption that we are rational beings who always think before we act, and then base our actions on a careful calculation of the gains and losses involved." ... As the plurality noted in *Thompson*, "[t]he likelihood that the teenage offender has made the kind of cost-benefit analysis that attaches any weight to the possibility of execution is so remote as to be virtually nonexistent." First, juveniles "have less capacity ... to think in long-range terms than adults," and their careful weighing of a distant, uncertain, and indeed highly unlikely consequence prior to action is most improbable. In addition, juveniles have little fear of death, because they have "a profound conviction of their own omnipotence and immortality." ... Because imposition of the death penalty on persons for offenses committed under the age of 18 makes no measurable contribution to the goals of either retribution or deterrence, it is "nothing more than the purposeless and needless imposition of pain and suffering," *Coker*, and is thus excessive and unconstitutional.

V

There are strong indications that the execution of juvenile offenders violates contemporary standards of decency: a majority of States decline to permit juveniles to be sentenced to death; imposition of the sentence upon minors is very unusual even in those States that permit it; and respected organizations with expertise in relevant areas regard the execution of juveniles as unacceptable, as does international opinion. These indicators serve to confirm in my view my conclusion that the Eighth Amendment prohibits the execution of persons for offenses they committed while below the age of 18, because the death penalty is disproportionate when applied to such young offenders and fails measurably to serve the goals of capital punishment. I dissent.

Chapter 23

Insane Convicts
May Not Be Executed—
Ford v. Wainwright (1986)

Ford v. Wainwright, 477 U.S. 399, 106 S. Ct. 2595, 91 L. Ed.2d 335 (1986) (5–4, the Eighth Amendment prohibits the execution of a defendant who is convicted and sentenced to death but is insane at the time of execution).

Editor's comment: Insanity is ordinarily thought of as a defense to criminal charges. In such instances, the jury must determine the defendant's mental state at the time of the crime. If found Not Guilty by Reason of Insanity, the accused may not be punished as a criminal, but may be civilly committed if dangerous. It is also possible to be insane, or "incompetent" to stand trial due to mental infirmity at the time of the trial, in which case there can be no trial for the duration of the infirmity. The case that follows presents yet one other possibility: a defendant who was neither insane when he committed the crime nor incompetent to be tried (as indicated by the fact that he was tried and found guilty), but who became insane at the point when the capital sentence was to be imposed.

The Court's discussion of the "common law" is a reference to the legal rules developed hundreds of years ago by English judges in the resolution of cases before them. These principles of law, synthesized in the writings of Blackstone (1723–1780) and Coke (pronounced "cook") (1552–1634), have had great influence on American law.

At the time of the *Ford* decision no state permitted the execution of the insane. However, the Supreme Court disapproved of the non-adversarial method Florida used to determine insanity. The Governor appointed three psychiatrists to examined Ford, and after receiving their reports, he signed the death warrant.

❖ ❖ ❖

OPINION OF JUSTICE MARSHALL FOR THE COURT

. . . This Court granted Ford's petition for certiorari in order to resolve the important issue whether the Eighth Amendment prohibits the execution of the insane . . .

II

Now that the Eighth Amendment has been recognized to affect significantly both the procedural and the substantive aspects of the death penalty, the question of executing the insane takes on a wholly different complexion. The adequacy of the procedures chosen by a State to determine sanity, therefore, will depend upon an issue that this Court has never addressed: whether the Constitution places a substantive restriction on the State's power to take the life of an insane prisoner.

There is now little room for doubt that the Eighth Amendment's ban on cruel and unusual punishment embraces, at a minimum, those modes or acts of punishment that had been considered cruel and unusual at the time that the Bill of Rights was adopted. . . .

Moreover, the Eighth Amendment's proscriptions are not limited to those practices condemned by the common law in 1789. Not bound by the sparing humanitarian concessions of our forebears, the Amendment also recognizes the "evolving standards of decency that mark the progress of a maturing society." In addition to considering the barbarous methods generally outlawed in the 18th century, therefore, this Court takes into account objective evidence of contemporary values before determining whether a particular punishment comports with the fundamental human dignity that the Amendment protects.

. . . A

We begin, then, with the common law. The bar against executing a prisoner who has lost his sanity bears impressive historical credentials; the practice consistently has been branded "savage and inhuman." 4 W. Blackstone, Commentaries 24–25. Blackstone explained:

> [I]diots and lunatics are not chargeable for their own acts, if committed when under these incapacities: no, not even for treason itself. Also, if a man in his sound memory commits a capital offence, and before arraignment for it, he becomes mad, he ought not to be arraigned for it: because he is not able to plead to it with that advice and caution that he ought. And if, after he has pleaded, the prisoner becomes mad, he shall not be tried: for how can he make his defence? If, after he be tried and found guilty, he loses his senses before judgment, judgment shall not be pronounced; and if, after judgment, he becomes of nonsane memory, execution shall be stayed: for peradventure, says

the humanity of the English law, had the prisoner been of sound memory, he might have alleged something in stay of judgment or execution.

Sir Edward Coke had earlier expressed the same view of the common law of England: "[B]y intendment of Law the execution of the offender is for example, . . . but so it is not when a mad man is executed, but should be a miserable spectacle, both against Law, and of extreme inhumanity and cruelty, and can be no example to others." 3 E. Coke, Institutes 6 (6th ed. 1680). Other recorders of the common law concurred. . . .

As is often true of common-law principles, the reasons for the rule are less sure and less uniform than the rule itself. One explanation is that the execution of an insane person simply offends humanity, another, that it provides no example to others and thus contributes nothing to whatever deterrence value is intended to be served by capital punishment. Other commentators postulate religious underpinnings: that it is uncharitable to dispatch an offender "into another world, when he is not of a capacity to fit himself for it." . . . It is also said that execution serves no purpose in these cases because madness is its own punishment: furiosus solo furore punitur. Blackstone. More recent commentators opine that the community's quest for "retribution"—the need to offset a criminal act by a punishment of equivalent "moral quality"—is not served by execution of an insane person, which has a "lesser value" than that of the crime for which he is to be punished. Hazard and Louisell, Death, the State, and the Insane: Stay of Execution, 9 UCLA L. Rev. 381, 387 (1962). Unanimity of rationale, therefore, we do not find. "But whatever the reason of the law is, it is plain the law is so." We know of virtually no authority condoning the execution of the insane at English common law.

Further indications suggest that this solid proscription was carried to America, where it was early observed that "the judge is bound" to stay the execution upon insanity of the prisoner. . . .

. . . B

This ancestral legacy has not outlived its time. Today, no State in the Union permits the execution of the insane.[2] It is clear that the ancient and humane limitation upon the State's ability to execute its sentences has as firm a hold upon the jurisprudence of today as it had centuries ago in England. The various reasons put forth in support of the common-law restriction have no less logical, moral,

---

[2] Of the 50 States, 41 have a death penalty or statutes governing execution procedures. Of those, 26 have statutes explicitly requiring the suspension of the execution of a prisoner who meets the legal test for incompetence. . . . Others have adopted the common-law rule by judicial decision. . . . Still others have more discretionary statutory procedures providing for the suspension of sentence and transfer to mental facilities for convicted prisoners who have developed mental illness. . . . The remaining four States having a death penalty have no specific procedure governing insanity, but have not repudiated the common-law rule.

and practical force than they did when first voiced. For today, no less than before, we may seriously question the retributive value of executing a person who has no comprehension of why he has been singled out and stripped of his fundamental right to life. Similarly, the natural abhorrence civilized societies feel at killing one who has no capacity to come to grips with his own conscience or deity is still vivid today. And the intuition that such an execution simply offends humanity is evidently shared across this Nation. Faced with such widespread evidence of a restriction upon sovereign power, this Court is compelled to conclude that the Eighth Amendment prohibits a State from carrying out a sentence of death upon a prisoner who is insane. Whether its aim be to protect the condemned from fear and pain without comfort of understanding, or to protect the dignity of society itself from the barbarity of exacting mindless vengeance, the restriction finds enforcement in the Eighth Amendment.

CONCURRING OPINION OF JUSTICE POWELL

... The more general concern of the common law—that executions of the insane are simply cruel—retains its vitality. It is as true today as when Coke lived that most men and women value the opportunity to prepare, mentally and spiritually, for their death. Moreover, today as at common law, one of the death penalty's critical justifications, its retributive force, depends on the defendant's awareness of the penalty's existence and purpose. Thus, it remains true that executions of the insane both impose a uniquely cruel penalty and are inconsistent with one of the chief purposes of executions generally. For precisely these reasons, Florida requires the Governor to stay executions of those who "d[o] not have the mental capacity to understand the nature of the death penalty and why it was imposed" on them. . . . A number of States have more rigorous standards.[3] but none disputes the need to require that those who are executed know the fact of their impending execution and the reason for it.

Such a standard appropriately defines the kind of mental deficiency that should trigger the Eighth Amendment prohibition. If the defendant perceives the connection between his crime and his punishment, the retributive goal of the criminal law is satisfied. And only if the defendant is aware that his death is approaching can he prepare himself for his passing. Accordingly, I would hold

---

[3] A number of States have remained faithful to Blackstone's view that a defendant cannot be executed unless he is able to assist in his own defense. . . . The majority of States appear not to have addressed the issue in their statutes. Modern case authority on this question is sparse, and while some older cases favor the Blackstone view, . . . those cases largely antedate the recent expansion of both the right to counsel and the availability of federal and state collateral review. Moreover, other cases suggest that the prevailing test is "whether the condemned man was aware of his conviction and the nature of his impending fate"—essentially the same test stated by Florida's statute. . . . Under these circumstances, I find no sound basis for constitutionalizing the broader definition of insanity, with its requirement that the defendant be able to assist in his own defense. States are obviously free to adopt a more expansive view of sanity in this context than the one the Eighth Amendment imposes as a constitutional minimum.

that the Eighth Amendment forbids the execution only of those who are unaware of the punishment they are about to suffer and why they are to suffer it.

Petitioner's claim of insanity plainly fits within this standard. According to petitioner's proffered psychiatric examination, petitioner does not know that he is to be executed, but rather believes that the death penalty has been invalidated. If this assessment is correct, petitioner cannot connect his execution to the crime for which he was convicted. Thus, the question is whether petitioner's evidence entitles him to a hearing in Federal District Court on his claim. . . .

OPINION OF JUSTICE O'CONNOR, JOINED BY JUSTICE WHITE, CONCURRING IN THE RESULT IN PART AND DISSENTING IN PART

I am in full agreement with Justice Rehnquist's conclusion that the Eighth amendment does not create a substantive right not to be executed while insane. Accordingly, I do not join the Court's reasoning or opinion. Because, however, the conclusion is for me inescapable that Florida positive law has created a protected liberty interest in avoiding execution while incompetent, and because Florida does not provide even those minimal procedural protections required by due process in this area, I would vacate the judgment and remand to the Court of Appeals with directions that the case be returned to the Florida system so that a hearing can be held in a manner consistent with the requirements of the Due Process Clause. I cannot agree, however, that the federal courts should have any role whatever in the substantive determination of a defendant's competency to be executed.

. . . I believe that one aspect of the Florida procedure for determining competency to be executed renders that procedure constitutionally deficient. If there is one "fundamental requisite" of due process, it is that an individual is entitled to an "opportunity to be heard." . . . As currently implemented, the Florida procedure for determining competency violates this bedrock principle. By Executive Order, the present Governor has provided that "[c]ounsel for the inmate and the State Attorney may be present [at the competency hearing] but shall not participate in the examination in any adversarial manner." . . . Indeed, respondent does not dispute that the Governor's office has steadfastly refused to acknowledge whether it would even review the extensive psychiatric materials submitted by petitioner concerning his present mental state. While I would not invariably require oral advocacy or even cross-examination, due process at the very least requires that the decision maker consider the prisoner's written submissions. I conclude therefore that Florida law has created a protected expectation that no execution will be carried out while the prisoner lacks the "mental capacity to understand the nature of the death penalty and why it was imposed on him." . . . Because Florida's procedures are inadequate to satisfy even the minimal requirements of due process in this context, I would vacate the judgment below with instructions that the case be returned to Florida so that it might assess petitioner's competency in a manner that accords with the command of the

Fourteenth Amendment. In my view, however, the only federal question presented in cases such as this is whether the State's positive law has created a liberty interest and whether its procedures are adequate to protect that interest from arbitrary deprivation. Once satisfied that the procedures were adequate, a federal court has no authority to second-guess a State's substantive competency determination.

DISSENTING OPINION OF JUSTICE REHNQUIST, JOINED BY CHIEF JUSTICE BURGER

The Court today holds that the Eighth Amendment prohibits a State from carrying out a lawfully imposed sentence of death upon a person who is currently insane. This holding is based almost entirely on two unremarkable observations. First, the Court states that it "know[s] of virtually no authority condoning the execution of the insane at English common law." Second, it notes that "[t]oday, no State in the Union permits the execution of the insane." Armed with these facts, and shielded by the claim that it is simply "keep[ing] faith with our common-law heritage," the Court proceeds to cast aside settled precedent and to significantly alter both the common-law and current practice of not executing the insane. It manages this feat by carefully ignoring the fact that the Florida scheme it finds unconstitutional, in which the Governor is assigned the ultimate responsibility of deciding whether a condemned prisoner is currently insane, is fully consistent with the "common-law heritage" and current practice on which the Court purports to rely.

The Court places great weight on the "impressive historical credentials" of the common-law bar against executing a prisoner who has lost his sanity. What it fails to mention, however, is the equally important and unchallenged fact that at common law it was the *executive* who passed upon the sanity of the condemned. See 1 N. Walker, Crime and Insanity in England 194–203 (1968). So when the Court today creates a constitutional right to a determination of sanity outside of the executive branch, it does so not in keeping with but at the expense of "our common-law heritage."

. . . Creating a constitutional right to a judicial determination of sanity before that sentence may be carried out, whether through the Eighth Amendment or the Due Process Clause, needlessly complicates and postpones still further any finality in this area of the law. The defendant has already had a full trial on the issue of guilt, and a trial on the issue of penalty; the requirement of still a third adjudication offers an invitation to those who have nothing to lose by accepting it to advance entirely spurious claims of insanity. A claim of insanity may be made at any time before sentence and, once rejected, may be raised again; a prisoner found sane two days before execution might claim to have lost his sanity the next day, thus necessitating another judicial determination of his sanity and presumably another stay of his execution. See *Nobles v. Georgia*, 168 U.S. 398, 405–406 (1897).

Since no State sanctions execution of the insane, the real battle being fought in this case is over what procedures must accompany the inquiry into sanity. The Court reaches the result it does by examining the common law, creating a constitutional right that no State seeks to violate, and then concluding that the common-law procedures are inadequate to protect the newly created but common-law based right. I find it unnecessary to "constitutionalize" the already uniform view that the insane should not be executed, and inappropriate to "selectively incorporate" the common-law practice. I therefore dissent.

Chapter 24

The Mentally Retarded May Not Be Executed— *Atkins v. Virginia* (2002)

Atkins v. Virginia, —U.S.—, 122 S. Ct. 2242 (2002) (6–3, executions of mentally retarded criminals are cruel and unusual punishments in violation of the Eighth Amendment).

Editor's comment: In *Penry v. Lynaugh*, 492 U.S. 302 (1989), a sharply divided Supreme Court held, 5–4, that executing a mildly to moderately retarded murderer did not offend the Eighth Amendment. In the thirteen year period between *Penry* and *Atkins*, however, sixteen states adopted statutory death penalty exemptions for the mentally retarded, bringing to eighteen the number of such laws. Although twenty death penalty states did not approve similar bans, the Court found a national consensus against executions of the retarded.

❖   ❖   ❖

OPINION OF JUSTICE STEVENS FOR THE COURT

Those mentally retarded persons who meet the law's requirements for criminal responsibility should be tried and punished when they commit crimes. Because of their disabilities in areas of reasoning, judgment, and control of their impulses, however, they do not act with the level of moral culpability that characterizes the most serious adult criminal conduct. Moreover, their impairments can jeopardize the reliability and fairness of capital proceedings against mentally retarded defendants. Presumably for these reasons, in the 13 years since we decided *Penry v. Lynaugh*, 492 U.S. 302 (1989), the American public, legislators, scholars, and judges have deliberated over the question whether the death penalty should ever be imposed on a mentally retarded criminal. The consensus reflected in those deliberations informs our answer to the question presented by this case: whether such executions are "cruel and unusual punishments" prohibited by the Eighth Amendment to the Federal Constitution.

255

I

Petitioner, Daryl Renard Atkins, was convicted of abduction, armed robbery, and capital murder, and sentenced to death. At approximately midnight on August 16, 1996, Atkins and William Jones, armed with a semiautomatic handgun, abducted Eric Nesbitt, robbed him of the money on his person, drove him to an automated teller machine in his pickup truck where cameras recorded their withdrawal of additional cash, then took him to an isolated location where he was shot eight times and killed.

Jones and Atkins both testified in the guilt phase of Atkins' trial. Each confirmed most of the details in the other's account of the incident, with the important exception that each stated that the other had actually shot and killed Nesbitt. Jones' testimony, which was both more coherent and credible than Atkins', was obviously credited by the jury and was sufficient to establish Atkins' guilt. At the penalty phase of the trial, the State introduced victim impact evidence and proved two aggravating circumstances: future dangerousness and "vileness of the offense." To prove future dangerousness, the State relied on Atkins' prior felony convictions as well as the testimony of four victims of earlier robberies and assaults. To prove the second aggravator, the prosecution relied upon the trial record, including pictures of the deceased's body and the autopsy report.

In the penalty phase, the defense relied on one witness, Dr. Evan Nelson, a forensic psychologist who had evaluated Atkins before trial and concluded that he was "mildly mentally retarded."[3] His conclusion was based on interviews with people who knew Atkins, a review of school and court records, and the administration of a standard intelligence test which indicated that Atkins had a full scale IQ of 59.

The jury sentenced Atkins to death, but the Virginia Supreme Court ordered a second sentencing hearing because the trial court had used a misleading verdict form. At the resentencing, Dr. Nelson again testified. The State presented an expert rebuttal witness, Dr. Stanton Samenow, who expressed the opinion that Atkins was not mentally retarded, but rather was of "average intelligence, at

---

[3] The American Association of Mental Retardation (AAMR) defines mental retardation as follows: "*Mental retardation* refers to substantial limitations in present functioning. It is characterized by significantly subaverage intellectual functioning, existing concurrently with related limitations in two or more of the following applicable adaptive skill areas: communication, self-care, home living, social skills, community use, self-direction, health and safety, functional academics, leisure, and work. Mental retardation manifests before age 18." Mental Retardation: Definition, Classification, and Systems of Supports 5 (9th ed. 1992).

The American Psychiatric Association's definition is similar: "The essential feature of Mental Retardation is significantly subaverage general intellectual functioning (Criterion A) that is accompanied by significant limitations in adaptive functioning in at least two of the following skill areas: communication, self-care, home living, social/interpersonal skills, use of community resources, self-direction, functional academic skills, work, leisure, health, and safety (Criterion B). The onset must occur before age 18 years (Criterion C). Mental Retardation has many different etiologies and may be seen as a final common pathway of various pathological processes that affect the functioning of the central nervous system." American Psychiatric Association, Diagnostic and Statistical Manual of Mental Disorders 41 (4th ed. 2000). "Mild" mental retardation is typically used to describe people with an IQ level of 50–55 to approximately 70. *Id.*, at 42–43.

least," and diagnosable as having antisocial personality disorder. The jury again sentenced Atkins to death.

The Supreme Court of Virginia affirmed the imposition of the death penalty. Atkins did not argue before the Virginia Supreme Court that his sentence was disproportionate to penalties imposed for similar crimes in Virginia, but he did contend "that he is mentally retarded and thus cannot be sentenced to death." The majority of the state court rejected this contention, relying on our holding in *Penry*. The Court was "not willing to commute Atkins' sentence of death to life imprisonment merely because of his IQ score."

Justice Hassell and Justice Koontz dissented. They rejected Dr. Samenow's opinion that Atkins possesses average intelligence as "incredulous as a matter of law," and concluded that "the imposition of the sentence of death upon a criminal defendant who has the mental age of a child between the ages of 9 and 12 is excessive." In their opinion, "it is indefensible to conclude that individuals who are mentally retarded are not to some degree less culpable for their criminal acts. By definition, such individuals have substantial limitations not shared by the general population. A moral and civilized society diminishes itself if its system of justice does not afford recognition and consideration of those limitations in a meaningful way."

Because of the gravity of the concerns expressed by the dissenters, and in light of the dramatic shift in the state legislative landscape that has occurred in the past 13 years, we granted certiorari to revisit the issue that we first addressed in the *Penry* case.

II

The Eighth Amendment succinctly prohibits "excessive" sanctions. It provides: "Excessive bail shall not be required, nor excessive fines imposed, nor cruel and unusual punishments inflicted." In *Weems* v. *United States*, 217 U.S. 349 (1910), we held that a punishment of 12 years jailed in irons at hard and painful labor for the crime of falsifying records was excessive. We explained "that it is a precept of justice that punishment for crime should be graduated and proportioned to the offense." We have repeatedly applied this proportionality precept in later cases interpreting the Eighth Amendment. See *Harmelin* v. *Michigan*, 501 U.S. 957 (1991). Thus, even though "imprisonment for ninety days is not, in the abstract, a punishment which is either cruel or unusual," it may not be imposed as a penalty for "the 'status' of narcotic addiction," *Robinson* v. *California*, 370 U.S. 660, 666 (1962), because such a sanction would be excessive. As Justice Stewart explained in *Robinson*: "Even one day in prison would be a cruel and unusual punishment for the 'crime' of having a common cold."

A claim that punishment is excessive is judged not by the standards that prevailed in 1685 when Lord Jeffreys presided over the "Bloody Assizes" or when the Bill of Rights was adopted, but rather by those that currently prevail. As Chief Justice Warren explained in his opinion in *Trop* v. *Dulles*, 356 U.S. 86 (1958): "The basic concept underlying the Eighth Amendment is nothing less than the dignity of man. . . . The Amendment must draw its meaning from the evolving standards of decency that mark the progress of a maturing society."

Proportionality review under those evolving standards should be informed by objective factors to the maximum possible extent. We have pinpointed that the clearest and most reliable objective evidence of contemporary values is the legislation enacted by the country's legislatures. Relying in part on such legislative evidence, we have held that death is an impermissibly excessive punishment for the rape of an adult woman, *Coker* v. *Georgia*, or for a defendant who neither took life, attempted to take life, nor intended to take life, *Enmund* v. *Florida*. In *Coker*, we focused primarily on the then-recent legislation that had been enacted in response to our decision 10 years earlier in *Furman* v. *Georgia* to support the conclusion that the "current judgment," though "not wholly unanimous," weighed very heavily on the side of rejecting capital punishment as a "suitable penalty for raping an adult woman." The "current legislative judgment" relevant to our decision in *Enmund* was less clear than in *Coker* but "nevertheless weighed on the side of rejecting capital punishment for the crime at issue."

We also acknowledged in *Coker* that the objective evidence, though of great importance, did not "wholly determine" the controversy, "for the Constitution contemplates that in the end our own judgment will be brought to bear on the question of the acceptability of the death penalty under the Eighth Amendment." For example, in *Enmund*, we concluded by expressing our own judgment about the issue. . . .

Thus, in cases involving a consensus, our own judgment is "brought to bear" by asking whether there is reason to disagree with the judgment reached by the citizenry and its legislators.

Guided by our approach in these cases, we shall first review the judgment of legislatures that have addressed the suitability of imposing the death penalty on the mentally retarded and then consider reasons for agreeing or disagreeing with their judgment.

III

The parties have not called our attention to any state legislative consideration of the suitability of imposing the death penalty on mentally retarded offenders prior to 1986. In that year, the public reaction to the execution of a mentally retarded murderer in Georgia apparently led to the enactment of the first state statute prohibiting such executions. In 1988, when Congress enacted legislation reinstating the federal death penalty, it expressly provided that a "sentence of death shall not be carried out upon a person who is mentally retarded." In 1989, Maryland enacted a similar prohibition. It was in that year that we decided *Penry*, and concluded that those two state enactments, "even when added to the 14 States that have rejected capital punishment completely, do not provide sufficient evidence at present of a national consensus."

Much has changed since then. Responding to the national attention received by the Bowden execution and our decision in *Penry*, state legislatures across the country began to address the issue. In 1990 Kentucky and Tennessee enacted statutes similar to those in Georgia and Maryland, as did New Mexico in 1991, and Arkansas, Colorado, Washington, Indiana, and Kansas in 1993 and 1994. In 1995, when New York reinstated its death penalty, it emulated the Federal Government by expressly exempting the mentally retarded. Nebraska followed suit in 1998. There appear to have been no similar enactments during the next two years, but in 2000 and 2001 six more States—South Dakota, Arizona, Connecticut, Florida, Missouri, and North Carolina—joined the procession. The Texas Legislature unanimously adopted a similar bill, and bills have passed at least one house in other States, including Virginia and Nevada.

It is not so much the number of these States that is significant, but the consistency of the direction of change.[18] Given the well-known fact that anticrime legislation is far more popular than legislation providing protections for persons guilty of violent crime, the large number of States prohibiting the execution of mentally retarded persons (and the complete absence of States passing legislation reinstating the power to conduct such executions) provides powerful evidence that today our society views mentally retarded offenders as categorically less culpable than the average criminal. The evidence carries even greater force when it is noted that the legislatures that have addressed the issue have voted overwhelmingly in favor of the prohibition. Moreover, even in those States that allow the execution of mentally retarded offenders, the practice is uncommon. Some States, for example New Hampshire and New Jersey, continue to authorize executions, but none have been carried out in decades. Thus there is little need to pursue legislation barring the execution of the mentally retarded in those States. And it appears that even among those States that regularly execute offenders and that have no prohibition with regard to the mentally retarded, only five have executed offenders possessing a known IQ less than 70 since we decided *Penry.* The practice, therefore, has become truly unusual, and it is fair to say that a national consensus has developed against it.[21]

---

[18] A comparison to *Stanford v. Kentucky,* in which we held that there was no national consensus prohibiting the execution of juvenile offenders over age 15, is telling. Although we decided *Stanford* on the same day as *Penry,* apparently only two state legislatures have raised the threshold age for imposition of the death penalty.

[21] Additional evidence makes it clear that this legislative judgment reflects a much broader social and professional consensus. For example, several organizations with germane expertise have adopted official positions opposing the imposition of the death penalty upon a mentally retarded offender. See Brief for American Psychological Association et al.; Brief for AAMR et al. In addition, representatives of widely diverse religious communities in the United States, reflecting Christian, Jewish, Muslim, and Buddhist traditions, have filed an amicus curiae brief explaining that even though their views about the death penalty differ, they all "share a conviction that the execution of persons with mental retardation cannot be morally justified." See Brief for United States Catholic Conference et al. Moreover, within the world community, the imposition of the death penalty for crimes committed by mentally retarded offenders is overwhelmingly disapproved. Brief for The European Union. Finally, polling data shows a widespread consensus among Americans, even those who support the death penalty, that executing the mentally retarded is wrong. Although these factors are by no means dispositive, their consistency with the legislative evidence lends further support to our conclusion that there is a consensus among those who have addressed the issue.

To the extent there is serious disagreement about the execution of mentally retarded offenders, it is in determining which offenders are in fact retarded. In this case, for instance, the Commonwealth of Virginia disputes that Atkins suffers from mental retardation. Not all people who claim to be mentally retarded will be so impaired as to fall within the range of mentally retarded offenders about whom there is a national consensus. As was our approach in *Ford* v. *Wainwright*, with regard to insanity, "we leave to the States the task of developing appropriate ways to enforce the constitutional restriction upon its execution of sentences."

IV

This consensus unquestionably reflects widespread judgment about the relative culpability of mentally retarded offenders, and the relationship between mental retardation and the penological purposes served by the death penalty. Additionally, it suggests that some characteristics of mental retardation undermine the strength of the procedural protections that our capital jurisprudence steadfastly guards.

As discussed above, clinical definitions of mental retardation require not only subaverage intellectual functioning, but also significant limitations in adaptive skills such as communication, self-care, and self-direction that became manifest before age 18. Mentally retarded persons frequently know the difference between right and wrong and are competent to stand trial. Because of their impairments, however, by definition they have diminished capacities to understand and process information, to communicate, to abstract from mistakes and learn from experience, to engage in logical reasoning, to control impulses, and to understand the reactions of others. There is no evidence that they are more likely to engage in criminal conduct than others, but there is abundant evidence that they often act on impulse rather than pursuant to a premeditated plan, and that in group settings they are followers rather than leaders. Their deficiencies do not warrant an exemption from criminal sanctions, but they do diminish their personal culpability.

In light of these deficiencies, our death penalty jurisprudence provides two reasons consistent with the legislative consensus that the mentally retarded should be categorically excluded from execution. First, there is a serious question as to whether either justification that we have recognized as a basis for the death penalty applies to mentally retarded offenders. *Gregg* v. *Georgia* identified "retribution and deterrence of capital crimes by prospective offenders" as the social purposes served by the death penalty. Unless the imposition of the death penalty on a mentally retarded person "measurably contributes to one or both of these goals, it 'is nothing more than the purposeless and needless imposition of pain and suffering,' and hence an unconstitutional punishment." *Enmund.*

With respect to retribution—the interest in seeing that the offender gets his "just deserts"—the severity of the appropriate punishment necessarily depends on the culpability of the offender. Since *Gregg*, our jurisprudence has consistently confined the imposition of the death penalty to a narrow category of the most serious crimes. For example, in *Godfrey* v. *Georgia*, 446 U.S. 420 (1980), we set aside a death sentence because the petitioner's crimes did not reflect "a consciousness materially more 'depraved' than that of any person guilty of murder." If the culpability of the average murderer is insufficient to justify the most extreme sanction available to the State, the lesser culpability of the mentally retarded offender surely does not merit that form of retribution. Thus, pursuant to our narrowing jurisprudence, which seeks to ensure that only the most deserving of execution are put to death, an exclusion for the mentally retarded is appropriate.

With respect to deterrence—the interest in preventing capital crimes by prospective offenders—it seems likely that capital punishment can serve as a deterrent only when murder is the result of premeditation and deliberation. Exempting the mentally retarded from that punishment will not affect the cold calculus that precedes the decision of other potential murderers. Indeed, that sort of calculus is at the opposite end of the spectrum from behavior of mentally retarded offenders. The theory of deterrence in capital sentencing is predicated upon the notion that the increased severity of the punishment will inhibit criminal actors from carrying out murderous conduct. Yet it is the same cognitive and behavioral impairments that make these defendants less morally culpable—for example, the diminished ability to understand and process information, to learn from experience, to engage in logical reasoning, or to control impulses—that also make it less likely that they can process the information of the possibility of execution as a penalty and, as a result, control their conduct based upon that information. Nor will exempting the mentally retarded from execution lessen the deterrent effect of the death penalty with respect to offenders who are not mentally retarded. Such individuals are unprotected by the exemption and will continue to face the threat of execution. Thus, executing the mentally retarded will not measurably further the goal of deterrence.

The reduced capacity of mentally retarded offenders provides a second justification for a categorical rule making such offenders ineligible for the death penalty. The risk that the death penalty will be imposed in spite of factors which may call for a less severe penalty is enhanced, not only by the possibility of false confessions,[25] but also by the lesser ability of mentally retarded defendants to make a persuasive showing of mitigation in the face of prosecutorial evidence of one or more aggravating factors. Mentally retarded defendants may be less able to give meaningful assistance to their counsel and are typically poor witnesses, and their demeanor may create an unwarranted impression of lack of remorse for their crimes. As *Penry* demonstrated, moreover, reliance on mental retardation as a mitigating factor can be a two-edged sword that may enhance the like-

---

[25] Despite the heavy burden that the prosecution must shoulder in capital cases, we cannot ignore the fact that in recent years a disturbing number of inmates on death row have been exonerated. As two recent high-profile cases demonstrate, these exonerations include mentally retarded persons who unwittingly confessed to crimes that they did not commit.

lihood that the aggravating factor of future dangerousness will be found by the jury. Mentally retarded defendants in the aggregate face a special risk of wrongful execution.

Our independent evaluation of the issue reveals no reason to disagree with the judgment of the legislatures that have recently addressed the matter and concluded that death is not a suitable punishment for a mentally retarded criminal. We are not persuaded that the execution of mentally retarded criminals will measurably advance the deterrent or the retributive purpose of the death penalty. Construing and applying the Eighth Amendment in the light of our "evolving standards of decency," we therefore conclude that such punishment is excessive and that the Constitution "places a substantive restriction on the State's power to take the life" of a mentally retarded offender.

The judgment of the Virginia Supreme Court is reversed and the case is remanded for further proceedings not inconsistent with this opinion.

It is so ordered.

DISSENTING OPINION OF CHIEF JUSTICE REHNQUIST JOINED BY JUSTICES SCALIA AND THOMAS

The question presented by this case is whether a national consensus deprives Virginia of the constitutional power to impose the death penalty on capital murder defendants like petitioner, *i.e.*, those defendants who indisputably are competent to stand trial, aware of the punishment they are about to suffer and why, and whose mental retardation has been found an insufficiently compelling reason to lessen their individual responsibility for the crime. The Court pronounces the punishment cruel and unusual primarily because 18 States recently have passed laws limiting the death eligibility of certain defendants based on mental retardation alone, despite the fact that the laws of 19 other States besides Virginia continue to leave the question of proper punishment to the individuated consideration of sentencing judges or juries familiar with the particular offender and his or her crime.

I agree with Justice Scalia that the Court's assessment of the current legislative judgment regarding the execution of defendants like petitioner more resembles a post hoc rationalization for the majority's subjectively preferred result rather than any objective effort to ascertain the content of an evolving standard of decency. I write separately, however, to call attention to the defects in the Court's decision to place weight on foreign laws, the views of professional and religious organizations, and opinion polls in reaching its conclusion. The Court's suggestion that these sources are relevant to the constitutional question finds little support in our precedents and, in my view, is antithetical to considerations of federalism, which instruct that any "permanent prohibition upon all units of democratic government must [be apparent] in the operative acts (laws and the application of laws) that the people have approved." *Stanford* v. *Kentucky*, 492 U.S. 361, 377 (1989) (plurality opinion). The Court's uncritical acceptance of the opinion poll data brought to our attention, moreover, warrants additional comment, because we lack sufficient information to conclude that the surveys were conducted in accordance with generally accepted scientific principles or are capable of supporting valid empirical inferences about the issue before us.

In my view, these two sources—the work product of legislatures and sentencing jury determinations—ought to be the sole indicators by which courts ascertain the contemporary American conceptions of decency for purposes of the Eighth Amendment. They are the only objective indicia of contemporary values firmly supported by our precedents. More importantly, however, they can be reconciled with the undeniable precepts that the democratic branches of government and individual sentencing juries are, by design, better suited than courts to evaluating and giving effect to the complex societal and moral considerations that inform the selection of publicly acceptable criminal punishments.

In reaching its conclusion today, the Court does not take notice of the fact that neither petitioner nor his amici have adduced any comprehensive statistics that would conclusively prove (or disprove) whether juries routinely consider death a disproportionate punishment for mentally retarded offenders like petitioner. Instead, it adverts to the fact that other countries have disapproved imposition of the death penalty for crimes committed by mentally retarded offenders. I fail to see, however, how the views of other countries regarding the punishment of their citizens provide any support for the Court's ultimate determination.

To further buttress its appraisal of contemporary societal values, the Court marshals public opinion poll results and evidence that several professional organizations and religious groups have adopted official positions opposing the imposition of the death penalty upon mentally retarded offenders. . . . In my view, none should be accorded any weight on the Eighth Amendment scale when the elected representatives of a State's populace have not deemed them persuasive enough to prompt legislative action. . . . For the Court to rely on such data today serves only to illustrate its willingness to proscribe by judicial fiat—at the behest of private organizations speaking only for themselves—a punishment about which no across-the-board consensus has developed through the workings of normal democratic processes in the laboratories of the States.

Even if I were to accept the legitimacy of the Court's decision to reach beyond the product of legislatures and practices of sentencing juries to discern a national standard of decency, I would take issue with the blind-faith credence it accords the opinion polls brought to our attention. An extensive body of social science literature describes how methodological and other errors can affect the reliability and validity of estimates about the opinions and attitudes of a population derived from various sampling techniques. Everything from variations in the survey methodology, such as the choice of the target population, the sampling design used, the questions asked, and the statistical analyses used to interpret the data can skew the results.

There are strong reasons for limiting our inquiry into what constitutes an evolving standard of decency under the Eighth Amendment to the laws passed by legislatures and the practices of sentencing juries in America. Here, the Court goes beyond these well-established objective indicators of contemporary values. It finds "further support to [its] conclusion" that a national consensus has developed against imposing the death penalty on all mentally retarded defendants in international opinion, the views of professional and religious organizations, and opinion polls not demonstrated to be reliable. Believing this view to be seriously mistaken, I dissent.

DISSENTING OPINION OF JUSTICE SCALIA JOINED BY CHIEF JUSTICE REHNQUIST AND JUSTICE THOMAS

Today's decision is the pinnacle of our Eighth Amendment death-is-different jurisprudence. Not only does it, like all of that jurisprudence, find no support in the text or history of the Eighth Amendment; it does not even have support in current social attitudes regarding the conditions that render an otherwise just death penalty inappropriate. Seldom has an opinion of this Court rested so obviously upon nothing but the personal views of its members.

II

... [P]etitioner's mental retardation was a *central issue* at sentencing. The jury concluded, however, that his alleged retardation was not a compelling reason to exempt him from the death penalty in light of the brutality of his crime and his long demonstrated propensity for violence. "In upsetting this particularized judgment on the basis of a constitutional absolute," the Court concludes that no one who is even slightly mentally retarded can have sufficient "moral responsibility to be subjected to capital punishment for any crime. As a sociological and moral conclusion that is implausible; and it is doubly implausible as an interpretation of the United States Constitution." *Thompson* v. *Oklahoma*, 487 U.S. 815, 863–864 (1988) (Scalia, J., dissenting).

Under our Eighth Amendment jurisprudence, a punishment is "cruel and unusual" if it falls within one of two categories: those modes or acts of punishment that had been considered cruel and unusual at the time that the Bill of Rights was adopted, and modes of punishment that are inconsistent with modern "standards of decency," as evinced by objective indicia, the most important of which is legislation enacted by the country's legislatures.

The Court makes no pretense that execution of the mildly mentally retarded would have been considered "cruel and unusual" in 1791. Only the *severely* or *profoundly* mentally retarded, commonly known as "idiots," enjoyed any special status under the law at that time. They, like lunatics, suffered a "deficiency in will" rendering them unable to tell right from wrong. 4 W. Blackstone, Commentaries on the Laws of England 24 (1769). ... Due to their incompetence, idiots were "excused from the guilt, and of course from the punishment, of any criminal action committed under such deprivation of the senses." Instead, they were often committed to civil confinement or made wards of the State, thereby preventing them from "going loose, to the terror of the king's subjects." Mentally retarded offenders with less severe impairments—those who were not "idiots"—suffered criminal prosecution and punishment, including capital punishment. . . .

The Court is left to argue, therefore, that execution of the mildly retarded is inconsistent with the "evolving standards of decency that mark the progress of a maturing society." *Trop.* Before today, our opinions consistently emphasized that Eighth Amendment judgments regarding the existence of social "standards" "should be informed by objective factors to the maximum possible extent" and "should not be, or appear to be, merely the subjective views of individual Justices." *Coker.* "First" among these objective factors are the "statutes passed by society's elected representatives," *Stanford,* because it "will rarely if ever be the case that the Members of this Court will have a better sense of the evolution in views of the American people than do their elected representatives." *Thompson.*

The Court pays lip service to these precedents as it miraculously extracts a "national consensus" forbidding execution of the mentally retarded from the fact that 18 States—less than *half* (47 percent) of the 38 States that permit capital punishment (for whom the issue exists)—have very recently enacted legislation barring execution of the mentally retarded. Even that 47 percent figure is a distorted one. If one is to say, as the Court does today, that *all* executions of the mentally retarded are so morally repugnant as to violate our national "standards of decency," surely the "consensus" it points to must be one that has set its righteous face against *all* such executions. Not 18 States, but only seven—18 percent of death penalty jurisdictions—have legislation of that scope. Eleven of those that the Court counts enacted statutes prohibiting execution of mentally retarded defendants *convicted after, or convicted of crimes committed after, the effective date* of the legislation; those already on death row, or consigned there before the statute's effective date, or even (in those States using the date of the crime as the criterion of retroactivity) tried in the future for murders committed many years ago, could be put to death. That is not a statement of absolute moral repugnance, but one of current preference between two tolerable approaches. Two of these States permit execution of the mentally retarded in other situations as well: Kansas apparently permits execution of all except the *severely* mentally retarded; New York permits execution of the mentally retarded who commit murder in a correctional facility.

But let us accept, for the sake of argument, the Court's faulty count. That bare number of States alone—*18*—should be enough to convince any reasonable person that no "national consensus" exists. How is it possible that agreement among 47 percent of the death penalty jurisdictions amounts to "consensus"? Our prior cases have generally required a much higher degree of agreement before finding a punishment cruel and unusual on "evolving standards" grounds. In *Coker,* we proscribed the death penalty for rape of an adult woman after finding that only one jurisdiction, Georgia, authorized such a punishment. In *Enmund,* we invalidated the death penalty for mere participation in a robbery in which an accomplice took a life, a punishment not permitted in 28 of the death penalty States (78 percent). In *Ford*, we supported the common-law prohibition of execution of the insane with the observation that "this ancestral legacy has not outlived its time," since not a single State authorizes such punishment. In *Solem* v. *Helm*, we invalidated a life sentence without parole under a recidivist statute by which the criminal "was treated more severely than he would have been in any other State." What the Court calls evidence of "consensus" in the present case (a fudged 47 percent) more closely resembles evidence that we found *inadequate* to establish consensus in earlier cases. *Tison* v. *Arizona* upheld a state law authorizing capital punishment for major participation in a felony with reckless indifference to life where only 11 of the 37 death penalty States (30 percent) prohibited such punishment. *Stanford* upheld a state law permitting execution of defendants who committed a capital crime at age 16 where only 15 of the 36 death penalty States (42 percent) prohibited death for such offenders.

Moreover, a major factor that the Court entirely disregards is that the legislation of all 18 States it relies on is still in its infancy. The oldest of the statutes is only 14 years old; five were enacted last year; over half were enacted within the past eight years. Few, if any, of the States have had sufficient experience with these laws to know whether they are sensible in the long term. It is "myopic to base sweeping constitutional principles upon the narrow experience of [a few] years." *Coker* (Burger, C. J., dissenting).

The Court attempts to bolster its embarrassingly feeble evidence of "consensus" with the following: "It is not so much the number of these States that is significant, but the *consistency* of the direction of change." But in what *other* direction *could we possibly* see change? Given that 14 years ago *all* the death penalty statutes included the mentally retarded, *any* change (except precipitate undoing of what had just been done) was *bound to be* in the one direction the Court finds significant enough to overcome the lack of real consensus. That is to say, to be accurate the Court's "*consistency*-of-the-direction-of-change" point should be recast into the following unimpressive observation: "No State has yet undone its exemption of the mentally retarded, one for as long as 14 whole years." In any event, reliance upon "trends," even those of much longer duration than a mere 14 years, is a perilous basis for constitutional adjudication, as Justice O'Connor eloquently explained in *Thompson*:

> In 1846, Michigan became the first State to abolish the death penalty. . . . In succeeding decades, other American States continued the trend towards abolition. . . . Later, and particularly after World War II, there ensued a steady and dramatic decline in executions. . . . In the 1950's and 1960's, more States abolished or radically restricted capital punishment, and executions ceased completely for several years beginning in 1968. . . .
>
> In 1972, when this Court heard arguments on the constitutionality of the death penalty, such statistics might have suggested that the practice had become a relic, implicitly rejected by a new societal consensus. . . . We now know that any inference of a societal consensus rejecting the death penalty would have been mistaken. But had this Court then declared the existence of such a consensus, and outlawed capital punishment, legislatures would very likely not have been able to revive it. The mistaken premise of the decision

would have been frozen into constitutional law, making it difficult to refute and even more difficult to reject.

Her words demonstrate, of course, not merely the peril of riding a trend, but also the peril of discerning a consensus where there is none. The Court's thrashing about for evidence of "consensus" includes reliance upon the margins by which state legislatures have enacted bans on execution of the retarded. Presumably, in applying our Eighth Amendment "evolving-standards-of-decency" jurisprudence, we will henceforth weigh not only how many States have agreed, but how many States have agreed *by how much.* Of course if the percentage of legislators voting for the bill is significant, surely the number of people *represented* by the legislators voting for the bill is also significant: the fact that 49 percent of the legislators in a State with a population of 60 million voted *against* the bill should be more impressive than the fact that 90 percent of the legislators in a state with a population of 2 million voted *for* it. (By the way, the population of the death penalty States that exclude the mentally retarded is only 44 percent of the population of all death penalty States.) This is quite absurd. What we have looked for in the past to "evolve" the Eighth Amendment is a consensus of the same sort as the consensus that *adopted* the Eighth Amendment: a consensus of the sovereign States that form the Union, not a nose count of Americans for and against.

Even less compelling (if possible) is the Court's argument that evidence of "national consensus" is to be found in the infrequency with which retarded persons are executed in States that do not bar their execution. To begin with, what the Court takes as true is in fact quite doubtful. It is not at all clear that execution of the mentally retarded is "uncommon," as even the sources cited by the Court suggest. *If,* however, execution of the mentally retarded *is* "uncommon"; and if it is not a sufficient explanation of this that the retarded comprise a tiny fraction of society (1 percent to 3 percent), then surely the explanation is that mental retardation is a constitutionally mandated mitigating factor at sentencing. For that reason, even if there were uniform national sentiment in *favor* of executing the retarded in appropriate cases, one would still expect execution of the mentally retarded to be "uncommon." To adapt to the present case what the Court itself said in *Stanford:* "It is not only possible, but overwhelmingly probable, that the very considerations which induce [today's majority] to believe that death should *never* be imposed on [mentally retarded] offenders . . . cause prosecutors and juries to believe that it should *rarely* be imposed."

But the Prize for the Court's Most Feeble Effort to fabricate "national consensus" must go to its appeal (deservedly relegated to a footnote) to the views of assorted professional and religious organizations, members of the so-called "world community," and respondents to opinion polls. I agree with the Chief Justice that the views of professional and religious organizations and the results of opinion polls are irrelevant. Equally irrelevant are the practices of the "world community," whose notions of justice are (thankfully) not always those of our people. "We must never forget that it is a Constitution for the United States of America that we are expounding. . . . Where there is not first a settled consensus among our own people, the views of other nations, however enlightened the Justices of this Court may think them to be, cannot be imposed upon Americans through the Constitution." *Thompson* (Scalia, J., dissenting).

III

Beyond the empty talk of a "national consensus," the Court gives us a brief glimpse of what really underlies today's decision: pretension to a power confined *neither* by the moral sentiments originally enshrined in the Eighth Amendment (its original meaning) *nor even* by the current moral sentiments of the American people. "The Constitution," the Court says, "contemplates that in the end *our own judgment* will be brought to bear on the question of the acceptability of the death penalty under the Eighth Amendment." (The unexpressed reason for this unexpressed "contemplation" of the Constitution is presumably that really good lawyers have moral sentiments superior to those of the common herd, whether in 1791 or today.) The arrogance of this assumption of power takes one's breath away. And it explains, of course, why the Court can be so cavalier about the evidence of consensus. It is just a game, after all. "In the end," it is the *feelings* and *intuition* of a majority of the Justices that count—"the perceptions of decency, or of penology, or of mercy, entertained . . . by a majority of the small and unrepresentative segment of our society that sits on this Court." *Thompson* (Scalia, J., dissenting).

The genuinely operative portion of the opinion, then, is the Court's statement of the reasons why it agrees with the contrived consensus it has found, that the "diminished capacities" of the mentally retarded render the death penalty excessive. The Court's analysis rests on two fundamental assumptions: (1) that the Eighth Amendment prohibits excessive punishments, and (2) that sentencing juries or judges are unable to account properly for the "diminished capacities" of the retarded. The first assumption is wrong, as I explained at length in *Harmelin* v. *Michigan*. The Eighth Amendment is addressed to always-and-everywhere "cruel" punishments, such as the rack and the thumbscrew. But where the punishment is in itself permissible, "the Eighth Amendment is not a ratchet, whereby a temporary consensus on leniency for a particular crime fixes a permanent constitutional maximum, disabling the States from giving effect to altered beliefs and responding to changed social conditions." *Id*. The second assumption—inability of judges or juries to take proper account of mental retardation— is not only unsubstantiated, but contradicts the immemorial belief, here and in England, that they play an *indispensable* role in such matters:

> "It is very difficult to define the indivisible line that divides perfect and partial insanity; but it must rest upon circumstances duly to be weighed and considered both by the judge and jury, lest on the one side there be a kind of inhumanity towards the defects of human nature, or on the other side too great an indulgence given to great crimes. . . ." 1 Hale, Pleas of the Crown, at 30.

Proceeding from these faulty assumptions, the Court gives two reasons why the death penalty is an excessive punishment for all mentally retarded offenders. First, the "diminished capacities" of the mentally retarded raise a "serious question" whether their execution contributes to the "social purposes" of the death penalty, viz., retribution and deterrence. (The Court conveniently ignores a third "social purpose" of the death penalty—"incapacitation of dangerous criminals and the consequent prevention of crimes that they may otherwise commit in the future," *Gregg*. But never mind; its discussion of even the other two does not bear analysis.) Retribution is not advanced, the argument goes, because the mentally retarded are *no more culpable* than the average murderer, whom we have already held lacks sufficient culpability to warrant the death penalty, see *Godfrey* v. *Georgia*. Who says so? Is there an established correlation between mental acuity and the ability to conform one's conduct to the law in such a rudimentary matter as murder? Are the mentally retarded really more disposed (and hence more likely) to commit willfully cruel and serious crime than others? In my experience, the opposite is true: being childlike generally suggests innocence rather than brutality.

Assuming, however, that there is a direct connection between diminished intelligence and the inability to refrain from murder, what scientific analysis can possibly show that a mildly retarded individual who commits an exquisite torture-killing is "no more culpable" than the "average" murderer in a holdup-gone-wrong or a domestic dispute? Or a moderately retarded individual who commits a series of 20 exquisite torture-killings? Surely culpability, and deservedness of the most severe retribution, depends not merely (if at all) upon the mental capacity of the criminal (above the level where he is able to distinguish right from wrong) but also upon the depravity of the crime—which is precisely why this sort of question has traditionally been thought answerable not by a categorical rule of the sort the Court today imposes upon all trials, but rather by the sentencer's weighing of the circumstances (both degree of retardation and depravity of crime) in the particular case. The fact that juries continue to sentence mentally retarded offenders to death for extreme crimes shows that society's moral outrage sometimes demands execution of retarded offenders. By what principle of law, science, or logic can the Court pronounce that this is wrong? There is none. Once the Court admits (as it does) that mental retardation does not render the offender morally *blameless*, there is no basis for saying that the death penalty is *never* appropriate retribution, no matter *how* heinous the crime. As long as a mentally retarded offender knows "the difference between right and wrong," only the sentencer can assess whether his retardation reduces his culpability enough to exempt him from the death penalty for the particular murder in question.

As for the other social purpose of the death penalty that the Court discusses, deterrence: That is not advanced, the Court tells us, because the mentally retarded are "less likely" than their nonretarded counterparts to "process the information of the possibility of execution as a penalty and . . . control their conduct based upon that information." Of course this leads to the same conclusion discussed earlier—that the mentally retarded (because they are less deterred) are more likely to kill—which neither I nor the society at large believes. In any event, even the Court does not say that *all* mentally retarded individuals cannot "process the information of the possibility of execution as a penalty and . . . control their conduct based upon that information"; it merely asserts that they are "less likely" to be able to do so. But surely the deterrent effect of a penalty is adequately vindicated if it successfully deters many, but not all, of the target class. Virginia's death penalty, for example, does not fail of its deterrent effect simply because *some* criminals are unaware that Virginia *has* the death penalty. In other words, the supposed fact that *some* retarded criminals cannot fully appreciate the death penalty has nothing to do with the deterrence rationale, but is simply an echo of the arguments denying a retribution rationale, discussed and rejected above. I am not sure that a murderer is somehow less blameworthy if (though he knew his act was wrong) he did not fully appreciate that he could die for it; but if so, we should treat a mentally retarded murderer the way we treat an offender who may be "less likely" to respond to the death penalty because he was abused as a child. We do not hold him immune from capital punishment, but require his background to be considered by the sentencer as a mitigating factor.

The Court throws one last factor into its grab bag of reasons why execution of the retarded is "excessive" in all cases: Mentally retarded offenders "face a special risk of wrongful execution" because they are less able "to make a persuasive showing of mitigation," "to give meaningful assistance to their counsel," and to be effective witnesses. "Special risk" is pretty flabby language (even flabbier than "less likely")—and I suppose a similar "special risk" could be said to exist for just plain stupid people, inarticulate people, even ugly people. If this unsupported claim has any substance to it (which I doubt) it might support a due process claim in all criminal prosecutions of the mentally retarded; but it is hard to see how it has anything to do with an *Eighth Amendment* claim that execution of the mentally retarded is cruel and unusual. We have never before held it to be cruel and unusual punishment to impose a sentence in violation of some *other* constitutional imperative.

Today's opinion adds one more to the long list of substantive and procedural requirements impeding imposition of the death penalty imposed under this Court's assumed power to invent a death-is-different jurisprudence. None of those requirements existed when the Eighth Amendment was adopted, and some of them were not even supported by current moral consensus. They include prohibition of the death penalty for "ordinary" murder, *Godfrey*, for rape of an adult woman, *Coker*, and for felony murder absent a showing that the defendant possessed a sufficiently culpable state of mind, *Enmund*; prohibition of the death penalty for any person under the age of 16 at the time of the crime, *Thompson*; prohibition of the death penalty as the mandatory punishment for any crime, *Woodson* v. *North Carolina, Sumner* v. *Shuman*; a requirement that the sentencer not be given unguided discretion, *Furman*, a requirement that the sentencer be empowered to take into account all mitigating circumstances, *Lockett* v. *Ohio, Eddings* v. *Oklahoma*, and a requirement that the accused receive a judicial evaluation of his claim of insanity before the sentence can be executed, *Ford*. There is something to be said for popular abolition of the death penalty; there is nothing to be said for its incremental abolition by this Court.

This newest invention promises to be more effective than any of the others in turning the process of capital trial into a game. One need only read the definitions of mental retardation adopted by the American Association of Mental Retardation and the American Psychiatric Association to realize that the symptoms of this condition can readily be feigned. And whereas the capital defendant who feigns insanity risks commitment to a mental institution until he can be cured (and then tried and executed), the capital defendant who feigns mental retardation risks nothing at all. The mere pendency of the present case has brought us petitions by death row inmates claiming for the first time, after multiple habeas petitions, that they are retarded.

Perhaps these practical difficulties will not be experienced by the minority of capital-punishment States that have very recently changed mental retardation from a mitigating factor (to be accepted or rejected by the sentencer) to an absolute immunity. Time will tell—and the brief time those States have had the new disposition in place (an average of 6.8 years) is surely not enough. But if the practical difficulties do not appear, and if the other States share the Court's perceived moral consensus that *all* mental retardation renders the death penalty inappropriate for *all* crimes, then that majority will presumably follow suit. But there is no justification for this Court's pushing them into the experiment—and turning the experiment into a permanent practice—on constitutional pretext. Nothing has changed the accuracy of Matthew Hale's endorsement of the common law's traditional method for taking account of guilt-reducing factors, written over three centuries ago:

> [Determination of a person's incapacity] is a matter of great difficulty, partly
> from the easiness of counterfeiting this disability . . . and partly from the
> variety of the degrees of this infirmity, whereof some are sufficient, and some
> are insufficient to excuse persons in capital offenses. . . .
>
> Yet the law of England hath afforded the best method of trial, that is
> possible, of this and all other matters of fact, namely, by a jury of twelve men
> all concurring in the same judgment, by the testimony of witnesses . . . , and by
> the inspection and direction of the judge. 1 Hale, Pleas of the Crown, at 32–33.

I respectfully dissent.

Chapter 25

Race Discrimination and Capital Punishment— *McCleskey v. Kemp* (1987)

McCleskey v. Kemp, 481 U.S. 279, 107 S. Ct. 1756, 95 L. Ed.2d 262 (1987) (5–4, study showing that, in Georgia, black defendants who killed whites have the greatest likelihood of receiving the death penalty does not prove discrimination in violation of the Equal Protection Clause or arbitrariness in violation of the Eighth Amendment).

Editor's comment: Defendant McCleskey, a black man convicted and sentenced to death in Georgia for a robbery-murder, argued that the Georgia capital punishment scheme violated the Fourteenth Amendment Equal Protection Clause and the Eighth Amendment. His claim was based solely on statistical evidence from an elaborate study by Professor David Baldus of murder cases in Georgia over a five-year period, 1973–1978. Unlike studies of the death penalty during the period prior to the 1970's, which showed race discrimination against black defendants,[a] Baldus's study offered proof of discrimination against black murder *victims*: killers of blacks were statistically less likely to get the death sentence than the murderers of whites, and death sentences were especially likely where the murderers of whites were black. The U.S. District Court found the Baldus study flawed and suggested that the racial disparities could be explained by the greater incidence of aggravating factors in white-victim cases and of mitigating factors in black-victim cases. *McCleskey v. Zant*, 580 F. Supp. 338 (N.D. Ga. 1984). The Eleventh Circuit Court of Appeals assumed that the Baldus findings were valid, but nevertheless rejected McCleskey's constitutional contentions. *McCleskey v. Kemp*, 753 F.2d 877 (11th Cir. 1985).

The U.S. Supreme Court, like the Circuit Court, assumed the validity of the Baldus study, but disallowed the constitutional claims. To under-

---

[a] For example, M. Wolfgang and M. Reidel, "Race, Judicial Discretion, and the Death Penalty," 407 Annals of the American Academy of Political and Social Science 119–133 (1973) (studying rape cases in 11 southern states during the period 1945 to 1965).

stand the "equal protection of the laws" issue, the reader should know that the Court has, for many years, demanded proof of purposeful or intentional discrimination. Mere racially disproportionate impact is not enough. The leading case establishing this was *Washington v. Davis*, 426 U.S. 229 (1976), where the Court held that the fact that a higher percentage of blacks than whites failed a police officer's test was insufficient to prove the discriminatory racial purpose essential to demonstrate an equal protection violation. Although statistical evidence of different treatment of blacks and whites is sometimes acceptable proof of discriminatory intent, the Baldus statistics were judged insufficient in this case. For additional statistics on race and the death penalty, see Appendix A.

❖   ❖   ❖

OPINION OF JUSTICE POWELL FOR THE COURT

This case presents the question whether a complex statistical study that indicates a risk that racial considerations enter into capital sentencing determinations proves that petitioner McCleskey's capital sentence is unconstitutional under the Eighth or Fourteenth Amendment.

I

McCleskey, a black man, was convicted of two counts of armed robbery and one count of murder in the Superior Court of Fulton County, Georgia, on October 12, 1978. McCleskey's convictions arose out of the robbery of a furniture store and the killing of a white police officer during the course of the robbery. . . .

In support of his claim, McCleskey proffered a statistical study performed by Professors David C. Baldus, Charles Pulaski, and George Woodworth (the Baldus study), that purports to show a disparity in the imposition of the death sentence in Georgia based on the race of the murder victim and, to a lesser extent, the race of the defendant. The Baldus study is actually two sophisticated statistical studies that examine over 2,000 murder cases that occurred in Georgia during the 1970's. The raw numbers collected by Professor Baldus indicate that defendants charged with killing white persons received the death penalty in 11 percent of the cases, but defendants charged with killing blacks received the death penalty in only 1 percent of the cases. The raw numbers also indicate a reverse racial disparity according to the race of the defendant: 4 percent of the black defendants received the death penalty, as opposed to 7 percent of the white defendants.

Baldus also divided the cases according to the combination of the race of the defendant and the race of the victim. He found that the death penalty was assessed in 22 percent of the cases involving black defendants and white victims;

8 percent of the cases involving white defendants and white victims; 1 percent of the cases involving black defendants and black victims; and 3 percent of the cases involving white defendants and black victims. Similarly, Baldus found that prosecutors sought the death penalty in 70 percent of the cases involving black defendants and white victims; 32 percent of the cases involving white defendants and white victims; 15 percent of the cases involving black defendants and black victims; and 19 percent of the cases involving white defendants and black victims.

Baldus subjected his data to an extensive analysis, taking account of 230 variables that could have explained the disparities on nonracial grounds. One of his models concludes that, even after taking account of 39 nonracial variables, defendants charged with killing white victims were 4.3 times as likely to receive a death sentence as defendants charged with killing blacks. According to this model, black defendants were 1.1 times as likely to receive a death sentence as other defendants. Thus, the Baldus study indicates that black defendants, such as McCleskey, who kill white victims have the greatest likelihood of receiving the death penalty.[5] . . .

II

McCleskey's first claim is that the Georgia capital punishment statute violates the Equal Protection Clause of the Fourteenth Amendment.[7] He argues that race has infected the administration of Georgia's statute in two ways: persons who murder whites are more likely to be sentenced to death than persons who murder blacks, and black murderers are more likely to be sentenced to death than white murderers. As a black defendant who killed a white victim, McCleskey claims that the Baldus study demonstrates that he was discriminated against because of his race and because of the race of his victim. In its broadest form, McCleskey's claim of discrimination extends to every actor in the Georgia capital sentencing

---

[5] Baldus' 230-variable model divided cases into eight different ranges, according to the estimated aggravation level of the offense. Baldus argued in his testimony to the District Court that the effects of racial bias were most striking in the midrange cases. "[W]hen the cases become tremendously aggravated so that everybody would agree that if we're going to have a death sentence, these are the cases that should get it, the race effects go away. It's only in the midrange of cases where the decision makers have a real choice as to what to do. If there's room for the exercise of discretion, then the [racial] factors begin to play a role." . . .

Under this model, Baldus found that 14.4 percent of the black-victim midrange cases received the death penalty, and 34.4 percent of the white-victim cases received the death penalty. . . . According to Baldus, the facts of McCleskey's case placed it within the midrange. . . .

[7] Although the District Court rejected the findings of the Baldus study as flawed, the Court of Appeals assumed that the study is valid and reached the constitutional issues. Accordingly, those issues are before us. As did the Court of Appeals, we assume the study is valid statistically without reviewing the factual findings of the District Court. Our assumption that the Baldus study is statistically valid does not include the assumption that the study shows that racial considerations actually enter into any sentencing decisions in Georgia. Even a sophisticated multiple-regression analysis such as the Baldus study can only demonstrate a risk that the factor of race entered into some capital sentencing decisions and a necessarily lesser risk that race entered into any particular sentencing decision.

process, from the prosecutor who sought the death penalty and the jury that imposed the sentence, to the State itself that enacted the capital punishment statute and allows it to remain in effect despite its allegedly discriminatory application. We agree with the Court of Appeals, and every other court that has considered such a challenge, that this claim must fail.

II–A

Our analysis begins with the basic principle that a defendant who alleges an equal protection violation has the burden of proving "the existence of purposeful discrimination." . . . A corollary to this principle is that a criminal defendant must prove that the purposeful discrimination "had a discriminatory effect" on him. . . . Thus, to prevail under the Equal Protection Clause, McCleskey must prove that the decision makers in his case acted with discriminatory purpose. He offers no evidence specific to his own case that would support an inference that racial considerations played a part in his sentence. Instead, he relies solely on the Baldus study.

McCleskey argues that the Baldus study compels an inference that his sentence rests on purposeful discrimination. McCleskey's claim that these statistics are sufficient proof of discrimination, without regard to the facts of a particular case, would extend to all capital cases in Georgia, at least where the victim was white and the defendant is black.

The Court has accepted statistics as proof of intent to discriminate in certain limited contexts. First, this Court has accepted statistical disparities as proof of an equal protection violation in the selection of the jury venire in a particular district. Although statistical proof normally must present a "stark" pattern to be accepted as the sole proof of discriminatory intent under the Constitution, . . . "[b]ecause of the nature of the jury-selection task, . . . we have permitted a finding of constitutional violation even when the statistical pattern does not approach [such] extremes." . . . Second, this Court has accepted statistics in the form of multiple regression analysis to prove statutory violations under Title VII of the Civil Rights Act of 1964. *Bazemore v. Friday,* [478 U.S. 385 (1986)].

But the nature of the capital sentencing decision, and the relationship of the statistics to that decision, are fundamentally different from the corresponding elements in the venire-selection or Title VII cases. Most importantly, each particular decision to impose the death penalty is made by a petit jury selected from a properly constituted venire. Each jury is unique in its composition, and the Constitution requires that its decision rest on consideration of innumerable factors that vary according to the characteristics of the individual defendant and the facts of the particular capital offense. . . . Thus, the application of an inference drawn from the general statistics to a specific decision in a trial and sentencing simply is not comparable to the application of an inference drawn from general statistics to a specific venire-selection or Title VII case. In those cases, the statistics relate to fewer entities,[14] and fewer variables are relevant to the challenged decisions.

Another important difference between the cases in which we have accepted statistics as proof of discriminatory intent and this case is that, in the venire-selection and Title VII contexts, the decision maker has an opportunity to explain the statistical disparity. . . . Here, the State has no practical opportunity to rebut the Baldus study. "[C]ontrolling considerations of . . . public policy," . . . dictate that jurors "cannot be called . . . to testify to the motives and influences that led to their verdict." . . . Similarly, the policy considerations behind a prosecutor's traditionally "wide discretion" suggest the impropriety of our requiring prosecutors to defend their decisions to seek death penalties, "often years after they were made." . . . Moreover, absent far stronger proof, it is unnecessary to seek such a rebuttal, because a legitimate and unchallenged explanation for the decision is apparent from the record: McCleskey committed an act for which the United States Constitution and Georgia laws permit imposition of the death penalty.

Finally, McCleskey's statistical proffer must be viewed in the context of his challenge. McCleskey challenges decisions at the heart of the State's criminal justice system. "[O]ne of society's most basic tasks is that of protecting the lives of its citizens and one of the most basic ways in which it achieves the task is through criminal laws against murder." *Gregg.* Implementation of these laws necessarily requires discretionary judgments. Because discretion is essential to the criminal justice process, we would demand exceptionally clear proof before we would infer that the discretion has been abused. The unique nature of the decisions at issue in this case also counsels against adopting such an inference from the disparities indicated by the Baldus study. Accordingly, we hold that the Baldus study is clearly insufficient to support an inference that any of the decision makers in McCleskey's case acted with discriminatory purpose.

II-B

McCleskey also suggests that the Baldus study proves that the State as a whole has acted with a discriminatory purpose. He appears to argue that the State has violated the Equal Protection Clause by adopting the capital punishment statute

---

[14] . . . The Baldus study seeks to deduce a state "policy" by studying the combined effects of the decisions of hundreds of juries that are unique in their composition. It is incomparably more difficult to deduce a consistent policy by studying the decisions of these many unique entities. It is also questionable whether any consistent policy can be derived by studying the decisions of prosecutors. The District Attorney is elected by the voters in a particular county. Since decisions whether to prosecute and what to charge necessarily are individualized and involve infinite factual variations, coordination among district attorney offices across a State would be relatively meaningless. Thus, any inference from statewide statistics to a prosecutorial "policy" is of doubtful relevance. Moreover, the statistics in Fulton County alone represent the disposition of far fewer cases than the statewide statistics. Even assuming the statistical validity of the Baldus study as a whole, the weight to be given the results gleaned from this small sample is limited.

and allowing it to remain in force despite its allegedly discriminatory application. But " '[d]iscriminatory purpose' . . . implies more than intent as volition or intent as awareness of consequences. It implies that the decision maker, in this case a state legislature, selected or reaffirmed a particular course of action at least in part 'because of,' not merely 'in spite of,' its adverse effects upon an identifiable group." . . . For this claim to prevail, McCleskey would have to prove that the Georgia Legislature enacted or maintained the death penalty statute because of an anticipated racially discriminatory effect. In *Gregg v. Georgia*, this Court found that the Georgia capital sentencing system could operate in a fair and neutral manner. There was no evidence then, and there is none now, that the Georgia Legislature enacted the capital punishment statute to further a racially discriminatory purpose.[20]

Nor has McCleskey demonstrated that the legislature maintains the capital punishment statute because of the racially disproportionate impact suggested by the Baldus study. As legislatures necessarily have wide discretion in the choice of criminal laws and penalties, and as there were legitimate reasons for the Georgia Legislature to adopt and maintain capital punishment, see *Gregg*, we will not infer a discriminatory purpose on the part of the State of Georgia. Accordingly, we reject McCleskey's equal protection claims.

III

McCleskey also argues that the Baldus study demonstrates that the Georgia capital sentencing system violates the Eighth Amendment. . . .

IV–A

In light of our precedents under the Eighth Amendment, McCleskey cannot argue successfully that his sentence is "disproportionate to the crime in the traditional sense." See *Pulley v. Harris*. He does not deny that he committed a murder in the course of a planned robbery, a crime for which this Court has determined that the death penalty constitutionally may be imposed. His disproportionality claim "is of a different sort." *Gregg*. McCleskey argues that the sentence in his case is disproportionate to the sentence in his case is disproportionate to the sentences in other murder cases. *Pulley*.

On the one hand, he cannot base a constitutional claim on an argument that his case differs from other cases in which defendants did receive the death penalty. On automatic appeal, the Georgia Supreme Court found that

---

[20] McCleskey relies on "historical evidence" to support his claim of purposeful discrimination by the State. This evidence focuses on Georgia laws in force during and just after the Civil War. Of course, the "historical background of the decision is one evidentiary source" for proof of intentional discrimination. . . . But unless historical evidence is reasonably contemporaneous with the challenged decision, it has little probative value. Although the history of racial discrimination in this country is undeniable, we cannot accept official actions taken long ago as evidence of current intent.

McCleskey's death sentence was not disproportionate to other death sentences imposed in the State.... The court supported this conclusion with an appendix containing citations to 13 cases involving generally similar murders.... Moreover, where the statutory procedures adequately channel the sentencer's discretion, such proportionality review is not constitutionally required. *Pulley.*

On the other hand, absent a showing that the Georgia capital punishment system operates in an arbitrary and capricious manner, McCleskey cannot prove a constitutional violation by demonstrating that other defendants who may be similarly situated did not receive the death penalty....

Because McCleskey's sentence was imposed under Georgia sentencing procedures that focus discretion "on the particularized nature of the crime and the particularized characteristics of the individual defendant," ... we lawfully may presume that McCleskey's death sentence was not "wantonly and freakishly" imposed, ... and thus that the sentence is not disproportionate within any recognized meaning under the Eighth Amendment.

IV–B

Although our decision in Gregg as to the facial validity of the Georgia capital punishment statute appears to foreclose McCleskey's disproportionality argument, he further contends that the Georgia capital punishment system is arbitrary and capricious in application, and therefore his sentence is excessive, because racial considerations may influence capital sentencing decisions in Georgia. We now address this claim.

To evaluate McCleskey's challenge, we must examine exactly what the Baldus study may show. Even Professor Baldus does not contend that his statistics prove that race enters into any capital sentencing decisions or that race was a factor in McCleskey's particular case. Statistics at most may show only a likelihood that a particular factor entered into some decisions. There is, of course, some risk of racial prejudice influencing a jury's decision in a criminal case. There are similar risks that other kinds of prejudice will influence other criminal trials. The question "is at what point that risk becomes constitutionally unacceptable." *Turner v. Murray.* McCleskey asks us to accept the likelihood allegedly shown by the Baldus study as the constitutional measure of an unacceptable risk of racial prejudice influencing capital sentencing decisions. This we decline to do.

Because of the risk that the factor of race may enter the criminal justice process, we have engaged in "unceasing efforts" to eradicate racial prejudice from our criminal justice system.... Our efforts have been guided by our recognition that "the inestimable privilege of trial by jury ... is a vital principle, underlying the whole administration of criminal justice." ... Thus, it is the jury that is a criminal defendant's fundamental "protection of life and liberty against race or color prejudice." ... Specifically, a capital sentencing jury representative of a criminal defendant's community assures a " 'diffused impartiality,' " ... in the jury's task of "express[ing] the conscience of the community on the ultimate question of life or death." *Witherspoon v. Illinois.*

Individual jurors bring to their deliberations "qualities of human nature and varieties of human experience, the range of which is unknown and perhaps unknowable." ... The capital sentencing decision requires the individual jurors to focus their collective judgment on the unique characteristics of a particular criminal defendant. It is not surprising that such collective judgments often are difficult to explain. But the inherent lack of predictability of jury decisions does not justify their condemnation. On the contrary, it is the jury's function to make the difficult and uniquely human judgments that defy codification and that "buil[d] discretion, equity, and flexibility into a legal system." H. Kalven and H. Zeisel, The American Jury 498 (1966).

McCleskey's argument that the Constitution condemns the discretion allowed decision makers in the Georgia capital sentencing system is antithetical to the fundamental role of discretion in our criminal justice system. Discretion in the criminal justice system offers substantial benefits to the criminal defendant. Not only can a jury decline to impose the death sentence, it can decline to convict or choose to convict of a lesser offense. Whereas decisions against a defendant's interest may be reversed by the trial judge or on appeal, these discretionary exercises of leniency are final and unreviewable. Similarly, the capacity of prosecutorial discretion to provide individualized justice is "firmly entrenched in American law." ... As we have noted, a prosecutor can decline to charge, offer a plea bargain, or decline to seek a death sentence in any particular case. ... Of course, "the power to be lenient [also] is the power to discriminate," ... but a capital punishment system that did not allow for discretionary acts of leniency "would be totally alien to our notions of criminal justice." ...

IV–C

At most, the Baldus study indicates a discrepancy that appears to correlate with race. Apparent disparities in sentencing are an inevitable part of our criminal justice system. The discrepancy indicated by the Baldus study is "a far cry from the major systemic defects identified in *Furman*," *Pulley v. Harris.* As this Court has recognized, any mode for determining guilt or punishment "has its weaknesses and the potential for misuse." ... Specifically, "there can be 'no perfect procedure for deciding in which cases governmental authority should be used to impose death.'" ... Despite these imperfections, our consistent rule has been that constitutional guarantees are met when "the mode [for determining guilt or punishment] itself has been surrounded with safeguards to make it as fair as possible." ... Where the discretion that is fundamental to our criminal process is involved, we decline to assume that what is unexplained is invidious. In light of the safeguards designed to minimize racial bias in the process, the fundamental value of jury trial in our criminal justice system, and the benefits that discretion provides to criminal defendants, we hold that the Baldus study does not demonstrate a constitutionally significant risk of racial bias affecting the Georgia capital sentencing process.[37]

V

Two additional concerns inform our decision in this case. First, McCleskey's claim, taken to its logical conclusion, throws into serious question the principles

---

[37] Justice Brennan's eloquent dissent of course reflects his often repeated opposition to the death sentence. His views, that also are shared by Justice Marshall, are principled and entitled to respect. Nevertheless, since *Gregg* was decided in 1976, seven Members of this Court consistently have upheld sentences of death under *Gregg*-type statutes providing for meticulous review of each sentence in both state and federal courts.

The ultimate thrust of Justice Brennan's dissent is that *Gregg* and its progeny should be overruled. He does not, however, expressly call for the overruling of any prior decision. Rather, relying on the Baldus study, Justice Brennan, joined by Justices Marshall, Blackmun, and Stevens, questions the very heart of our criminal justice system: the traditional discretion that prosecutors and juries necessarily must have. We have held that discretion in a capital punishment system is necessary to satisfy the Constitution. *Woodson v. North Carolina.* . . . Yet, the dissent now claims that the "discretion afforded prosecutors and jurors in the Georgia capital sentencing system" violates the Constitution by creating "opportunities for racial considerations to influence criminal proceedings." . . . The dissent contends that in Georgia "[n]o guidelines govern prosecutorial decisions . . . and [that] Georgia provides juries with no list of aggravating and mitigating factors, nor any standard for balancing them against one another." . . . Prosecutorial decisions necessarily involve both judgmental and factual decisions that vary from case to case. . . . Thus, it is difficult to imagine guidelines that would produce the predictability sought by the dissent without sacrificing the discretion essential to a humane and fair system of criminal justice. Indeed, the dissent suggests no such guidelines for prosecutorial discretion.

The reference to the failure to provide juries with the list of aggravating and mitigating factors is curious. The aggravating circumstances are set forth in detail in the Georgia statute. . . . The jury is not provided with a list of aggravating circumstances because not all of them are relevant to any particular crime. Instead, the prosecutor must choose the relevant circumstances and the State must prove to the jury that at least one exists beyond a reasonable doubt before the jury can even consider imposing the death sentence. It would be improper and often prejudicial to allow jurors to speculate as to aggravating circumstances wholly without support in the evidence. The dissent's argument that a list of mitigating factors is required is particularly anomalous. We have held that the Constitution requires that juries be allowed to consider "any relevant mitigating factor," even if it is not included in a statutory list. *Eddings v. Oklahoma.* See *Lockett v. Ohio.* The dissent does not attempt to harmonize its criticism with this constitutional principle. The dissent also does not suggest any standard, much less a workable one, for balancing aggravating and mitigating factors. If capital defendants are to be treated as "uniquely individual human beings," *Woodson,* then discretion to evaluate and weigh the circumstances relevant to the particular defendant and the crime he committed is essential.

The dissent repeatedly emphasizes the need for "a uniquely high degree of rationality in imposing the death penalty." . . . Again, no suggestion is made as to how greater "rationality" could be achieved under any type of statute that authorizes capital punishment. The *Gregg*-type statute imposes unprecedented safeguards in the special context of capital punishment. These include: (i) a bifurcated sentencing proceeding; (ii) the threshold requirement of one or more aggravating circumstances; and (iii) mandatory State Supreme Court review. All of these are administered pursuant to this Court's decisions interpreting the limits of the Eighth Amendment on the imposition of the death penalty, and all are subject to ultimate review by this Court. These ensure a degree of care in the imposition of the sentence of death that can be described only as unique.

Given these safeguards already inherent in the imposition and review of capital sentences, the dissent's call for greater rationality is no less than a claim that a capital punishment system cannot be administered in accord with the Constitution. As we reiterate, *infra,* the requirement of heightened rationality in the imposition of capital punishment does not "plac[e] totally unrealistic conditions on its use." *Gregg.*

that underlie our entire criminal justice system. The Eighth Amendment is not limited in application to capital punishment, but applies to all penalties. *Solem v. Helm* . . . Thus, if we accepted McCleskey's claim that racial bias has impermissibly tainted the capital sentencing decision, we could soon be faced with similar claims as to other types of penalty. Moreover, the claim that his sentence rests on the irrelevant factor of race easily could be extended to apply to claims based on unexplained discrepancies that correlate to membership in other minority groups, and even to gender. Similarly, since McCleskey's claims relates to the race of his victim, other claims could apply with equally logical force to statistical disparities that correlate with the race or sex of other actors in the criminal justice system, such as defense attorneys or judges. Also, there is no logical reason that such a claim need be limited to racial or sexual bias. If arbitrary and capricious punishment is the touchstone under the Eighth Amendment, such a claim could—at least in theory—be based upon any arbitrary variable, such as the defendant's facial characteristics, or the physical attractiveness of the defendant or the victim, that some statistical study indicates may be influential in jury decision making. As these examples illustrate, there is no limiting principle to the type of challenge brought by McCleskey. The Constitution does not require that a State eliminate any demonstrable disparity that correlates with a potentially irrelevant factor in order to operate a criminal justice system that includes capital punishment. As we have stated specifically in the context of capital punishment, the Constitution does not "plac[e] totally unrealistic conditions on its use." *Gregg.*

Second, McCleskey's arguments are best presented to the legislative bodies. It is not the responsibility—or indeed even the right—of this Court to determine the appropriate punishment for particular crimes. It is the legislatures, the elected representatives of the people, that are "constituted to respond to the will and consequently the moral values of the people." *Furman v. Georgia*, 408 U.S., at 383 (Burger, C.J., dissenting). Legislatures also are better qualified to weight and "evaluate the results of statistical studies in terms of their own local conditions and with a flexibility of approach that is not available to the courts," *Gregg.* Capital punishment is now the law in more than two-thirds of our States. It is the ultimate duty of courts to determine on a case-by-case basis whether these laws are applied consistently with the Constitution. Despite McCleskey's wide-ranging arguments that basically challenge the validity of capital punishment in our multiracial society, the only question before us is whether in his case, the law of Georgia was properly applied. We agree with the District Court and the Court of Appeals for the Eleventh Circuit that this was carefully and correctly done in this case. . . .

DISSENTING OPINION OF JUSTICE BRENNAN, JOINED BY JUSTICES MARSHALL, BLACKMUN, AND STEVENS

II

At some point in this case, Warren McCleskey doubtless asked his lawyer whether a jury was likely to sentence him to die. A candid reply to this question would have been disturbing. First, counsel would have to tell McCleskey that few of the details of the crime or of McCleskey's past criminal conduct were more important than the fact that his victim was white. . . . Furthermore, counsel would feel bound to tell McCleskey that defendants charged with killing white victims in Georgia are 4.3 times as likely to be sentenced to death as defendants charged with killing blacks. . . . In addition, frankness would compel the disclosure that it was more likely than not that the race of McCleskey's victim would determine whether he received a death sentence: 6 of every 11 defendants convicted of killing a white person would not have received the death penalty if their victims had been black, while, among defendants with aggravating and mitigating factors comparable to McCleskey's, 20 of every 34 would not have been sentenced to die if their victims had been black. . . . Finally, the assessment would not be complete without the information that cases involving black defendants and white victims are more likely to result in a death sentence than cases featuring any other racial combination of defendant and victim. . . . The story could be told in a variety of ways, but McCleskey could not fail to grasp its essential narrative line: there was a significant chance that race would play a prominent role in determining if he lived or died.

The Court today holds that Warren McCleskey's sentence was constitutionally imposed. It finds no fault in a system in which lawyers must tell their clients that race casts a large shadow on the capital sentencing process. The Court arrives at this conclusion by stating that the Baldus study cannot "prove that race enters into any capital sentencing decisions or that race was a factor in McCleskey's particular case." . . . Since, according to Professor Baldus, we cannot say "to a moral certainty" that race influenced a decision, we can identify only "a likelihood that a particular factor entered into some decisions," and "a discrepancy that appears to correlate with race." . . . This "likelihood" and "discrepancy," holds the Court, is insufficient to establish a constitutional violation. The Court reaches this conclusion by placing four factors on the scales opposite McCleskey's evidence: The desire to encourage sentencing discretion, the existence of "statutory safeguards" in the Georgia scheme, the fear of encouraging wide-spread challenges to other sentencing decisions, and the limits of the judicial role. The Court's evaluation of the significance of petitioner's evidence is fundamentally at odds with our consistent concern for rationality in capital sentencing, and the considerations that the majority invokes to discount that evidence cannot justify ignoring its force.

III–A

It is important to emphasize at the outset that the Court's observation that McCleskey cannot prove the influence of race on any particular sentencing decision is irrelevant in evaluating his Eighth Amendment claim. Since *Furman v. Georgia*, the Court has been concerned with the risk of the imposition of an arbitrary sentence, rather than the proven fact of one. *Furman* held that the death penalty "may not be imposed under sentencing procedures that create a substantial risk that the punishment will be inflicted in an arbitrary and capricious manner." . . . This emphasis on risk acknowledges the difficulty of divining the jury's motivation in an individual case. In addition, it reflects the fact that concern for arbitrariness focuses on the rationality of the system as a whole, and that a system that features a significant probability that sentencing decisions are influenced by impermissible considerations cannot be regarded as rational. As we said in *Gregg v. Georgia*, "the petitioner looks to the sentencing system as a whole (as the Court did in *Furman* and we do today)": a constitutional violation is established if a plaintiff demonstrates a "pattern of arbitrary and capricious sentencing." *Id.* . . .

The Court assumes the statistical validity of the Baldus study, and acknowledges that McCleskey has demonstrated a risk that racial prejudice plays a role in capital sentencing in Georgia. . . . Nonetheless, it finds the probability of prejudice insufficient to create constitutional concern. Close analysis of the Baldus study, however, in light of both statistical principles and human experience, reveals that the risk that race influenced McCleskey's sentence is intolerable by any imaginable standard.

III–B

The Baldus study indicates that, after taking into account some 230 nonracial factors that might legitimately influence a sentencer, the jury more likely than not would have spared McCleskey's life had his victim been black. The study distinguishes between those cases in which (1) the jury exercises virtually no discretion because the strength or weakness of aggravating factors usually suggests that only one outcome is appropriate; and (2) cases reflecting an "intermediate" level of aggravation, in which the jury has considerable discretion in choosing a sentence. McCleskey's case falls into the intermediate range. In such cases, death is imposed in 34 percent of white-victim crimes and 14 percent of black-victim crimes, a difference of 139 percent in the rate of imposition of the death penalty. . . . In other words, just under 59 percent—almost 6 in 10—defendants comparable to McCleskey would not have received the death penalty if their victims had been black.

Furthermore, even examination of the sentencing system as a whole, factoring in those cases in which the jury exercises little discretion, indicates the influence of race on capital sentencing. For the Georgia system as a whole, race accounts for a 6 percentage point difference in the rate at which capital punishment is imposed. Since death is imposed in 11 percent of all white-victim cases, the rate in comparably aggravated black-victim cases is 5 percent. The rate of capital sentencing in a white-victim case is thus 120 percent greater than the rate in a black-victim case. Put another way, over half—55 percent—of defendants in white-victim crimes in Georgia would not have been sentenced to die if their victims had been black. Of the more than 200 variables potentially relevant to a sentencing decision, race of the victim is a powerful explanation for variation in death sentence rates—as powerful as nonracial aggravating factors such as a prior murder conviction or acting as the principal planner of the homicide. These adjusted figures are only the most conservative indication of the risk that race will influence the death sentences of defendants in Georgia. Data unadjusted for the mitigating or aggravating effect of other factors show an even more pronounced disparity by race. The capital sentencing rate for all white-victim cases was almost 11 times greater than the rate for black-victim cases.... Furthermore, blacks who kill whites are sentenced to death at nearly 22 times the rate of blacks who kill blacks, and more than 7 times the rate of whites who kill blacks.... In addition, prosecutors seek the death penalty for 70 percent of black defendants with white victims, but for only 15 percent of black defendants with black victims, and only 19 percent of white defendants with black victims.... Since our decision upholding the Georgia capital sentencing system in *Gregg*, the State has executed seven persons. All of the seven were convicted of killing whites, and six of the seven executed were black. Such execution figures are especially striking in light of the fact that, during the period encompassed by the Baldus study, only 9.2 percent of Georgia homicides involved black defendants and white victims, while 60.7 percent involved black victims.

McCleskey's statistics have particular force because most of them are the product of sophisticated multiple-regression analysis. Such analysis is designed precisely to identify patterns in the aggregate, even though we may not be able to reconstitute with certainty any individual decision that goes to make up that pattern. Multiple-regression analysis is particularly well suited to identify the influence of impermissible considerations in sentencing, since it is able to control for permissible factors that may explain an apparent arbitrary pattern. While the decision-making process of a body such as a jury may be complex, the Baldus study provides a massive compilation of the details that are most relevant to that decision. As we held in the context of Title VII of the Civil Rights Act of 1964 last term in *Bazemore v. Friday*, 478 U.S. 385 (1986), a multiple-regression analysis need not include every conceivable variable to establish a party's case, as long as it includes those variables that account for the major factors that are likely to influence decisions. In this case, Professor Baldus in fact conducted additional regression analyses in response to criticisms and suggestions by the District Court, all of which confirmed, and some of which even strengthened, the study's original conclusions.

The statistical evidence in this case thus relentlessly documents the risk that McCleskey's sentence was influenced by racial considerations. This evidence shows that there is a better than even chance in Georgia that race will influence the decision to impose the death penalty: a majority of defendants in white-victim crimes would not have been sentenced to die if their victims had been black. In determining whether this risk is acceptable, our judgment must be shaped by the awareness that "[t]he risk of racial prejudice infecting a capital sentencing proceeding is especially serious in light of the complete finality of the death sentence," *Turner v. Murray*, and that "[i]t is of vital importance to the defendant and to the community that any decision to impose the death sentence be, and appear to be, based on reason rather than caprice or emotion." *Gardner v. Florida*, 430 U.S. 349 (1977). In determining the guilt of a defendant, a State must prove its case beyond a reasonable doubt. That is, we refuse to convict if the chance of error is simply less likely than not. Surely, we should not be willing to take a person's life if the chance that his death sentence was irrationally imposed is more likely than not. In light of the gravity of the interest at stake, petitioner's statistics on their face are a powerful demonstration of the type of risk that our Eighth Amendment jurisprudence has consistently condemned.

III–C

Evaluation of McCleskey's evidence cannot rest solely on the numbers themselves. We must also ask whether the conclusion suggested by those numbers is consonant with our understanding of history and human experience. Georgia's legacy of a race-conscious criminal justice system, as well as this Court's own recognition of the persistent danger that racial attitudes may affect criminal proceedings, indicates that McCleskey's claim is not a fanciful product of mere statistical artifice.

For many years, Georgia operated openly and formally precisely the type of dual system the evidence shows is still effectively in place. The criminal law expressly differentiated between crimes committed by and against blacks and whites, distinctions whose lineage traced back to the time of slavery. During the colonial period, black slaves who killed whites in Georgia, regardless of whether in self-defense or in defense of another, were automatically executed.

. . . The discretion afforded prosecutors and jurors in the Georgia capital sentencing system creates . . . opportunities [for racial considerations]. No guidelines govern prosecutorial decisions to seek the death penalty, and Georgia provides juries with no list of aggravating and mitigating factors, nor any standard for balancing them against one another. Once a jury identifies one aggravating factor, it has complete discretion in choosing life or death, and need not articulate its basis for selecting life imprisonment. The Georgia sentencing system therefore provides considerable opportunity for racial considerations, however subtle and unconscious, to influence charging and sentencing decisions.

History and its continuing legacy thus buttress the probative force of McCleskey's statistics. Formal dual criminal laws may no longer be in effect, and intentional discrimination may no longer be prominent. Nonetheless, as we acknowledged in *Turner*, "subtle, less consciously held racial attitudes" continue to be of concern, and the Georgia system gives such attitudes considerable room to operate. The conclusions drawn from McCleskey's statistical evidence are therefore consistent with the lessons of social experience.

The majority thus misreads our Eighth Amendment jurisprudence in concluding that McCleskey has not demonstrated a degree of risk sufficient to raise constitutional concern. The determination of the significance of his evidence is at its core an exercise in human moral judgment, not a mechanical statistical analysis. It must first and foremost be informed by awareness of the fact that death is irrevocable, and that as a result "the qualitative difference of death from all other punishments requires a greater degree of scrutiny of the capital sentencing determination." . . . For this reason, we have demanded a uniquely high degree of rationality in imposing the death penalty. A capital sentencing system in which race more likely than not plays a role does not meet this standard. It is true that every nuance of decision cannot be statistically captured, nor can any individual judgment be plumbed with absolute certainty. Yet the fact that we must always act without the illumination of complete knowledge cannot induce paralysis when we confront what is literally an issue of life and death. Sentencing data, history, and experience all counsel that Georgia has provided insufficient assurance of the heightened rationality we have required in order to take a human life.

IV

The Court cites four reasons for shrinking from the implications of McCleskey's evidence: the desirability of discretion for actors in the criminal justice system, the existence of statutory safeguards against abuse of that discretion, the potential consequences for broader challenges to criminal sentencing, and an understanding of the contours of the judicial role. While these concerns underscore the need for sober deliberation, they do not justify rejecting evidence as convincing as McCleskey has presented.

The Court maintains that petitioner's claim "is antithetical to the fundamental role of discretion in our criminal justice system." It states that "[w]here the discretion that is fundamental to our criminal process is involved, we decline to assume that what is unexplained is invidious." . . . Reliance on race in imposing capital punishment, however, is antithetical to the very rationale for granting sentencing discretion. Discretion is a means, not an end. It is bestowed in order to permit the sentencer to "trea[t] each defendant in a capital case with that degree of respect due the uniqueness of the individual." *Lockett*. The decision to impose the punishment of death must be based on a "particularized consideration of relevant aspects of the character and record of each convicted defendant." *Woodson*. Failure to conduct such an individualized moral inquiry "treats all persons convicted of a designated offense not as unique individual human beings, but as members of a faceless, undifferentiated mass to be subjected to the blind infliction of the penalty of death." *Id.*

Considering the race of a defendant or victim in deciding if the death penalty should be imposed is completely at odds with this concern that an individual be evaluated as a unique human being. Decisions influenced by race rest in part on a categorical assessment of the worth of human beings according to color, insensitive to whatever qualities the individuals in question may possess.

Enhanced willingness to impose the death sentence on black defendants, or diminished willingness to render such a sentence when blacks are victims, reflects a devaluation of the lives of black persons. When confronted with evidence that race more likely than not plays such a role in a capital sentencing system, it is plainly insufficient to say that the importance of discretion demands that the risk be higher before we will act—for in such a case the very end that discretion is designed to serve is being undermined.

Our desire for individualized moral judgments may lead us to accept some inconsistencies in sentencing outcomes. Since such decisions are not reducible to mathematical formulae, we are willing to assume that a certain degree of variation reflects the fact that no two defendants are completely alike. There is thus a presumption that actors in the criminal justice system exercise their discretion in responsible fashion, and we do not automatically infer that sentencing patterns that do not comport with ideal rationality are suspect.

As we made clear in *Batson v. Kentucky*, 476 U.S. 79 (1986), however, that presumption is rebuttable. *Batson* dealt with another arena in which considerable discretion traditionally has been afforded, the exercise of peremptory challenges. Those challenges are normally exercised without any indication whatsoever of the grounds for doing so. The rationale for this deference has been a belief that the unique characteristics of particular prospective jurors may raise concern on the part of the prosecution or defense, despite the fact that counsel may not be able to articulate that concern in a manner sufficient to support exclusion for cause. As with sentencing, therefore, peremptory challenges are justified as an occasion for particularized determinations related to specific individuals, and, as with sentencing, we presume that such challenges normally are not made on the basis of a factor such as race. As we said in *Batson*, however, such features do not justify imposing a "crippling burden of proof," *id.*, in order to rebut that presumption. The Court in this case apparently seeks to do just that. On the basis of the need for individualized decisions, it rejects evidence, drawn from the most sophisticated capital sentencing analysis ever performed, that reveals that race more likely than not infects capital sentencing decisions. The Court's position converts a rebuttable presumption into a virtually conclusive one.

The Court also declines to find McCleskey's evidence sufficient in view of "the safeguards designed to minimize racial bias in the [capital sentencing] process." . . . It is clear that *Gregg* bestowed no permanent approval on the Georgia system. It simply held that the State's statutory safeguards were assumed sufficient to channel discretion without evidence otherwise.

It has now been over 13 years since Georgia adopted the provisions upheld in *Gregg*. Professor Baldus and his colleagues have compiled data on almost 2,500 homicides committed during the period 1973–1979. They have taken into account the influence of 230 nonracial variables, using a multitude of data from the State itself, and have produced striking evidence that the odds of being sentenced to death are significantly greater than average if a defendant is black or his or her victim is white. The challenge to the Georgia system is not speculative or theoretical; it is empirical. As a result, the Court cannot rely on the statutory safeguards in discounting McCleskey's evidence, for it is the very effectiveness of those safeguards that such evidence calls into question. While we may hope that a model of procedural fairness will curb the influence of race on sentencing, "we cannot simply assume that the model works as intended; we must critique its performance in terms of its results." . . .

The Court next states that its unwillingness to regard petitioner's evidence as sufficient is based in part on the fear that recognition of McCleskey's claim would open the door to widespread challenges to all aspects of criminal sentencing. . . . Taken on its face, such a statement seems to suggest a fear of too much justice. Yet surely the majority would acknowledge that if striking evidence indicated that other minority groups, or women, or even persons with blond hair, were disproportionately sentenced to death, such a state of affairs would be repugnant to deeply rooted conceptions of fairness. The prospect that there may be more widespread abuse than McCleskey documents may be dismaying, but it does not justify complete abdication of our judicial role. The Constitution was framed fundamentally as a bulwark against governmental power, and preventing the arbitrary administration of punishment is a basic ideal of any society that purports to be governed by the rule of law.

In fairness, the Court's fear that McCleskey's claim is an invitation to descend a slippery slope also rests on the realization that any humanly imposed system of penalties will exhibit some imperfection. Yet to reject McCleskey's powerful evidence on this basis is to ignore both the qualitatively different character of the death penalty and the particular repugnance of racial discrimination, considerations which may properly be taken into account in determining whether various punishments are "cruel and unusual." Furthermore, it fails to take account of the unprecedented refinement and strength of the Baldus study.

It hardly needs reiteration that this Court has consistently acknowledged the uniqueness of the punishment of death. "Death, in its finality, differs more from life imprisonment than a 100-year prison term differs from one of only a year or two. Because of that qualitative difference, there is a corresponding difference in the need for reliability in the determination that death is the appropriate punishment." *Woodson.* Furthermore, the relative interests of the state and the defendant differ dramatically in the death penalty context. The marginal benefits accruing to the state from obtaining the death penalty rather than life imprisonment are considerably less than the marginal difference to the defendant between death and life in prison. Such a disparity is an additional reason for tolerating scant arbitrariness in capital sentencing. Even those who believe that society can impose the death penalty in a manner sufficiently rational to justify its continuation must acknowledge that the level of rationality that is considered satisfactory must be uniquely high. As a result, the degree of arbitrariness that may be adequate to render the death penalty "cruel and unusual" punishment may not be adequate to invalidate lesser penalties. What these relative degrees of arbitrariness might be in other cases need not concern us here; the point is that the majority's fear of wholesale invalidation of criminal sentences is unfounded.

The Court also maintains that accepting McCleskey's claim would pose a threat to all sentencing because of the prospect that a correlation might be demonstrated between sentencing outcomes and other personal characteristics.

Again, such a view is indifferent to the considerations that enter into a determination whether punishment is "cruel and unusual." Race is a consideration whose influence is expressly constitutionally proscribed. We have expressed a moral commitment, as embodied in our fundamental law, that this specific characteristic should not be the basis for allotting burdens and benefits. Three constitutional amendments, and numerous statutes, have been prompted specifically by the desire to address the effects of racism. "Over the years, this Court has consistently repudiated '[d]istinctions between citizens solely because of their ancestry' as being 'odious to a free people whose institutions are founded upon the doctrine of equality.'" . . . Furthermore, we have explicitly acknowledged the illegitimacy of race as a consideration in capital sentencing. *Zant v. Stephens*, 462 U.S. 862, 885 (1983). That a decision to impose the death penalty could be influenced by race is thus a particularly repugnant prospect, and evidence that race may play even a modest role in levying a death sentence should be enough to characterize that sentence as "cruel and unusual."

Certainly, a factor that we would regard as morally irrelevant, such as hair color, at least theoretically could be associated with sentencing results to such an extent that we would regard as arbitrary a system in which that factor played a significant role. As I have said above, however, the evaluation of evidence suggesting such a correlation must be informed not merely by statistics, but by history and experience. One could hardly contend that this Nation has on the basis of hair color inflicted upon persons deprivation comparable to that imposed on the basis of race. Recognition of this fact would necessarily influence the evaluation of data suggesting the influence of hair color on sentencing, and would require evidence of statistical correlation even more powerful than that presented by the Baldus study.

Furthermore, the Court's fear of the expansive ramifications of a holding for McCleskey in this case is unfounded because it fails to recognize the uniquely sophisticated nature of the Baldus study. McCleskey presents evidence that is far and away the most refined data ever assembled on any system of punishment, data not readily replicated through casual effort. Moreover, that evidence depicts not merely arguable tendencies, but striking correlations, all the more powerful because nonracial explanations have been eliminated. Acceptance of petitioner's evidence would therefore establish a remarkably stringent standard of statistical evidence unlikely to be satisfied with any frequency.

The Court's projection of apocalyptic consequences for criminal sentencing is thus greatly exaggerated. The Court can indulge in such speculation only by ignoring its own jurisprudence demanding the highest scrutiny on issues of death and race. As a result, it fails to do justice to a claim in which both those elements are intertwined—an occasion calling for the most sensitive inquiry a court can conduct. Despite its acceptance of the validity of Warren McCleskey's evidence, the Court is willing to let his death sentence stand because it fears that we cannot successfully define a different standard for lesser punishments. This fear is baseless.

Finally, the Court justifies its rejection of McCleskey's claim by cautioning against usurpation of the legislatures' role in devising and monitoring criminal punishment. The Court is, of course, correct to emphasize the gravity of constitutional intervention and the importance that it be sparingly employed. The fact that "[c]apital punishment is now the law in more than two thirds of our States," *ante*, however, does not diminish the fact that capital punishment is the most awesome act that a State can perform. The judiciary's role in this society counts for little if the use of governmental power to extinguish life does not elicit close scrutiny. . . .

Those whom we would banish from society or from the human community itself often speak in too faint a voice to be heard above society's demand for punishment. It is the particular role of courts to hear these voices, for the Constitution declares that the majoritarian chorus may not alone dictate the conditions of social life. The Court thus fulfills, rather than disrupts, the scheme of separation of powers by closely scrutinizing the imposition of the death penalty, for no decision of a society is more deserving of "sober second thought." . . .

V

. . . Warren McCleskey's evidence confronts us with the subtle and persistent influence of the past. His message is a disturbing one to a society that has formally repudiated racism, and a frustrating one to a Nation accustomed to regarding its destiny as the product of its own will. Nonetheless, we ignore him at our peril, for we remain imprisoned by the past as long as we deny its influence in the present.

It is tempting to pretend that minorities on death row share a fate in no way connected to our own, that our treatment of them sounds no echoes beyond the chambers in which they die. Such an illusion is ultimately corrosive, for the reverberations of injustice are not so easily confined. "The destinies of the two races in this country are indissolubly linked together," . . . and the way in which we choose those who will die reveals the depth of moral commitment among the living.

The Court's decision today will not change what attorneys in Georgia tell other Warren McCleskeys about their chances of execution. Nothing will soften the harsh message they must convey, nor alter the prospect that race undoubtedly will continue to be a topic of discussion. McCleskey's evidence will not have obtained judicial acceptance, but that will not affect what is said on death row. However many criticisms of today's decision may be rendered, these painful conversations will serve as the most eloquent dissents of all.

[The dissenting opinions of Justice Blackmun and Justice Stevens are omitted.]

Chapter 26

"Innocence" and Federal Habeas Corpus— *Herrera v. Collins* (1993)

Herrera v. Collins, 506 U.S. 390, 113 S. Ct. 853, 122 L. Ed.2d 203 (1993) (6-3, death row defendant's claim of innocence was insufficiently supported by evidence to serve as the constitutional basis for the issuance of a federal writ of habeas corpus).

Editor's comment: The federal writ of habeas corpus is usually the last stage in the postconviction process in death penalty cases. (See Chapter 1.) If the writ is denied, only the Governor's clemency power (or, in a federal prosecution, the President's) can prevent the execution. The writ may issue only for violations of the Constitution (or federal laws or treaties, rarely at issue in state prosecutions). The *Herrera* case raises the question whether a defendant who asserts that he is innocent (commonly supported by evidence discovered after the trial) is making the necessary *constitutional* claim for federal habeas purposes. Would it, for example, be cruel and unusual punishment in violation of the Eighth Amendment to execute (or perhaps even imprison) an innocent person?

The Court's answer seems to be a highly qualified "yes." If no state remedy, such as gubernatorial clemency, is available to the inmate, and if he can cross an "extraordinarily high" threshold (*i.e.*, make a very persuasive initial showing of support for the claim), then the *Herrera* majority assumed (without deciding) that a constitutional foundation for the writ would be established.

Such claims are highly uncommon. It is not unusual, however, to have innocence claims in habeas petitions accompanied by other, more commonplace, constitutional arguments. The Supreme Court actually encouraged this practice. In the 1980's, the Court tried to prevent inmates from filing successive habeas petitions (as a way of delaying execution) by tightening the rules for federal court review. However, the Court established an exception to these restrictions. It allowed repeated habeas petitions if review was necessary to avoid a miscarriage of justice, *i.e.,* if the petitioner claimed actual innocence. Thus, a claim of innocence became a means of avoiding the limitations on repeated habeas filings. This is what the *Herrera* Court meant when it said that a claim of actual innocence could serve as "a gateway through which a habeas petitioner must pass to have his otherwise barred constitutional claim considered on the merits." In short, freestanding claims of innocence are highly disfavored as the basis for federal habeas, but coupling innocence with other constitutional claims may enable an inmate to file repeated applications as a delaying tactic.

Three years after *Herrera,* Congress tried to close the door to multiple habeas petitions with the Antiterrorism and Effective Death Penalty Act of 1996 (AEDPA). AEDPA's barrier to successive claims is higher than the Supreme Court's, but whether or not it will survive court challenges is uncertain.

❖ ❖ ❖

OPINION OF CHIEF JUSTICE REHNQUIST FOR THE COURT

Petitioner Leonel Torres Herrera was convicted of capital murder and sentenced to death in January 1982. He unsuccessfully challenged the conviction on direct appeal and state collateral proceedings in the Texas state courts, and in a federal habeas petition. In February 1992—10 years after his conviction—he urged in a second federal habeas petition that he was "actually innocent" of the murder for which he was sentenced to death, and that the Eighth Amendment's prohibition against cruel and unusual punishment and the Fourteenth Amendment's guarantee of due process of law therefore forbid his execution. He supported this claim with affidavits tending to show that his now-dead brother, rather than he, had been the perpetrator of the crime. Petitioner urges us to hold that this showing of innocence entitles him to relief in this federal habeas proceeding. We hold that it does not.

Shortly before 11 P.M. on an evening in late September 1981, the body of Texas Department of Public Safety Officer David Rucker was found by a passerby on a stretch of highway about six miles east of Los Fresnos, Texas, a few miles north of Brownsville in the Rio Grande Valley. Rucker's body was lying beside his patrol car. He had been shot in the head.

At about the same time, Los Fresnos Police Officer Enrique Carrisalez observed a speeding vehicle traveling west towards Los Fresnos, away from the place where Rucker's body had been found, along the same road. Carrisalez, who was accompanied in his patrol car by Enrique Hernandez, turned on his flashing red lights and pursued the speeding vehicle. After the car had stopped briefly at a red light, it signaled that it would pull over and did so. The patrol car pulled up behind it. Carrisalez took a flashlight and walked toward the car of the speeder. The driver opened his door and exchanged a few words with Carrisalez before firing at least one shot at Carrisalez' chest. The officer died nine days later.

Petitioner Herrera was arrested a few days after the shootings and charged with the capital murder of both Carrisalez and Rucker. He was tried and found guilty of the capital murder of Carrisalez in January 1982, and sentenced to death. In July 1982, petitioner pleaded guilty to the murder of Rucker.

At petitioner's trial for the murder of Carrisalez, Hernandez, who had witnessed Carrisalez' slaying from the officer's patrol car, identified petitioner as the person who had wielded the gun. A declaration by Officer Carrisalez to the same effect, made while he was in the hospital, was also admitted. Through a license plate check, it was shown that the speeding car involved in Carrisalez' murder was registered to petitioner's "live-in" girlfriend. Petitioner was known to drive this car, and he had a set of keys to the car in his pants pocket when he was arrested. Hernandez identified the car as the vehicle from which the murderer had emerged to fire the fatal shot. He also testified that there had been only one person in the car that night.

The evidence showed that Herrera's Social Security card had been found alongside Rucker's patrol car on the night he was killed. Splatters of blood on the car identified as the vehicle involved in the shootings, and on petitioner's blue jeans and wallet, were identified as type A blood—the same type which Rucker had. (Herrera has type O blood.) Similar evidence with respect to strands of hair found in the car indicated that the hair was Rucker's and not Herrera's. A handwritten letter was also found on the person of petitioner when he was arrested, which strongly implied that he had killed Rucker.[1]

---

[1] The letter read:

"To whom it may concern: I am terribly sorry for those I have brought grief to their lives. Who knows why? We cannot change the future's problems with problems from the past. What I did was for a cause and purpose. One law runs others, and in the world we live in, that's the way it is.

"I'm not a tormented person. . . . I believe in the law. What would it be without this [sic] men that risk their lives for others, and that's what they should be doing—protecting life, property, and the pursuit of happiness. Sometimes, the law gets too involved with other things that profit them. The most laws that they make for people to break them, in other words, to encourage crime.

"What happened to Rucker was for a certain reason. I knew him as Mike Tatum. He was in my business, and he violated some of its laws and suffered the penalty, like the one you have for me when the time comes.

"My personal life, which has been a conspiracy since my high school days, has nothing to do with what has happened. The other officer that became part of our lives, me and Rucker's (Tatum), that night had not to do in this [sic]. He was out to do what he had to do, protect, but that's life. There's a lot of us that wear different faces in lives every day, and that is what causes problems for all [unintelligible word].

"You have wrote all you want of my life, but think about yours, also.

[Signed Leonel Herrera].

"I have tapes and pictures to prove what I have said. I will prove my side if you accept to listen. You [unintelligible word] freedom of speech, even a criminal has that right. I will present myself if this is read word for word over the media, I will turn myself in; if not, don't have millions of men out there working just on me while others—robbers, rapists, or burglars—are taking advantage of the law's time. Excuse my spelling and writing. It's hard at times like this."

Petitioner appealed his conviction and sentence, arguing, among other things, that Hernandez' and Carrisalez' identifications were unreliable and improperly admitted. The Texas Court of Criminal Appeals affirmed and we denied certiorari. Petitioner's application for state habeas relief was denied. Petitioner then filed a federal habeas petition, again challenging the identifications offered against him at trial. This petition was denied and we again denied certiorari.

Petitioner next returned to state court and filed a second habeas petition, raising, among other things, a claim of "actual innocence" based on newly discovered evidence. In support of this claim petitioner presented the affidavits of Hector Villarreal, an attorney who had represented petitioner's brother, Raul Herrera Senior, and of Juan Franco Palacious, one of Raul Senior's former cellmates. Both individuals claimed that Raul Senior, who died in 1984, had told them that he—and not petitioner—had killed Officers Rucker and Carrisalez. The State District Court denied this application, finding that "no evidence at trial remotely suggest[ed] that anyone other than [petitioner] committed the offense." The Texas Court of Criminal Appeals affirmed and we denied certiorari.

In February 1992, petitioner lodged the instant habeas petition—his second—in federal court, alleging, among other things, that he is innocent of the murders of Rucker and Carrisalez, and that his execution would thus violate the Eighth and Fourteenth Amendments. In addition to proffering the above affidavits, petitioner presented the affidavits of Raul Herrera Junior, Raul Senior's son, and Jose Ybarra Junior, a schoolmate of the Herrera brothers. Raul Junior averred that he had witnessed his father shoot Officers Rucker and Carrisalez and petitioner was not present. Raul Junior was nine years old at the time of the killings. Ybarra alleged that Raul Senior told him one summer night in 1983 that he had shot the two police officers.

The District Court dismissed most of petitioner's claims as an abuse of the writ. However, "in order to ensure that Petitioner can assert his constitutional claims and out of a sense of fairness and due process," the District Court granted petitioner's request for a stay of execution so that he could present his claim of actual innocence, along with the Raul Junior and Ybarra affidavits, in state court.

The Court of Appeals vacated the stay of execution. Absent an accompanying constitutional violation, the Court of Appeals held that petitioner's claim of actual innocence was not cognizable because, under *Townsend v. Sain*, 372 U.S. 293 (1963), "the existence merely of newly discovered evidence relevant to the guilt of a state prisoner is not a ground for relief on federal habeas corpus." We granted certiorari and the Texas Court of Criminal Appeals stayed petitioner's execution. We now affirm.

Petitioner asserts that the Eighth and Fourteenth Amendments to the United States Constitution prohibit the execution of a person who is innocent of the crime for which he was convicted. This proposition has an elemental appeal, as would the similar proposition that the Constitution prohibits the imprisonment of one who is innocent of the crime for which he was convicted. After all, the central purpose of any system of criminal justice is to convict the guilty and free the innocent. But the evidence upon which petitioner's claim of innocence rests was not produced at his trial, but rather eight years later. In any system of criminal justice, "innocence" or "guilt" must be determined in some sort of a judicial proceeding. Petitioner's showing of innocence, and indeed his constitutional claim for relief based upon that showing, must be evaluated in the light of the previous proceedings in this case, which have stretched over a span of 10 years.

A person when first charged with a crime is entitled to a presumption of innocence, and may insist that his guilt be established beyond a reasonable doubt. *In re Winship*, 397 U.S. 358 (1970). Other constitutional provisions also have the effect of ensuring against the risk of convicting an innocent person. . . . In capital cases, we have required additional protections because of the nature of the penalty at stake. See, *e.g.*, *Beck v. Alabama*, 447 U.S. 625 (1980) (jury must be given option of convicting the defendant of a lesser offense). All of these constitutional safeguards, of course, make it more difficult for the State to rebut and finally overturn the presumption of innocence which attaches to every criminal defendant. But we have also observed that "[d]ue process does not require that every conceivable step be taken, at whatever cost, to eliminate the possibility of convicting an innocent person." *Patterson v. New York*, 432 U.S. 197 (1977). To conclude otherwise would all but paralyze our system for enforcement of the criminal law.

Once a defendant has been afforded a fair trial and convicted of the offense for which he was charged, the presumption of innocence disappears. Cf. *Ross v. Moffitt*, 417 U.S. 600 (1974) ("The purpose of the trial stage from the State's point of view is to convert a criminal defendant from a person presumed innocent to one found guilty beyond a reasonable doubt"). Here, it is not disputed that the State met its burden of proving at trial that petitioner was guilty of the capital murder of Officer Carrisalez beyond a reasonable doubt. Thus, in the eyes of the law, petitioner does not come before the Court as one who is "innocent," but, on the contrary, as one who has been convicted by due process of law of two brutal murders.

Based on affidavits here filed, petitioner claims that evidence never presented to the trial court proves him innocent notwithstanding the verdict reached at his trial. Such a claim is not cognizable in the state courts of Texas. For to obtain a new trial based on newly discovered evidence, a defendant must file a motion within 30 days after imposition or suspension of sentence. The Texas courts have construed this 30-day time limit as jurisdictional.

Claims of actual innocence based on newly discovered evidence have never been held to state a ground for federal habeas relief absent an independent constitutional violation occurring in the underlying state criminal proceeding. Chief Justice Warren made this clear in *Townsend v. Sain*, 372 U.S., at 317:

> "Where newly discovered evidence is alleged in a habeas application, evidence which could not reasonably have been presented to the state trier of facts, the federal court must grant an evidentiary hearing. Of course, such evidence must bear upon the constitutionality of the applicant's detention; the existence merely of newly discovered evidence relevant to the guilt of a state prisoner is not a ground for relief on federal habeas corpus."

This rule is grounded in the principle that federal habeas courts sit to ensure that individuals are not imprisoned in violation of the Constitution—not to correct errors of fact. . . . Few rulings would be more disruptive of our federal system than to provide for federal habeas review of freestanding claims of actual innocence.

Our decision in *Jackson v. Virginia*, 443 U.S. 307 (1979), comes as close to authorizing evidentiary review of a state-court conviction on federal habeas as any of our cases. There, we held that a federal habeas court may review a claim that the evidence adduced at a state trial was not sufficient to convict a criminal defendant beyond a reasonable doubt. But in so holding, we emphasized:

> "[T]his inquiry does not require a court to 'ask itself whether it believes that the evidence at the trial established guilt beyond a reasonable doubt.' Instead, the relevant question is whether, after viewing the evidence in the light most favorable to the prosecution, any rational trier of fact could have found the essential elements of the crime beyond a reasonable doubt. This familiar standard gives full play to the responsibility of the trier of fact fairly to resolve conflicts in the testimony, to weigh the evidence, and to draw reasonable inferences from basic facts to ultimate facts." *Id.*, at 318–319.

We specifically noted that "the standard announced . . . does not permit a court to make its own subjective determination of guilt or innocence." *Id.*, at 320, n. 13.

The type of federal habeas review sought by petitioner here is different in critical respects than that authorized by *Jackson*. First, the *Jackson* inquiry is aimed at determining whether there has been an independent constitutional violation—*i.e.*, a conviction based on evidence that fails to meet the *Winship* standard [of proof beyond a reasonable doubt]. Thus, federal habeas courts act in their historic capacity—to assure that the habeas petitioner is not being held in violation of his or her federal constitutional rights. Second, the sufficiency of the evidence review authorized by *Jackson* is limited to "record evidence." *Jackson* does not extend to nonrecord evidence, including newly discovered evidence. Finally, the *Jackson* inquiry does not focus on whether the trier of fact made the correct guilt or innocence determination, but rather whether it made a rational decision to convict or acquit.

Petitioner is understandably imprecise in describing the sort of federal relief to which a suitable showing of actual innocence would entitle him. In his brief he states that the federal habeas court should have "an important initial opportunity to hear the evidence and resolve the merits of Petitioner's claim." Acceptance of this view would presumably require the habeas court to hear testimony from the witnesses who testified at trial as well as those who made the statements in the affidavits which petitioner has presented, and to determine anew whether or not petitioner is guilty of the murder of Officer Carrisalez. Indeed, the dissent's approach differs little from that hypothesized here.

The dissent would place the burden on petitioner to show that he is "probably" innocent. Although petitioner would not be entitled to discovery "as a matter of right," the District Court would retain its "discretion to order discovery . . . when it would help the court make a reliable determination with respect to the prisoner's claim." And although the District Court would not be required to hear testimony from the witnesses who testified at trial or the affiants upon whom petitioner relies, the dissent would allow the District Court to do so "if the petition warrants a hearing." At the end of the day, the dissent would have the District Court "make a case-by-case determination about the reliability of the newly discovered evidence under the circumstances," and then "weigh the evidence in favor of the prisoner against the evidence of his guilt."

The dissent fails to articulate the relief that would be available if petitioner were to meet its "probable innocence" standard. Would it be commutation of petitioner's death sentence, new trial, or unconditional release from imprisonment? The typical relief granted in federal habeas corpus is a conditional order of release unless the State elects to retry the successful habeas petitioner, or in a capital case a similar conditional order vacating the death sentence. Were petitioner to satisfy the dissent's "probable innocence" standard, therefore, the District Court would presumably be required to grant a conditional order of relief, which would in effect require the State to retry petitioner 10 years after his first trial, not because of any constitutional violation which had occurred at the first trial, but simply because of a belief that in light of petitioner's new-found evidence a jury might find him not guilty at a second trial.

Yet there is no guarantee that the guilt or innocence determination would be any more exact. To the contrary, the passage of time only diminishes the reliability of criminal adjudications. . . . Under the dissent's approach, the District Court would be placed in the even more difficult position of having to weigh the probative value of "hot" and "cold" evidence on petitioner's guilt or innocence.

This is not to say that our habeas jurisprudence casts a blind eye toward innocence. In a series of cases culminating with *Sawyer v. Whitley*, 505 U.S. 333 (1992), decided last Term, we have held that a petitioner otherwise subject to defenses of abusive or successive use of the writ may have his federal constitutional claim considered on the merits if he makes a proper showing of actual innocence. This rule, or fundamental miscarriage of justice exception, is grounded in the "equitable discretion" of habeas courts to see that federal constitutional errors do not result in the incarceration of innocent persons. But this body of our habeas jurisprudence makes clear that a claim of "actual innocence" is not itself a constitutional claim, but instead a gateway through which a habeas petitioner must pass to have his otherwise barred constitutional claim considered on the merits.

Petitioner in this case is simply not entitled to habeas relief based on the reasoning of this line of cases. For he does not seek excusal of a procedural error so that he may bring an independent constitutional claim challenging his conviction or sentence, but rather argues that he is entitled to habeas relief because newly discovered evidence shows that his conviction is factually incorrect. The fundamental miscarriage of justice exception is available "only where the prisoner supplements his constitutional claim with a colorable showing of factual innocence." *Kuhlmann* [*v. Wilson*, 477 U.S. 436,] at 454 [(1986) (plurality opinion)]. We have never held that it extends to freestanding claims of actual innocence. Therefore, the exception is inapplicable here.

Petitioner asserts that this case is different because he has been sentenced to death. But we have "refused to hold that the fact that a death sentence has been imposed requires a different standard of review on federal habeas corpus." *Murray v. Giarratano*, 492 U.S. 1 (1989) (plurality opinion). We have, of course, held that the Eighth Amendment requires increased reliability of the process by which capital punishment may be imposed. See, *e.g.*, *McKoy v. North Carolina*, 494 U.S. 433 (1990) (unanimity requirement impermissibly limits jurors' consideration of mitigating evidence); *Eddings v. Oklahoma*, 455 U.S. 104 (1982) (jury must be allowed to consider all of a capital defendant's mitigating character evidence); *Lockett v. Ohio*, 438 U.S. 586 (1978) (plurality opinion) (same). But petitioner's claim does not fit well into the doctrine of these cases, since, as we have pointed out, it is far from clear that a second trial 10 years after the first trial would produce a more reliable result.

Perhaps mindful of this, petitioner urges not that he necessarily receive a new trial, but that his death sentence simply be vacated if a federal habeas court deems that a satisfactory showing of "actual innocence" has been made. But such a result is scarcely logical; petitioner's claim is not that some error was made in imposing a capital sentence upon him, but that a fundamental error was made in finding him guilty of the underlying murder in the first place. It would be a rather strange jurisprudence, in these circumstances, which held that under our Constitution he could not be executed, but that he could spend the rest of his life in prison.

Alternatively, petitioner invokes the Fourteenth Amendment's guarantee of due process of law in support of his claim that his showing of actual innocence entitles him to a new trial, or at least to a vacation of his death sentence. "[B]ecause the States have considerable expertise in matters of criminal procedure and the criminal process is grounded in centuries of common-law tradition," we have "exercis[ed] substantial deference to legislative judgments in this area." *Medina v. California*, 505 U.S. 437, 445–446 (1992). Thus, we have found criminal process lacking only where it "offends some principle of justice so rooted in the traditions and conscience of our people as to be ranked as fundamental." *Ibid.* [quoting *Patterson v. New York*, 432 U.S. 197, 202 (1977)]. "Historical practice is probative of whether a procedural rule can be characterized as fundamental." 505 U.S., at 446 . . .

[The Court here made the following points regarding time limits on the filing of motions for a new trial based on newly discovered evidence. Historically, the common-law rule was that a new trial could be granted "only during the term of court in which the final judgment was entered." In 1946, the Supreme Court adopted Rule 33 of the Federal Rules of Criminal Procedure, setting a two-year time limit for filing a motion for a new trial. This has remained the rule in federal courts. Contemporary state practice is "divergent." Texas is one of 17 states that requires a motion within 60 days of judgment. One state adheres to the common-law rule. Eighteen jurisdictions have time limits ranging between one and three years. Fifteen States allow a motion to be filed more than three years after conviction. Of these states, four have waivable time limits of less than 120 days, two have waivable time limits of more than 120 days, and nine states have no time limits.]

In light of the historical availability of new trials, our own . . . Rule 33, and the contemporary practice in the States, we cannot say that Texas' refusal to entertain petitioner's newly discovered evidence eight years after his conviction transgresses a principle of fundamental fairness "rooted in the traditions and conscience of our people." This is not to say, however, that petitioner is left without a forum to raise his actual innocence claim. For under Texas law, petitioner may file a request for executive clemency. Clemency[12] is deeply rooted in our Anglo-American tradition of law, and is the historic remedy for preventing miscarriages of justice where judicial process has been exhausted.

In England, the clemency power was vested in the Crown and can be traced back to the 700's. W. Humbert, *The Pardoning Power of the President* 9 (1941). Blackstone thought this "one of the great advantages of monarchy in general, above any other form of government; that there is a magistrate, who has it in his power to extend mercy, wherever he thinks it is deserved: holding a court of equity in his own breast, to soften the rigour of the general law, in such criminal cases as merit an exemption from punishment." 4 W. Blackstone, *Commentaries*. Clemency provided the principal avenue of relief for individuals convicted of criminal offenses—most of which were capital—because there was no right of appeal until 1907. 1 L. Radzinowicz, *A History of English Criminal Law* 122 (1948). It was the only means by which one could challenge his conviction on the ground of innocence. *United States* Dept. of Justice, 3 *Attorney General's Survey of Release Procedures* 73 (1939).

Our Constitution adopts the British model and gives to the President the "Power to grant Reprieves and Pardons for Offences against the United States." Art. II, § 2, cl. 1. In *United States v. Wilson*, 32 U.S. (7 Pet.) 150, 160–61, 8 L. Ed. 640 (1833), Chief Justice Marshall expounded on the President's pardon power:

> "As this power had been exercised from time immemorial by the executive of that nation whose language is our language, and to whose judicial institutions ours bear a close resemblance; we adopt their principles respecting the operation and effect of a pardon, and look into their books for the rules prescribing the manner in which it is to be used by the person who would avail himself of it.
>
> "A pardon is an act of grace, proceeding from the power entrusted with the execution of the laws, which exempts the individual, on whom it is bestowed, from the punishment the law inflicts for a crime he has committed. It is the private, though official act of the executive magistrate, delivered to the individual for whose benefit it is intended, and not communicated officially to the court. It is a constituent part of the judicial system, that the judge sees only with judicial eyes, and knows nothing respecting any particular case, of which he is not informed judicially. A private deed, not communicated to him, whatever may be its character, whether a pardon or release, is totally unknown and cannot be acted on. The looseness which would be introduced into judicial

---

[12] The term "clemency" refers not only to full or conditional pardons, but also commutations, remissions of fines, and reprieves. See Kobil, "The Quality of Mercy Strained: Wresting the Pardoning Power from the King," 69 Texas L. Rev. 569, 575–578 (1991).

proceedings, would prove fatal to the great principles of justice, if the judge might notice and act upon facts not brought regularly into the cause. Such a proceeding, in ordinary cases, would subvert the best established principles, and overturn those rules which have been settled by the wisdom of ages."

See also *Ex parte Garland*, 71 U.S. (4 Wall.) 333, 38–381, 18 L. Ed. 366 (1867); *The Federalist* No. 74, pp. 447–449 (C. Rossiter ed. 1961) (A. Hamilton) ("The criminal code of every country partakes so much of necessary severity that without an easy access to exceptions in favor of unfortunate guilt, justice would wear a countenance too sanguinary and cruel").

Of course, although the Constitution vests in the President a pardon power, it does not require the States to enact a clemency mechanism. Yet since the British Colonies were founded, clemency has been available in America. C. Jensen, *The Pardoning Power in the American States* 3–4 (1922). The original States were reluctant to vest the clemency power in the executive. And although this power has gravitated toward the executive over time, several States have split the clemency power between the Governor and an advisory board selected by the legislature. See *Survey of Release Procedures, supra*, at 91–98. Today, all 36 States that authorize capital punishment have constitutional or statutory provisions for clemency.

Executive clemency has provided the "fail safe" in our criminal justice system. K. Moore, *Pardons: Justice, Mercy, and the Public Interest* 131 (1989). It is an unalterable fact that our judicial system, like the human beings who administer it, is fallible. But history is replete with examples of wrongfully convicted persons who have been pardoned in the wake of after-discovered evidence establishing their innocence. In his classic work, Professor Edwin Borchard compiled 65 cases in which it was later determined that individuals had been wrongfully convicted of crimes. Clemency provided the relief mechanism in 47 of these cases; the remaining cases ended in judgments of acquittals after new trials. E. Borchard, *Convicting the Innocent* (1932). Recent authority confirms that over the past century clemency has been exercised frequently in capital cases in which demonstrations of "actual innocence" have been made. See M. Radelet, H. Bedau, & C. Putnam, *In Spite of Innocence* 282–356 (1992).[15]

In Texas, the Governor has the power, upon the recommendation of a majority of the Board of Pardons and Paroles, to grant clemency. The board's consideration is triggered upon request of the individual sentenced to death, his or her representative, or the Governor herself. In capital cases, a request may be made for a full pardon, a commutation of death sentence to life imprisonment or appro-

---

[15] The dissent points to one study concluding that 23 innocent persons have been executed in the United States this century as support for the proposition that clemency requests by persons believed to be innocent are not always granted (citing Bedau and Radelet, "Miscarriages of Justice in Potentially Capital Cases," 40 Stan. L. Rev. 21 (1987)). Although we do not doubt that clemency—like the criminal justice system itself—is fallible, we note that scholars have taken issue with this study. See Markman and Cassell, "Protecting the Innocent: A Response to the Bedau-Radelet Study," 41 Stan. L. Rev. 121 (1988).

priate maximum penalty, or a reprieve of execution. The Governor has the sole authority to grant one reprieve in any capital case not exceeding 30 days. The Texas clemency procedures contain specific guidelines for pardons on the ground of innocence. The board will entertain applications for a recommendation of full pardon because of innocence upon receipt of the following: "(1) a written unanimous recommendation of the current trial officials of the court of conviction; and/or (2) a certified order or judgment of a court having jurisdiction accompanied by certified copy of the findings of fact (if any); and (3) affidavits of witnesses upon which the finding of innocence is based." In this case, petitioner has apparently sought a 30-day reprieve from the Governor, but has yet to apply for a pardon, or even a commutation, on the ground of innocence or otherwise.

As the foregoing discussion illustrates, in state criminal proceedings the trial is the paramount event for determining the guilt or innocence of the defendant. Federal habeas review of state convictions has traditionally been limited to claims of constitutional violations occurring in the course of the underlying state criminal proceedings. Our federal habeas cases have treated claims of "actual innocence," not as an independent constitutional claim, but as a basis upon which a habeas petitioner may have an independent constitutional claim considered on the merits, even though his habeas petition would otherwise be regarded as successive or abusive. History shows that the traditional remedy for claims of innocence based on new evidence, discovered too late in the day to file a new trial motion, has been executive clemency.

We may assume, for the sake of argument in deciding this case, that in a capital case a truly persuasive demonstration of "actual innocence" made after trial would render the execution of a defendant unconstitutional, and warrant federal habeas relief if there were no state avenue open to process such a claim. But because of the very disruptive effect that entertaining claims of actual innocence would have on the need for finality in capital cases, and the enormous burden that having to retry cases based on often stale evidence would place on the States, the threshold showing for such an assumed right would necessarily be extraordinarily high. The showing made by petitioner in this case falls far short of any such threshold.

Petitioner's newly discovered evidence consists of affidavits. In the new trial context, motions based solely upon affidavits are disfavored because the affiants' statements are obtained without the benefit of cross-examination and an opportunity to make credibility determinations. Petitioner's affidavits are particularly suspect in this regard because, with the exception of Raul Herrera Junior's affidavit, they consist of hearsay. Likewise, in reviewing petitioner's new evidence, we are mindful that defendants often abuse new trial motions "as a method of delaying enforcement of just sentences." Although we are not presented with a new trial motion *per se*, we believe the likelihood of abuse is as great—or greater—here.

The affidavits filed in this habeas proceeding were given over eight years after petitioner's trial. No satisfactory explanation has been given as to why the affiants waited until the 11th hour—and, indeed, until after the alleged perpetrator of the murders himself was dead—to make their statements. . . . Equally troubling, no explanation has been offered as to why petitioner, by hypothesis an innocent man, pleaded guilty to the murder of Rucker.

Moreover, the affidavits themselves contain inconsistencies, and therefore fail to provide a convincing account of what took place on the night Officers Rucker and Carrisalez were killed. For instance, the affidavit of Raul Junior, who was nine years old at the time, indicates that there were three people in the speeding car from which the murderer emerged, whereas Hector Villarreal attested that Raul Senior told him that there were two people in the car that night. Of course, Hernandez testified at petitioner's trial that the murderer was the only occupant of the car. The affidavits also conflict as to the direction in which the vehicle was heading when the murders took place and petitioner's whereabouts on the night of the killings.

Finally, the affidavits must be considered in light of the proof of petitioner's guilt at trial—proof which included two eyewitness identifications, numerous pieces of circumstantial evidence, and a handwritten letter in which petitioner apologized for killing the officers and offered to turn himself in under certain conditions. That proof, even when considered alongside petitioner's belated affidavits, points strongly to petitioner's guilt.

This is not to say that petitioner's affidavits are without probative value. Had this sort of testimony been offered at trial, it could have been weighed by the jury, along with the evidence offered by the State and petitioner, in deliberating upon its verdict. Since the statements in the affidavits contradict the evidence received at trial, the jury would have had to decide important issues of credibility. But coming 10 years after petitioner's trial, this showing of innocence falls far short of that which would have to be made in order to trigger the sort of constitutional claim which we have assumed, arguendo, to exist.

The judgment of the Court of Appeals is Affirmed.

CONCURRING OPINION OF JUSTICE O'CONNOR, JOINED BY JUSTICE KENNEDY

I cannot disagree with the fundamental legal principle that executing the innocent is inconsistent with the Constitution. Regardless of the verbal formula employed—"contrary to contemporary standards of decency," "shocking to the conscience," or offensive to a "principle of justice so rooted in the traditions and conscience of our people as to be ranked as fundamental,"—the execution of a legally and factually innocent person would be a constitutionally intolerable event. Dispositive to this case, however, is an equally fundamental fact: Petitioner is not innocent, in any sense of the word.

As the Court explains, petitioner is not innocent in the eyes of the law because, in our system of justice, "the trial is the paramount event for determining the guilt or innocence of the defendant." In petitioner's case, that paramount event occurred 10 years ago. He was tried before a jury of his peers, with the full panoply of protections that our Constitution affords criminal defendants. At the conclusion of that trial, the jury found petitioner guilty beyond a reasonable doubt. Petitioner therefore does not appear before us as an innocent man on the verge of execution. He is instead a legally guilty one who, refusing to accept the jury's verdict, demands a hearing in which to have his culpability determined once again.

Consequently, the issue before us is not whether a State can execute the innocent. It is, as the Court notes, whether a fairly convicted and therefore legally guilty person is constitutionally entitled to yet another judicial proceeding in which to adjudicate his guilt anew, 10 years after conviction, notwithstanding his failure to demonstrate that constitutional error infected his trial. In most circumstances, that question would answer itself in the negative. Our society has a high degree of confidence in its criminal trials, in no small part because the Constitution offers unparalleled protections against convicting the innocent. The question similarly would be answered in the negative today, except for the disturbing nature of the claim before us. Petitioner contends not only that the Constitution's protections "sometimes fail," but that their failure in his case will result in his execution— even though he is factually innocent and has evidence to prove it.

Exercising restraint, the Court and Justice White assume for the sake of argument that, if a prisoner were to make an exceptionally strong showing of actual innocence, the execution could not go forward. Justice Blackmun, in contrast, would expressly so hold; he would also announce the precise burden of proof. . . . Resolving the issue is neither necessary nor advisable in this case. The question is a sensitive and, to say the least, troubling one. It implicates not just the life of a single individual, but also the State's powerful and legitimate interest in punishing the guilty, and the nature of state-federal relations. Indeed, as the Court persuasively demonstrates, throughout our history the federal courts have assumed that they should not and could not intervene to prevent an execution so long as the prisoner had been convicted after a constitutionally adequate trial. The prisoner's sole remedy was a pardon or clemency.

Nonetheless, the proper disposition of this case is neither difficult nor troubling. No matter what the Court might say about claims of actual innocence today, petitioner could not obtain relief. The record overwhelmingly demonstrates that petitioner deliberately shot and killed Officers Rucker and Carrisalez the night of September 29, 1981; petitioner's new evidence is bereft of credibility. Indeed, despite its stinging criticism of the Court's decision, not even the dissent expresses a belief that petitioner might possibly be actually innocent. Nor could it: The record makes it abundantly clear that petitioner is not somehow the future victim of "simple murder," (dissenting opinion), but instead himself the established perpetrator of two brutal and tragic ones.

Now, 10 years after being convicted on that seemingly dispositive evidence, petitioner has collected four affidavits that he claims prove his innocence. The affidavits allege that petitioner's brother, who died six years before the affidavits were executed, was the killer—and that petitioner was not. Affidavits like these are not uncommon, especially in capital cases. They are an unfortunate although understandable occurrence. It seems that, when a prisoner's life is at stake, he often can find someone new to vouch for him. Experience has shown, however, that such affidavits are to be treated with a fair degree of skepticism.

These affidavits are no exception. They are suspect, produced as they were at the 11th hour with no reasonable explanation for the nearly decade-long delay. Worse, they conveniently blame a dead man—someone who will neither contest the allegations nor suffer punishment as a result of them. Moreover, they contradict each other on numerous points, including the number of people in the murderer's car and the direction it was heading when Officer Carrisalez stopped it. They do not even agree on when Officer Rucker was killed. . . . And the affidavits are inconsistent with petitioner's own admission of guilt. The affidavits blame petitioner's deceased brother for both the Rucker and Carrisalez homicides—even though petitioner pleaded guilty to murdering Rucker and contested only the Carrisalez slaying.

Most critical of all, however, the affidavits pale when compared to the proof at trial. While some bits of circumstantial evidence can be explained, petitioner offers no plausible excuse for the most damaging piece of evidence, the signed letter in which petitioner confessed and offered to turn himself in. One could hardly ask for more unimpeachable—or more unimpeached—evidence of guilt.

The conclusion seems inescapable: Petitioner is guilty. The dissent does not contend otherwise. Instead, it urges us to defer to the District Court's determination that petitioner's evidence was not "so insubstantial that it could be dismissed without any hearing at all." I do not read the District Court's decision as making any such determination. Nowhere in its opinion did the District Court question the accuracy of the jury's verdict. Nor did it pass on the sufficiency of the affidavits. The District Court did not even suggest that it wished to hold an evidentiary hearing on petitioner's actual innocence claims. Indeed, the District Court apparently believed that a hearing would be futile because the court could offer no relief in any event. As the court explained, claims of "newly discovered evidence bearing directly upon guilt or innocence" are not cognizable on habeas corpus "unless the petition implicates a constitutional violation."

Unless federal proceedings and relief—if they are to be had at all—are reserved for "extraordinarily high" and "truly persuasive demonstration[s] of 'actual innocence'" that cannot be presented to state authorities, the federal courts will be deluged with frivolous claims of actual innocence. Justice Jackson explained the dangers of such circumstances some 40 years ago:

> "It must prejudice the occasional meritorious application to be buried in a flood of worthless ones. He who must search a haystack for a needle is likely to end up with the attitude that the needle is not worth the search." *Brown v. Allen*, 344 U.S. 443, 537 (1953) (concurring in result).

If the federal courts are to entertain claims of actual innocence, their attention, efforts, and energy must be reserved for the truly extraordinary case; they ought not be forced to sort through the insubstantial and the incredible as well.

Ultimately, two things about this case are clear. First is what the Court does not hold. Nowhere does the Court state that the Constitution permits the execution of an actually innocent person. Instead, the Court assumes for the sake of argument that a truly persuasive demonstration of actual innocence would render any such execution unconstitutional and that federal habeas relief would be warranted if no state avenue were open to process the claim. Second is what petitioner has not demonstrated. Petitioner has failed to make a persuasive showing of actual innocence. Not one judge—no state court judge, not the District Court Judge, none of the three judges of the Court of Appeals, and none of the Justices of this Court—has expressed doubt about petitioner's guilt. Accordingly, the Court has no reason to pass on, and appropriately reserves, the question whether federal courts may entertain convincing claims of actual innocence. That difficult question remains open. If the Constitution's guarantees of fair procedure and the safeguards of clemency and pardon fulfill their historical mission, it may never require resolution at all.

CONCURRING OPINION OF JUSTICE SCALIA, JOINED BY JUSTICE THOMAS

We granted certiorari on the question whether it violates due process or constitutes cruel and unusual punishment for a State to execute a person who, having been convicted of murder after a full and fair trial, later alleges that newly discovered evidence shows him to be "actually innocent." I would have preferred to decide that question, particularly since, as the Court's discussion shows, it is perfectly clear what the answer is: There is no basis in text, tradition, or even in contemporary practice (if that were enough) for finding in the Constitution a right to demand judicial consideration of newly discovered evidence of innocence brought forward after conviction. In saying that such a right exists, the dissenters apply nothing but their personal opinions to invalidate the rules of more than two-thirds of the States, and a Federal Rule of Criminal Procedure for which this Court itself is responsible. If the system that has been in place for 200 years (and remains widely approved) "shock[s]" the dissenters' consciences, perhaps they should doubt the calibration of their consciences, or, better still, the usefulness of "conscience shocking" as a legal test.

I nonetheless join the entirety of the Court's opinion, including the final portion—because there is no legal error in deciding a case by assuming, arguendo, that an asserted constitutional right exists, and because I can understand, or at least am accustomed to, the reluctance of the present Court to admit publicly that Our Perfect Constitution* lets stand any injustice, much less the execution of an innocent man who has received, though to no avail, all the process that our society has traditionally deemed adequate. With any luck, we shall avoid ever having to face this embarrassing question again, since it is improbable that evidence of innocence as convincing as today's opinion requires would fail to produce an executive pardon.

---

* My reference is to an article by Professor Monaghan, which discusses the unhappy truth that not every problem was meant to be solved by the United States Constitution, nor can be. See Monaghan, "Our Perfect Constitution," 56 N.Y.U. L. Rev. 353 (1981).

My concern is that in making life easier for ourselves we not appear to make it harder for the lower federal courts, imposing upon them the burden of regularly analyzing newly-discovered-evidence-of-innocence claims in capital cases (in which event such federal claims, it can confidently be predicted, will become routine and even repetitive). A number of Courts of Appeals have hitherto held, largely in reliance on our unelaborated statement in *Townsend v. Sain*, 372 U.S. 293 (1963), that newly discovered evidence relevant only to a state prisoner's guilt or innocence is not a basis for federal habeas corpus relief. I do not understand it to be the import of today's decision that those holdings are to be replaced with a strange regime that assumes permanently, though only "arguendo," that a constitutional right exists, and expends substantial judicial resources on that assumption. The Court's extensive and scholarly discussion of the question presented in the present case does nothing but support our statement in *Townsend* and strengthen the validity of the holdings based upon it.

CONCURRING OPINION OF JUSTICE WHITE

In voting to affirm, I assume that a persuasive showing of "actual innocence" made after trial, even though made after the expiration of the time provided by law for the presentation of newly discovered evidence, would render unconstitutional the execution of petitioner in this case. To be entitled to relief, however, petitioner would at the very least be required to show that based on proffered newly discovered evidence and the entire record before the jury that convicted him, "no rational trier of fact could [find] proof of guilt beyond a reasonable doubt." *Jackson v. Virginia*, 443 U.S. 307 (1979). For the reasons stated in the Court's opinion, petitioner's showing falls far short of satisfying even that standard, and I therefore concur in the judgment.

DISSENTING OPINION OF JUSTICE BLACKMUN, JOINED IN PARTS I-IV BY JUSTICE STEVENS AND SOUTER

Nothing could be more contrary to contemporary standards of decency, or more shocking to the conscience, than to execute a person who is actually innocent.

I therefore must disagree with the long and general discussion that precedes the Court's disposition of this case. That discussion, of course, is dictum because the Court assumes, "for the sake of argument in deciding this case, that in a capital case a truly persuasive demonstration of 'actual innocence' made after trial would render the execution of a defendant unconstitutional." Without articulating the standard it is applying, however, the Court then decides that this petitioner has not made a sufficiently persuasive case. Because I believe that in the first instance the District Court should decide whether petitioner is entitled to a hearing and whether he is entitled to relief on the merits of his claim, I would reverse the order of the Court of Appeals and remand this case for further proceedings in the District Court.

I

The Court's enumeration of the constitutional rights of criminal defendants surely is entirely beside the point. These protections sometimes fail.[1] We really are being asked to decide whether the Constitution forbids the execution of a person who has been validly convicted and sentenced but who, nonetheless, can prove his innocence with newly discovered evidence. Despite the State of Texas' astonishing protestation to the contrary, I do not see how the answer can be anything but "yes."

A. The Eighth Amendment prohibits "cruel and unusual punishments." This proscription is not static but rather reflects evolving standards of decency. I think it is crystal clear that the execution of an innocent person is "at odds with contemporary standards of fairness and decency." *Spaziano v. Florida*, 468 U.S. 447, 465 (1984). Indeed, it is at odds with any standard of decency that I can imagine.

This Court has ruled that punishment is excessive and unconstitutional if it is "nothing more than the purposeless and needless imposition of pain and suffering," or if it is "grossly out of proportion to the severity of the crime." *Coker v. Georgia*, 433 U.S. 584, 592 (1977) (plurality opinion); *Gregg v. Georgia*, 428 U.S., at 173 (opinion of Stewart, Powell, and Stevens, JJ). It has held that death is an excessive punishment for rape, *Coker*, and for mere participation in a robbery during which a killing takes place, *Enmund*. If it is violative of the Eighth Amendment to execute someone who is guilty of those crimes, then it plainly is violative of the Eighth Amendment to execute a person who is actually innocent. Executing an innocent person epitomizes "the purposeless and needless imposition of pain and suffering." *Coker*.[2]

---

[1] One impressive study has concluded that 23 innocent people have been executed in the United States in this century, including one as recently as 1984. Bedau and Radelet, "Miscarriages of Justice in Potentially Capital Cases," 40 Stan. L. Rev. 21, 36, 173–179 (1987); Radelet, Bedau, and Putnam, *In Spite of Innocence* 282–356 (1992). The majority cites this study to show that clemency has been exercised frequently in capital cases when showings of actual innocence have been made. But the study also shows that requests for clemency by persons the authors believe were innocent have been refused. See, *e.g.*, Bedau and Radelet, 40 Stan. L. Rev., at 91 (discussing James Adams who was executed in Florida on May 10, 1984); Radelet, Bedau, and Putnam, *In Spite of Innocence*, at 5–10 (same).

[2] It also may violate the Eighth Amendment to imprison someone who is actually innocent. See *Robinson v. California*, 370 U.S. 660, 667 (1962) ("Even one day in prison would be a cruel and unusual punishment for the 'crime' of having a common cold"). On the other hand, this Court has noted that "'death is a different kind of punishment from any other which may be imposed in this country.... From the point of view of the defendant, it is different in both its severity and its finality.'" We are not asked to decide in this case whether petitioner's continued imprisonment would violate the Constitution if he actually is innocent, and I do not address that question.

The protection of the Eighth Amendment does not end once a defendant has been validly convicted and sentenced. In *Johnson v. Mississippi*, 486 U.S. 578 (1988), the petitioner had been convicted of murder and sentenced to death on the basis of three aggravating circumstances. One of those circumstances was that he previously had been convicted of a violent felony in the State of New York. After Johnson had been sentenced to death, the New York Court of Appeals reversed his prior conviction. Although there was no question that the prior conviction was valid at the time of Johnson's sentencing, this Court held that the Eighth Amendment required review of the sentence because "the jury was allowed to consider evidence that has been revealed to be materially inaccurate." In *Ford v. Wainwright*, the petitioner had been convicted of murder and sentenced to death. There was no suggestion that he was incompetent at the time of his offense, at trial, or at sentencing, but subsequently he exhibited changes in behavior that raised doubts about his sanity. This Court held that Florida was required under the Eighth Amendment to provide an additional hearing to determine whether Ford was mentally competent, and that he could not be executed if he were incompetent. Both *Johnson* and *Ford* recognize that capital defendants may be entitled to further proceedings because of an intervening development even though they have been validly convicted and sentenced to death.

Respondent and the United States as amicus curiae argue that the Eighth Amendment does not apply to petitioner because he is challenging his guilt, not his punishment. The majority attempts to distinguish *Ford* on that basis. Such reasoning, however, . . . fundamentally misconceives the nature of petitioner's argument. Whether petitioner is viewed as challenging simply his death sentence or also his continued detention, he still is challenging the State's right to punish him. Respondent and the United States would impose a clear line between guilt and punishment, reasoning that every claim that concerns guilt necessarily does not involve punishment. Such a division is far too facile. What respondent and the United States fail to recognize is that the legitimacy of punishment is inextricably intertwined with guilt.

Beck [v. Alabama, 447 U.S. 625 (1980)] makes this clear. In *Beck*, the petitioner was convicted of the capital crime of robbery-intentional killing. Under Alabama law, however, the trial court was prohibited from giving the jury the option of convicting him of the lesser included offense of felony murder. We held that precluding the instruction injected an impermissible element of uncertainty into the guilt phase of the trial.

> "To insure that the death penalty is indeed imposed on the basis of 'reason rather than caprice or emotion,' we have invalidated procedural rules that tended to diminish the reliability of the sentencing determination. The same reasoning must apply to rules that diminish the reliability of the guilt determination. Thus, if the unavailability of a lesser included offense instruction enhances the risk of an unwarranted conviction, [the State] is constitutionally prohibited from withdrawing that option in a capital case." *Id.*, at 638 (footnote omitted).

The decision in *Beck* establishes that, at least in capital cases, the Eighth Amendment requires more than reliability in sentencing. It also mandates a reliable determination of guilt. See also *Spaziano v. Florida*, 468 U.S., at 456.

The Court also suggests that allowing petitioner to raise his claim of innocence would not serve society's interest in the reliable imposition of the death penalty because it might require a new trial that would be less accurate than the first. This suggestion misses the point entirely. The question is not whether a second trial would be more reliable than the first but whether, in light of new evidence, the result of the first trial is sufficiently reliable for the State to carry out a death sentence. Furthermore, it is far from clear that a State will seek to retry the rare prisoner who prevails on a claim of actual innocence. As explained in Part III, I believe a prisoner must show not just that there was probably a reasonable doubt about his guilt but that he is probably actually innocent. I find it difficult to believe that any State would choose to retry a person who meets this standard.

I believe it contrary to any standard of decency to execute someone who is actually innocent. Because the Eighth Amendment applies to questions of guilt or innocence, and to persons upon whom a valid sentence of death has been imposed, I also believe that petitioner may raise an Eighth Amendment challenge to his punishment on the ground that he is actually innocent.

B. Execution of the innocent is equally offensive to the Due Process Clause of the Fourteenth Amendment. The majority's discussion misinterprets petitioner's Fourteenth Amendment claim as raising a procedural, rather than a substantive, due process challenge.

"The Due Process Clause of the Fifth Amendment provides that 'No person shall be deprived of life, liberty, or property, without due process of law.' This Court has held that the Due Process Clause protects individuals against two types of government action. So-called 'substantive due process' prevents the government from engaging in conduct that 'shocks the conscience,' or interferes with rights 'implicit in the concept of ordered liberty.' "

Petitioner's claim falls within our due process precedents. In *Rochin [v. California*, 342 U.S. 165, 172 (1952)]*, deputy sheriffs investigating narcotics sales broke into Rochin's room and observed him put two capsules in his mouth. The deputies attempted to remove the capsules from his mouth and, having failed, took Rochin to a hospital and had his stomach pumped. The capsules were found to contain morphine. The Court held that the deputies' conduct "shock[ed] the conscience" and violated due process. 342 U.S., at 172. "Illegally breaking into the privacy of the petitioner, the struggle to open his mouth and remove what was there, the forcible extraction of his stomach's contents—this course of proceeding by agents of government to obtain evidence is bound to offend even hardened sensibilities. They are methods too close to the rack and the screw to permit of constitutional differentiation." *Ibid.* The lethal injection that petitioner faces as an allegedly innocent person is certainly closer to the rack and the screw than the stomach pump condemned in *Rochin*. Execution of an innocent person is the ultimate "arbitrary impositio[n]." It is an imposition from which one never recovers and for which one can never be compensated. Thus, I also believe that petitioner may raise a substantive due process challenge to his punishment on the ground that he is actually innocent.

C.   Given my conclusion that it violates the Eighth and Fourteenth Amendments to execute a person who is actually innocent, I find no bar in *Townsend v. Sain* to consideration of an actual-innocence claim. Newly discovered evidence of petitioner's innocence does bear on the constitutionality of his execution. Of course, it could be argued this is in some tension with *Townsend*'s statement, that "the existence merely of newly discovered evidence relevant to the guilt of a state prisoner is not a ground for relief on federal habeas corpus." That statement, however, is no more than distant dictum here, for we never had been asked to consider whether the execution of an innocent person violates the Constitution.

II

The majority's discussion of petitioner's constitutional claims is even more perverse when viewed in the light of this Court's recent habeas jurisprudence. Beginning with a trio of decisions in 1986, this Court shifted the focus of federal habeas review of successive, abusive, or defaulted claims away from the preservation of constitutional rights to a fact-based inquiry into the habeas petitioner's guilt or innocence. See *Kuhlmann v. Wilson, Murray v. Carrier, Smith v. Murray*. The Court sought to strike a balance between the State's interest in the finality of its criminal judgments and the prisoner's interest in access to a forum to test the basic justice of his sentence. In striking this balance, the Court adopted the view of Judge Friendly that there should be an exception to the concept of finality when a prisoner can make a colorable claim of actual innocence. Friendly, "Is Innocence Irrelevant? Collateral Attack on Criminal Judgments," 38 U. Chi. L. Rev. 142, 160 (1970).

   Justice Powell, writing for the plurality in *Wilson*, explained the reason for focusing on innocence:

> "The prisoner may have a vital interest in having a second chance to test the fundamental justice of his incarceration. Even where, as here, the many judges who have reviewed the prisoner's claims in several proceedings provided by the State and on his first petition for federal habeas corpus have determined that his trial was free from constitutional error, a prisoner retains a powerful and legitimate interest in obtaining his release from custody if he is innocent of the charge for which he was incarcerated. That interest does not extend, however, to prisoners whose guilt is conceded or plain." 477 U.S., at 452.

In other words, even a prisoner who appears to have had a constitutionally perfect trial "retains a powerful and legitimate interest in obtaining his release from custody if he is innocent of the charge for which he was incarcerated." It is obvious that this reasoning extends beyond the context of successive, abusive, or defaulted claims to substantive claims of actual innocence. Indeed, Judge Friendly recognized that substantive claims of actual innocence should be cognizable on federal habeas.

Having adopted an "actual-innocence" requirement for review of abusive, successive, or defaulted claims, however, the majority would now take the position that "a claim of 'actual innocence' is not itself a constitutional claim, but instead a gateway through which a habeas petitioner must pass to have his otherwise barred constitutional claim considered on the merits." In other words, having held that a prisoner who is incarcerated in violation of the Constitution must show he is actually innocent to obtain relief, the majority would now hold that a prisoner who is actually innocent must show a constitutional violation to obtain relief. The only principle that would appear to reconcile these two positions is the principle that habeas relief should be denied whenever possible.

III

The Eighth and Fourteenth Amendments, of course, are binding on the States, and one would normally expect the States to adopt procedures to consider claims of actual innocence based on newly discovered evidence. The majority's disposition of this case, however, leaves the States uncertain of their constitutional obligations.

A. Whatever procedures a State might adopt to hear actual-innocence claims, one thing is certain: The possibility of executive clemency is not sufficient to satisfy the requirements of the Eighth and Fourteenth Amendments. The majority correctly points out: "A pardon is an act of grace." The vindication of rights guaranteed by the Constitution has never been made to turn on the unreviewable discretion of an executive official or administrative tribunal. Indeed, in *Ford v. Wainwright*, we explicitly rejected the argument that executive clemency was adequate to vindicate the Eighth Amendment right not to be executed if one is insane. The possibility of executive clemency "exists in every case in which a defendant challenges his sentence under the Eighth Amendment. Recognition of such a bare possibility would make judicial review under the Eighth Amendment meaningless." *Solem v. Helm*, 463 U.S. 277, 303 (1983).

"The government of the United States has been emphatically termed a government of laws, and not of men. It will certainly cease to deserve this high appellation, if the laws furnish no remedy for the violation of a vested legal right." *Marbury v. Madison*, 5 U.S. (1 Cranch) 137, 163, 2 L. Ed. 60 (1803). If the exercise of a legal right turns on "an act of grace," then we no longer live under a government of laws. "The very purpose of a Bill of Rights was to withdraw certain subjects from the vicissitudes of political controversy, to place them beyond the reach of majorities and officials and to establish them as legal principles to be applied by the courts." *West Virginia Bd. of Ed. v. Barnette*, 319 U.S. 624, 638 (1943). It is understandable, therefore, that the majority does not say that the vindication of petitioner's constitutional rights may be left to executive clemency.

C.   The question that remains is what showing should be required to obtain relief on the merits of an Eighth or Fourteenth Amendment claim of actual innocence.

I would hold that, to obtain relief on a claim of actual innocence, the petitioner must show that he probably is innocent.

It should be clear that the standard I would adopt would not convert the federal courts into "forums in which to relitigate state trials." It would not "require the habeas court to hear testimony from the witnesses who testified at trial," though, if the petition warrants a hearing, it may require the habeas court to hear the testimony of "those who made the statements in the affidavits which petitioner has presented." I believe that if a prisoner can show that he is probably actually innocent, in light of all the evidence, then he has made "a truly persuasive demonstration," and his execution would violate the Constitution. I would so hold.

IV

. . . In one of the affidavits, Hector Villarreal, a licensed attorney and former state court judge, swears under penalty of perjury that his client Raul Herrera Senior confessed that he, and not petitioner, committed the murders. No matter what the majority may think of the inconsistencies in the affidavits or the strength of the evidence presented at trial, this affidavit alone is sufficient to raise factual questions concerning petitioner's innocence that cannot be resolved simply by examining the affidavits and the petition.

I do not understand why the majority so severely faults petitioner for relying only on affidavits. It is common to rely on affidavits at the preliminary-consideration stage of a habeas proceeding. The opportunity for cross-examination and credibility determinations comes at the hearing, assuming that the petitioner is entitled to one. It makes no sense for this Court to impugn the reliability of petitioner's evidence on the ground that its credibility has not been tested when the reason its credibility has not been tested is that petitioner's habeas proceeding has been truncated by the Court of Appeals and now by this Court. In its haste to deny petitioner relief, the majority seems to confuse the question whether the petition may be dismissed summarily with the question whether petitioner is entitled to relief on the merits of his claim.

V

I have voiced disappointment over this Court's obvious eagerness to do away with any restriction on the States' power to execute whomever and however they please. I have also expressed doubts about whether, in the absence of such restrictions, capital punishment remains constitutional at all. Of one thing, however, I am certain. Just as an execution without adequate safeguards is unacceptable, so too is an execution when the condemned prisoner can prove that he is innocent. The execution of a person who can show that he is innocent comes perilously close to simple murder.

Appendix A

Facts and Figures on Murder and the Death Penalty

HOMICIDES[a]

Homicide rates in the United States doubled from the mid-1960's to the late 1970's, peaking in 1980 and 1991. (See Figure 1.) Rates then declined sharply, reaching mid-1960s levels in 1999. In 1991, there had been 24,700 homicides, for a rate of 9.8 per 100,000. In 1999, there were 15,553 homicides, for a rate of 5.7.

Figure 1. Homicide victimization, 1950–1999; Rate per 100,000 population

[a] Unless otherwise indicated, this section of the Appendix relies on data for the period 1976 to 1999 from the U.S. Department of Justice, Bureau of Justice Statistics, *Homicide Trends in the United States*. These data are regularly updated and are available at http://www.ojp.usdoj.gov/bjs/.

HOMICIDE OFFENDERS[b]

Age

Nearly half the killers were under the age of 25. Eighteen- to 24-year-olds have the highest homicide rate of any age group—between three and four times the rate for the national population.

The rate for 14- to 17-year-olds soared in the mid-1980's, exceeding that of even the 35- to 49-year-old age group. (See Figure 2.) The eligibility for the death penalty of 14- to 17-year-olds is a matter of controversy.

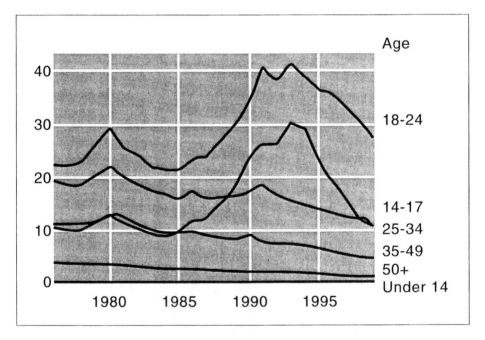

Figure 2. Homicide offending by age, 1976–1999; Rate per 100,000 population

---

[b] The Justice Department defines "homicide" as murder or nonnegligent manslaughter as determined by police investigation. The ultimate disposition of these offenses is not known. It would not be proper to identify these offenses as "murder" in the legal sense, nor to assume that the perpetrators faced capital charges.

Race

Although blacks make up 12.1 percent of the U.S. population (1990 and 2000 Censuses), they committed more than half (51.5 percent) the homicides in the United States.

The black homicide rate is seven to nine times that of whites. (See Figure 3.)

Blacks were the offenders in six out of ten "felony-murders" (homicides contemporaneous with another felony) and 67 percent of drug-related homicides. Offenders who kill during the commission of another offense (an aggravating factor) may be eligible for the death penalty.

Hispanics (of any race) comprised 20 percent of those accused of murder in the largest counties, where they made up 26 percent of the population.[c]

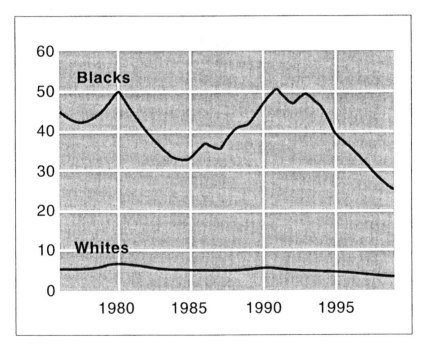

Figure 3. Homocide offending by race, 1976–1999; Rate per 100,000 population

[c] U.S. Department of Justice, Bureau of Justice Statistics, *Felony Defendants in Large Urban Counties,* 1998, pp. 5, 43.

Sex

Killers overwhelmingly are males—88 percent from 1976 to 1999. (See Figure 4.)

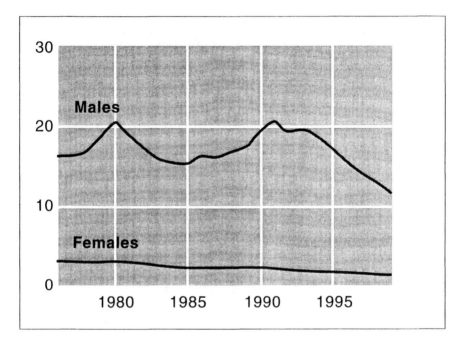

Figure 4.   Homicide offending by gender, 1976–1999; Rate per 100,000 population

HOMICIDE VICTIMS

Age

Homicide victims are somewhat older than the killers, but still relatively young. Nearly 30 percent of the victims were between the ages of 25 and 34, the most victimized age group. Eighteen to 24-year-olds and 35–49-year-olds each constituted roughly 23 percent of the victims.

Among victimized children under age five, 61 percent were killed by a parent, only 3 percent by a stranger.

Victimization of the elderly has been declining since the 1980's. Five percent of all homicides involve the death of someone 65 or older.

(See Figure 5.)

Figure 5. Homicide victimization by age, 1976–1999; Rate per 100,000 population

Race

Nearly 47 percent of all homicide victims have been black. Ninety-four percent of the black victims were killed by blacks. Eighty-six percent of white victims were killed by whites.

In 1999, 46 percent of all homicides involved white perpetrators and white victims; 42 percent involved blacks killing blacks; 8 percent were black on white and 3 percent were white on black. These figures are fairly typical for the 1976–1999 period.

(See Figures 6 and 7.)

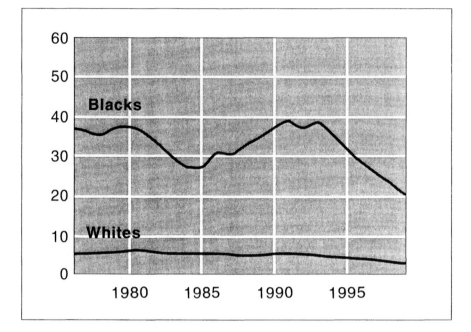

Figure 6.   Homicide victimization by race, 1976–1999; Rate per 100,000 population

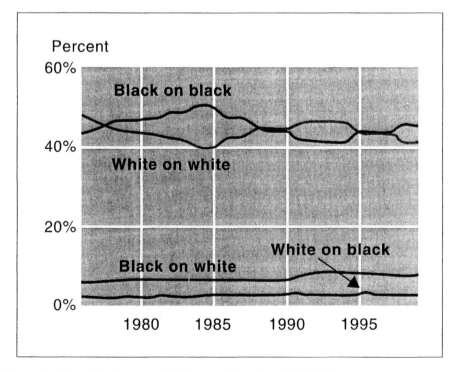

Figure 7.   Homicides by race of offender and victim, 1976–1999

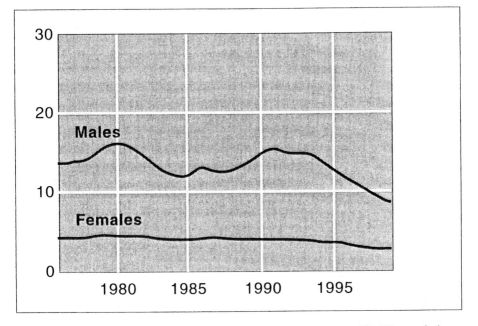

Figure 8. Homicide victimization by gender, 1976–1999; Rate per 100,000 population

Sex

More than three-quarters of all homicide victims were males. Females were 62 percent of the victims in killings by intimates. The number of men murdered by intimates dropped 69 percent since 1976, whereas the number of women killed by intimates was stable for two decades and declined after 1993. Females were the victims in 81 percent of the sex-related killings. (See Figure 8.)

Among all homicides, 65 percent involved males killing males, 22 percent were males killing females, 10 percent were female offender/male victim, and 2 percent were female offender/female victim.

HOMICIDE CIRCUMSTANCES

From 1976 to 1999, 14 percent of all homicides were by strangers, 20 percent by family members. About one-third of the victims were acquaintances of the assailant.

Two-thirds of all homicides were committed with guns, mostly handguns.

Big cities account for over 57 percent of all homicides. However, in the late 1990's, homicide rates in cities of over one million declined to the level of cities with one-quarter to one-half million people. (See Figure 9.)

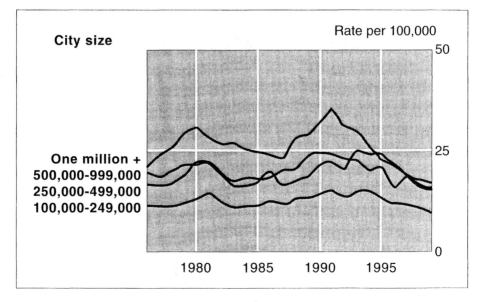

Figure 9.   Homicide victimization rates for cities over 100,000 population, 1976–1999

Over 1,800 law enforcement officers were killed from 1976 to 1999, but the trend is down (134 died in 1976, 42 in 1999). Murder of a police officer is commonly treated as an aggravating circumstance establishing eligibility for the death penalty.

Arguments (such as over money or property, and sometimes associated with drinking or drug use) are the major cause of homicide. Such homicides are less likely to be "aggravated" and therefore are less death penalty eligible than homicides occurring during the commission of a felony. (See Figure 10.)

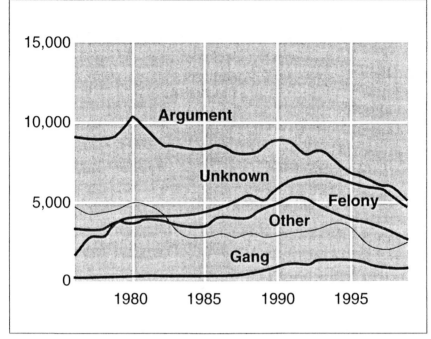

Figure 10. Homicide by circumstance, 1976–1999; Number of Victims

MURDER ARRESTS, CONVICTIONS, AND SENTENCES[d]

A 1988 survey of murder arrests in the most populous urban counties of the United States indicated the following:

- Of those arrested for murder, 63 percent were convicted of murder; 10 percent were convicted of some other crime.
- Of those convicted of murder, 74 percent received prison terms less than life, with an average sentence of 14 years. Eighteen percent were sentenced to life in prison, and 2 percent received a death sentence.
- Eight percent of those arrested for murder were charged with capital murder. All capital defendants were convicted of some offense: 31 percent received prison terms, 51 percent were sentenced to life, and 12 percent got death sentences.
- Whites constituted 77 percent of the total population of the sampled counties and 36 percent of those arrested for murder. Blacks were 20 percent of the population and 62 percent of the murder arrestees.
- Of whites arrested for murder, 25 percent were not convicted of any crime. 56 percent received less than life prison sentences, with an average sentence

[d] U.S. Department of Justice, Bureau of Justice Statistics, *Murder in Large Urban Counties*, 1988.

of 14 years. Ten percent were sentenced to life, and 2 percent got death sentences.

• Of blacks arrested for murder, 29 percent were not convicted of any crime. Fifty-two percent received less than life prison sentences, with an average sentence of 14 years. Twelve percent were sentenced to life, and 1 percent got death sentences.

EXECUTIONS[e]

• From 1930 to the end of 2000, 4,542 prisoners were executed by nonmilitary authority in the United States (see Figure 11). The peak year for executions was 1935, with 199.

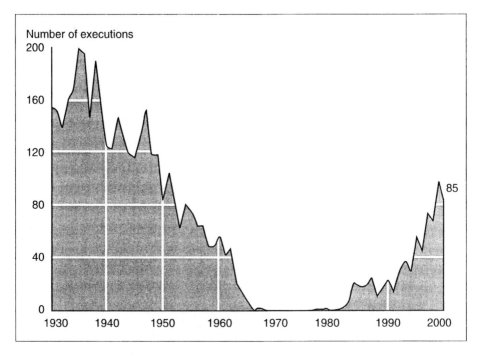

Figure 11.   Persons executed, 1930–2000

• From 1968 to 1976, no executions took place in the United States. The Supreme Court's ruling in *Furman v. Georgia*, which struck down the death penalty as then applied, was announced in 1972. *Gregg v. Georgia*, which upheld the death penalty, was decided in 1976. Between 1977 and 2000, there were 6,588 death sentences and 683 executions in 31 states.

[e] This section of the Appendix was drawn from the U.S. Department of Justice, Bureau of Justice Statistics, *Capital Punishment 2000* (2001). This publication is available at http://www.ojp.usdoj.gov/bjs/ and is updated annually.

- Thirty-eight states have a death penalty; 12 states and the District of Columbia have no death penalty. The states with no death penalty are: Alaska, Hawaii, Iowa, Maine, Massachusetts, Michigan, Minnesota, North Dakota, Rhode Island, Vermont, West Virginia, and Wisconsin.
- Texas leads all states in total executions, with 239 from 1977 through 2000. This is more than one third of all executions in the United States (239/683 = .349). Next are Virginia (81), Florida (50), and Missouri (46).
- As of year-end 2000, 36 states authorized executions by lethal injection; half of these states provided an alternative means as well. Eleven states authorized electrocution, 4 lethal gas, 3 hanging, and 3 a firing squad.
- Fourteen states and the Federal Government set 18 as the minimum age for execution. Four states extend the age to 17. Thirteen states permit 16-year-olds to receive the death penalty. 7 states do not specify a minimum age.
- Of the 6,588 death sentences from 1977 to the end of 2000, 3,243 (49 percent) were imposed on whites, 2,722 (41 percent) on blacks, 524 (8 percent) on Hispanics, and 99 (2 percent) on all other races.
- Of the 683 executions from 1977 through 2000, 377 (55 percent) were of whites, 246 (36 percent) were of blacks, 49 (7 percent) were of Hispanics, and 11 (2 percent) were of all other races.
- At year end 2000, there were 3,593 prisoners under sentence of death. 98.5 percent were men and 1.5 percent (55 prisoners) were women. 55.4 percent were white, 42.7 percent were black and 1.9 percent were of other races, such as Asians or American Indians. 10.6 percent of the inmates were Hispanic. For racial trends in capital sentences, see Figure 12.

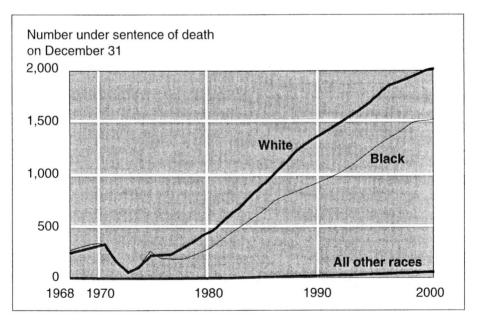

Figure 12. Persons under sentence of death, by race, 1968–2000

- For the 85 executions that occurred in 2000, the average time between sentence and execution was 11 years, 5 months. Since 1994, the average wait on death row has been over 10 years. From 1977–1983, it was 4 years, 3 months.
- Of 6,930 death sentences imposed between 1973 and 2000, there were (by year-end 2000) 683 executions (10 percent), 223 deaths due to other causes (3 percent), 2,244 appeals court reversals (32 percent), and 157 sentence commutations (2 percent). At the beginning of 2001, 3,593 inmates (52 percent) were still on death row. (See Table 1.)

Table 1 Prisoners sentenced to death and the outcome sentence by year of sentencing, 1978–2000

Year of sentence	Number sentenced to death	Execution	Other death	Appeal or higher court overturned			Sentence commuted	Other or unknown reasons	Under sentence of death 12/31/00
				Death Penalty Statute	Conviction	Sentence			
1973	42	2	0	14	9	8	9	0	0
1974	149	10	4	65	15	30	22	1	2
1975	298	6	4	171	24	67	21	2	3
1976	233	14	5	136	17	43	15	0	3
1977	137	19	3	40	26	32	7	0	10
1978	185	35	6	21	36	62	8	0	17
1979	152	28	13	2	28	58	5	1	17
1980	173	42	13	3	29	48	7	0	31
1981	224	51	13	0	42	73	5	1	39
1982	266	55	14	0	36	68	7	1	85
1983	252	57	15	1	26	59	7	2	85
1984	285	51	10	2	39	61	6	8	108
1985	267	34	6	1	42	69	4	3	108
1986	300	47	19	0	45	52	6	5	126

Number of prisoners removed from under sentence of death

Table 1 *Continued*

Year of sentence	Number sentenced to death	Number of prisoners removed from under sentence of death								Under sentence of death 12/31/00
		Execution	Other death	Appeal or higher court overturned			Sentence commuted	Other or unknown reasons	
				Death Penalty Statute	Conviction	Sentence			
1987	289	38	15	5	36	57	2	6	130
1988	292	37	12	0	33	54	3	0	153
1989	259	26	10	0	29	50	4	0	140
1990	253	26	8	0	33	37	2	0	147
1991	266	21	9	0	31	33	3	0	169
1992	288	21	9	0	21	36	5	0	196
1993	289	20	11	0	17	22	5	0	214
1994	318	14	7	0	21	23	2	0	251
1995	320	16	8	0	15	21	1	0	259
1996	318	9	4	0	14	27	1	0	263
1997	278	1	3	0	13	9	0	0	252
1998	303	3	2	0	3	3	0	0	292
1999	280	0	0	0	1	0	0	0	279
2000	214	0	0	0	0	0	0	0	214
Total	6930	683	223	461	681	1102	157	30	3593

Note: For those persons sentenced to death more than once, the numbers are based on the most recent death sentence.

PUBLIC OPINION[f]

- Surveys of American public opinion in 2001 show that two-thirds of the public approves capital punishment. This marks a softening of support since 1994, when 80 percent favored the death penalty. (See Table 2.)

Table 2 Attitudes toward the death penalty for persons convicted of murder

United States, selected years 1953–2001[a]
Question: "Are you in favor of the death penalty for a person convicted of murder?"

	Yes, in favor	No, not in favor	No opinion[b]
1953	69	25	7
1956	53	34	13
1957	47	34	18
1960	53	36	11
1965	45	43	12
1966	42	47	11
1967	54	38	8
1969	51	40	9
1971	49	40	11
March 1972	50	41	9
November 1972	57	32	11
1976	66	26	8
1978	62	27	11
1981	66	25	9
January 1985	72	20	8
November 1985	75	17	8
1986	70	22	8
1988	79	16	5
1991	76	18	6
1994	80	16	4
1995	77	13	10
1999	71	22	7
2000	66	28	6
2001	67	25	8

[a] Percents may not add up to 100 because of rounding.
[b] May include other response categories such as "depends" or "refused."
Data Source: The Gallup Organization, Inc., *The Gallup Poll* [Online]. Available: http://www.gallup.com/poll/releases/pr010302.asp [Mar. 2, 2001]. Reprinted by permission.

[f] Data for this section of the Appendix was obtained from U.S. Dept of Justice, *Sourcebook of Criminal Justice Statistics—2000*, available at http://www.albany.edu/sourcebook/

Table 3 Attitudes toward the penalty for murder, United States, selected years 1985–2001[a]

Question: "What do you think should be the penalty for murder—the death penalty or life imprisonment with absolutely no possibility of parole?"

	Death penalty	Life imprisonment without possibility of parole	No opinion[b]
1985	56	34	10
1986	55	35	10
1991	53	35	11
1992	50	37	13
1993	59	29	12
1994	50	32	18
1997	61	29	10
1999	56	38	6
2000	52	37	11
2001	57	41	3

Note: Sample sizes vary from year to year; the data for 2001 are based on telephone interviews with a randomly selected national sample of 1,016, 18 years of age and older. Conducted Feb. 19, 2001.
[a] Percents may not add up to 100 because of rounding.
[b] Includes volunteered responses such as "other," "neither," and "depends."
Data Source: The Gallup Organization, Inc., *The Gallup Poll* [Online]. Available: http://www.gallup.com/poll/releases/pr010302.asp [Mar. 2, 2001]. Reprinted by permission.

- Approval of the death penalty drops to under 60 percent when respondents are given a choice between death and life without parole. (See Table 3.)
- Surveys since 1953 indicate sharp divisions over the death penalty in the mid-1960's. Public support for capital punishment rose after 1976, when the Supreme Court upheld its constitutionality. From the mid-1980's to the end of the century, approval was very strong, always exceeding 70 percent. (See Table 2.) It may be significant that murder and violent crime rates soared from the mid-1960's to the mid-1970's, remaining high until the mid-1990's.
- Support for the death penalty varies with the subgroup. Whites are more supportive than nonwhites, men more than women, older people more than younger, wealthier more than poorer, and Republicans more than Democrats. (See Table 4.)

Table 4 Attitudes toward the death penalty for persons convicted of murder

By demographic characteristics, United States, 2001
Question: "Are you in favor of the death penalty for a person convicted of murder?"

	Yes, in favor	No, not in favor	Don't know/ refused
Sex			
Male	73	20	7
Female	63	29	8
Race			
White	73	20	7
Black	24	62	15
Nonwhite[a]	37	52	11
Age			
18–29 years	63	34	3
30–49 years	69	20	11
50–64 years	69	26	5
65 years and older	69	26	5
Education			
College post graduate	61	35	4
College graduate	73	23	4
Some college	67	23	10
High school graduate or less	68	24	8
Income			
$75,000 and over	76	22	2
$50,000 and over[b]	74	22	4
$30,000 to $49,000	73	20	7
$20,000 to $29,000	63	20	17
Under $20,000	56	36	8
Community			
Urban area	62	31	7
Suburban area	66	25	9
Rural area	77	18	5
Region			
East	59	29	12
Midwest	73	21	6
South	66	26	8
West	74	23	3
Politics			
Republican	79	16	5
Democrat	52	40	8
Independent	69	22	9

[a] Includes black responses.
[b] Includes $75,000 and over category.
Data Source: The Gallup Organization, Inc., Reprinted by permission.

• Among those who favor the death penalty, nearly half cite retributive concepts (*e.g.*, "an eye for an eye") as justification. Only 10 percent give deterrence as a reason. (See Table 5.) Fifty-two percent of Americans think that executions do not have much deterrent effect. Forty-two percent believe that it deters murderers.

Table 5 Reported reasons for favoring the death penalty for persons convicted of murder

United States, 2001
Question: "Why do you favor the death penalty for persons convicted of murder?"

Reasons for favoring	
An eye for an eye/they took a life/fits the crime	48%
Save taxpayers money/cost associated with prison	20
Deterrent for potential crimes/set an example	10
They deserve it	6
Support/believe in death penalty	6
Depends on the type of crime they commit	6
They will repeat their crimes/keep them from repeating it	6
Biblical reasons	3
Relieves prison overcrowding	2
If there's no doubt the person committed the crime	2
Life sentences don't always mean life in prison	2
Don't believe they can be rehabilitated	2
Serve justice	1
Fair punishment	1
Would help/benefit families of victims	1
Other	3
No opinion	1

Data Source: The Gallup Organization, Inc., *The Gallup Poll* [Online]. Available: http://www.gallup.com/poll/releases/pr010302.asp [Mar. 2, 2001]. Reprinted by permission.

Appendix B

Selected Death Penalty Statutes

ARKANSAS

Arkansas Code, Section 5-4-602

§ 5-4-602 Capital murder charge—Trial procedure.
The following procedures shall govern trials of persons charged with capital murder:

(1) The jury shall first hear all evidence relevant to the charge or charges and shall then retire to reach a verdict of guilt or innocence.

(2) If the defendant is found not guilty of the capital offense charged but guilty of a lesser included offense, sentence shall be determined and imposed as provided by law.

(3) If the defendant is found guilty of capital murder, the same jury shall sit again in order to hear additional evidence as provided by subdivision (4) of this section, and to determine sentence in the manner provided by § 5-4-603; except that, if the state waives the death penalty, stipulates that no aggravating circumstance exists, or stipulates that mitigating circumstances outweigh aggravating circumstances, no such hearing shall be required, and the trial court shall sentence the defendant to life imprisonment without parole.

(4) In determining sentence, evidence may be presented to the jury as to any matters relating to aggravating circumstances enumerated in § 5-4-604, any mitigating circumstances, or any other matter relevant to punishment, including, but not limited to, victim impact evidence, provided that the defendant and the state are accorded an opportunity to rebut such evidence. Evidence as to any mitigating circumstances may be presented by either the state or the defendant regardless of its admissibility under the rules governing admission of evidence in trials of criminal matters, but mitigation evidence must be relevant to the issue of punishment, including, but not limited to, the nature and circumstances of the crime, and the defendant's character, background, history, and mental and physical condition as set forth in § 5-4-605. The admissibility of evidence relevant to the aggravating circumstances set forth in § 5-4-604 shall be governed by the rules governing the admission of evidence in trials of criminal matters. Any evidence

admitted at the trial relevant to punishment may be considered by the jury without the necessity of reintroducing it at the sentencing proceeding. The state and the defendant or his counsel shall be permitted to present argument respecting sentencing. The state shall open the argument. The defendant shall be permitted to reply. The state shall then be permitted to reply in rebuttal.

Arkansas Code, Section 5-4-603

5-4-603 Findings required for death sentence—Harmless error review.
  (a) The jury shall impose a sentence of death if it unanimously returns written findings that:
    (1) Aggravating circumstances exist beyond a reasonable doubt; and
    (2) Aggravating circumstances outweigh beyond a reasonable doubt all mitigating circumstances found to exist; and
    (3) Aggravating circumstances justify a sentence of death beyond a reasonable doubt.
  (b) The jury shall impose a sentence of life imprisonment without parole if it finds that:
    (1) Aggravating circumstances do not exist beyond a reasonable doubt; or
    (2) Aggravating circumstances do not outweigh beyond a reasonable doubt all mitigating circumstances found to exist; or
    (3) Aggravating circumstances do not justify a sentence of death beyond a reasonable doubt.
  (c) If the jury does not make all findings required by subsection (a) of this section, the court shall impose a sentence of life imprisonment without parole.
  (d) On appellate review of a death sentence, if the Arkansas Supreme Court finds that the jury erred in finding the existence of any aggravating circumstance or circumstances for any reason and if the jury found no mitigating circumstances, the Arkansas Supreme Court shall conduct a harmless error review of the defendant's death sentence. The Arkansas Supreme Court shall conduct this harmless error review by:
    (1) Determining that the remaining aggravating circumstance or circumstances exist beyond a reasonable doubt; and
    (2) Determining that the remaining aggravating circumstance or circumstances justify a sentence of death beyond a reasonable doubt.
  (e) If the Arkansas Supreme Court concludes that the erroneous finding of any aggravating circumstances by the jury would not have changed the jury's decision to impose the death penalty on the defendant, then a simple majority of the court may vote to affirm the defendant's death sentence.

Arkansas Code, Section 5-4-604

5-4-604. Aggravating circumstances.
  Aggravating circumstances shall be limited to the following:

(1) The capital murder was committed by a person imprisoned as a result of a felony conviction;

(2) The capital murder was committed by a person unlawfully at liberty after being sentenced to imprisonment as a result of a felony conviction;

(3) The person previously committed another felony, an element of which was the use or threat of violence to another person or the creation of a substantial risk of death or serious physical injury to another person;

(4) The person in the commission of the capital murder knowingly created a great risk of death to a person other than the victim or caused the death of more than one (1) person in the same criminal episode;

(5) The capital murder was committed for the purpose of avoiding or preventing an arrest or effecting an escape from custody;

(6) The capital murder was committed for pecuniary gain;

(7) The capital murder was committed for the purpose of disrupting or hindering the lawful exercise of any government or political function;

(8)

(A) The capital murder was committed in an especially cruel or depraved manner.

(B) For purposes of this subdivision (8), a capital murder is committed in an especially cruel manner when, as part of a course of conduct intended to inflict mental anguish, serious physical abuse, or torture upon the victim prior to the victim's death, mental anguish, serious physical abuse, or torture is inflicted. "Mental anguish" is defined as the victim's uncertainty as to his ultimate fate. "Serious physical abuse" is defined as physical abuse that creates a substantial risk of death or that causes protracted impairment of health, or loss or protracted impairment of the function of any bodily member or organ. "Torture" is defined as the infliction of extreme physical pain for a prolonged period of time prior to the victim's death.

(C) For purposes of this subdivision (8), a capital murder is committed in an especially depraved manner when the person relishes the murder, evidencing debasement or perversion, or shows an indifference to the suffering of the victim and evidences a sense of pleasure in committing the murder;

(9) The capital murder was committed by means of a destructive device, bomb, explosive, or similar device which the person planted, hid, or concealed in any place, area, dwelling, building, or structure, or mailed or delivered, or caused to be planted, hidden, concealed, mailed, or delivered, and the person knew that his act or acts would create a great risk of death to human life; or

(10) The capital murder was committed against a person whom the defendant knew or reasonably should have known was especially vulnerable to the attack because:

(A) Of either a temporary or permanent severe physical or mental disability which would interfere with the victim's ability to flee or to defend himself; or

(B) The person was twelve (12) years of age or younger.

FLORIDA

Florida Statutes, Section 921.141

921.141. Sentence of death or life imprisonment for capital felonies; further proceedings to determine sentence
(1) Separate proceedings on issue of penalty.—Upon conviction or adjudication of guilt of a defendant of a capital felony, the court shall conduct a separate sentencing proceeding to determine whether the defendant should be sentenced to death or life imprisonment as authorized by s. 775.082. The proceeding shall be conducted by the trial judge before the trial jury as soon as practicable. If, through impossibility or inability, the trial jury is unable to reconvene for a hearing on the issue of penalty, having determined the guilt of the accused, the trial judge may summon a special juror or jurors as provided in chapter 913 to determine the issue of the imposition of the penalty. If the trial jury has been waived, or if the defendant pleaded guilty, the sentencing proceeding shall be conducted before a jury impaneled for that purpose, unless waived by the defendant. In the proceeding, evidence may be presented as to any matter that the court deems relevant to the nature of the crime and the character of the defendant and shall include matters relating to any of the aggravating or mitigating circumstances enumerated in subsections (5) and (6). Any such evidence which the court deems to have probative value may be received, regardless of its admissibility under the exclusionary rules of evidence, provided the defendant is accorded a fair opportunity to rebut any hearsay statements. However, this subsection shall not be construed to authorize the introduction of any evidence secured in violation of the Constitution of the United States or the Constitution of the State of Florida. The state and the defendant or the defendant's counsel shall be permitted to present argument for or against sentence of death.
(2) Advisory sentence by the jury.—After hearing all the evidence, the jury shall deliberate and render an advisory sentence to the court, based upon the following matters:
(a) Whether sufficient aggravating circumstances exist as enumerated in subsection (5);
(b) Whether sufficient mitigating circumstances exist which outweigh the aggravating circumstances found to exist; and
(c) Based on these considerations, whether the defendant should be sentenced to life imprisonment or death.
(3) Findings in support of sentence of death.—Notwithstanding the recommendation of a majority of the jury, the court, after weighing the aggravating and mitigating circumstances, shall enter a sentence of life imprisonment or death, but if the court imposes a sentence of death, it shall set forth in writing its findings upon which the sentence of death is based as to the facts:
(a) That sufficient aggravating circumstances exist as enumerated in subsection (5), and
(b) That there are insufficient mitigating circumstances to outweigh the aggravating circumstances.

In each case in which the court imposes the death sentence, the determination of the court shall be supported by specific written findings of fact based upon the circumstances in subsections (5) and (6) and upon the records of the trial and the sentencing proceedings. If the court does not make the findings requiring the death sentence within 30 days after the rendition of the judgment and sentence, the court shall impose sentence of life imprisonment in accordance with s. 775.082.

(4) Review of judgment and sentence.—The judgment of conviction and sentence of death shall be subject to automatic review by the Supreme Court of Florida and disposition rendered within 2 years after the filing of a notice of appeal. Such review by the Supreme Court shall have priority over all other cases and shall be heard in accordance with rules promulgated by the Supreme Court.

(5) Aggravating circumstances.—Aggravating circumstances shall be limited to the following:

(a) The capital felony was committed by a person previously convicted of a felony and under sentence of imprisonment or placed on community control or on felony probation.

(b) The defendant was previously convicted of another capital felony or of a felony involving the use or threat of violence to the person.

(c) The defendant knowingly created a great risk of death to many persons.

(d) The capital felony was committed while the defendant was engaged, or was an accomplice, in the commission of, or an attempt to commit, or flight after committing or attempting to commit, any: robbery; sexual battery; aggravated child abuse; abuse of an elderly person or disabled adult resulting in great bodily harm, permanent disability, or permanent disfigurement; arson; burglary; kidnapping; aircraft piracy; or unlawful throwing, placing, or discharging of a destructive device or bomb.

(e) The capital felony was committed for the purpose of avoiding or preventing a lawful arrest or effecting an escape from custody.

(f) The capital felony was committed for pecuniary gain.

(g) The capital felony was committed to disrupt or hinder the lawful exercise of any governmental function or the enforcement of laws.

(h) The capital felony was especially heinous, atrocious, or cruel.

(i) The capital felony was a homicide and was committed in a cold, calculated, and premeditated manner without any pretense of moral or legal justification.

(j) The victim of the capital felony was a law enforcement officer engaged in the performance of his or her official duties.

(k) The victim of the capital felony was an elected or appointed public official engaged in the performance of his or her official duties if the motive for the capital felony was related, in whole or in part, to the victim's official capacity.

(l) The victim of the capital felony was a person less than 12 years of age.

(m) The victim of the capital felony was particularly vulnerable due to advanced age or disability, or because the defendant stood in a position of familial or custodial authority over the victim.

(n) The capital felony was committed by a criminal street gang member, as defined in s. 874.03.

(6) Mitigating circumstances.—Mitigating circumstances shall be the following:

(a) The defendant has no significant history of prior criminal activity.

(b) The capital felony was committed while the defendant was under the influence of extreme mental or emotional disturbance.

(c) The victim was a participant in the defendant's conduct or consented to the act.

(d) The defendant was an accomplice in the capital felony committed by another person and his or her participation was relatively minor.

(e) The defendant acted under extreme duress or under the substantial domination of another person.

(f) The capacity of the defendant to appreciate the criminality of his or her conduct or to conform his or her conduct to the requirements of law was substantially impaired.

(g) The age of the defendant at the time of the crime.

(h) The existence of any other factors in the defendant's background that would mitigate against imposition of the death penalty.

(7) Victim impact evidence.—Once the prosecution has provided evidence of the existence of one or more aggravating circumstances as described in subsection (5), the prosecution may introduce, and subsequently argue, victim impact evidence. Such evidence shall be designed to demonstrate the victim's uniqueness as an individual human being and the resultant loss to the community's members by the victim's death. Characterizations and opinions about the crime, the defendant, and the appropriate sentence shall not be permitted as a part of victim impact evidence.

(8) Applicability.—This section does not apply to a person convicted or adjudicated guilty of a capital drug trafficking felony under s. 893.135.

GEORGIA

Code of Georgia, 17-10-30

17-10-30 Procedure for imposition of death penalty generally.

(a) The death penalty may be imposed for the offenses of aircraft hijacking or treason in any case.

(b) In all cases of other offenses for which the death penalty may be authorized, the judge shall consider, or he shall include in his instructions to the jury for it to consider, any mitigating circumstances or aggravating circumstances otherwise authorized by law and any of the following statutory aggravating circumstances which may be supported by the evidence:

(1) The offense of murder, rape, armed robbery, or kidnapping was committed by a person with a prior record of conviction for a capital felony;

(2) The offense of murder, rape, armed robbery, or kidnapping was committed while the offender was engaged in the commission of another capital felony or aggravated battery, or the offense of murder was committed while the offender was engaged in the commission of burglary or arson in the first degree;

(3) The offender, by his act of murder, armed robbery, or kidnapping, knowingly created a great risk of death to more than one person in a public place by means of a weapon or device which would normally be hazardous to the lives of more than one person;

(4) The offender committed the offense of murder for himself or another, for the purpose of receiving money or any other thing of monetary value;

(5) The murder of a judicial officer, former judicial officer, district attorney or solicitor-general, or former district attorney, solicitor, or solicitor-general was committed during or because of the exercise of his or her official duties;

(6) The offender caused or directed another to commit murder or committed murder as an agent or employee of another person;

(7) The offense of murder, rape, armed robbery, or kidnapping was outrageously or wantonly vile, horrible, or inhuman in that it involved torture, depravity of mind, or an aggravated battery to the victim;

(8) The offense of murder was committed against any peace officer, corrections employee, or fireman while engaged in the performance of his official duties;

(9) The offense of murder was committed by a person in, or who has escaped from, the lawful custody of a peace officer or place of lawful confinement; or

(10) The murder was committed for the purpose of avoiding, interfering with, or preventing a lawful arrest or custody in a place of lawful confinement, of himself or another.

(c) The statutory instructions as determined by the trial judge to be warranted by the evidence shall be given in charge and in writing to the jury for its deliberation. The jury, if its verdict is a recommendation of death, shall designate in writing, signed by the foreman of the jury, the aggravating circumstance or circumstances which it found beyond a reasonable doubt. In nonjury cases the judge shall make such designation. Except in cases of treason or aircraft hijacking, unless at least one of the statutory aggravating circumstances enumerated in subsection (b) of this Code section is so found, the death penalty shall not be imposed.

Code of Georgia, 17-10-31

17-10-31 Requirement of jury finding of aggravating circumstance and recommendation of death penalty prior to imposition.

Where, upon a trial by jury, a person is convicted of an offense which may be punishable by death, a sentence of death shall not be imposed unless the jury verdict includes a finding of at least one statutory aggravating circumstance and a recommendation that such sentence be imposed. Where a statutory aggravating circumstance is found and a recommendation of death is made, the court shall sentence the defendant to death. Where a sentence of death is not recommended by the jury, the court shall sentence the defendant to imprisonment as provided by law. Unless the jury trying the case makes a finding of at least one statutory aggravating circumstance and recommends the death sentence in its verdict, the court shall not sentence the defendant to death, provided that no such finding of statutory aggravating circumstance shall be necessary in offenses of treason or aircraft hijacking. This Code section shall not affect a sentence when the case is tried without a jury or when the judge accepts a plea of guilty.

PENNSYLVANIA

Pennsylvania Consolidated Statutes, Title 42, Section 9711

§ *9711. Sentencing procedure for murder of the first degree.*
    (a) Procedure in jury trials.—
        (1) After a verdict of murder of the first degree is recorded and before the jury is discharged, the court shall conduct a separate sentencing hearing in which the jury shall determine whether the defendant shall be sentenced to death or life imprisonment.
        (2) In the sentencing hearing, evidence concerning the victim and the impact that the death of the victim has had on the family of the victim is admissible. Additionally, evidence may be presented as to any other matter that the court deems relevant and admissible on the question of the sentence to be imposed. Evidence shall include matters relating to any of the aggravating or mitigating circumstances specified in subsections (d) and (e), and information concerning the victim and the impact that the death of the victim has had on the family of the victim. Evidence of aggravating circumstances shall be limited to those circumstances specified in subsection (d).
        (3) After the presentation of evidence, the court shall permit counsel to present argument for or against the sentence of death. The court shall then instruct the jury in accordance with subsection (c).
        (4) Failure of the jury to unanimously agree upon a sentence shall not impeach or in any way affect the guilty verdict previously recorded.
    (b) Procedure in nonjury trials and guilty pleas.—If the defendant has waived a jury trial or pleaded guilty, the sentencing proceeding shall be conducted before a jury impaneled for that purpose unless waived by the defendant with the consent of the Commonwealth, in which case the trial judge shall hear the evidence and determine the penalty in the same manner as would a jury as provided in subsection (a).
    (c) Instructions to jury.—
        (1) Before the jury retires to consider the sentencing verdict, the court shall instruct the jury on the following matters:

(i) the aggravating circumstances specified in subsection (d) as to which there is some evidence.

(ii) the mitigating circumstances specified in subsection (e) as to which there is some evidence.

(iii) aggravating circumstances must be proved by the Commonwealth beyond a reasonable doubt; mitigating circumstances must be proved by the defendant by a preponderance of the evidence.

(iv) the verdict must be a sentence of death if the jury unanimously finds at least one aggravating circumstance specified in subsection (d) and no mitigating circumstance or if the jury unanimously finds one or more aggravating circumstances which outweigh any mitigating circumstances. The verdict must be a sentence of life imprisonment in all other cases.

(v) the court may, in its discretion, discharge the jury if it is of the opinion that further deliberation will not result in a unanimous agreement as to the sentence, in which case the court shall sentence the defendant to life imprisonment.

(2) The court shall instruct the jury that if it finds at least one aggravating circumstance and at least one mitigating circumstance, it shall consider, in weighing the aggravating and mitigating circumstances, any evidence presented about the victim and about the impact of the murder on the victim's family. The court shall also instruct the jury on any other matter that may be just and proper under the circumstances.

(d) Aggravating circumstances.—Aggravating circumstances shall be limited to the following:

(1) The victim was a firefighter, peace officer, public servant concerned in official detention, as defined in 18 Pa.C.S. § 5121 (relating to escape), judge of any court in the unified judicial system, the Attorney General of Pennsylvania, a deputy attorney general, district attorney, assistant district attorney, member of the General Assembly, Governor, Lieutenant Governor, Auditor General, State Treasurer, State law enforcement official, local law enforcement official, Federal law enforcement official or person employed to assist or assisting any law enforcement official in the performance of his duties, who was killed in the performance of his duties or as a result of his official position.

(2) The defendant paid or was paid by another person or had contracted to pay or be paid by another person or had conspired to pay or be paid by another person for the killing of the victim.

(3) The victim was being held by the defendant for ransom or reward, or as a shield or hostage.

(4) The death of the victim occurred while defendant was engaged in the hijacking of an aircraft.

(5) The victim was a prosecution witness to a murder or other felony committed by the defendant and was killed for the purpose of preventing his testimony against the defendant in any grand jury or criminal proceeding involving such offenses.

(6) The defendant committed a killing while in the perpetration of a felony.

(7) In the commission of the offense the defendant knowingly created a grave risk of death to another person in addition to the victim of the offense.

(8) The offense was committed by means of torture.

(9) The defendant has a significant history of felony convictions involving the use or threat of violence to the person.

(10) The defendant has been convicted of another Federal or State offense, committed either before or at the time of the offense at issue, for which a sentence of life imprisonment or death was imposable or the defendant was undergoing a sentence of life imprisonment for any reason at the time of the commission of the offense.

(11) The defendant has been convicted of another murder committed in any jurisdiction and committed either before or at the time of the offense at issue.

(12) The defendant has been convicted of voluntary manslaughter, as defined in 18 Pa.C.S. § 2503 (relating to voluntary manslaughter), or a substantially equivalent crime in any other jurisdiction, committed either before or at the time of the offense at issue.

(13) The defendant committed the killing or was an accomplice in the killing, as defined in 18 Pa.C.S. § 306(c) (relating to liability for conduct of another; complicity), while in the perpetration of a felony under the provisions of the act of April 14, 1972 (P.L. 233, No. 64), known as The Controlled Substance, Drug, Device and Cosmetic Act, and punishable under the provisions of 18 Pa.C.S. § 7508 (relating to drug trafficking sentencing and penalties).

(14) At the time of the killing, the victim was or had been involved, associated or in competition with the defendant in the sale, manufacture, distribution or delivery of any controlled substance or counterfeit controlled substance in violation of The Controlled Substance, Drug, Device and Cosmetic Act or similar law of any other state, the District of Columbia or the United States, and the defendant committed the killing or was an accomplice to the killing as defined in 18 Pa.C.S. § 306(c), and the killing resulted from or was related to that association, involvement or competition to promote the defendant's activities in selling, manufacturing, distributing or delivering controlled substances or counterfeit controlled substances.

(15) At the time of the killing, the victim was or had been a nongovernmental informant or had otherwise provided any investigative, law enforcement or police agency with information concerning criminal activity and the defendant committed the killing or was an accomplice to the killing as defined in 18 Pa.C.S. § 306(c), and the killing was in retaliation for the victim's activities as a nongovernmental informant or in providing information concerning criminal activity to an investigative, law enforcement or police agency.

(16) The victim was a child under 12 years of age.

(17) At the time of the killing, the victim was in her third trimester of pregnancy or the defendant had knowledge of the victim's pregnancy.

(18) At the time of the killing the defendant was subject to a court order restricting in any way the defendant's behavior toward the victim pursuant to 23 Pa.C.S. Ch. 61 (relating to protection from abuse) or any other order of a court of common pleas or of the minor judiciary designed in whole or in part to protect the victim from the defendant.

(e) Mitigating circumstances.—Mitigating circumstances shall include the following:

(1) The defendant has no significant history of prior criminal convictions.

(2) The defendant was under the influence of extreme mental or emotional disturbance.

(3) The capacity of the defendant to appreciate the criminality of his conduct or to conform his conduct to the requirements of law was substantially impaired.

(4) The age of the defendant at the time of the crime.

(5) The defendant acted under extreme duress, although not such duress as to constitute a defense to prosecution under 18 Pa.C.S. § 309 (relating to duress), or acted under the substantial domination of another person.

(6) The victim was a participant in the defendant's homicidal conduct or consented to the homicidal acts.

(7) The defendant's participation in the homicidal act was relatively minor.

(8) Any other evidence of mitigation concerning the character and record of the defendant and the circumstances of his offense.

(f) Sentencing verdict by the jury.—

(1) After hearing all the evidence and receiving the instructions from the court, the jury shall deliberate and render a sentencing verdict. In rendering the verdict, if the sentence is death, the jury shall set forth in such form as designated by the court the findings upon which the sentence is based.

(2) Based upon these findings, the jury shall set forth in writing whether the sentence is death or life imprisonment. . . .

TEXAS

Texas Code of Criminal Procedure, Article 37.071

Art. 37.071. Procedure in capital case.

Sec. 2

(a)

(1) If a defendant is tried for a capital offense in which the state seeks the death penalty, on a finding that the defendant is guilty of a capital offense,

the court shall conduct a separate sentencing proceeding to determine whether the defendant shall be sentenced to death or life imprisonment. The proceeding shall be conducted in the trial court and, except as provided by Article 44.29(c) of this code, before the trial jury as soon as practicable. In the proceeding, evidence may be presented by the state and the defendant or the defendant's counsel as to any matter that the court deems relevant to sentence, including evidence of the defendant's background or character or the circumstances of the offense that mitigates against the imposition of the death penalty. This subdivision shall not be construed to authorize the introduction of any evidence secured in violation of the Constitution of the United States or of the State of Texas. The state and the defendant or the defendant's counsel shall be permitted to present argument for or against sentence of death. The court, the attorney representing the state, the defendant, or the defendant's counsel may not inform a juror or a prospective juror of the effect of a failure of a jury to agree on issues submitted under Subsection (c) or (e) of this article.

(2) Notwithstanding Subdivision (1), evidence may not be offered by the state to establish that the race or ethnicity of the defendant makes it likely that the defendant will engage in future criminal conduct.

(b) On conclusion of the presentation of the evidence, the court shall submit the following issues to the jury:

(1) whether there is a probability that the defendant would commit criminal acts of violence that would constitute a continuing threat to society; and

(2) in cases in which the jury charge at the guilt or innocence stage permitted the jury to find the defendant guilty as a party under Sections 7.01 and 7.02, Penal Code, whether the defendant actually caused the death of the deceased or did not actually cause the death of the deceased but intended to kill the deceased or another or anticipated that a human life would be taken.

(c) The state must prove each issue submitted under Subsection (b) of this article beyond a reasonable doubt, and the jury shall return a special verdict of "yes" or "no" on each issue submitted under Subsection (b) of this Article.

(d) The court shall charge the jury that:

(1) in deliberating on the issues submitted under Subsection (b) of this article, it shall consider all evidence admitted at the guilt or innocence stage and the punishment stage, including evidence of the defendant's background or character or the circumstances of the offense that mitigates for or mitigates against the imposition of the death penalty;

(2) it may not answer any issue submitted under Subsection (b) of this article "yes" unless it agrees unanimously and it may not answer any issue "no" unless 10 or more jurors agree; and

(3) members of the jury need not agree on what particular evidence supports a negative answer to any issue submitted under Subsection (b) of this article.

(e)

(1) The court shall instruct the jury that if the jury returns an affirmative finding to each issue submitted under Subsection (b) of this article, it shall answer the following issue: Whether, taking into consideration all of the evidence, including the circumstances of the offense, the defendant's character and background, and the personal moral culpability of the defendant, there is a sufficient mitigating circumstance or circumstances to warrant that a sentence of life imprisonment rather than a death sentence be imposed.

(2) The court, on the written request of the attorney representing the defendant, shall:

(A) instruct the jury that if the jury answers that a circumstance or circumstances warrant that a sentence of life imprisonment rather than a death sentence be imposed, the court will sentence the defendant to imprisonment in the institutional division of the Texas Department of Criminal Justice for life; and

(B) charge the jury in writing as follows:

"Under the law applicable in this case, if the defendant is sentenced to imprisonment in the institutional division of the Texas Department of Criminal Justice for life, the defendant will become eligible for release on parole, but not until the actual time served by the defendant equals 40 years, without consideration of any good conduct time. It cannot accurately be predicted how the parole laws might be applied to this defendant if the defendant is sentenced to a term of imprisonment for life because the application of those laws will depend on decisions made by prison and parole authorities, but eligibility for parole does not guarantee that parole will be granted."

(f) The court shall charge the jury that in answering the issue submitted under Subsection;

(g) of this article, the jury:

(1) shall answer the issue "yes" or "no";

(2) may not answer the issue "no" unless it agrees unanimously and may not answer the issue "yes" unless 10 or more jurors agree;

(3) need not agree on what particular evidence supports an affirmative finding on the issue; and

(4) shall consider mitigating evidence to be evidence that a juror might regard as reducing the defendant's moral blameworthiness.

(h) If the jury returns an affirmative finding on each issue submitted under Subsection (b) of this article and a negative finding on an issue submitted under Subsection (g) of this article, the court shall sentence the defendant to death. If the jury returns a negative finding on any issue submitted under Subsection (b) of this article or an affirmative finding on an issue submitted under Subsection (g) of this article or is unable to answer any issue submitted under Subsection (b) or (g) of this article, the court shall sentence the defendant to confinement in the institutional division of the Texas Department of Criminal Justice for life.

(i) The judgment of conviction and sentence of death shall be subject to automatic review by the Court of Criminal Appeals.

(j) This article applies to the sentencing procedure in a capital case for an offense that is committed on or after September 1, 1991. For the purposes of this section, an offense is committed on or after September 1, 1991, if any element of that offense occurs on or after that date.